ACT ONE

MOSS HART

ACT ONE

An Autobiography

RANDOM HOUSE, NEW YORK

For my wife,

Kitty Carlisle

The book that she asked for

These memories, which are my life—for we possess nothing certainly except the past—were always with me. Like the pigeons of St. Mark's, they were everywhere under my feet, singly, in pairs, in little honey-voiced congregations, nodding, strutting, winking, rolling the tender feathers of their necks, perching sometimes, if I stood still, on my shoulder or pecking a broken biscuit from between my lips; until, suddenly, the noon gun boomed and in a moment, with a flutter and sweep of wings, the pavement was bare and the whole sky above dark with a tumult of fowl.

EVELYN WAUGH

PART
ONE

THAT AFTERNOON, I went to work at the music store as usual. It was just around the corner from where we lived, and I worked there every afternoon from three o'clock until seven, while its owner, a violin and piano teacher on the side, gave the lessons which more or less supported the store. There was apparently no great passion for music in the Bronx at that time, and the sparseness of the customers, other than Mr. Levenson's pupils themselves, allowed me to finish my homework as rapidly as possible and then pore greedily over as many copies of *Theatre Magazine* as the library would allow me to take out at one time.

It was, as far as I was concerned, the perfect job. There was usually even enough time, before Mr. Levenson returned at seven o'clock, for a good half-hour or so of pure, idle dreaming; a necessity as basic to a twelve-year-old boy as food and drink. I was thoroughly conscious of the fact that my own dreams of glory were quite unlike those of the other boys on the block, for the fantasies and speculations I indulged in, after I had reluctantly turned the last page of *Theatre Magazine,* were always of Broadway. They were fantasies because though I had been born in and had lived in New York City all of my life, I had never actually seen Broadway.

In my twelve-year-old world it was permissible to work after school; it was, in fact, rather a necessity. The four dollars I earned every week was an item that counted heavily in the shaky family budget, but the rules did not permit my going downtown alone. True, I had passed underneath Broadway many times in the subway on the way to visit relatives in the far reaches of Brooklyn, but the family had never yielded to my entreaties that we get out at Times Square and have a quick look around, and the anguish of being directly underneath my goal and yet not able to see it was well-nigh insupportable.

This afternoon, however, a kind fate was arranging a far more impressive look for me than I ever could have arranged for myself. As I entered the store, and before I could even toss my books and magazines on the counter, Mr. Levenson was speaking. Apparently he had been waiting impatiently for me to arrive.

"Do you think," he said, while I was still in the doorway, "your mother would let you go downtown alone, just this once? I need some music for tomorrow's lessons. All you have to do is to get off the subway at Times Square, walk two blocks east to Schirmer's, pick up the music, and then get on the subway again. Do you think she would let you do it? I don't want you to go without telling your mother."

I nodded solemnly, not wishing to put into words what I knew was going to be a barefaced lie. I had no idea, of course, of asking for my mother's consent. This was the excuse I had been longing for. I took the slip of paper he held out to me, tossed my books onto the counter, and bolted straight for the subway station, by-passing our house on the dangerous chance that my mother might be looking out the window or talking to a neighbor on the stoop.

On the journey downtown I determined to pick up the music at Schirmer's as quickly as possible and then have a long and glorious look around. I can still recall my excitement as the subway doors opened at Times Square, and I shall certainly never forget the picture that greeted me as I dashed up the stairs and stood gaping at my first sight of Broadway and 42nd Street. A swirling mob of happy, laughing people filled the streets, and others hung from the windows of nearly every building. Vendors moved among the crowd selling confetti, noisemakers and paper streamers, and policemen on horseback circled slowly and good-naturedly around the Times Building, pressing the throngs, with no great success, out of the street and onto the jammed sidewalks. Nor can I deny that my first

[4]

thought was, "Of course! That's just the way I thought it would be!"

In that first breathless look it seemed completely right somehow that the glittering Broadway of my fantasy should be as dazzling as this even in broad daylight, but what I took to be an everyday occurrence was Broadway waiting to celebrate the election of either Charles Evans Hughes or Woodrow Wilson as the next President of the United States. I had merely stumbled into a historic moment. It was the first of many disappointments inevitable to the stage-struck, and after helplessly trying to push my way through that solid mass of humanity, I got into the subway again and rode glumly back to the Bronx.

I have thought it fitting to begin this book with my first glimpse of Broadway, since I have spent most of my adult working life in and about its gaudy locale, and if this opening anecdote falls too quickly into the time-honored tradition of theatrical memoirs, then let the unwary reader beware at the very outset—these annals are not for those unsentimental about the theatre or untouched by its idiocies as well as its glories.

There is no point whatever in writing or reading a book of theatrical reminiscences if either the writer or the reader is to be hampered by incredulity, an aversion to melodrama, or even the somewhat foolish glow of the incorrigibly stage-struck. Like it or not, the credulous eye and the quixotic heart are part and parcel of the theatre. The theatre is not so much a profession as a disease, and my first look at Broadway was the beginning of a lifelong infection.

The most interesting aspect of that twelve-year-old self was not the naïveté expressed in the fantasy of what Broadway would be like, but the already strong sense of dedication in that childish figure on the subway steps.

Why? How does it occur? It is an interesting speculation, for I know of no greater race of fanatics, no more severely lost or dedicated a tribe, than the people of the theatre.

What special need masks those simple words "stage-struck"? How explain the strength of what usually amounts to a lifelong

[5]

obsession? What sets the trigger on the inner mechanism that produces actors, actresses or playwrights—what is the nature of the compelling force that marks those particular human beings and sets them apart for the rest of their lives? It is somewhat easier to understand the dedication of a scientist or a man of the church, but the grubby rewards the theatre offers, except to the privileged few, make it hard to understand the undaunted loyalty it calls forth or the passion with which it is pursued.

I have a pet theory of my own, probably invalid, that the theatre is an inevitable refuge of the unhappy child. Like most pet theories, this one also contains the fallacy of too broad a generalization. But certainly the first retreat a child makes to alleviate his unhappiness is to contrive a world of his own, and it is but a small step out of his private world into the fantasy world of the theatre. We have all seen children create imaginary companions or even imaginary parents. The daydream of attending our own funeral and savoring the abiding satisfaction of having our contrite and conscience-stricken parents stand weeping over our coffin is so usual a fantasy of childhood as to be almost obligatory, and it disappears with the other flights and fancies of childhood. But to the deeply disturbed child caught in a situation that he cannot resolve, the first wonder of the theatre comes as a revelation and a resolution of his unconscious difficulties. Here on a brightly lit stage, before a hushed and admiring audience, are people doing the very things he has played out in his own fantasies: assuming heroic or villainous guises, bathing in the applause and love of a hitherto hostile world. Suddenly he perceives that his secret goal is attainable—to be himself and yet be somebody else, and in the very act of doing so, to be loved and admired; to stand gloriously in a spotlight undimmed by the rivalry of brothers or sisters and to be relieved of his sense of guilt by the waves of applause that roll over the footlights to those wonderful creatures on the stage. After all, is not the essence of acting the art of being somebody else? Is not the craft of the playwright the ability to make a fantasy of his own creation so true to the lives of the characters he is depicting that the audience accepts it as reality? And what is any play but the expression of its author's conscious fantasy at that particular moment. I would hazard a guess that no play idea is ever completely accidental, and I would hazard a further guess that the temperament, the tantrums and the utter childishness of theatre people in general, is neither accidental nor a necessary weapon of their profession. It has nothing to do with so-called "artistic temperament." The explanation, I think, is a far simpler one. For the most part, they are impaled in childhood like a fly in amber.

I have set down the foregoing not altogether without guile, for it allows me to come somewhat circuitously to my own childhood. Inevitably, I sheer away from the hackneyed picture of the unhappy child in poor circumstances who triumphed over difficulties and achieved success. Yet the hackneyed is sometimes relevant, for how else is one to understand the figure of the Sunday interview, or the press agent's program notes, if there is not a more conventional picture of his beginnings? Hackneyed or not, beginnings are necessary —and mine were certainly conventional enough.

I GREW UP in an atmosphere of unrelieved poverty, with what Ruth Gordon describes as "the dark brown taste of being poor" forever in my mouth and the grim smell of actual want always at the end of my nose. It was not, as may be gathered, a very happy childhood and the atmosphere was not improved by the family cast of characters. I cannot remember who it was who said that a family was a dictatorship ruled over by its sickest member—he certainly could not have known my grandfather—but it was some such symbol he must have had in mind when he made the remark, for my grandfather, whom I adored, towered over my first seven years like an Everest of Victorian tyranny. He was, in many ways, quite an extraordinary man, and his effect on me in those early and crucial years was, I suppose, incalculable. I am certain I still bear the marks. He was a cigarmaker by trade, and he worked side by side on the same bench with his closest friend, Samuel Gompers. Together they hatched out the first early dream of an American Federation of Labor, and for a while it was a tossup as to who would lead the crusade, my grandfather or Samuel Gompers. The family legend is that they quarreled bitterly and their friendship ended on the somewhat comic grounds of who was to carry the briefcase in to union meetings—the one briefcase they owned between them. I am quite prepared to believe this story as not entirely apocryphal. It sounds, indeed, very much like my grandfather, and exactly the way he was likely to behave.

[8]

He most certainly behaved that way at home. His two daughters, my mother and my Aunt Kate, he looked upon as indentured servants sent to serve him by some fine beneficent natural law. I think he accepted my father's dim presence in the house with the passing annoyance of a GI watching a jungle fungus grow on his boot, and he returned my adoration of him with a deep devotion of his own. To do him strict justice, he had no easy time of it himself, and the sorry state of shabby gentility in which he lived out most of his life, though due entirely to his own truculence and innate bad temper, was not what he had been born to. He was, as a matter of fact, the black sheep of a large and quite wealthy family of English Jews, and he had apparently at a very early age alienated himself from each and every one of them, finally ending all family ties in a burst of rebellion that settled him for good and all in America.

He was a man of considerable personal charm, with an alert and inquiring mind, but since he was always superior to the life he was forced to live, it served to further sour a nature already steeped in arrogance and gall. The bitterness and disappointments of his daily life he of course took out on his immediate family, and though I never knew my grandmother (she died shortly before I was born), the tales I have heard of her life with him were hair-raising and a little terrifying.

He had married beneath him in the best tradition of the black sheep, and my grandmother could neither read nor write. His financial circumstances from the very moment of their marriage were extremely straitened, and since there was very little left over for entertainment of any kind, the great pleasure of my grandmother's life was to have my grandfather read aloud to her in the evening. Charles Dickens was at the height of his fame then as a novelist and his works were her abiding passion. My mother has told me that there were difficult times when my grandmother seemed to survive only for the evenings, and the most vivid recollection of her own early childhood was my grandfather's voice reading Dickens aloud, and later on her most terrifying memory was when he would *not*—and the house would be completely silent, for when he was in a rage or fit of depression he would punish my grandmother by not reading for days and sometimes weeks at a time and would sit evening after evening without uttering a word. There would be silence throughout the evening meal and complete silence afterward, for he would talk to no one and would allow no word to be spoken by his wife or daughters. He sulked until the fit was over. Worse still, he would never pick up where he had left off. Dickens was published serially in America in those days, and he would start the readings again with the latest installment, so that my grandmother was forever in the dark about large portions of David Copperfield's life and did not know until long afterwards what happened to Little Emily. Perhaps I inherited from my grandmother my abhorrence of people who sulk, for it is the one quirk or quality in people I cannot abide and do not suffer gladly.

Another tale my mother told me of this perverse and unpredictable man, was his reception of the news that my grandmother had saved, after twenty years of scrounging, enough money to take them all on a trip to England. How she managed to save any such sum out of the meager amount she was allotted to make ends meet, God knows, even though it took her twenty years to do it. How many untold small and large privations that money represented is painful to think of—daily existence must have been harsh enough in itself. But save it she did, with some involuted feminine logic that men are unable to contemplate or understand. And she brought it forth and offered it to her husband because he had been out of work for eight months and in such a state of melancholia, according to my mother, that they all feared for his reason. They needn't have. When my grandmother, at one of those silent evening meals, proposed that they break his streak of bad luck by sailing to London and that she had the money for their passage, he flew into one of his monumental rages. How dared she, he thundered, let him walk around with the seat hanging out of his pants and one frayed shirt to his name! It did her no good to protest that she had saved it for just some such crisis and that she was offering it all to him now. He sulked in terrible silence for another two weeks and then they sailed for London, all freshly and fashionably outfitted; for it was not my grandfather's way to let his rich family have the least hint that he had been anything but a complete success in his adopted country. And my mother never forgot the grand airs he gave himself or the new and unfailing courtesy to his wife and daughters, a side of his they had never before seen and which was revealed in full flower from the moment the boat docked at Southampton.

The trip was not without fateful consequences of its own. My mother and father met in London—he followed her to America a year later. And on my Aunt Kate the trip produced so profound an impression that she never recovered from it for the rest of her life. She was twenty at the time and my mother eighteen, and for both of them it was a glimpse of a kind of life they had never known or were to know again. To my poor Aunt Kate, an incurable romantic, this whiff of how the other half lived was like some fearful narcotic. From that moment onward, she behaved like a lady of fashion, disdaining work of any sort, and was supported for the rest of her days—she lived to be sixty-odd—first by my grandfather and then by my father, whom she detested and who detested her in return. It was a rather strange obsession, but one that remained unshakable, in spite of the fact that she sometimes had to read her inevitable novel by candlelight, since there wasn't always a quarter to put in the gas meter. One of the most vivid memories of my own childhood is seeing her trail into her room with her bottle of smelling salts and a book or the Sunday papers, and hearing the lock click shut. Her behavior remained unchanged, while my mother cooked, cleaned and did the washing and ironing not only for ourselves but for the boarders we took in to help pay the rent. It drove my father crazy, as well it might, for she never lifted a finger to help in any way, not so much as by drying a single dish. Yet it was she who opened up the world of the theatre to me and I loved her and am forever grateful to her. It was she, too, who was largely responsible for the powerful effect my grandfather was to have on my early years.

Shortly after the family returned to America, my grandmother died—heaving, I imagine, a sigh of relief that must have pushed her halfway to heaven—and my mother took over the role of house-keeper for my grandfather. This circumstance was an unfortunate blow to my father's courtship, for it was some ten years before my mother could be pried loose from my grandfather and allowed to marry. He was not precisely the man to let love interfere with his creature comforts. Besides, my mother acted as a daily keeper of the peace between her father and her sister, who reacted fearfully on each other's nerves—a part she was also to play for many years with her sister and her future husband, though she could not have known it then. Knowing my father as I do now, it does not strike me as at all strange that he should have been willing to sit out patiently an engagement of ten years. It was, on the contrary, rather typical of him. He is a man who has made a lifelong hobby of unruffled self-preservation. At any rate, the long engagement finally ended. They were married and set up a ménage of their own, leaving my grandfather and his remaining daughter in a state of armed and un-easy truce.

My mother and father were not to be alone for long, however. About a month before I was born, my grandfather appeared at their door at two o'clock in the morning, and roused them out of their bed. He was in a wild state and threatened that if my mother did not move back with him he would kill himself or Kate, one or the other. He could not and would not stand another day of it. In some awful way I can sympathize with him. I have a rough idea of what my Aunt Kate's housekeeping must have been like, since I once or twice sampled her cooking, and her own room, no matter how tidied up by my mother, always gave the impression of a countryside ravaged by a long and fierce war. I can't think how my mother and father ever agreed to this foolish and tragic plan. Certainly neither they nor their marriage ever recovered from it and my mother never ceased to look wistfully back on the only time she ever spent alone with my father in their thirty years of married life.

Thus it was that I was born in my grandfather's house, and I am told that I had no sooner entered into the world with that age-old wail of protest, than I was picked up bodily by this seventy-nine-

year-old autocrat and became his sole and jealously guarded possession. How clearly he still stands out in my memory and how much
of him remains!

I can see him now, with absolute clarity, bending over my bed,
lifting me high up in his arms, then putting me on his shoulder,
taking me into the dining room and standing me in the center of
the dining-room table. And I can still dimly see the ring of upturned
faces smiling at me. The faces belonged to the Friday Evening
Literary Society, of which he was president, which convened, as
per its title, every Friday evening at our house. Supper was always
served at ten thirty, and before the cloth was spread, he would
march into my room, wake me up and carry me into the dining
room. I would stand on the table, rubbing the sleep out of my eyes,
and as soon as I could collect myself, I would proceed to recite one
of his favorite bits from *A Christmas Carol,* which he had taught
me during the preceding week, and once, I believe, at the age of
five, I did him proud by belting into *Hamlet.*

Still earlier, I have another vivid memory of the terrible day he
took me to the barber and had all my hair cut off. Without a word
to my mother, of course. I was not quite three at the time, and my
curls, which were the fashion then for little boys, were my mother's
particular pride. But he had humored her, apparently, as long as he
intended to, and since he never asked approval for anything he did,
much less discussed it beforehand, he had simply taken me to the
barber and returned me, *fait accompli,* to my mother. It was the
only time, I think, she ever talked back to him and then only through
her sobs, while my father was dispatched to the barber shop to try
to retrieve a curl from the floor; which he did, and which my grandfather promptly flushed down the toilet. Scenes like this were the
rule rather than the exception in my grandfather's daily life; he
generated high drama as his key turned in the door, and I was
usually the storm center of both his violence and his tenderness.

Years later, another memory of him was brought sharply back to
me on a very eventful night in my own life. My first play was being
given a spring tryout in Brighton Beach. I was hurrying along
the boardwalk to the theatre, when I stopped and stared at a ram-

shackle building which had become a public bathhouse. Suddenly I remembered a sweltering August night long ago when my grandfather had led us all into this same building, then a kind of boardwalk night club, and like a flash of summer lightning illuminating a dark landscape, that whole agonizing time rushed into my mind: the terrible heat, the oppressive silence that had filled our house for so many weeks, the blind panic a child can feel when he senses a crisis in the family—it all flooded back as I stopped and stared at that building.

The crisis which I sensed but could not understand, nor do I suppose they could have explained it to a child of six, was that modern industrial methods had finally caught up with the ancient trade of cigarmaking. A machine had been invented to turn out cigars from the tobacco leaf to the finished, banded and boxed product, and the craft of making cigars by hand was suddenly and overnight revolutionized. My grandfather and my father, a cigarmaker by trade also, had been out of work for months. We lived as best we could on the paltry benefits doled out by the Cigarmakers Union, never a very rich union at best, and I have never forgotten, nor shall I, the plight of these two men whose trade had suddenly been snatched away from them. My grandfather was too old to try anything else, my father too frail. They tried desperately at first to hang on to their only means of livelihood by buying raw tobacco, making cigars in the kitchen, and peddling them from door to door; but competition with machine-made cigars was a pathetically lost cause.

Finally, in this terrible summer I speak of, they had stopped trying altogether and sat helplessly all day around the house, a growing fear in my grandfather's eyes and a tightness about his lips that frightened me. Even I, who could do anything with him, could not penetrate his cold despair, and this particular night he had shut himself in his room and had not appeared for the evening meal, nor did my entreaties or repeated knocks on the door, when I was sent to fetch him, call forth an answer. I remember I had wandered out to the fire escape, my mother, father and aunt sitting in heavy silence in the stifling room behind me, when my grandfather's door suddenly opened and he shouted to my mother, "Lily—how much money is there in the house?" She told him, and he called back, "Give it to me and get your hats on! We're going to Brighton Beach! I've had enough of this!" He knew, of course, that it was not only all the money in the house, but all the money they possessed in the world; but he had had enough of fear and despair, and off we went to the seashore and a boardwalk floor show in the very building I was standing in front of now. I had adored him more than ever that night, and I thought, as I walked away from the place, what delight it would have given him to know that I had written a play—what infinite pleasure he would have taken in hurrying along to the theatre with me and watching the curtain go up. He was a very dramatic fellow himself.

He died just a year later, when I was seven years old, in the same week that my brother was born, and with him went the only things that I remember with any pleasure of my childhood. It may be that I have made him sound faintly like a monster, and it cannot be denied that he was certainly monstrous to have around the house, but by the same token he was a unique figure of enormous vitality, color and salt. Every memory I have of him is vivid and alive, from the Sunday morning ritual of standing on a chair beside him while he dyed his hair, mustache and goatee a jet-black—he was as vain as he was bad-tempered—to the recollection of watching him try to catch a butterfly for me with his Panama hat, while a delighted crowd of Central Park strollers looked on, laughing their heads off. I think perhaps that I gave him the only peaceful and untroubled emotion he ever knew in his turbulent and unhappy life, and he gave me in return, for good or ill, a relish for people of thunder and lightning and a distaste for the humdrum. After his death, I turned not to my mother or father, but to my Aunt Kate, and like all seemingly innocent happenings which afterward shape our destiny, this unconscious turning to my aunt was the most important event of my boyhood.

I SUPPOSE it is a trifle too easy and, in fact, a little simple-minded to look down the long corridor of one's life and say with any degree of surety, "Here is how it happened—here is where the door opened—this was the turning point." After all, how does one know? Suppose, for instance, there had been no Aunt Kate, or presume she had been a less strange person than she was; would the door have opened differently, the path turned the other way? Perhaps. I cannot be certain. But my aunt, in her own way, had the same streak of iron in her that my grandfather had in him, and though the iron emerged in my aunt's case as a kind of childish and permanent romanticism, her influence on my awakening mind and senses, particularly in the void left by my grandfather's death, was a powerful and determining factor in all the young years that followed.

To the casual eye, she must have seemed a foolish, if not a downright ridiculous woman. She was full of airs and graces that were faintly grotesque considering the lowly orbit in which she moved; but apart from her obsession, which was pathological and worsened with the years, she was extremely intelligent. It is both sad and strange that this often silly woman, dressed usually in a most idiotic attire, was in fact an immensely shrewd and sensitive human being. The two are not mutually exclusive. I sat in a theatre a few years ago at the out-of-town opening of a now famous play and watched, fascinated and puzzled, as the actress on the stage played out the tragic destiny of the playwright's imagining. There was something about the character of this woman on the stage that tolled the bell of remembrance within me. It was almost as though I had known this woman myself—echo after echo reminded me of someone I had known in my own life—and suddenly I knew who it was I was remembering. Aunt Kate. The play that brought her back to me so sharply was *A Streetcar Named Desire* and the character was the unforgettable Blanche Du Bois. I do not mean to suggest that the story of Blanche was my aunt's story or that she was anything like the twisted and tormented Blanche; but there was enough of Blanche in my Aunt Kate—a touching combination of the sane and the ludicrous along with some secret splendor within herself— that re-awakened long-forgotten memories. I think Tennessee Williams would have understood my Aunt Kate at once—perhaps far better than I did, for in those early years I confess I was a little ashamed of her. She was too strange a figure for the conforming little beasts that children usually are for me to have been completely comfortable about her. I always looked straight ahead when we passed other children that I knew in the street and swallowed my discomfort as best I could.

It was a hazard I willingly undertook, for when we walked out together we were almost always on the way to the theatre, and that delightful prospect was enough to make me run any gantlet. I did not know until long afterward how she managed these excursions to the theatre for herself and me, and the method she used was, I think, very characteristic of her. Quite simply, she managed them through pure blackmail. After my grandfather's death, my father continued to support my aunt in the style, such as it was, that she was accustomed to. Poor as we were, this was somehow taken for granted—I do not pretend to understand why. However, Aunt Kate's style was of necessity somewhat curtailed now that my father was the sole wage earner. It could not possibly include the theatre and novels, two items she found as necessary to living as breathing and eating. So she promptly sat down and wrote a fine blackmailing letter to the rich relatives in London, outlining in the best tear-drenched tradition of the period, I am sure, her sad plight as the now orphaned daughter, and shaming them into a small monthly allowance. This she used exclusively for theatre tickets and books, and come hell or high water not one penny of it was ever touched otherwise.

I can well remember the times we went to bed in the dark because there was no quarter to put in the gas meter; or even more vividly, some evening meals eaten by candlelight for the same reason, after which Aunt Kate would emerge from her room, attired in what she considered proper fashion, and be on her way to David Belasco's production of *The Darling of the Gods* or the equivalent hit of the moment. Incredible as it may seem, never once did she offer to forgo the theatre, no matter how dire the financial crisis might be and, equally astonishing, it seems to me, was the fact that she was not expected to. In some curious way I think the answer is that we were grateful for this small patch of lunatic brightness in the unending drabness of those years. Just as she never admitted to herself the poverty in which we lived, so through her passion for the theatre she made us forget it for a little while, too.

My mother and I always waited up for her return, and then she would re-create the entire evening for us. She was a wonderful reporter. She had a fine eye for irrelevant detail and a good critical sense of acting values. Her passion for the theatre did not include being overwhelmed by it, nor was she a blind idolater of stars. She always sat in the gallery, of course, but she always got to the theatre early enough to stand in the lobby and watch the audience go in—in order, as she expressed it, to get all there was to get! She must have been a strange figure indeed, standing in the lobby, her eyes darting about, "getting" everything there was to get, her conversation, if she spoke to anyone, a mixture of Clyde Fitch and Thomas Hardy; her own clothes a parody of the fashionable ladies going into the theatre. But little indeed did escape her and she regaled us with all of it, from the audience arriving to the footlights dimming, and then the story of the play itself. She would smooth out the program on the kitchen table, and there we would sit, sometimes until two o'clock in the morning, reliving the play with her, goggle-eyed at the second-act climax, as ready to applaud the curtain calls as the audience itself had been.

It is hard to realize now in these days of television, movies, radio and organized play groups what all this meant to a child of those days. It was not only the one available source of pleasure and wonder, it was all of them rolled into one. I remember my constant entreaty was, "When will you take me?" And then my aunt decided, with the knowledge kept from my father of course, that I was old enough to go. I was too young to be taken downtown to see plays, but from the time I was seven years old I was kept out of school every Thursday afternoon and taken to the Alhambra Theatre—to which my aunt had a season subscription ticket each year—where I watched, sober-faced, all the great vaudeville headliners. Then, still in conspiracy against my father, I graduated to Saturday matinées at the local stock company and a little later to touring companies at the Bronx Opera House. Not unnaturally I lived for those wonderful Thursday and Saturday afternoons, and in between waited out the days for those evenings when my aunt returned from the greater world of Broadway.

The effect of all this on the curious and aloof little boy that I must have been is not hard to imagine. Psychologically, of course, it was less than salutary, and I paid the price for it in my adult life. A target for a child's love and affection is a basic necessity to the security of his early years, and my childhood world was a bewildering battlefield of conflicting loyalties. My aunt and my father were in a state of constant daily warfare. My mother seemed to live only to appease them, a role not unnoticed by me and deplorable to me even then. Even the beloved figure of my grandfather had been in some ways a terrifying one. As a consequence, the world outside my home was seen through the filter of waiting for those two glorious afternoons. At school I was a lonely and alien figure. My given name, to begin with, was a strange one, and children are quick to hold suspect and to damn anything different from themselves, even a name. Added to this was the fact that I spoke with a faint English accent; and my manner of speaking, I'm afraid, was a trifle too literate, if not downright theatrical—the one a heritage from my family, the other a carry-over from Thursday and Saturday afternoons at the Alhambra Theatre and the Bronx Opera House.

It is easy to understand how my aunt became for me a refuge against the world of reality and how the fantasy world of the theatre quickly became an escape and a solace. Increasingly, that world assumed for me more reality than the hostile world in which I lived—and then suddenly both refuges, my aunt and the theatre, crashed about my head. I was ten years old at the time and it was a Sunday morning, and I can still remember the sound and even the smell of that morning.

We had taken in boarders long since to eke out my father's meager earnings, and I might add that boarders in those days received a full measure for their weekly room rent. Along with the room there were included two meals, breakfast and dinner, and laundry. All of this my mother did, as well as taking care of my brother and myself, and serving separate meals to Aunt Kate in her own room. My aunt, of course, weaved through the various boarders, who moved in and out, like royalty visiting a slum, and complicated the life of the household not only by the separate meals in her room, but by locking herself in the bathroom at the busiest hours of traffic and refusing to budge—another bit of Blanche Du Bois—a rather good example, I think, of life imitating art.

We were all at breakfast that Sunday morning, except my aunt, who was already entrenched in the bathroom, when a telegram came for one of the boarders. He must return to St. Louis at once—a dying uncle or some such. He hurriedly packed his things, and as a parting gesture to my father, whom he liked, he left behind a number of books. My father was very pleased. He was not a great reader himself, but he had received so few gifts in his life that I think it was the idea of being given something that gave him a feeling of possession for those books and marked them as some sort of symbol for him.

In the afternoon my father went downtown to put a "room to let" advertisement in the papers, and when he returned, went directly to the late boarder's room to collect his books. They were gone.

Aunt Kate had taken them and blithely given them to a neighbor upstairs. At first he couldn't believe it—then he demanded that she go upstairs and get the books back. She merely laughed at the very suggestion of doing such a thing. One did not ask for a gift to be returned. The fact that they were not hers to give she blandly passed by—and then herself produced the straw that finally broke the camel's back. "Just some old socialist stuff by Eugene Debs," she scoffed. "Lucky to have it out of the house."

It was unfair and unkind, and it was the last time she ever baited my father. All the accumulated years of rage and frustration came out in a great burst of violence. It was frightening to see the reservoir of hate in this mild little man spill over. Frightening and astonishing, both. I had hardly been aware of my father before. But Debs was his hero, and somehow his name was the touchstone that set off all the indignities and failures of my father's own life. I had never seen him like that before, nor have I since that day. He ordered my aunt from the house and stood over her while she packed. For once my mother's tears availed her nothing, and while I watched horrified, my wonderful Aunt Kate dwindled before my eyes to a frightened old maid, gathering her bits of foolish finery together and dropping her beloved programs from trembling hands all over the floor. It was a terrible scene and I'm not sure that I have ever forgiven my father for it, right though he was. She left the house that day and never returned, and for many years I was not allowed to see her.

It is difficult to recapture now the full impact that quarrel had upon me. A child's world is made up of the immediate and the absolute. He does not look past today or tomorrow—the tragedy of the moment is an all-enveloping one, and in a very real sense my aunt's leave-taking represented both a tragedy and a crisis in my life. It marked an end and a beginning. All through those early years I had had no real relationship with either my father or my mother. The two dominant figures in my life had been first my grandfather and then my aunt. I had literally been taken over— alienated, if you will, from my parents at the very beginning. We faced a dilemma now, my parents and I, that was not easy to resolve, nor am I sure that we ever did resolve it. For the first time in my life I was entirely theirs—and we were strangers to each other, almost as though I had been kept in some foreign country and had just returned to them.

I realize now that it was as hard for them as it was for me, but then I was bereft and vengeful. I needed someone to blame and I blamed my father. I think I dimly knew that he was a good man, but the gulf between us was a wide one. My aunt and the world she opened to me had come to mean a great deal. Now it was cut off— both she and it ceased to exist as though they had never been. I blamed him not only for the exile of my aunt but for the poverty in which we lived. Later on, I blamed him for the fact that I was unable to graduate from public school. I went to work the summer I reached the eighth grade, and never returned to school. It was obvious that I could not go back—the money I brought home during that summer vacation was too sorely needed. I hated school, but I desperately wanted to graduate; even the poorest families in the neighborhood saw to it that at least the eldest son or daughter graduated. It had little to do with the idea of education; it was the gesture that counted, and the gesture had meaning. It was a sign that however poor, no family was too poor for that. My bitterness and my sense of shame remained fresh for a long time. I lied when anyone asked me about my schooling, and each time I lied I blamed my father anew.

Children are not creatures of justice—they lay blame and praise about them as their needs demand. Somehow, I think he knew or sensed this in some instinctive way, and although he had never heard of Freud, he made what efforts he could within the harsh realities of daily existence to regain his son; but the damage had been done. Only once did I ever feel close to him and then I was unable to express what I felt or let him know that I understood.

It was the Christmas after my aunt had left the house, and since it was she who always supplied the tree and the presents for my brother and myself, this first Christmas without her was a bleak and empty one. I remember that I was more or less reconciled to it, because my father had worked only spasmodically throughout the year. Two of our rooms were vacant of boarders and my mother was doing her marketing farther and farther away from our neighborhood. This was always a sign that we were dangerously close to rock bottom, and each time it occurred I came to dread it more. It was one of the vicious landmarks of poverty that I had come to know well and the one I hated the most. As the bills at our regular grocer and butcher went unpaid, and my mother dared not even be seen at the stores lest they come to the doorways and yell after her publicly, she would trudge ten or twelve blocks to a whole new neighborhood, tell the new grocer or butcher that we had just moved in to some fictitious address around the corner, and establish credit for as long as she could. Thus we were able to exist until my father found work again, or all the rooms were rented, and she could pay our own grocer and butcher, and gradually the others. This time, however, they had all of them gone unpaid and my mother was walking twenty blocks or more for a bottle of milk.

Obviously Christmas was out of the question—we were barely staying alive. On Christmas Eve my father was very silent during the evening meal. Then he surprised and startled me by turning to me and saying, "Let's take a walk." He had never suggested such a thing before, and moreover it was a very cold winter's night. I was even more surprised when he said as we left the house, "Let's go down to a Hundred Forty-ninth Street and Westchester Avenue." My heart leapt within me. That was the section where all the big stores were, where at Christmastime open pushcarts full of toys stood packed end-to-end for blocks at a stretch. On other Christmas Eves I had often gone there with my aunt, and from our tour of the carts she had gathered what I wanted the most. My father had known of this, of course, and I joyously concluded that this walk could mean only one thing—he was going to buy me a Christmas present.

On the walk down I was beside myself with delight and an inner relief. It had been a bad year for me, that year of my aunt's going, and I wanted a Christmas present terribly—not a present merely, but a symbol, a token of some sort. I needed some sign from my father or mother that they knew what I was going through and

[23]

cared for me as much as my aunt and my grandfather did. I am sure they were giving me what mute signs they could, but I did not see them. The idea that my father had managed a Christmas present for me in spite of everything filled me with a sudden peace and lightness of heart I had not known in months.

We hurried on, our heads bent against the wind, to the cluster of lights ahead that was 149th Street and Westchester Avenue, and those lights seemed to me the brightest lights I had ever seen. Tugging at my father's coat, I started down the line of pushcarts. There were all kinds of things that I wanted, but since nothing had been said by my father about buying a present, I would merely pause before a pushcart to say, with as much control as I could muster, "Look at that chemistry set!" or, "There's a stamp album!" or, "Look at the printing press!" Each time my father would pause and ask the pushcart man the price. Then without a word we would move on to the next pushcart. Once or twice he would pick up a toy of some kind and look at it and then at me, as if to suggest this might be something I might like, but I was ten years old and a good deal beyond just a toy; my heart was set on a chemistry set or a printing press. There they were on every pushcart we stopped at, but the price was always the same and soon I looked up and saw we were nearing the end of the line. Only two or three more pushcarts remained. My father looked up, too, and I heard him jingle some coins in his pocket. In a flash I knew it all. He'd gotten together about seventy-five cents to buy me a Christmas present, and he hadn't dared say so in case there was nothing to be had for so small a sum.

As I looked up at him I saw a look of despair and disappointment in his eyes that brought me closer to him than I had ever been in my life. I wanted to throw my arms around him and say, "It doesn't matter . . . I understand . . . this is better than a chemistry set or a printing press . . . I love you." But instead we stood shivering beside each other for a moment—then turned away from the last two pushcarts and started silently back home. I don't know why the words remained choked up within me. I didn't even take his hand on the way home nor did he take mine. We were not on that

[24]

basis. Nor did I ever tell him how close to him I felt that night—that for a little while the concrete wall between father and son had crumbled away and I knew that we were two lonely people struggling to reach each other.

I came close to telling him many years later, but again the moment passed. Again it was Christmas and I was on my way to visit him in Florida. My father was a bright and blooming ninety-one years of age now and I arrived in Florida with my wife to spend Christmas and New Year's with him. On Christmas Eve we sat in his living room, and while my wife chatted with his nurse and companion, I sat on a sofa across the room with my father, showing him the pictures of his two grandchildren. Suddenly I felt his hand slip into mine. It was the first time in our lives that either of us had ever touched the other. No words were spoken and I went right on turning the pages of the picture album, but my hand remained over his. A few years before I might have withdrawn mine after a moment or two, but now my hand remained; nor did I tell him what I was thinking and feeling. The moment was enough. It had taken forty years for the gulf that separated us to close.

With my mother the gulf that parted us was even wider, and it remained so forever. I felt sorrow for her, I admired her, but I did not like her. If this seems like a heartless impertinence I do not mean it so. It is said in terms of compassion and not of complaint. Within her limitations she was a woman of decent instincts and exemplary behavior, and her lot was a hard one. The days of her life were spent in a constant battle of keeping peace between her father and her sister, and later on, after my grandfather died, between her sister and her husband. The struggle robbed her of her children—people who spend their lives in appeasing others have little left to give in the way of love. It was her tragedy, as well as my brother's and my own. At a certain age, sometimes early, sometimes late, children make up their minds about their parents. They decide, not always justly, the kind of people their mothers and fathers are, and the judgment can be a stern one; as cruel, perhaps, as mine was, for it was maintained through the years and was not lessened by the fact that to the end of her days my mother showed not the faintest sign of understanding either the man she had married or the sons she had produced.

Thus the scene is set. This was the world I lived in and these were the people who shaped and formed the human being I was to become.

There were two other motivating influences—two compelling forces in my life at that time which, though intangible and inanimate, served as sharply as the people around me to mold the direction that all the years that followed were to take. The first was a goad. The second, a goal.

The goad, in a nutshell, was poverty. Now, there is nothing about poverty in itself that is in any way disgraceful, and I have noticed that children of poor families do not in any way seem to feel humiliated or hampered by it. Indeed, in many ways they lead a freer and less thwarted life than the constantly supervised children of the well-to-do. Moreover, since all the other children they know are also poor, they take it for granted that this is the way the world is, and it is not until the awakening years of adolescence that an awareness comes that the world is somewhat unevenly divided between the rich and the poor.

Somehow this did not hold true in my case. I have never been able to explain satisfactorily to myself or to others just why I hated poverty so passionately and savagely. I can only remember that my childhood from quite early on was filled with a series of bitter resolves to get myself out of it—to escape to a less wretched world than the one I knew. I recall a few years ago having a heated argument on the pronunciation of the word "squalor" with someone who insisted that it was pronounced squay-lor. I argued that it was pronounced squah-lor, and finally to prove my point I said, "When I lived in it, it was squalor!"

Poverty was always a living and evil thing to me, and from the moment in my teens when I could scrape a few pennies together I tried, for however brief a time, to disguise the face of poverty as best I could. I used to go without lunch for a week or ten days until I had accumulated enough to eat in a restaurant that had tablecloths instead of having a frankfurter or hamburger at a Sixth Avenue sidewalk orange-juice stand, which was the usual. Or I would stroll into the lobby of a fashionable hotel and walk around for as long as I dared, making believe that I belonged there. If all of this has a faintly ignominious and snobbish air, I do not defend it. That is the way it was, and doubtless there must have been another side to me too—less foolish and perhaps more admirable. Perhaps all this accounts in some measure for the extravagant way I have lived from the moment large sums of money began to pour in. I know my profligacy has been a cause of head-shaking among my friends, but my hatred for those years I am now speaking of was bound to affect me one way or the other. Either it would make me afraid of ever being poor again and therefore cautious and miserly, or it would send me sprawling among the gaudy and foolish goods the world has to offer, leaving a trail of greenbacks flowing heedlessly behind me. The latter is what happened and I prefer it so. I have built needless wings on my house in the country and planted thousands of trees on my land, so that the late Alexander Woollcott was prompted to remark a little contemptuously, "Just what God would have done if He had the money." I did not mind. I am not a fool about money but I do not live in fear of it. That fear I lived with in my childhood, and then I was through with it for good and all. That, indeed, was the goad and it served its purpose.

The goal, of course, was Broadway and the theatre. I had no idea how I was to achieve it, but I knew at once there was no other world possible for me. I believed this with all the dedication and the mysticism of a religious. The struggle to reach that world is the story I have chosen to tell; for I have no wish to merely set down a succession of theatrical anecdotes with famous names splattered among the pages in gossip-column fashion. I have never understood the avidity with which people read about the celebrated, and though I have known most of the famous literary and theatrical figures of my time, it is not my intention to reduce these friendships to a pleasant reportage. If the reader has read this far, perhaps he will already know that I consider the memories and pledges that were part of the struggle that preceded success the vital ones, and that I must set them down as though what happened was of great importance, as indeed it was to me, and I have set the stage accordingly. My feet were embedded in the Upper Bronx, but my eyes were set firmly toward Broadway.

I WANTED, of course, to be an actor. It never occurred to me that these godlike creatures did not themselves make up the words that flowed so effortlessly and magnificently from their lips. I think I believed they created a play as they went along—a belief, I am convinced, that some portions of a matinée audience still cling to. More than once, sitting in the audience at a play of mine, I have heard the lady behind me exclaim, "The clever things actors say! Aren't they wonderful!" And I have been tempted to say, "Not *that* wonderful, madame!" But I have understood her bewitchment. Not even in my wildest dreams of glory did I ever imagine that I would one day write the words for actors to speak on the stage, and not until long afterward did I come to know that there were more important figures in the theatre than the gods of my idolatry.

Had I had the wit to perceive it, there was already a hint that I was a dramatist; even then I could dramatize a story and hold an audience, and when I inadvertently stumbled on this gift, I used it the way other boys use a good pitching arm or a long reach in basketball. It gave me the only standing I was ever to have in the tough and ruthless world of boys of my own age, and I wielded the tiny sense of power it gave me hungrily and shrewdly. Even in the long-ago days when I was growing up, the cult of "toughness" in American life was beginning to blossom and flower. The non-athletic boy, the youngster who liked to read or listen to music, who could not fight or was afraid to, or the boy who had some special interest that was strange or alien to the rest, like the theatre in my case, was banished from the companionship of the others by rules of the "tough" world that was already beginning to prevail.

It is a mistake to believe that this cult of "toughness" was limited to the poor neighborhood in which we lived. It had begun to pervade other levels of American life, and I suspect that today's bland dismissal of the intellectual and the overwhelming emphasis placed on the necessity of competing and of success are due in part to the strange taboo we have set against that softness in ourselves which brings men closest to the angels. A nation of poets would be no more desirable than a nation of athletes, but I wonder if that toughness and competitiveness, which have become an ingrained part of our character as a people and a symbol of our way of life as a nation, are not a sign of weakness as well as of strength. Is our cultural life not robbed of a necessary dimension and our emotional life of an element of grace? And I wonder if the fear of a lack of toughness in our children does not sometimes rob them of an awakening awareness and sensitivity in the realm of the spirit that are each child's birthright and his weapon of rebellion against the accepted norm of his time. This lack of toughness and the inability to compete were a constant agony of my own childhood, and I lived it through as best I could.

A city child's summer is spent in the street in front of his home, and all through the long summer vacations I sat on the curb and watched the other boys on the block play baseball or prisoner's base or gutter hockey. I was never asked to take part even when one team had a member missing—not out of any special cruelty, but because they took it for granted I would be no good at it. They were right, of course. Yet much of the bitterness and envy and loneliness I suffered in those years could have been borne better if a single wise teacher or a knowledgeable parent had made me understand that there were compensations for the untough and the nonathletic; that the world would not always be bounded by the curbstone in front of the house.

One of those compensations I blundered into myself, and its effect was electric on both me and the tough world of the boys on the block. I have never forgotten the joy of that wonderful evening when it happened. There was no daylight-saving in those days, and the baseball and other games ended about eight or eight thirty, when it grew dark. Then it was the custom of the boys to retire to a little stoop that jutted out from the candy store on the corner and that somehow had become theirs through tribal right. No grownup ever sat there or attempted to. There the boys would sit, talking aimlessly for hours on end. There were the usual probings of sex and dirty jokes, not too well defined or clearly understood; but mostly the talk was of the games played during the day and of the game to be played tomorrow. Ultimately, long silences would fall and then the boys would wander off one by one. It was just after one of those long silences that my life as an outsider changed, and for one glorious summer I was accepted on my own terms as one of the tribe. I can no longer remember which boy it was that summer evening who broke the silence with a question; but whoever he was, I nod to him in gratitude now. "What's in those books you're always reading?" he asked idly. "Stories," I answered. "What kind?" asked somebody else without much interest.

Nor do I know what impelled me to behave as I did, for usually I just sat there in silence, glad enough to be allowed to remain among them; but instead of answering his question, I launched full tilt into the book I was immersed in at the moment. The book was *Sister Carrie* and I told them the story of Sister Carrie for two full hours. They listened bug-eyed and breathless. I must have told it well, but I think there was another and deeper reason that made them so flattering an audience. Listening to a tale being told in the dark is one of the most ancient of man's entertainments, but I was offering them as well, without being aware of doing it, a new and exciting experience.

The books they themselves read were the *Rover Boys* or *Tom Swift* or G. A. Henty. I had read them too, but at thirteen I had long since left them behind. Since I was much alone I had become an omnivorous reader and I had gone through the books-for-boys-series in one vast gulp. In those days there was no intermediate reading material between children's and grownups' books, or I could find none, and since there was no one to say me nay, I had gone right from *Tom Swift and His Flying Machine* to Theodore Dreiser and *Sister Carrie*. Dreiser had hit my young mind and senses with the impact of a thunderbolt, and they listened to me tell the story with some of the wonder that I had had in reading it.

It was, in part, the excitement of discovery—the discovery that there could be another kind of story that gave them a deeper kind of pleasure than the *Rover Boys*—blunderingly, I was giving them a glimpse of the riches contained outside the world of *Tom Swift*. Not one of them left the stoop until I had finished, and I went upstairs that wonderful evening not only a member of the tribe but a figure in my own right among them.

The next night and many nights thereafter, a kind of unspoken ritual took place. As it grew dark, I would take my place in the center of the stoop and, like Scheherazade, begin the evening's tale. Some nights, in order to savor my triumph more completely, I cheated. I would stop at the most exciting part of a story by Jack London or Frank Norris or Bret Harte, and without warning tell them that that was as far as I had gone in the book and it would have to be continued the following evening. It was not true, of course; but I had to make certain of my new-found power and position, and with a sense of drama that I did not know I possessed, I spun out the long summer evenings until school began again in the fall. Other words of mine have been listened to by larger and more fashionable audiences, but for that tough and grimy one that huddled on the stoop outside the candy store, I have an unreasoning affection that will last forever. It was a memorable summer, and it was the last I was to spend with the boys on the block.

The following summer, since I was now thirteen years old, I would be able to obtain "working papers" and get a job downtown for the summer months. The prospect of getting away from "the block," of nudging closer to that small shimmering area where Broadway lay, made life more endurable. All that winter I concocted grandiose dreams of getting a job as office boy for Klaw & Erlanger, or Florenz Ziegfeld, or Sam Harris, and somehow, some way, working my way down from the office and through the stage door. As the last days of school loomed ahead, I scanned the Sunday advertisements more and more desperately, searching for an ad that would read, "Office or errand boy wanted in theatrical office." There were none, of course. There were errand and office boy ads by the dozen, office and errand boys wanted by every other business under the sun; but no such ad as I looked for ever appeared, and in time to come I learned why none was ever likely to. Nepotism runs through the theatre with the grandeur of the Mississippi at flood time, and when an office boy is needed, there is always a nephew on hand; if a secretary is wanted, a niece or a cousin magically appears. This may account in part for the fact that theatrical telephone messages are inevitably garbled, manuscripts go unread, and theatrical correspondence continues to be a whimsical affair that goes largely unanswered. But all this I did not know then. I persisted in believing the ad I dreamed of would certainly appear the following Sunday.

School closed and still I stubbornly waited, until it became imperative that I take whatever job I could get if I was going to work at all that summer. In desperation I even boldly considered the idea of marching into a theatrical office and asking point-blank for a job; but I lacked the courage and, as a matter of fact, I didn't even know where any of the offices were. By the time I was ready to concede defeat, all the best jobs were gone and I took the only job I could get. It was quite a distance from Broadway, and the heavy steel door I pushed open and closed fifty times a day as part of my job was a far cry from the stage door I had fondly hoped to pass through; but I was working "downtown" and a step nearer my goal. If I looked northward from 14th Street, as I stood on the steps of the subway station each night, I could see the golden glow of Times Square in the distance.

I worked in the storage vault of a large wholesale furrier, and my job was to open the vault as the hampers of wet skins were brought in and then hang the furs on racks to dry. It was tedious work, but it was cool inside the vault and I had ample time to read. It had another compensation, that job, and I took full advantage of it once I stoically accepted the fact that people were likely to hold their noses and walk rapidly away if they happened to pass within ten feet of me. They had good reason to. I possessed only one suit of clothes and that suit I wore to work every day. Not that it would have made much difference if I had owned a dozen suits and worn a different one each day, for after eight hours in a vault with un-cured skins any article of clothing, even a handkerchief, emerged smelling to high heaven.

Out of the vault I would come at the end of each day, into the steaming midsummer heat, every day smelling progressively worse, and make my way down the subway stairs, grimly reconciled to the nightly battle of pushing and shoving my way into the Bronx Express. And therein lay the compensation. The inhuman crush in the subway during the rush hours was just as great then as it is now, and like the rest of the wretched subway riders, I would fight my way into the train and then fight again for enough elbow space to read my book on the long ride uptown. Things changed for the better as I began to smell really awful and the weather grew hotter. Avenues of space would open up around me, and sometimes if I resolutely leaned over a lady who was sitting down, she would give up by 125th Street and I would sink down into her seat with plenty of room on either side of me. I could not smell myself, fortunately, for my olfactory senses had been anesthetized by the daily smell of the vault, and after the first shock of having someone yell at me, "Boy, you stink out loud!" I pretended not to hear either the mut-tered threats or the imprecations of my fellow subway riders and would gaze innocently around me for a moment as though trying to discover who it was that smelled so bad, and then bury my face in my book or newspaper.

A new excitement had come into my reading life—the newspaper. Not just any newspaper, but the finest newspaper of its era and, for my part, one of the finest journalistic achievements of our time. The newspaper was the New York *World,* which at the time I speak of, and for some years following, was in its full power and glory. I devoured it daily. It would be truer to say I savored it daily, for I read the news section cover-to-cover on the way downtown in the morning and sternly resisted the temptation to look at the page opposite the editorial page until the journey uptown at night. I saved and hoarded that section like the proverbial stick of candy. It was the high moment of my day and that was why I needed space around me and sufficient concentration to enjoy it to the full. All my new gods were on that page. Heywood Broun and then Alexander Woollcott, doing dramatic criticism; Deems Taylor, music; Laurence Stallings, book reviews; William Bolitho, writing about everything under the sun; and finally, F.P.A. and "The Conning Tower," illuminating not only the world of the theatre, but the world of wit and laughter as well, and making them both seem even more desirable. Every Saturday morning his "Diary of Our Own Samuel Pepys" appeared, and I would breathlessly go through the week with him on a round of opening nights, opening-night parties afterward, lunches at the Algonquin Round Table, poker parties at the Swopes', and all kinds of high jinks at Neysa McNein's studio, where all these giants seemed constantly to forgather as if by magic and spin out the nights in a spate of insults and ribaldry. Famous initials and names spattered the diary like a translucent Milky Way: G.S.K. and Beatrice—A.W. and Harpo—Alice Duer Miller and Smeed—Benchley and Dottie—Bob Sherwood and Marc—I. Berlin and J. Kern—H. Ross and Sullivan—H.B.S. and Maggie. The initiate knew that G.S.K. was George S. Kaufman; Dottie was Dorothy Parker; H.B.S. was Herbert Bayard Swope; and so on ad infinitum. If all this has the faint air of a star-struck movie fan standing in the forecourt of Grauman's Chinese Theatre and gazing down at the footsteps of his favorites preserved in cement, I suppose that is exactly what I was doing, only with newsprint instead of cement, and with, I need hardly point out, a slightly superior product.

Yet no movie I have ever seen has dared to be as gauche and idiotically Cinderella-like as life itself dares to be and is. Even I, with my head full of wild dreams of glory as I closed the door of the vault behind me each day, would have had to stretch credulity to its limits to believe all the lucky accidents and the fortunate coincidences that lay in the life just ahead of me. I make no pretense about it and I never have—I have been extremely lucky. Such talent as I possess I have used well and industriously, but talent alone is not enough. I do not mean to suggest that luck *per se* plays the major part in success, theatrical or otherwise; but I venture to guess that in the grand design of any successful career the element of luck has been a powerful factor. Perhaps luck is too easy a word—too all-inclusive. A sense of timing would be more accurate— or perhaps a quirk of character that enables its fortunate possessor to tread the main path and never swerve from it. Every successful person I have ever known has had it—actor or businessman, writer or politician. It is that instinct or ability to sense and seize the right moment without wavering or playing safe, and without it many gifted people flicker brilliantly and briefly and then fade into oblivion in spite of their undoubted talents.

It would have been hard to convince me then that I was one of the lucky ones, however; for week after week the door of the vault closed behind me and the weeks finally lengthened out into months.

And then it happened. In one day—actually in one after, noon. My fantasy of getting a job in a theatrical office turned into reality, and it seemed not at all strange to me that it should. At the believing age, the old saw that "dreams come true" is taken quite as a matter of course by the very young. It happened none too soon. I had been two and a half years in the storage vault by this time. I was almost seventeen and the lingering look I turned toward the lights of Broadway each evening before I plunged down the subway steps, was growing daily more bitter.

One morning in the early fall I decided in the darkness of the vault that when I went out for lunch that day that steel door was going to swing behind me for the last time. Perhaps it was because my head was full of the accounts in the papers of the new theatrical season just beginning—yet another season that I was not even a microscopic part of. Perhaps it was the sharp sting of going from the brilliant September sunshine into the darkness of the vault that made my lot seem downright insupportable. Whatever it was, I made my decision. I would not return to that vault, stack those skins for another day, if we all starved!

At twelve o'clock I took down my lunch box, gave a last look around and walked out. I didn't give notice or say good-bye. I hated everyone and everything at A. L. Neuburger Furs, Inc. I ate my lunch on a bench in Union Square and tried to feel a lift of the heart or a slight taste of my new-found freedom. I could do neither.

I well knew that I could not afford to be out of work for so much as a week, with the present state of things at home. For a moment I wavered, but not for more than a moment. Character is destiny, and even then I did not believe in second chances. I snapped the lunch box shut and stood up. I had gone over the Help Wanted ads while I ate. One job was more miserable than the other. Packers, stockroom boys, shipping clerks were all wanted in abundance. The halfway decent jobs (what there were of them) all starkly proclaimed, "High school education necessary"—so that avenue was closed to me. Like Scarlett O'Hara, then not yet even born in Margaret Mitchell's mind, I resolved to think of all that tomorrow. Right now, I turned my face toward Times Square and started walking. This afternoon, at least, I'd have an authentic smell of Broadway, the real thing.

I decided to pay a visit to my one and only link with the theatre, thin though that link was. My friend, George Steinberg, who lived in the apartment next to ours, had the very job I coveted above all jobs. He was an office boy in a theatrical office. I cultivated his friendship shamelessly, though it seemed to me an unjust caprice of fate that George, who cared nothing whatever about the theatre, should have an Aunt Belle who worked in a theatrical office, while the only relative I had who was even remotely connected with the theatre, was a cousin who painted posters for a movie house in Brooklyn. Moreover, George actually hated working in a theatrical office. He was as incapable of understanding my fascination for his job as I was of understanding his loathing of it. In an irritated way I think I dimly grasped why he felt as he did, for George was by all odds the shyest human being I've ever known—"painfully shy" was a phrase that fit him exactly—and I think the flamboyancy of actors, actresses and theatre people in general embarrassed him. Almost every evening we would meet after dinner for a long walk, and my questions were never-ending. Why he endured them and how our friendship continued I do not profess to understand, for I was avid for every small detail of the office, and to make him talk about it seemed to increase his dislike of the job threefold.

I thought of all this as I walked toward 42nd Street—the gods were blind indeed—and as I finally stood looking up at the façade of the New Amsterdam Theatre I sighed. Imagine going to work every day by walking through a lobby where the Ziegfeld *Follies* was playing instead of having a steel door clang shut behind you! I stood in the lobby and looked at the pictures for a moment before I pressed the elevator button. There they all were—Marilyn Miller, Will Rogers, Fanny Brice, W. C. Fields—and on the office directory next to the elevator, the magical names: Florenz Ziegfeld, George Tyler, A. L. Erlanger, Aarons & Freedly, and a horde of others.

When the elevator door opened, it would not have surprised me at all to see Marilyn Miller step out on the arm of Florenz Ziegfeld; but it was empty. I got in and managed to blurt out, "Eighth floor, please." As the elevator shot upward I sniffed delightedly. I am not certain that it is so, but it has always seemed to me that theatres, both backstage and front, have a very special odor of their own. It is an odor as definite to my nostrils as the smell of a hospital or a ship. I have always been immediately conscious of it, and I was aware of it then.

When I got out at the eighth floor I hesitated. What in the world was I going to say to George? My sudden appearance would be certain to plunge him into a paroxysm of shyness. But I was determined to go through with it. I opened the door marked "Augustus Pitou, Theatrical Enterprises" and walked in. I recognized Aunt Belle immediately in the tiny outer office, just as George had described it. She sat typing fiercely, her head bent over the machine. Without looking up and before the door had even closed behind me, she barked out, "No casting today. Come back in two weeks." She finished the letter, ripped it out of the roller, and as she inserted the envelope she spoke again, still without looking up. "Didn't you hear me? No casting today."

"May I speak to George, please?" I said.

"George isn't here," she answered, her fingers never stopping, her head still bent over the typewriter. It had never occurred to me that George might be out on some errand. If I left now, without even a glimpse of the office, I would have to start looking for a new job, and the chance would most certainly not occur soon again.

"Could I wait for him, please?" I pleaded.

"He won't be here any more. He quit today."

"He quit? You mean he gave up the job?" My voice must have had a note of such incredulity in it that Aunt Belle looked up for the first time.

"Who are you? A friend of George's?"

I nodded. "We live next door to each other."

"Well, he quit," said Aunt Belle. "Try and do good for your relatives!"

She glared at me in annoyance, and as I still stood there staring at her, she said, "Well, good-bye. I'm busy. Maybe he'll explain to *you* why he walked out of an easy job that pays fifteen dollars a week." Her head bent over the machine again.

In a dazzling moment, I saw the finger of fate beckoning me on. I took a deep breath and plunged. "Miss Belle," I said, "could I have the job? I just quit my old job today, too."

The typewriter stopped and she looked at me again. "Sure, why not? Save putting an ad in the paper, and I got no more nephews, thank God. Go in and see Mr. Pitou and ask him if it's all right if you're the new office boy. Don't tell him you're a friend of George's—make like you just came around looking for a job."

I stood there immobilized.

"Go ahead," she said irritably, "you want the job or don't you?"

Did I want the job!

I walked past her and knocked on Mr. Pitou's door. It seemed an unconscionable time until a voice said, "Come in." Mr. Pitou was seated with his back to the door, his head bent over a long booking-route sheet, and like Aunt Belle, he did not look up. In fact, he did not so much as glance at me throughout the entire interview, if such it may be termed.

"What is it?" he said, after a long moment.

"Miss Belle sent me in to see you, Mr. Pitou," I replied. "Is it all right for me to be the new office boy?" Again I waited. Mr. Pitou seemed not to have heard and I did not dare to speak again. Suppose he wanted someone who had worked in a theatrical office before; or suppose he had a nephew himself? My voice quavered a bit as I finally felt impelled to break the silence.

"I'm sure I could do it," I said, "because I'm crazy about the theatre." Fortunately this remark was lost on Mr. Pitou, for at that moment he seemed to be having trouble finding a paper on his desk.

"What?" he said.

He paused, and for a terrible moment I thought a waft of my unmistakable aroma had reached him. He lifted his head and seemed to be sniffing the air. I moved away and stood by the open window. He sneezed—and my heart stopped pounding. It started to pound again when he spoke.

"Fifteen dollars a week," he said. "Could you start tomorrow morning?"

"I could start now, sir," I said. I had difficulty not shouting it at him.

"That's good," he said. "What's your name?"

"Moss Hart," I replied.

"Mouse?" he said, mispronouncing the name immediately. "Take this booking sheet down to George Tyler. He's on the fourth floor. And take this note up to Goldie, Mr. Ziegfeld's secretary—that's on the floor above this. And wait for an answer in both places."

He handed me the booking sheet and the letter without looking up, already lost in what I came to know as his daily bible, the *Railway Guide*.

I closed the door behind me. "I got it, Miss Belle!" This time I actually did shout. *"I got it!"*

She looked up, a little startled. "What's the matter?" she asked.

"I got the job," I said, waving the papers in my hand.

"Well, that's good," said Miss Belle. "You can run out first and get me a container of coffee and some aspirin. My head is splitting."

I did not realize until much later how fitting it was, that I should make my entry into the theatre with a container of black coffee in one hand and an aspirin in the other, but the future has seldom held the same roseate glow as it did for me at that particular moment.

As it turned out, I couldn't have contrived a better beginning in the theatre than to start as an office boy for Augustus Pitou. True, Mr. Pitou was not exactly a "Broadway" producer, but his was a theatrical office nonetheless, and it was in the New Amsterdam Theatre Building, smack among the great ones, to boot.

Augustus Pitou, Jr. (to give him his full name), and his father before him, was known as the "King of the One Night Stands." Mr. Pitou, Sr., had long since passed on, but he had left to Augustus Pitou, Jr., a stable of stars, a map of the United States, the *Official Railway Guide,* and the route sheets. The stars were: Chauncey Olcott, Fiske O'Hara, May Robson, Elsa Ryan, Joseph Regan and Gerald Griffin. With the possible exception of Chauncey Olcott, Fiske O'Hara and May Robson, I doubt if the theatregoing public of New York had ever heard of them; but to the residents of Fond du Lac and Eau Claire, Wisconsin, their annual one-night stand was an event not to be missed.

Each year, beginning on Labor Day, six companies with six different stars spread out over the land, bearing the imprint "Augustus Pitou, Jr., presents . . . " and from Labor Day until the following June 30, they played engagements of one night each in hamlets scattered north, east, south and west. Occasionally, in cities like Los Angeles, San Francisco and Seattle, they settled in for the luxury of a three-day or a week's stand; but other than that, it was: "Tonight, Huron, Michigan . . . tomorrow night, Green Bay."

They left for the railroad station as the curtain fell or on the six o'clock train out the next morning, rode all day, and got to the next theatre barely in time to slap on some make-up and take their places on the stage. When one considers that Fiske O'Hara invariably sang ten or twelve songs during the course of his performance each evening, and that May Robson—already nearly sixty—was duly expected, as the star of her production, never to leave the stage for more than a few moments, the conclusion that a more rugged breed of actors existed in those days is inescapable.

True, they complained a good deal, almost daily. A letter would arrive at the office from one star or another denouncing this season's bookings; for Mr. Pitou, in spite of his wizardry with the *Railway Guide,* sometimes cut things awfully close to the knuckle. There would be a week now and then when the poor creatures would never get near a bed at all, but would sleep sitting up during the day on the train and exist on chocolate bars and apples. In spite of this, the office was always crowded with actors, eager to take the long tour —a further proof, if one is needed, that the profession was quite as lunatic then as it is now.

Nor can I ever recall an instance of May Robson's or Fiske O'Hara's missing a performance. And, of course, there was no such thing as an understudy. When the good folk of Butte, Montana, bought their tickets each year to see May Robson, it would have been a brave stage manager indeed who could have come out in front of the curtain to announce that the understudy was going on that night. Sick or well, exhausted or hungry, the curtain went up every night from September until the following June 30, and that was that.

More astonishing still was the fact that one single playwright wrote all the plays. Each separate star had a new vehicle tailored for him each season, and one person executed every one of them. Her name was Anne Nichols. It was a sad day, indeed—nay, a cataclysmic one—for Mr. Pitou when *Abie's Irish Rose* miraculously turned into a success. It ruined him in more ways than one; and the triumph of that incredible play was to change my own fate considerably, too.

At this happy moment, however, Augustus Pitou was safely enthroned forever, or so it seemed, as King of the One Night Stands. Each evening as he left the office he would write on a small slip of paper his estimate of the evening's receipts of each of the shows, fold it over and hand it to me. And sure enough, the following morning when I opened the telegrams sent in by the various company managers from all parts of the country, Mr. Pitou's shrewd guess would be right almost to the very dollar. He even knew how much a hog-calling contest in Sheboygan would affect the receipts if the show played Sheboygan the same evening; or if a parade of the Sons of Erin in St. Louis would keep them outdoors too late to get them to the theatre to see Fiske O'Hara. He would smile happily at the telegrams, riffle through his mail, attend to such details as needed immediate attention, and then settle back contentedly behind the *Railway Guide* and the booking sheet.

It was the one and only thing he really enjoyed doing in a business that he hated. It took me a little time to realize this and at first I could not believe it. But Mr. Pitou loathed the theatre almost more than George did, if such a thing were possible. Indeed, the one thing that made it bearable for him at all was the fact that once the companies were launched on Labor Day, he need never lay eyes on another actor again for six whole months and could nestle down with the mosaic-like task of putting together next year's bookings.

As June came on, and with it the approach of the returning companies, he grew increasingly nervous; and during July and August, the time of casting and rehearsing the next season's output—which also meant dealing with the stars themselves—he was at his wits' end. But by mid-September he was himself again. The white-covered *Railway Guide* appeared once more, and the voice of the turtle—and of May Robson and Fiske O'Hara—was heard throughout the land.

I have thought it necessary to describe at some length the particular kind of theatrical enterprise Mr. Pitou engaged in, for it illuminates how deeply the theatre has changed in a comparatively short period of time, and it makes quickly apparent the fact that I was still a somewhat far cry from being entangled with "Broadway." Yet this first active attachment to the theatre, removed though it was from the larger world of Times Square, had the effect on me of that first stiff drink on a reformed alcoholic.

There may have been more efficient office boys than I was, but there was certainly not a happier one. Though I was not expected to open the office until nine o'clock each morning, I got there a full hour before—not through any sense of industry on my part, but simply because I delighted in just being there. Likewise, when Mr. Pitou left to take the 5:30 train to Bayside, Long Island, I was free to go also; but I seldom left the office before seven o'clock. Though I never learned in two and a half years how to stack skins correctly in their respective racks, I was able with ridiculous ease to use the complicated *Railway Guide* and lay out a booking route like a professional in no time at all. Even the dullest aspects of the job I found enjoyable.

There was one thing, however, that I could not seem to learn, try as I would, and it almost cost me my precious job. I could not for the life of me say, "No casting today. Come back in two weeks," to the stream of actors that poured into the office. I had never actually seen an actor before, other than on the stage, and now that I was suddenly face to face with these wonderful beings, it seemed literally impossible for me to turn them away. Instead, I first asked them to sit down and wait for a while—perhaps Mr. Pitou could see them later. Then I discussed the various plays that Mr. Pitou would be doing and the possibilities of parts they might be suitable for, and while they blissfully waited we discussed everything they had done on the stage to date, from tentative beginnings clean through to minor triumphs and eventual hopes. It may be easily imagined what effect this unorthodox reception had on a people long used to being buffeted in and out of offices or summarily dismissed.

Within a few days the news was about that Mr. Pitou would see anyone and everyone, that he was about to invade Broadway (a rumor for which I was not entirely blameless), and that a fine array of choice parts and splendid salaries awaited even newcomers with little or no experience. The consequence was that the office was jammed throughout the entire day.

Mr. Pitou fought his way in in the morning, and what was worse still, he had to fight his way out every time he wanted to go to the bathroom, which was down the hall. Mr. Pitou, a slow-moving man, did not at first connect me with what he took to be a sudden, bewildering phenomenon or at the least a mistake on the part of the hapless actors; but quickly enough it dawned on him that I was the culprit. I was called in and sternly ordered to clear the outside office and keep it cleared. I did my best, but in spite of myself, the words, "No casting today, come back in two weeks," somehow always seemed to emerge as an invitation to sit down and talk about the theatre.

Finally, one morning Miss Belle announced tartly, "Mr. Pitou says that if the office is not empty when he goes to the bathroom today, we get a new office boy."

Thus ended forever, I should imagine, the last dim spark of gallantry among theatrical office boys. I managed under that dire threat to keep the office free of actors from then on, but I found it hard indeed to say "no" and turn them away. I still do.

Even now, by far the most difficult aspect of a production of mine which calls for a large cast is always the weeks of casting, and if it is a musical, the auditions. I still find it fairly agonizing to walk into a theatre or office jammed with actors and know that of the fifty and sometimes one hundred or so eagerly awaiting, no more than two or three at best will even get a chance to read for the part, though they must all be talked to or listened to and given some sort of reason for the rejection.

I know I have maddened the various producers I have worked with through the years by the amount of time I seem to take in saying "no" to actors who are obviously wrong for the part at first glance. Yet I persist in believing that the particular way one says "no" to an actor on a certain day, may very well give him the courage to go on in a hazardous and difficult profession.

It is equally true that after listening to a wearisome lot of people with no talent whatever for the theatre, men and women who would be better advised to marry at once or sell knitted ties in a haberdashery, I feel far sorrier for myself than I do for them. But there can be no denying the fact that offering one's physical self for inspection, exposing one's talent to the test of standing alone on a bare stage and speaking out into the void of a dark and empty auditorium, is a harsh and cruel way of pursuing one's life work.

I have always marveled at how actors survive, year after year, this inhuman aspect of their profession. Of course, stars and established players are not usually asked to read for a part; but in the main, most actors accept the necessity for doing so. It is unfortunately a necessity, for most authors and directors, myself included, insist on a reading, sometimes even with leading players, before deciding definitely on the actor.

It has, it must be noted, its brighter side. Sometimes an inexperienced tyro reading for the first time will capture a part against experienced professionals. But to me it still remains the most difficult of all hazards in a profession studded with varying degrees of humiliation. The playwright, the composer and the other artisans of the theatre, all face exposure of some sort or another in a deeply personal sense. It is their work that is exposed, however, and not their physical self. That is the difference—and a large difference it is. It has always placed me squarely on the actor's side and I think I have profited by it.

For the moment, nevertheless, I had to learn to say a brisk and authoritative "no" to all unfortunates who opened the office door, and once an open path to the bathroom down the hall was secured, I quickly became indispensable to Mr. Pitou. I am ashamed to relate that within six months' time I displaced the formidable Miss Belle and became his secretary myself. This was not quite as ruthless as it may appear to be, since Miss Belle worked for two other entrepreneurs in the adjoining office as well as for Mr. Pitou, though I doubt she thought any the more kindly of me for taking over her job. I did not give too much thought to her feelings, however, for by this time a whole new life had opened for me.

I had early on joined the confederation of office boys who worked on 42nd Street, a sharp and knowing crew, the main by-product of whose jobs was the free tickets they dispensed to their bosses' shows: Freddie Kohlmar, of A. H. Woods' office; Jimmy, of the Selwyns'; Irving Morrison, of George Tyler's; the famous Goldie, of the Ziegfeld office; and a score of others. I could offer them no free tickets on my own, since the closest our shows ever came to New York was Albany, but I managed little favors, nevertheless, and very soon I was wallowing in what was for me ambrosia. In the first six months of my tenure with Mr. Pitou, and for the next year and a half afterward, I went solemnly to the theatre every evening, with the exception of Saturday nights, when the free list was suspended even for the flops.

Again, I could not have arranged a better time to have a gate swing open. It was the heyday of a flourishing New York theatre—the early 1920's. Seventy theatres were going full blast during the height of the season, and such pathfinders as the Provincetown, the Greenwich Village Theatre and the Neighborhood Playhouse were part of this largesse as well. One memorable week eleven new plays all opened on the same night. So crowded was the time that some new plays were offered only at special matinées on days when the play already in the theatre did not give one. It was thus that Eugene O'Neill was first introduced to uptown audiences.

It was that extraordinary time, too, when a number of exciting new playwrights all seemed to emerge in a burst of heedless exuberance and plenty. Though the imprint of Max Marcin, Sam Shipman and Edward Childs Carpenter still lay rather heavily on the theatre of the early twenties, names like Vincent Lawrence, Robert Sherwood, Sidney Howard, S. N. Behrman and Maxwell Anderson were appearing or were soon to make their appearance, to say nothing of Rodgers and Hart, Vincent Youmans and George Gershwin in the musical field. With my name on a "free list" every evening, I saw everything. I saw the failures first, of course. I was by no means fastidious in my choice. Just walking into a theatre and waiting for the curtain to go up was all I asked for. During the summer months, as the free lists to the hits opened up, I managed to wangle my name onto them—but I should like to wager that for a space of two years I witnessed more plays that closed in less than a week than any other living mortal, barring the critics who reviewed them.

This was not without some value, I believe. I am not suggesting that witnessing a spate of appallingly bad plays is a creditable method of learning how to write a good one, but it has its points. Though I had no idea whatever of writing plays at that time—the thought never crossed my mind—I am certain that some of those expository first acts, some of the ineptitudes of those second-act climaxes, and some of the stunning lack of invention in those third acts must somehow have seeped into my inner consciousness. The big "hit" of any season always seems absurdly simple; so effortlessly does it unfold, that it almost seems as though it could not have been written any other way. Watch a failure on the same subject, and you will see by what a slim margin the mistakes have been by-passed, the cul-de-sacs averted in the hit. I am inclined to think those wretched plays I sat through stood me in good stead long after I'd forgotten what they were even about.

I was grateful for the free tickets for quite another and more personal reason. Those free tickets brought Aunt Kate back into my life. Once I had tasted the joy of being able to go to the theatre with-out paying for it, and of sitting in the orchestra to boot, I was deter-mined to find Aunt Kate and escort her grandly into the orchestra. I knew that she had never sat anywhere but in the gallery all of her playgoing life. Seven years had passed since I had seen her, and nothing had been heard of her at our house since that terrible Sun-day when she left. Her name was not allowed to be mentioned. I knew she was still alive, for we certainly should have heard other-wise, and I had long since suspected that my mother received an occasional furtive letter from her; but she never spoke of it and I did not dare ask.

One Saturday evening, since I was bereft of the theatre, I paid a visit to the cousins in Brooklyn and made some discreet inquiries. Aunt Kate, of all things, was working only a few blocks away from the New Amsterdam Theatre. She had ultimately worn out her welcome with all the relatives she could visit for long stays, though she had managed to spin out these visits for five years by a carefully timed rotation, and for the last two years she had been custodian of linens in the Clara De Hirsch Home for Working Girls.

The next afternoon after lunch I went to the drug store on the corner and telephoned her. While I waited for her to be called to the phone, my mind raced ahead to the wonderful evenings we would have together and to the remembrance of those old evenings in the kitchen, and of how much she and they had meant to me. Then a voice said, "Hello." It was unmistakably Aunt Kate. She managed still to put into the simple word "Hello" all the archaic grandeur, all the necessary hauteur of a lady of fashion. Of sheets and pillowcases, and the fact that she had been forced to go to work for the first time in her life at the age of sixty, there was no hint. There was still all of Ouida and Mrs. Humphry Ward in that "Hello," and I could have hugged her!

When I said, "This is Moss, Aunt Kate," there was a glacial silence, and when she spoke again her voice was distant and cold. She had been very hurt, there was no doubt of that, by my failure to get in touch with her all these years, in spite of my father. But my eager-ness to see her again was so unmistakable and my pleasure at the prospect of taking her to the theatre so patent, that in a few moments she relented and we were interrupting each other quite like old times, until my nickels ran out.

What a joy it was to hear those grandiloquent and noble phrases roll forth once again after all the years of silence! What a pleasure it was going to be for me to have someone in my life once more whose passion for the theatre matched my own. And how satisfactory her reception was of the news that I was an office boy in a theatrical office—she received it as though I had announced my appointment as Ambassador to the Court of St. James's! With a sudden pang I realized all at once how deeply I had missed her. I wanted to run to the subway straight off and meet her that very afternoon, but this was one of her "working Sundays in," she grandly explained, so we agreed to meet on the following Tuesday evening. I had some lunch money saved up and I pleaded to take her to dinner before the theatre, but she insisted I come to dinner with her at the Clara De Hirsch Home first and then go on to the theatre afterward. While I was still urging her to let me take her to dinner, the operator cut us off and so our meeting was left as she had arranged it.

This turned out to be one of the most misbegotten ideas ever spawned by Aunt Kate, in a life not overly concerned with the fitness of things; but I did not know it then, of course, and I looked forward to Tuesday in a state of high excitement. Sunday and Monday dragged by somehow, and on Tuesday morning Mr. Pitou announced to my chagrin that he was not taking the 5:30 back to Bayside that afternoon, but was staying in town to take Mrs. Pitou to the theatre and would I mind working a little later. There was nothing I could do but agree, of course. Why I did not telephone my aunt that I would be delayed I have no idea, but I did not do so and I was well over a half-hour late for our appointment when Mr. Pitou finally left the office.

Once more I looked up the address in the telephone book to make sure and then I hurried out. The Clara De Hirsch Home for Working Girls was an estimable enterprise charitably run by good people to provide unattached and homeless girls with decent food and shelter in a city not much interested in their welfare. Yet as I hurried toward the building at the corner of Third Avenue, I wondered if any edifice need actually look so cheerless and desolate. Why do worthy institutions or good causes always lack any single element of gaiety or joy? The thought was a fleeting one, for there was a figure on the steps staring anxiously toward me.

It was a thin and emaciated woman who stood there, a woman who bore no resemblance to the bosomy and buxom Aunt Kate that I remembered. In a crowded street or subway I would have passed her by without a backward glance, for this was not Aunt Kate but a stranger. In a moment I was ascending the steps and I saw that it was indeed she. She was too upset at the moment, I think, to notice the astonished and unbelieving look of recognition on my face as I leaned over to kiss her, and now that I was here, some of the strain left her face and it seemed less gaunt and pinched.

I came to know later on that I had constituted her sole topic of conversation with the staff and the girls from the moment she had set foot in the place. No doubt her inventions and tales about me were as unlikely as the romantic and fashionable welter of stories that she made up about herself, but it was a touching proof of how much she had loved me. And when I had finally and at last called her and it seemed she could produce me in person for all to see, her excitement had been immense. God knows what tall tales she had told them about my present position in the theatre. If I knew Aunt Kate, nothing so plebeian as "office boy" would pass her lips. Thus, when I was over a half-hour late, she must have stood there in an agony of waiting for fear that I had forgotten or would not appear at all.

As we walked toward the door, I stole a sideways glance at her. The clothes were the same, pathetically grand and foolish, but they hung loosely on her, and if they had been ludicrous before, they were now almost grotesque. As she opened the door and stood waiting for me to pass her, I made myself look straight at the ravaged face. Surely these few years of work could not have wreaked such havoc, no matter how she hated it. Suddenly it struck me that she was dying, and with terrible certainty I knew that I had hit upon the truth.

We were inside now and the din was incredible. Opening off the main hall was the dining room to which Aunt Kate was leading me. It was filled to overflowing with about three hundred girls of all ages, and as Aunt Kate appeared with me beside her in the doorway, a silence fell as loud as the din that had preceded it.

As we walked to a table at the far end of the room, six hundred eyes followed us in silence, and then a cacophony of giggles and smothered laughter began to flow over the room and over me like molten lava. By the time we reached the staff table, a walk that I thought would never end, I was in an anguish of embarrassment and rage. Why, oh why, had she done this to me? I forgot about how ill she looked and how much I loved her. I could only smother my anger, wipe the perspiration from my face, and sit there tongue-tied, staring at the plate in front of me. The ladies of the staff were kind souls, no doubt, and the questions they plied me with were well intentioned, but I refused to speak or look up; I nodded or grunted disagreeably, and I could feel my aunt's dismay as this frightful meal proceeded. I tried to recover but I could not, for every so often a girl stifling a giggle would come over to the table and ask to be introduced, and my aunt would ring out my name like some terrible master of ceremonies at a Rotary meeting.

Somehow the meal ground to a finish—and ground is the proper simile, for even Aunt Kate sat in utter silence at the end. I knew I had been a wretched failure for her, but I could not speak. All I could think of was the gantlet to be run when we left the dining room—not a girl appeared to have moved from any table. They seemed, in fact, to be waiting for our exit. I kept hoping, vainly, that the staff would all rise from the table together and I might somehow lose myself among them, but that was not to be.

Aunt Kate, once again the grand lady of fashion, proclaimed in a ringing voice, "We shall be late for the theatre," and rose from her chair. Immediately silence fell over the entire room. Knives and forks clattered against plates and then were still. And as we had entered, so we left, only this time the laughter and giggles that accompanied our steps were less well concealed. I could have wrung their necks singly and with pleasure, though my aunt seemed to notice nothing.

We were outside now and neither of us spoke. She was furious with me, I knew, but I was still too anguished to speak and offer some explanation for my behavior. I doubt if I could have. In a dismal silence we walked toward the theatre. Had I been a few years younger I would have been tempted to burst into tears. How eagerly I had looked forward to this meeting and how thoroughly she had managed to ruin it for both of us by the folly of meeting in that dining room! Why need she always be so ridiculous a figure, so strange and different from anybody else? The laughter of those wretched girls rang in my ears, melting into the laughter of the kids on the block as they used to laugh when my aunt walked by, and I cringed. How could I have known that it was her own uniqueness that gave me so much that I treasured and that no one else could have given? I could not, of course; so we walked on in silence.

It was not until we reached the theatre that either of us spoke, and as we walked into the lobby, Aunt Kate instinctively turned toward the steps leading up to the gallery. Without a word I took her arm and steered her toward the orchestra door, and as we handed our stubs to the usher I said, "From now on we sit in the orchestra." For the first time that evening she smiled; and the sight of Aunt Kate sweeping through the orchestra doors, just as I had imagined she would, was magical. In a moment everything was forgotten and forgiven by both of us in the glory of sitting "down front." Aunt Kate sailed down the aisle like a great ship coming into port and sank into her orchestra seat, with a quiet sigh of being home at long last. It mattered not a bit to either one of us that we were almost alone in the theatre, for the play was one of the most notorious failures of the season and people could not be enticed into the theatre even with free tickets. We sat there with vast empty spaces all around us, utterly oblivious and content.

From that memorable evening on, we were inseparable. I said nothing at home about our meeting, of course, but each day I called Aunt Kate from the office and almost every evening we trotted off happily together to dinner and the theatre. I never went near the Clara De Hirsch Home for Working Girls again. In unspoken agreement, we never mentioned the place, but went instead to a restaurant called Lorber's on Broadway at 41st Street, directly opposite the Metropolitan Opera House.

Lorber's was a leftover relic of the nineties, and not long for the bustling world of the twenties, but in its own anachronistic way it suited Aunt Kate exactly. The walls were satin-covered, and little pink lamps stood on each table; an astonishingly good table d'hote dinner could be had for seventy-five cents.

Somehow at Lorber's Aunt Kate did not seem out of place. No heads turned to look at her strange garb as we took our places at the table, and the old waiters never raised an eyebrow at the stentorian voice with which she ordered the meal. Curiously enough, she herself behaved less strangely in Lorber's than anywhere else. The sense of belonging at last, of being in a proper setting, seemed to soothe her troubled spirit—for once she was not fighting the world, but was a part of it. She talked sensibly and shrewdly. She even discussed my father and herself with acute perception and understanding, and once she took my hand in a rare moment of tenderness and said, "Some day I hope you'll be as good a son to your mother as you've been to me." I doubt that I ever was, but I have never forgotten that remark or the way that she said it. It illuminated so much that was dark in all of our lives.

All in all, that year marked a turning point in my life. She died at the end of it. I have always been grateful that the final year of her life was, I think, her happiest one; and of all the good things the theatre has given me, I count as not the least those free tickets that enabled me to give Aunt Kate that last wonderful year.

I SUPPOSE EVERYONE has at some time or other speculated on the curious and sometimes frightening chain of events set in motion by a single and seemingly innocent act of one's own. I have often been bemused by the fact that two people have met and married, children have been born, and lives channeled in an entirely different direction by the tiny beginning of an idea for a play that passed fleetingly through my mind while I was shaving or brushing my teeth in the morning. True, those actors who married each other after meeting in a play of mine might just as easily have met and married in a play of somebody else's, but the fact remains that it was at rehearsals of my play that they first met, and who is to say it might not have been quite otherwise had they met in the rehearsal of another play and at another time? It is an idle speculation, of course, and one that must forever remain unproved, for fate is an implacable strategist.

Still, how strange a quirk of fate it is that as Anne Nichols wrote the opening lines of *Abie's Irish Rose* she was also changing unalterably the life of an obscure office boy named Moss Hart. Miss Nichols' play, which had opened to almost unanimous critical disdain, had not at this moment of its incredible career turned the corner that was to make it a lasting theatrical phenomenon, but it was showing enough signs of staggering through the season to alert Mr. Pitou to the direct possibility that Anne Nichols might not be available to produce the next season's output for his stars. Miss

Nichols' faith in her concoction, however, was monumental and unshakable. Her belief that the critics were wrong and she was right is a legend, and since it turned out that she was correct, countless backers of plays have lost untold fortunes.

Mr. Pitou's predicament was a very real one. He was certain, as was everyone else, that *Abie's Irish Rose* was doomed to ignominious failure, but so long as Anne Nichols persisted in the folly of believing that it was going to turn into a success, she could not or would not give any thought to getting on with the writing of those new plays that were so necessary a part of Mr. Pitou's business. I do not believe that Mr. Pitou wished *Abie's Irish Rose* to fail; he very humanly wanted the very obvious handwriting on the wall to transpose itself into a closing notice as quickly as possible, so that Miss Nichols could get cozily back to her proper knitting for him. But *Abie's Irish Rose* stubbornly refused to die, with a miraculous stubbornness that was to turn Anne Nichols into a millionaire.

In the interim, while this maddening period of waiting was going on, there was one historic moment when Miss Nichols, in desperate need of money to keep the play going, offered Mr. Pitou a half-interest in *Abie's Irish Rose* for $5,000. It is my impression that he was quite willing to give Miss Nichols $5,000 purely as a token of friendship, for he needed her good will. Nevertheless, in order to make some show of putting things on a purely business basis, he agreed to go to the Saturday matinée, look at the play again, and then make his decision. Theatrical decisions, however, then as now, always hang by the proverbial thread. This mighty decision was not made by him, but by Mrs. Pitou instead, and I was an accidental witness to it.

On that crucial Saturday morning, Mr. Pitou instructed me to meet him after the second act of *Abie's Irish Rose* and bring with me the telegrams of the grosses of the matinées of our shows on the road. At four thirty, I was waiting in the lobby of the theatre with the telegrams in hand as Mr. and Mrs. Pitou emerged from the auditorium. I stood beside them as Mr. Pitou read through the telegrams, and when he had finished, Mrs. Pitou, who had stood silently by, suddenly spoke up sharply and, with an involuted feminine logic that was unanswerable, said, "Gus, if you put five thousand dollars into this terrible play, don't you ever dare say no to me when I want a new dress or a new fur coat for the rest of my life." I like to think of that heartfelt and thoroughly justified sentence as one of the most expensive remarks in theatrical history, for Mr. Pitou did not buy that half-interest in *Abie's Irish Rose* for $5,000, and Anne Nichols enjoyed her millions alone. She deserved them, for she sold her house, pawned her jewelry and steadfastly refused to write anything else until her faith in that nonsensical bit of dramaturgy was thoroughly justified. It is extremely foolish, as Mr. Mencken so sagely pointed out, ever to underestimate the low taste of the American public.

Mr. Pitou finally faced up to the inevitable. New writers were engaged to grind out the next season's output, and the plays were launched on Labor Day as usual—not, I might add, with overpoweringly good results. The Nichols touch, such as it was, was a tried and true one, and the merchandise of this new season ranged from indifferent to just passable. There was one play among them, however, that even the good citizens of Butte, Montana, could not stomach. It starred a young Irish tenor named Joseph Regan—whom Mr. Pitou was grooming to follow in the footsteps of Fiske O'Hara —and was, in a word, unforgivable. It is hard to imagine that out in the vastnesses of the hinterland a play's reputation would precede it so damningly that it could not get in and out of a town in one night without the inhabitants' knowing how terrible it was beforehand. Yet know it they did, whether advised by thoughtful friends from neighboring towns who had had the misfortune to have seen it, or through that plain sixth sense which somehow tells good folk to stay away from the theatre—but stay away from it they did in successively greater numbers.

By the time the company had wended its noisome way through Illinois, the receipts were so alarming that Mr. Pitou considered the situation desperate enough to ask me to take plays home with me to read, in the hope of uncovering a new script he could finish out the season with. It was under these circumstances and after reading batch after batch of manuscripts, one more footling and foolish than the other, that the terrible idea occurred to me that was to prove my undoing.

It was a Sunday afternoon and I remember it well. The moment was not accompanied by any such sensible thought as, "Why, I could write a better play than any of these myself." I was simply bored to distraction by the trash I had been thumbing through all day, and without thinking too much about it, I simply sat down at a battered typewriter that I had rescued from the ash-heap of a Brooklyn relative's largesse and wrote on a piece of paper, "Act One. Scene One." By twelve o'clock that night Act One was completed and the next morning I took it into the office with me. Some demon of mischief was already at work, however, for on the title page I did not put my own name, but instead strung together the first three names of some of the boys on the block and listed as the author of the play "Robert Arnold Conrad." Candor compels me to reveal that the title was *The Beloved Bandit,* a secret I have arranged to keep rather well through the years. But I do not believe the demands of candor decree that I reveal any more of the play than that.

The next morning I handed the act to Mr. Pitou, and with a proper edge of the casual in my voice said, "I read an act of a play last night that I think is very good. You ought to read it."

"Who wrote it?" asked Mr. Pitou.

"A fellow named Robert Arnold Conrad," I replied. "He's a friend of mine."

"All right, I'll read it this evening. Put it in my briefcase," he said. And that was that.

I do not believe I gave it even a passing thought during the rest of that day or evening. I'm certain to this day that I meant it to be no more than a mild joke between us to enliven the drudgery we were going through in the search for the new vehicle. But I was utterly unprepared for what happened the following morning when Mr. Pitou entered the office. With his hat still on his head, he slapped the act down on the desk, turned to me triumphantly and said, "We found it. Don't have to look any further. This is it. If the second and third acts hold up anything like as well, we're home. When can I get the second act?"

"Tomorrow morning," I replied, too stunned to know what I was saying.

"Great," said Mr. Pitou. "Take a letter to Mr. Conrad—will you be seeing him tonight?"

"I guess so," I replied, truthfully enough I suppose.

"Well, if you don't," said Mr. Pitou, still under the spell of being out of the woods at last, "mail it special delivery so that he gets it first thing in the morning. I want to point out a few things he ought to do in the second act."

Still stunned, I sat down at the typewriter and solemnly took the long letter to Robert Arnold Conrad that Mr. Pitou poured forth. Why I did not tell Mr. Pitou the truth then and there escapes me even now. Perhaps I was too startled by his completely unexpected enthusiasm to puncture the bubble so quickly, or it may be I was suddenly titillated by the idea of carrying the joke through to the end; but whatever it was that possessed me to keep silent in those first few minutes set in motion a chain of events that I was powerless afterward to stop. By the time he signed the letter and handed it over to me, I knew I was doomed to go on.

That night I went home and wrote Act II. It took me until almost five o'clock in the morning to do it, but unbelievable as it may sound, I finished it that night. Bleary-eyed, I handed it to Mr. Pitou the next morning. He promptly turned off the telephone and read it at once. This time his enthusiasm was even greater.

"Mouse," he said, "telephone your friend and ask him to come and see me this afternoon, or give me his number—I'd like to speak to him myself."

Panic-stricken, I managed to blurt out, "Oh, he's very seldom in his office, Mr. Pitou. He's in court most of the day. He's a lawyer." Quick thinking and an unholy gift of invention seem to spring to the aid of all liars at moments like these.

"Well, ask him to come in and see me tomorrow," said Mr. Pitou after a moment. "And when do you think he'll have the third act finished? Did he say anything to you about it?"

"No, he didn't," I replied a little haltingly, "but I guess he could have it for you by tomorrow."

"Fine, fine," said Mr. Pitou. "He writes fast, just what we need right now. Better take a letter and give it to him tonight in case you can't get him on the phone."

And there poured forth under my panic-frozen fingers another four-page single-spaced letter from Mr. Pitou. Glassy-eyed, I watched him sign it, and in a moment of sweet clarity the thought flashed through my mind: "You've got to tell him now." But before I could screw up sufficient courage to speak, Mr. Pitou spoke instead.

"You know, Mouse," he said, a satisfied smile on his lips, "I don't often go around giving myself pats on the back, but I think my letter helped Mr. Conrad. I wish I had kept a copy of it. As a matter of fact, I wish you'd make a copy of this one right now. I'd like to take it home and show it to Mrs. Pitou tonight. I've been telling the family how you discovered this young fellow just in the nick of time."

That did it, of course. To confess to Mr. Pitou that he had been writing these wonderful letters to his office boy was bad enough; but to make him out an utter fool in the eyes of his family was something I could not face. Any kind of delay would give me time to think—something was bound to happen to make that terrible moment of confession a little less awful than it seemed to me just then.

That night I went home and tackled the third act. Alas, third acts are notoriously tough even for hardened veterans, and Robert Arnold Conrad, a tired and sorry spectacle by this time, did not finish the act that night. The next day another and still longer letter was tolled off to Mr. Conrad—longer, I believe, because Mr. Pitou was daily growing more proud of his new-found prowess as a teacher of play-writing, the while I sat there miserably taking it all down. During the day there was again the same insistence on Mr. Pitou's part of wanting to see Mr. Conrad or at least talk to him on the telephone, and I fended this off as best I could by muttering, "He's on a case—in court—he'll be finished in a couple of days." I was almost too tired to care. All I wanted was to finish the third act, tell Mr. Pitou the truth, and have it over with. All I cared about now was not losing my wonderful job as a consequence of this miserable joke. I silently prayed for a propitious moment for telling him. If only I could get that act finished quickly, so that there need be no more letters, each one of which, of course, could only make him feel more foolish as he remembered sitting there and dictating them to me, all might not be lost.

That night I went to sleep after dinner and slept until midnight. Then I got up, sat down at the typewriter, and did not get up until I had typed "The curtain falls." It was eight o'clock in the morning. Now that it was done and I could tell Mr. Pitou at last, I felt strangely awake and refreshed. I could hardly wait to get down to the office and face him with the truth at last. When I walked in at nine o'clock Mr. Pitou was already there. I was surprised to see him there so early, for he usually arrived at the office between ten and ten thirty and he looked immensely pleased with himself into the bargain. Oh, God, not another letter! I thought. I must tell him immediately. He spoke while I was still in the doorway.

"Got that third act?" he said. I nodded and handed it to him.

"Mr. Pitou," I began—but I got no further than that.

"Get your friend on the phone right away," he interrupted, "the damnedest thing has happened. I showed these two acts to Mrs. Henry B. Harris last night, and you know what? She says this play is too good for the road—she wants to co-produce it with me and do it on Broadway. I'm going to bring the company back to New York, rehearse the play here, open in Rochester, play Chicago for four weeks, and then we'll bring it in. It will be my first New York production, so get your friend on the phone right away and tell him to come up here and sign the contract—I'm going downstairs to the booking office to book the time."

I stared numbly after him as he passed me in the doorway. After a moment, I sat down in a chair and tried hard to think, but I could not think; I could only keep looking around the office as though I were seeing it for the last time. I was still sitting there transfixed in the chair when Mr. Pitou returned from the booking office.

"What time is Mr. Conrad coming in?" he asked. "The theatres are all set. What time is he coming in?"

[61]

"Two o'clock," I replied, promptly and automatically, as though somebody else were using my voice.

"Fine," said Mr. Pitou, "let's get going—we've got a lot to do before lunch and I want to read that third act before he gets here."

The enormity of what I had done settled over me like a suit of mail. It is bad enough to make a man look foolish within the confines of his family, but quite another thing to make him a figure of ridicule outside, for I had no doubt that he had told Mrs. Harris the whole story and had showed her his letters to Robert Arnold Conrad as well. I stared so hard at Mr. Pitou that he finally became aware of it and said, "What is it? Were you going to say something?" I shook my head. There are certain moments when the process of thinking is frozen, when the ability to act, speak or move is completely and totally paralyzed. I could no more have told Mr. Pitou the truth right then, or even have given him the correct time had he asked me to, if my life had depended on it. I took down the telegrams, went through the morning's mail, and did the various other office chores without speaking and actually without quite knowing what I was doing.

When Mr. Pitou went out for lunch, taking the third act with him, I again sat down in the chair and stared unseeingly around the office. I was still sitting there when Mr. Pitou returned from lunch a little before two o'clock.

"It's just right," he said as he closed the door behind him. "He certainly read my letters carefully." He looked at his watch. "You said he was coming in at two o'clock, didn't you?" I nodded. "I'm kind of anxious to meet him now," he said, as he picked up the *Railway Guide* and settled back to wait.

I sat silently in the chair and watched the moments drag by. Finally he put the *Railway Guide* back on the desk and looked at his watch unbelievingly. "Why, it's three o'clock," he said. "Where is he?"

This time I had to speak—tell the last lie to fend off approaching doom if only for a little while longer. "He must have been held up in court, Mr. Pitou. Sometimes they don't recess until four o'clock," I said, pulling out a legal term from God knows where.

For the first time Mr. Pitou looked hard at me. He had, of course, no suspicion of the truth, but he sensed something was wrong. He rose from the desk and reached for his hat and coat. "Get your coat, Mouse," he said, "we'll go down to his office and wait for him, if we have to wait there all day. I'm bringing a company back from Omaha and I've got Rochester and Chicago booked. I've got to have those contracts signed. What's the matter with him, anyway? Come on, let's go." This last was added rather sharply, for I still sat there immobilized.

Somehow I put on my hat and coat and followed him to the elevator. I knew that I must tell him before we reached the lobby; I realized the terrible moment had come at last—for if we got to the street and he asked me for the address of the office where Robert Arnold Conrad worked, what in the world would I say? The moment had arrived—there could be no more delay. I was trapped and I knew it. We got into the elevator and it started down. I made my revelation between the eighth and fifth floors as the elevator shot downward, and I remember every word I spoke, for the two short declarative sentences I managed to get out had an enviable economy and a dramatic brevity that I was not able to appreciate fully until long afterward.

"Mr. Pitou," I began, "I have a confession to make."

Mr. Pitou turned and looked at me a little wonderingly, as well he might have, for my voice had gone at least two octaves higher and seemed even to my own ears to be coming through an echo chamber some great distance away. I swallowed and got the rest of it out.

"Mr. Pitou," I said, "*I* am Robert Arnold Conrad."

The elevator doors opened and we both stepped out into the lobby. In silence we walked the length of the lobby and out into 42nd Street. Only then did Mr. Pitou give any indication that he had heard me.

"Mouse," he said at last, "I don't know whether you know it or not, but when an author writes his first play he doesn't get the regular royalties."

I could hardly believe my ears. "You mean—it's all right, Mr. Pitou?" I faltered.

"Certainly it's all right," he replied, "as long as you understand that a new author doesn't get the regular royalties. We'll have to make out new contracts. I guess I'd better go over and see Mrs. Harris and tell her the good news."

He patted me on the shoulder paternally, smiled down at me, and started off briskly toward 44th Street. I stood stock-still for a moment, and my first emotion, if such it may be called, was one of hunger. Suddenly I seemed to be literally starving. I could not remember having eaten anything at all for the last three days. I walked to the Nedick's orange-juice stand on the corner and ate one frankfurter after another, until all my money except the subway fare I needed to get home ran out. I must have eaten at least ten frankfurters, for the counterman finally said, "You'll be sick, buddy—better knock off."

He was right. I just managed to get back to the office and into the bathroom in time. My debut as a playwright was a portent for the future: I have been sick in the men's room every opening night of a play of mine in theatres all over the country.

The next day I was officially presented to Mrs. Harris, and my dual career as office boy and built-in playwright swung into full gear. It did not seem at all extraordinary to me that I should go about my duties as office boy in the morning, emerge as playwright in the afternoon, then revert to the role of office boy again at the end of the day: closing the windows, emptying the wastebaskets, stamping the mail and then taking it to the post office on my way to the subway. Neither Mr. Pitou nor I myself, for that matter, seemed to feel that any great change of status had taken place, which was exactly what I had prayed for. My relief that I still retained my job was so great that had Mr. Pitou asked me, he could easily have had the play for no royalties at all.

By the same token, the news at home that I had written a play was received with hardly a lift of an eyebrow. I think that my mother and father, utterly unaware of the ways of the theatre, simply concluded it was some sort of homework I had done in the evenings that I had not finished during the day at the office.

[64]

Only Mrs. Henry B. Harris seemed to gather a secret amusement from the situation, and she treated me from our first meeting on with a grave outward courtesy that was belied only by the twinkle in her eye. Mrs. Harris was rich, racy, colorful and of infinite good humor. She was a survivor of the *Titanic* disaster. Her husband, Henry B. Harris, the producer of such famous plays as *The Lion and the Mouse,* having perished in that tragedy, she now owned the Hudson Theatre on 44th Street, a yacht and a stable of horses. She mentioned to Mr. Pitou at our first meeting, I remember, that she had just turned down an offer of one million dollars for the Hudson Theatre, and I thought of this moment years later, when I heard that Mrs. Harris had come upon hard times.

Her inordinate liking for *The Beloved Bandit* was something I could not fathom then, nor can I understand it now, for she was theatrically shrewd and by no means a fool about plays in general— another proof, as though one were needed, that quite sensible people make fools of themselves about plays, with a relentless inevitability that fills half the theatres in New York each season with pure rubbish. In fact, her faith in *The Beloved Bandit* imbued us all with a foolish optimism and a ridiculous impatience to see the curtain rise as quickly as possible. Every afternoon we met in the large, beautifully appointed office above the Hudson Theatre, and once the director had been engaged, casting proceeded at a furious pace.

Priestly Morrison, an actor of great charm and quite a good director in his own right, was engaged to stage the play, and I suspected almost at once that he thought *The Beloved Bandit* was absolute nonsense. In those days, however, directors did not pick and choose or wait around for a play they liked or respected. They took more or less what came their way, and since the theatre was in a wildly flourishing state, it was common practice for a director to do as many as four or five plays in a season. If one or two of them were decent efforts, or if one of the five happened to turn out a hit, that was all to the good—and Onward and Upward with the Arts for the following season. Directors did not occupy the hallowed place they do now in the theatre—that place was the playwright's alone.

In spite of my suspicions, Priestly Morrison did nothing to diminish Mrs. Harris' or Mr. Pitou's enthusiasm—he merely nodded and smiled at their grandiose plans for the play, and during the slight rewriting he demanded of me, he was scrupulously polite and non-committal.

In ten days from the fateful morning I had handed Mr. Pitou the third act, the company had been brought back to New York and the play was in rehearsal. Joseph Regan, an actor whose performance on any given night might have been presented as an appropriate gift to two people celebrating their wooden wedding anniversary, remained the star; but an entirely new cast was engaged. I was allowed the morning off to attend the first reading, but thereafter I remained in the office until four o'clock in the afternoon, when both Mr. Pitou and I would ceremoniously attend rehearsals.

It must have been somewhat bewildering to the cast, or at the very least slightly unorthodox, to see the author of the play called to across the rehearsal hall and sent out to get a package of cigarettes or a container of coffee for the producer. But whatever they thought of this curious arrangement, they kept it to themselves and were always unfailingly kind to me. No actor, not even Joseph Regan himself, ever asked me to run out and get him coffee or cigarettes—a small consideration, but one which I was grateful for nevertheless. Only the stage manager, a hardened soul whose name escapes me, took an exceedingly dim view of the entire proceedings and not even Priestly Morrison's unflagging good humor could make him feel that anything but disaster lay ahead. His displeasure with the play was not verbal—he would merely emit long, doleful sighs from time to time, like a sheep dog settling down in front of the fireplace for a long nap—and when questioned about his heavy state of gloom he would simply raise his eyes heavenward and tap the manuscript of the play with a finger of doom.

In spite of our dolorous stage manager, rehearsals were indomitably cheerful. Mrs. Harris did not appear at rehearsals until the first run-through, and under the spell of her delighted and ringing laughter, the actors outdid themselves and the play seemed to catch fire and spring to life. Even Mr. Pitou on that splendid afternoon forgot to send me out for coffee, and Mrs. Harris shook my hand and prophesied a rosy future for me. Three days later the company, the producers and the author left for the opening performance in Rochester, New York, all of them as usual magnificently optimistic and each one filled with hope and dreams of glory.

THERE ARE many "firsts" in one's life when one is young and at the beginning of things; but there are certain "firsts" that remain forever memorable. I had never been outside New York City itself. I had never ridden in a Pullman train or eaten in a dining car, and I had never stayed overnight in a hotel. All of these things now took place in glittering succession.

When the train roared out of Grand Central station and emerged from the tunnel at 96th Street, I sat in my seat at the window and watched the squalid tenements rush past me, in one of which, though I could not see it, I had lived all my life. I have never emerged from the tunnel since then without thinking of that first ride. I sat there not quite daring to hope that the time would come when I would never have to return to the Bronx and the poverty that dulled and demeaned each day.

In the dining car I sat opposite Mrs. Harris and Mr. Pitou, and sensed what it was like to order the food that tickled one's palate at a particular moment without thinking of what it cost. And when I settled into my room at the hotel in Rochester, I sat for a long moment on the bed drinking in a joyous sense of privacy that I had never before experienced. I would sleep alone in a room that night for the first time in my life. I did not know until that moment how starved I had been for privacy, what a precious refreshment to the spirit it is; there is no such indulgence in the realms of poverty, and only those who have lived without it can know what a prime luxury privacy is. From that moment on I began to fight savagely for the blessed solace of a door closing behind me in a room of my own. It was a long time before I could rouse myself sufficiently to leave and go to the theatre where the dress rehearsal was about to begin.

The play was in only one set, a prime requisite of any Augustus Pitou production, and since the scope of the action was limited and the props almost primitively simple (another requisite), it was taken for granted that the dress rehearsal would be a simple and smooth one. I have learned since that the gods who hover over dress rehearsals are perverse, deceptive and wildly unpredictable. The most complicated shows sometimes move with a blessed smoothness, and the simplest ones, the ones in which nothing could conceivably go wrong, turn without warning into hell's own acre. I have learned, too, that a play with which everything is going to go well, a play which is destined to be a hit almost from the moment the curtain rises, is preceded in its out-of-town birth pangs by a series of unrelated but inevitable omens that I have come to look upon with superstitious awe when they appear and a grim foreboding when they do not.

When the tide is running right, the room service at the hotel is swift, the food piping hot and delicious, and the waiters silent and matchlessly efficient. The telephone service and the bellboys are expert and bright, the elevator doors swing magically open without a moment of waiting as you press the button, and the traffic lights turn green as you step to the curb.

Skulk lightly around the outskirts of a play that is in trouble in its out-of-town tryout and you will hear the agonized pleas to room service that the order was given over an hour ago, God damn it! You will notice the glazed eye, its owner already late for rehearsal, watching the dials of the elevator indicator as it remains stuck at the top floor; and you will hear the waiter, his dirty thumb in the plate as he serves the soup, discourse at great length on what is wrong with the theatre. There will be no porters to carry the bags up to the room as you check in. The telephone operators will take a "No Disturb" call as a challenge to their ingenuity as to what early hour to wake you up, and, of course, there will be a taxi strike on and a convention in town. There is nothing more painful to an author with a play in trouble out of town than the spectacle of middle-aged men with fezzes on their heads and noisemakers in their hands, drunkenly greeting him in the hotel corridor as he makes his way desperately to his room for an all-night session of rewriting, knowing full well that the voices of this little group singing "Sweet Adeline" and "By the Old Mill Stream" will vibrate through the halls until the small hours of the morning.

Not all of these omens were in operation when we arrived, nor would I have recognized them if they were. But the dress rehearsal that night was chaos of a kind to give anyone pause. Nothing went right. The theatre curtain jammed going up as the lights dimmed, and the set, of a hideous green color that I have never seen duplicated, buckled during the first five minutes of dialogue and nearly brained the character man. There was an unholy wait until it was secured and made fast, and the entrance of the star, trilling a lilting Irish ballad, was somewhat marred as he tripped over a stage brace and sprawled full length, all six Irish feet of him, smack into the fireplace. As he picked himself up, cursing, the rain which had been coming down in torrents all day turned into hail, and for the next half-hour not a word was to be heard—a small mercy for which I was not then sufficiently grateful.

Nothing worked. If an actor went to open a door, it stuck. And at one point, when the leading lady, with a loud cry of passion, rushed to the window to open it and call after the star, the window came off the frame and she was left standing with the entire window in her hands. It was a nightmare of the proverbial bad dress rehearsal. By the second act, the actors were dithering about the stage, hopelessly lost in their lines, hollowly waiting for the next calamity to descend, and sure enough, Joseph Regan, making his second-act entrance through the same door, tripped again over the same stage brace—only this time the fireplace crumpled under the impact and fell in a shambles all around him. Even Priestly Morrison's unfailing good spirits and courtly manners deserted him at this point and he stalked up the aisle muttering imprecations against the Irish and Irish tenors in particular.

[70]

Only Mrs. Harris remained unperturbed. She sat there, unwavering, as each successive disaster on the stage made the play seem a mass of pure absurdity; leaning over to the perspiring Mr. Pitou from time to time, she would say quietly, "I'm glad it's going this way, Gus. A bad dress rehearsal means a good opening night. I've never seen it fail."

Through the years I have heard that phrase repeated over and over, and it is my firm conviction hardened by experience that a bad dress rehearsal with rare exceptions invariably means a ragged opening night. It is one of those theatrical shibboleths that have no basis whatever in fact; but I did not know it then and I clung to the good cheer that Mrs. Harris exuded.

Somehow the third act dragged through with only the minor casualty of the juvenile being hit in the eye by a flying piece of teacup that shattered as he banged it down on the table, and when the bleeding subsided, the play proceeded uneventfully until the end. Mr. Regan did not trip over the stage brace in his third-act entrance, for the simple reason that it had been removed during the intermission, though the stagehand holding up the door was plainly and incongruously visible and the damaged fireplace still swayed dangerously every so often. It fell again with a tremendous crash just as the curtain came down, rousing Priestly Morrison from the depths of his seat, where he had sunk so low that only the top of his hat was visible. He uncurled himself slowly and came up the aisle to Mr. Pitou and Mrs. Harris. He raised his hat to them both and said, "I'm not going to give any notes to the actors tonight. I'm going to church early tomorrow morning and offer up a little prayer. I suggest everyone do the same." He bowed slightly and disappeared up the dark aisle.

Mrs. Harris rose from her seat and laughed. "This is how I like 'em," she said. "Terrible at the dress rehearsal, great on the opening night. I've never seen it fail." Her golden opportunity lay just ahead!

We walked back to the hotel through the sleeping city, too tired and exhausted for even a cup of coffee. I have often walked back to my hotel through a dark city after a bad dress rehearsal and looked up at the shuttered and peaceful windows of its inhabitants, some

[71]

of them no doubt likely to be part of the opening-night audience the following evening. I have wondered if they ever thought enviously of the rewards both financial and otherwise that come with great success in the theatre. I have wondered, too, if they ever glimpsed the other side of the coin—the tremendous toll the theatre takes in return in nerves, in strain, in stamina—that it takes almost as much as it gives and that those who court its wayward favor must be made of stern stuff indeed.

Now I turned the key in the lock of my hotel bedroom and looked at the bed with something like alarm. The privacy I so longed for seemed a dubious gift right now; though I was thoroughly exhausted, I felt wildly awake. That terrible "second wind" was gathering momentum and I knew that sleep was going to be impossible. In those days, sleeping pills, that basic out-of-town necessity of the theatrical profession, had not yet been invented; or if they had, I had never heard of them. I left the light on and did not even bother to undress.

I paced up and down the room and thought of the dread consequences for me if the play were to fail. I did not give a damn about the play—my own name was not even listed as author—and I felt absolutely no pride or sense of ownership in it. What I cared about was losing my job, and I knew Mr. Pitou well enough by this time to know that he would ultimately place the blame not on his misjudgment or Mrs. Harris', but on the trick I had played upon him. I did not particularly blame him—I blamed myself and the insane moment when I had launched blindly and unthinkingly into the whole idiotic business. I castigated myself for my own folly, until I fell asleep with my clothes still on and dreamed a sweet dream that the play was a glorious success.

The early morning sunlight streaming through the windows brought me back to reality. It was a bitter cold winter's day, but at least the sun was shining. Perhaps they would be grateful to be out of the cold tonight, and in a warm theatre they might be a generous and receptive audience. I was already beginning to count on small omens.

There was an eleven o'clock rehearsal at the theatre, and this time, to do Mrs. Harris full justice, the proceedings on the stage resembled something more closely akin to sanity than they had last night. Nothing, of course, could change the nauseous color of the set, but the stage brace had been set farther back of the door, so that Joseph Regan at least remained upright each time he entered the doorway. The window was bolted into the frame, and the juvenile and the character man, though a little the worse for wear, met with no further mishaps. A curious hypnotic state now fell upon everyone connected with *The Beloved Bandit,* actors and producers alike; and I have seen the same thing happen often since then. Because the horror of last night was not repeated, or was at least greatly lessened, everyone concerned seemed to be utterly blinded to the deficiencies and lacks of the play itself. The mere fact that the play proceeded from one act to another without disaster seemed to lull all minds, including my own, into a sense of sweet euphoria that dissipated any kind of valid judgment or even plain common sense. Before the rehearsal was half over, witless optimism was again flowing through the theatre like May wine, and since everyone was drunk with it, Mrs. Harris was being congratulated on all sides for her shrewd perception and her unshakable faith in the play.

Before dinner that evening, in Mrs. Harris' room, I had my first martini. It was thought proper that I should, since a congratulatory toast was being raised to me; but I had never had hard liquor before, and the second martini made me quite drunk. I remember a great many congratulatory toasts being drunk all around, including a special one raised to himself by Mr. Pitou for having discovered Robert Arnold Conrad. We were all in a state of ebullient good spirits as we started for the theatre. In my mildly drunken state I thought the audience looked delightful as I stood in the lobby watching them file into the theatre, and for a brief moment I had a drunken fantasy of rising from my seat in the third row of the orchestra as the final curtain fell and making a graceful little speech to the audience, climaxing with that deathless sentence, "Ladies and gentlemen—*I* am Robert Arnold Conrad."

I took my seat just as the lights dimmed and the curtain rose.

The audience seemed slightly stunned as the set stood revealed in its full ghastliness, but there was only the slightest murmur among them and they settled back generously to enjoy themselves. In the first fifteen minutes of a play an audience is the most malleable group in the world. Give them the slightest token that they are going to be entertained or moved and they become a receptive instrument that both playwright and actors can play upon at will. Then a curious thing happens. Somehow at the end of that first fifteen minutes an invisible bell seems to ring in the theatre, and if the play has not captured them by then en masse, they become a disparate group of people who are never welded together again. One can almost feel the moment when it arrives, and the inner ear can hear that bell tolling soundlessly.

In the first fifteen minutes of *The Beloved Bandit* they sat pleasantly enough, hoping against hope (or so it seemed to me) that they had not been drawn out of their homes on a bitter cold night only to be made fools of. Had the play had the slightest merit or even a redeeming scene or two to lift it out of the mire of its own monotony, I believe they would have responded immediately. As it was, they sat there in utter and complete silence. I do not know of any silence more devastating. I have sat through it more than once and it is a searing experience. Yet I have always marveled at the infinite politeness of an American audience. When it is perfectly plain to them that they have been sold down the river, that they have paid their money and they have been humbugged and are in for an evening of crushing boredom into the bargain, they do not become impolite or unruly—they sit there in a rather apathetic silence, and as the curtain falls on each act, they stride heavily up the aisle, the hope written plain on their faces that the next act will be better.

They have in addition a kind of idiot genius as a group; they can detect falsity and reject the spurious with a lightning-like precision, without knowing why, of course, or saying a word to each other. But they are the surest barometer of a play's weakness or an actor's inadequacy that I know of. They knew what was wrong with *The Beloved Bandit* before the first act was half over.

[74]

It was a fake. It was a composite of all the plays Anne Nichols had written for Fiske O'Hara, and while I doubt that any of those efforts would have won an accolade from a student of play-writing, they were at least true to their genre. Of their kind, they at least had the virtue of honesty—and *The Beloved Bandit* was a dishonest facsimile.

As the first-act curtain descended to an ominous silence, I sat for a moment trying to clear my head of the two martinis. I had no wish to go up the aisle and see Mr. Pitou, Mrs. Harris or Priestly Morrison, but I wanted to be told by somebody that it hadn't gone as badly as I thought it had. I decided to mingle with the audience in the lobby and listen for their comments. It was a mistake. I moved as rapidly as I could from group to group, and it was as though they had not been at the theatre at all. They were talking about everything else under the sun, but of the act they had just seen not one person said a word. I think I would have felt better about it if I had heard someone say, "Isn't it terrible," or, "Worst thing I've ever seen"—but I did not. The contemptuous dismissal of what they had seen as not being worth discussion was much harder to bear.

In too short a time for comfort, the gong in the lobby signaled them back into the theatre. I was reluctant to go back to my seat, but I had no place else to go. I had not then discovered the release of pacing endlessly up and down at the back of the orchestra, nor the trick of ducking into a bar down the street for that stiff drink which enabled one to face the punishment that was coming. I sat through the second and third acts in the same grim silence the audience did. As the final curtain fell, a mass exodus started, as though twenty-dollar gold pieces were being distributed free in the street outside. There was not even a smattering of applause. The actors bowed to a solid phalanx of retreating backs, and the stage manager, his prophecy proved true at last, mercifully raised the curtain only once.

I made my way slowly backstage, in order to postpone for as long as possible that inevitable face-to-face meeting with Mr. Pitou and Mrs. Harris, but when I got there they were nowhere to be seen.

The stage manager, cheerful for the first time since rehearsals began, waved a hearty greeting to me. "Never saw one go worse," he said smilingly. "I've seen them go all kinds of ways," he continued, "but this was like spraying ether. You looking for the management?" I nodded. "They fled before the curtain came down. They said to tell you there was a conference in Mrs. Harris' room at the hotel and to get over there as fast as you could."

As I started to walk away he called after me, "I wouldn't wait up for the notices, if I were you. I know one of the critics here and he waits all year for one to come along like this."

I managed a miserable smile back at him and made my way out, but not before I had been accosted by the character man, who shook my hand fervently and said, "Went rather well, didn't you think?" I stared at him, not quite certain if this were not some sort of cruel joke, but he seemed to be quite serious.

There is always one actor in every company, I have found, who no matter how badly a play has gone always thinks or pretends to think that it has been received splendidly and moreover takes the trouble to waylay you and tell you so. He stands next to you at the hotel desk as you ask for the key to your room. He seeks you out in the drug store as you purchase an extra supply of headache tablets. He's invariably in the elevator with you late at night as you wearily and at last wend your way to the solitude of your room, and always with that ingratiating smile on his face and those absurd words on his lips. Whether this is done with an eye on future plays the playwright may have up his sleeve or simply to endear himself to those in power at a moment of crisis, I do not know; but this barefaced and foolish lie is always somehow harder to bear than the forthright disdain of an honest stage manager.

I was prepared for the very worst when I knocked on the door of Mrs. Harris' suite, but to my surprise I heard the ringing laugh of Mrs. Harris coming unmistakably through the transom.

I opened the door on my first theatrical conference. The conference back at the hotel after the opening-night performance out of town is a theatrical tribal rite, whose unchanging ritual persists

[76]

through the years like the Hopi Indians' rain dance. The setting is usually the producer's or the author's suite, and depending upon the fame of the author or the importance of the play, it is attended not only by those most intimately connected with the production but also by what is technically referred to as "the wrecking crew": those friends or well-wishers who have journeyed up from New York in order to be the first ones back with the news of the play's chances of success or, preferably, in order to provide a more juicy ride back on the late train, its probable failure.

If the play has the earmarks of a hit, the room is jammed, noisy, blue with cigarette smoke and agents, and the telephone rings with the constancy of election night in campaign headquarters. If the play has gone badly, it is as though the room were suddenly radio-active and only the author and the management were immune to the deadly fall-out. A hardy soul or two from New York, their faces wreathed in gritty smiles of pitiable determination, will appear long enough to declare with a false brightness, "It needs work, of course," and then flee, the sigh of their relief blowing them halfway down the corridor like a gust of March wind.

There is always a table from room service in a corner of the room, on which stand beer bottles, whiskey, sandwiches and endless pots of coffee, glacially cold and notably rancid. Since room service in hotels in most tryout towns closes down at nine o'clock, this tribal repast is always ordered by the company manager at about four o'clock in the afternoon; and although the food is not delivered until midnight, the sandwiches have been made in late afternoon and wrapped in a damp napkin, where they repose cold and wet until the conference begins. The sight of these pathetic bits of bread, no longer white but now a pale gray color, with slivers of rubbery ham and soapy cheese limply overlapping the wet edges, is enough to turn an author's stomach if the play has gone well—but the sight of them after a bad opening out of town is enough to make him physically ill. Usually, the butter has been placed separately in little disk-shaped china butter plates so dear to every hotel dining room, and during the conference, these become scattered all over the room. Cigarettes are stubbed out in unused pats of butter, and chewing gum is also disposed of thereby. If the conference has been held in the author's suite, the next morning, as he makes his way to the door to pick up the newspapers and read the first bad notices for the show, he is greeted by the sight of empty beer bottles, half-finished glasses of Scotch, and cigarette stubs swimming in melted butter. I have always considered it an appropriate setting in which to perform this grisly ceremony, and in some way I cannot clearly define, the horror of the room seems somehow to relieve, rather than add to, the pain of the occasion.

This first hotel-room conference that I was to participate in differed only in degree from all the others that were to stretch down the years. Since both author and play were equally unimportant, there were no well-wishers up from New York to witness the opening performance, and since the debacle at the theatre had been complete, all faces with the exception of Mrs. Harris' bore the imprint of a deep sense of guilt and a look of public disgrace, as though one among them had raped a ten-year-old girl and buried her body in the woods, and the others had helped to dig the grave. Other than that, however, the ritual was the same. There was the table in the corner, with the beer bottles, the pots of coffee, the limp sandwiches with the gray bread already beginning to curl around the edges, the little china butter plates with a goodly supply of half-smoked cigarettes already stubbed out in the butter, and the butt of the company manager's cigar floating unconcerned in the half-full highball glass that stood at his elbow.

Mr. Pitou sat slumped in a chair, a heavy figure of gloom, and Priestly Morrison seemed engrossed to the exclusion of all else in a series of elaborate drawings he was executing on the blotter of the desk. But Mrs. Harris, a cigarette dangling from the corner of her mouth and a glass of beer in her hand, strode up and down the room as chirpy and cheerful as though the audience had acclaimed the play with sixteen curtain calls. She waved a hand to me as I came in and continued with what she had been saying.

"I'll tell you something, boys," she said, addressing me now as well as the others, "the way it went tonight doesn't bother me one bit. Not a bit. You know why? First, this is Rochester—and what the hell does Rochester know about anything except Kodaks? Second, this is an audience play. I knew it when I read it and I still believe it. Give this play a chance with its own audience, boys, and you won't know you're watching the same play you saw tonight."

There was a heavy silence for a moment and then Priestly Morrison spoke in a mild voice. "Just what city do you think the audience for this play is hiding in?" he said, without looking up from his doodling.

"Chicago," cried Mrs. Harris triumphantly. "And after Chicago, New York. I don't have to remind you of *Abie's Irish Rose,* do I, boys?"

A grimace of pain flitted across Mr. Pitou's face and he shifted uneasily in his chair. He said nothing.

"I tell you what I'm going to do, Gus," she went on, addressing him directly, "and I'd advise you to do the same. I'm going to get out of here on the morning train. I'm not just going to sit and look at a play for a whole week that I know more about than the audience does. Priestly and Moss can watch the performance and do whatever they think necessary. Then you and I will jump on to Chicago next Monday night, and if the Chicago audience doesn't eat this play up, I'll eat my hat in the lobby. Come on, Moss, have a glass of beer and some sandwiches—you look pea-green, or it's these lights."

Again I found that extreme emotion induced a monumental hunger, and I wolfed more than half of those horrible sandwiches and drained two bottles of beer almost without stopping to breathe. I dared not look at Mr. Pitou and I sat as far away as possible from him. Mrs. Harris chatted merrily on and my relief was enormous when Mr. Pitou finally arose from the chair and said, "Well, Priestly, I'll see you and Moss in Chicago next Monday. If it goes any better during the week give me a call. Otherwise, I'll be standing in the lobby in Chicago watching Mrs. Harris eat her hat." He laughed mirthlessly at his little joke and slammed the door behind him.

The week that followed in Rochester was perhaps the most dismal week I have ever spent with a play. There have been other weeks in my theatrical life out of town that involved more pain and moments of crisis, but I can remember none that was so completely melancholy. There is something infinitely sad about a theatre with an audience of perhaps twenty or thirty disconsolate people scattered through its seats, and there is a touch of the sepulchral about actors booming out their lines into the vast reaches of an almost empty auditorium. I have often wondered what curious necessities bring these few masochistic souls to sit and watch what they have obviously been warned against as a dreary and unsatisfactory play. And why twenty or thirty? Why not two or ten or two hundred? Yet inevitably with even the worst play there are always somehow twenty or thirty people sitting almost obscenely alone in a large theatre and making it obligatory for the curtain to rise.

During the entire week in Rochester I do not believe that more than thirty people at the most ever filed through the doors into the theatre for a single performance, and the sight of them, huddled in lonely groups of two and three, cast a pall of misery over the theatre even before the curtain rose. They sat in silence throughout the performance, and as the final curtain fell, they clumped silently up the aisle and left the theatre in the same glum fashion they had entered it, leaving behind them the mystery of why they had bothered to come at all. By the end of the week, my very bones ached with the monotony and the indescribable boredom of watching *The Beloved Bandit* through each and every performance—for I felt I was honor-bound to sit through each performance and make what suggestions I could to Priestly Morrison.

I have never been able to understand the enjoyment of some playwrights who are able to visit the theatre night after night during the run of a play in New York and with obvious relish sit entranced before the magic of their own creation. True, *The Beloved Bandit* was not a play to fill an author's heart with pride, but I have never been able, once a play of mine has opened in New York, however great a success it may have achieved, to sit through an entire performance. I have been able to drop into the theatre and watch a favorite scene or two, but I know I would find it torturous to watch the play in its entirety, or even to watch a large portion of it with any degree of pleasure. It may be that *The Beloved Bandit* filled me with a lifelong antipathy for watching my own works performed, and if this is true, it is the only mark in its favor that I can find.

Somehow the days dragged through until Saturday night—there is an old and fond phrase in the theatre which actors whisper to each other on opening nights: "Eleven o'clock always comes"—and with something like a relief and even a glimmering of hope, I got onto the sleeper to Chicago with the company. Chicago certainly couldn't be worse than Rochester.

We arrived at Chicago late Sunday afternoon and I made straight for the Adelphi Theatre, where *The Beloved Bandit* was to open the following night. Performances are played on Sunday nights in Chicago, and as the author of the incoming play, I was entitled to the courtesy of "free tickets" for Sunday evening. *Beggar on Horseback*, by George S. Kaufman and Marc Connelly, was playing its last performance and I wanted very much to see it. It was one of the hits I had not been able to wedge my way into during its New York run. I ate a hurried dinner and then went back to the theatre. What a difference it was to stand in this crowded lobby and listen to the buzz of anticipation of a fashionable audience eager to go through the doors to their seats and enjoy the play. The very atmosphere crackled with that unmistakable and wonderful sound of an audience certain of the fare about to be spread before them and eager for the curtain to rise. It is one of the jolliest sounds in the world.

Before I knew quite what had happened, I forgot my own perilous state and lost myself in the glow of the crowded theatre and the sudden hush that pervaded the audience as the footlights dimmed *Beggar on Horseback* remains still one of the landmarks of satirical writing for the American stage, and I sat rapt and bug-eyed with admiration in front of it. Its gifted approach to the satirical and the fantastic aspects of our national life and culture must have awakened some kinship to the satirical and the fantastic within me, and for the first time I glimpsed that there might be a deeper sense of fulfillment in the art of the writer than in that of the actor. It was a fleeting thought only, but on the way back to the hotel I thought

[81]

again of what the world of Kaufman and Connelly must be like as opposed to the world of John and Lionel Barrymore.

The next morning, Mr. Pitou and Mrs. Harris arrived, and I learned with some dismay that I was being moved into Mr. Pitou's room. When the gods were not smiling, Mr. Pitou was apt to cut corners rather sharply to effect every possible economy, and I reflected with no little tinge of dread what it was going to be like to share a room with Mr. Pitou if the play went badly tonight.

That evening there was a gay and merry dinner for all in Mrs. Harris' suite, and while it was not quite so uninhibitedly convivial as the first dinner in Rochester, by the second martini and the third toast of mutual congratulations, even Mr. Pitou seemed to fall anew into the trap of false hope and glittering optimism. He even laughed aloud and joked in the taxi on the way to the theatre, and such is the ulfaltering faith of theatre folk that an unlikely miracle is certain to occur on opening nights, that by the time we reached the theatre we were one and all of us quite blind to the fact that this was the very same play that had played with such dire results in Rochester the week before.

My heart sank a little as I glanced over the audience coming down the aisle. There was a goodly smattering of evening dresses and black ties among them and they seemed to have that look of threatening benevolence so native to all first-night audiences. They would not, I thought, be nearly as polite in their disdain as the opening-night audience in Rochester. I was not wrong.

In Rochester they had greeted that appalling set in astonished silence, but as the curtain rose in Chicago, after an initial gasp of disbelief at what greeted their eyes, they broke as one into a gale of derisive laughter. The laughter lasted long enough to drown out the opening lines of dialogue, but just as the audience grew quiet again, Joseph Regan made his entrance in a way that he had never done before. It was his own impromptu invention and he never bothered, then or afterward, to explain why he did it. He came in through the fireplace and interpolated a line of his own authorship, the delicacy of whose phrasing I have forgotten, but which said something to the effect that: "Every day was Christmas when the

Irish came to town." The sight of Joseph Regan creeping in through the fireplace had numbed me to everything else for a few moments, but now I was conscious of a murmur going on all around me. The audience was laughing again, only now they were whispering to each other at the same time, and suddenly I became conscious of a gray-haired gentleman rising from his seat in the third row and walking up the aisle. A large portion of the audience seemed to follow his progress with such interest that I turned to Priestly Morrison and whispered, "Who is that and why is everyone watching him?"

"That," said Priestly Morrison, not even bothering to whisper, "is Ashton Stevens, Chicago's leading critic, and I believe he's going home."

What followed after is told quickly enough, for it happened with frightening rapidity. Before Joseph Regan had intoned too many more "macushlas" and "mavourneens" the audience started streaming up the aisle, and by the time the curtain of the first act fell, the seats all around me were empty and I knew that their occupants, like Ashton Stevens, were undoubtedly going home. This time I spared myself the anguish of going back into the theatre for the second and third acts. Instead, I walked around to the stage-door alley and remained there, walking up and down, until eleven o'clock.

Some perceptive fellow once remarked, "They find the draftiest place in town and then build a theatre around it." He was right. The wind from Lake Michigan whistled up the alley as though it had been sent there expressly by Ashton Stevens to find the author, but I hardly noticed it. Now that the worst had happened, I could think only of just how and when the blow I most feared would fall.

Mr. Pitou, a notably slow-moving man, moved with remarkable swiftness in certain areas, and the area of his pocketbook was one that always galvanized him into immediate action. If the result of *The Beloved Bandit* was the loss of my job, what lay ahead for me? The fur vault again? I knew I would never go back to that; but I knew too, more surely than I had ever known before, how hard come by was the job of office boy in a theatrical office. The prospect of landing another was almost impossible and I did not delude myself on that score. The lucky ones who had the jobs, relatives or no, held on to them for dear life.

It is noticeable, I think, that anyone who has tasted the heady wine of the theatre, even on its merest fringes or in the most menial of its jobs, is cut off from the outside world forever after. The world of the theatre is as closed a tribe and as removed from other civilian worlds as a Gypsy encampment, and those who enter it are spoiled for anything else and are tainted with its insidious lure for the rest of their lives. I could not or would not bring myself face to face with the fact that by this time next week I might well be a stockroom clerk or a messenger boy, and the world in which I had so fragile a toe hold would be closed to me once more—this time, for all I knew, for good and all.

I walked up and down the alley, turning over and over in my mind every avenue and possibility of escape and refusing with a mixture of stubbornness and rage to accept the fact that there was none. At eleven o'clock I started back to the hotel. I knocked on the door of Mrs. Harris' suite and walked in without waiting for an answer, for now there was no need to delay whatever might be in store for me.

The setting and the atmosphere were identical with the first conference in Rochester, but Mrs. Harris, to her everlasting credit, was valiant in defeat—a defeat which even her optimistic spirit had to concede was final and absolute.

"You just missed seeing me trying to eat my hat, Moss," she called to me as I came in. She laughed and crossed to where Mr. Pitou was slumped down in the depths of the sofa. "Gus," she said, "we guaranteed the theatre here for four weeks, didn't we?" He nodded without looking up at her. "Four thousand a week, wasn't it?" she asked. Again Mr. Pitou nodded, as though naming the actual amount would cause him acute physical pain.

"Well, Gus," she went on, "my suggestion is we pay the theatre off and close here tomorrow night. What would you say our total loss on the show would be, Gus? With the loss up to date and the guarantee and bringing the company back to New York and paying them off?"

Mr. Pitou took an envelope and pencil out of his pocket and slowly covered the back of it with figures. He seemed to take a long time about it, and while he scribbled, no one spoke. When he had finished, he looked up and laid the envelope on the sofa beside him.

"Well, how much is it, Gus?" Mrs. Harris asked a little impatiently.

His reply was so faint that Mrs. Harris had to ask him to repeat it, and when he did, the words emerged jerkily like a sore tooth being yanked by an inept dentist. "Forty-five thousand dollars," he said.

I swallowed painfully. I had started it all in a kitchen in the Bronx on a quiet Sunday afternoon!

"Can we leave the scenery here?" asked Mrs. Harris.

"Nope," said the company manager, speaking up for the first time. "We gotta cart it away from the theatre."

"Cart it away where?" asked Mrs. Harris.

"To the city dump," he replied. "Then you wait for a windy day on the dump and burn it. Gotta pay for that, too."

Mrs. Harris laughed. "Couldn't we find out where Ashton Stevens lives and leave it on his doorstep?" she said. And as an afterthought, she added, "That set and a dramatic critic deserve each other."

Priestly Morrison crossed to where I was standing and laid a hand on my shoulder. "I'd spare myself reading Ashton Stevens in the morning, Moss," he said kindly. "Anyway, you'll be coming back here with another one some day and make him eat his words, won't he, Gus?"

Mr. Pitou did not reply. He rose from the sofa and made his way slowly toward the door. His voice, when he finally spoke, was muted and forlorn. "Good night," he said, "I'm going to bed." He signaled to me from the doorway to follow him. I murmured a good night and closed the door after me.

I stood beside him in silence as we waited for the elevator and in silence he walked down the corridor to the room I was to share with him. He's waiting till we get inside, I thought, then he'll tell me.

Mr. Pitou unlocked the door and threw the key with something of a crash on the glass-top bureau; still in silence, he began to undress. There is something terribly disconcerting in seeing your employer, the man who holds your destiny in his hands, stand before you in long winter underwear. It is an article of apparel that can rob any situation of dignity and create an immediate atmosphere of absurdity. Fearful as I was of what he was about to say, I was suffused with so great an embarrassment that I did not catch the first few words of what he said when finally he spoke. To my surprise he was talking not about *The Beloved Bandit* but about the receipts of his other shows on the road.

"May Robson played to under a thousand in Flint, Michigan, Saturday night; and Fiske O'Hara played to four hundred in Saginaw," he was saying. "I don't know what the hell is happening. This is the height of the season, they never played to those kinds of grosses before." He went on to list the grosses of the other shows and the possible adverse conditions in each town, all of which he knew intimately, that might account for the alarming drop in receipts. But as he talked on, his bewilderment only grew greater, for there appeared to be no logical answer to the over-all slump.

What was happening, of course, though neither of us knew it then and the final grim answer was not to be a certainty until a few years later, was that "the road"—that staple and necessary adjunct of the theatre's lifeline in America—"the road" as the theatre knew it and counted on it at that time was disappearing with frightening swiftness. Talking pictures had not yet arrived, of course, but the silent movies and the magic of early radio were making enormous inroads on the cultural habits of theatregoing America. Also, the tremendous impact of the mass-produced automobile and the fact that communication between peoples in small towns was suddenly obtainable and with ease, all played a part, I suppose, in the hidden revolution that was to destroy both the road and that deeply entrenched kingpin of family entertainment, vaudeville. With their disappearance went a way of theatrical life and an irreplaceable training ground for young actors, for shoddy as some of the fare may have been, it provided a testing ground for actors that no school of acting, however high-minded its purpose, ever came close

[86]

to. There is no such thing as a substitute for acting before an audience, no matter how grubby the conditions may be, and with the passing of the road and vaudeville, a large and invaluable audience disappeared forever, too.

It occurred neither to Mr. Pitou nor apparently to anyone else in the theatre of that time that what they were witnessing was not a passing flurry of bad business but the end of an era, and the fearsome figures of A. L. Erlanger and E. F. Albee continued to rule over a domain that had already vanished.

What occurred to me quite sharply, listening to Mr. Pitou talk on and on, was the fact that he was not mentioning either *The Beloved Bandit* or myself. It took a few minutes for the full import of this to sink in, and then a great weight seemed to lift from my chest. It could mean, of course, only one thing—I was safe! My precarious footing in the theatre was still intact. I made a solemn vow to myself never again to type the words "Act One" on a piece of white paper as long as I lived. And my relief was so enormous that involuntarily I gave a huge yawn right in Mr. Pitou's face.

He looked at his watch and sighed. "It's almost four o'clock in the morning," he said. "Let's get to bed. I want to get the first train out of here tomorrow."

I slept soundly that night for the first time in a week.

Mr. Pitou was not the most cheerful of companions on the journey back to New York, but nothing could dampen my good spirits. Even Ashton Stevens' notice of *The Beloved Bandit,* which I read surreptitiously in the men's toilet on the train, failed to depress me unduly. He had not actually written a criticism of the play. He had run, instead, an obituary notice bordered in black, which began: "There died at the Adelphi Theatre last night . . ." and then went on to list the name of the play, the author and the actors. It was a cruel joke, of course, but I understood his irritation, which, I was forced to admit, was not entirely unmerited. Strangely enough, it didn't seem to matter very much. Nothing about *The Beloved Bandit* seemed to matter much now as long as I still had my job.

That foolish illusion was dispelled as the train roared into Grand

Central. As the lights flicked on, Mr. Pitou, who had seemed to be dozing in his chair, opened his eyes and spoke.

"The way things are, Mouse," he said slowly, "with business on the road so bad and all, I'll go back to sharing Miss Belle as secretary and have John, the elevator man, empty the wastepaper baskets and mail the letters."

I stared at him for a moment and then said, "Oh."

People were beginning to rise from their seats now, and the porter was between us getting the bags down from the racks overhead. I called across to Mr. Pitou, "Is it all right if I come up to see you once in a while—in case things change?"

"Oh, sure," he replied, "do that." He gathered up his things and started toward the door. "I'm going to have to make a run for it as soon as the train stops," he said over his shoulder. "I think I can just make my train to Bayside, so good-bye."

I watched him make his way toward the door. By the time I reached the platform he was lost in the swirl of people heading for the stairway. I stood for a few moments uncertainly, then I picked up my suitcase and headed for the stairway and the subway back to the Bronx.

N EW YORK is not a city to return to in defeat. Its walls of granite and glass are not inclined to reassure the fearful or console the despairing. I love the city of my birth and I always return to it with a lift of the heart. When I am away from it for any stretch of time, I grow querulous and unhappy, and with the real ache of the homesick I long to get back to it. But on this, my first return, the city seemed forbidding and impregnable. For the first time I felt as so many must feel who come from the little towns and hamlets to challenge the city—I felt swallowed up by it, erased; and I felt for the first time a hopelessness, a wretched awareness that the best thing I could do was to forget the theatre and take the first job offered to me tomorrow morning.

I think my deep and undying hatred of the New York subway stems from the ride home that night. I had always hated it, of course, as do most of its unfortunate straphangers; but it became to me that evening a symbol of all that I hated and a portent of the endless years stretching ahead of riding back at the end of each day to the Bronx. All the bitterness I felt seemed to be embodied in its noise, its filth, and etched indelibly in the lines of the faces of the close-packed people all around me. I walked down the steps of the subway station at Jackson Avenue, and as I started the three-block trudge home, I began to think with some degree of clarity for the first time since Mr. Pitou had revealed his stunning bit of news.

I decided not to tell my father or mother that I was without a job. That could well wait until the end of the week when I might have some other job and the blow would be softened by the sight of another pay check. I had had enough of bad news for one day without bringing more of it home with me. I knew, too, that the fact that my mother and father would completely fail to understand how much the loss of my job meant to me, would only add to the sense of hopelessness within me that was already heavier than the suitcase I carried in my hand.

Suddenly I stopped, astonished at the sight of my father sitting in the window of the small cigar store about a block from where we lived. It was a little hole-in-the-wall cigar store run by a Cuban man and his wife, and there was usually another little Cuban man sitting in the window from morning until late at night, endlessly cutting and rolling tobacco leaves into cheap cigars. It had been a grim family jest for my father to remark when things were particularly bad, "Well, if things get any worse, I'll have to go to work in the window around the corner." They had never quite come to that low pass, and I always shuddered a little at the prospect of that public humiliation. What could have happened in the two weeks that I had been away? The two boarders we were hanging onto for dear life must have left, or my mother or my brother must be ill. Doctor bills were an ever-present nightmare.

I hurried past the window. My father did not see me; he was bent over the cigar board, his fingers deftly rolling the leaves, and my heart went out to him. I knew he must have been there since eight o'clock in the morning. I always used to see the little Cuban man sitting there on my way to the subway each day. Cigar makers of that sort were paid not by the day but by the number of cigars they turned out, and my father was working very late indeed.

I would know what had happened soon enough—but why, oh why, I thought as I approached the house, did one disaster have to follow another, always in twos or threes? There was a very successful motion picture playing at that time called *Over the Hill to the Poorhouse,* and some sensible fellow was said to have remarked, "The poorhouse wasn't tough enough—they had to put a hill in front of it!" I did not hear this witticism until long afterward, but as I walked up the four flights to our apartment my feelings were more or less the same. My mother opened the door, and behind her I immediately saw my brother and the two boarders sitting at the kitchen table. In the same quick look I noticed her eyes were red-rimmed with weeping.

"What's the matter, Ma—what's happened?" I asked, still standing in the hallway. She pulled me gently in and shut the door behind us. Then she led me to the front room, which was my mother's and father's bedroom but which we disguised as the parlor with a series of throws and covers when company came. She sat down on the bed and motioned me to sit beside her.

"Aunt Kate died while you were away," she said and burst anew into quiet weeping. After a moment or two, she told me what little there was to tell. It had all happened in the space of a single night. They had been called to the hospital at two o'clock in the morning, and at four o'clock she had died as they sat beside her bed. It had been cancer but of the painless variety, and she had regained consciousness just a little before the end and had smiled at them and asked after me. My father, unforgiving while she had lived, had behaved with great gentleness and understanding with her death. She had not a penny of her own, of course, but he had insisted nevertheless on giving her the kind of funeral he knew she would have liked, and we were hopelessly in debt thereby. So that was why he sat in the window around the corner—he would sit there now day after day doing at last the one thing he feared and hated most, in order to see that a woman he had bitterly disliked was buried with decency and respect.

The first thought that flashed through my mind as my mother spoke was: "I should have told her," for I had not told Aunt Kate that a play of mine was to be produced. I had secretly nourished the fantasy of saying nothing until I escorted her to the theatre for the opening night in New York. Both the fantasy and Aunt Kate were gone now, but for the moment I could feel no sense of grief —I seemed to be drained of all emotion.

"How much did the funeral cost?" I asked my mother.

"Two hundred dollars," she answered. "We have to pay it off at ten dollars a week. It was wonderful of them to trust us, wasn't it?" I nodded. I must take the first job I could get tomorrow, I decided, without even shopping around. My mother stood up and wiped her eyes.

"We'd better not talk any more now," she said. "I was just starting to serve supper when you rang the bell. They've been very nice about everything"—she gestured toward the kitchen, indicating the boarders—"but we can't afford to have them leave now, we need every single penny."

I went to the room that I shared with my brother and unpacked my suitcase. There on the top lay the tattered and thumb-marked script of *The Beloved Bandit,* and carefully preserved between two shirts, was a clean program I had saved to show Aunt Kate. I tore it into little pieces and tossed the pieces out the window. Then I went to the bathroom and turned on the water taps full, so that no one might hear me crying.

The next morning I was in the subway by seven-thirty, marking out the want ads in the *New York Times* as I rode downtown. There were possibilities enough—none that I liked or wanted, of course, but I was not in a position to choose. Stockroom clerk, shipping-room packer, errand boy—it didn't really matter now which one I got.

I decided to start the rounds at 14th Street and work my way uptown, but at Times Square I got off the train. Almost before I knew what I was doing, I began to push my way to the door, but by the time I had wrenched my way out, I knew why I was getting off and what I was going to do. Before I settled down into drudgery, I was going out to the cemetery to make my own farewell.

I changed to the Brooklyn train, and on the long ride out to Cypress Hills I felt a wonderful quietude and peace settle over me. There were several different funerals wending their way slowly through the cemetery when I arrived, but I did not find the sight a depressing one. The panoply of death has never held any sadness for me or even touched me very greatly. I have always experienced my grief privately, and then it was done. The funeral has always left me unmoved. Such rites as I have attended, I have attended unwillingly and only as a mark of respect to the living and not to the dead. I have said my good-byes unpublicly; the coolly organized trappings of the funeral chapel have always seemed to me an outmoded and unnecessary ordeal.

It was a long walk to where Aunt Kate lay buried and I lost my way several times. I rather enjoyed it. The cemetery did not seem an unpleasant place to be after the subway. It was almost a spring-like day for the middle of winter, and though the trees were leafless, the well-kept lawns around the graves were a sparkling green. I came to the end of a little path and there in front of me was the grave of my aunt, some of the funeral greens still upon it. Next to it was the grave of my grandfather.

I stood there not knowing quite what to do. I had been impelled to come here by some force within me of terrible urgency, but now that I was here I did not know what to do. I could think only that here were the two people whose lives had meant the most to mine and what a pitiful waste their lives had been to themselves. They were both better, I knew, than life had allowed them to be; and standing there I thought of them more clearly than I ever had before. Fleeting words and moments with both of them came back to me with startling clarity and I suddenly realized how much of their hopes had been unconsciously pinned on me. I had been their bulwark against complete defeat. Far from feeling sorrow or self-pity, I began to shake with an uncontrollable rage. To take a job as shipping clerk or errand boy was no worse than hundreds of boys my own age and circumstances were doing every day of the week. But standing by the graves of my aunt and my grandfather, I was damned if I would. For all that they had been to me, I owed it to them not to; and out of my rage I resolved that come what may, I was sticking to the theatre and I would never turn back. And the truth of the matter is that from that actual moment on, I never did.

There are certain great disadvantages to the truth—one of them is that the truth sometimes emerges as hopelessly cliché. It would be a brave writer indeed or an extremely foolish one who would contrive a scene such as I have just described without the inescapable feeling that it was perhaps a little too pat. Yet life often imitates very bad plays or movies with a minimum of effort and a disquieting ease, and the only plausible explanation I can offer for this is an aphorism from Pascal I came across years afterward. He said: "The heart has reasons which the reason knows not of." I think that was true of me on this particular day. I think that it is true, too, that men are sometimes willing to die for the very same things they make fools of themselves over, so that when the truth comes out cliché there is nothing to do but set it down.

I made my way back to the subway, and I knew that I was getting off at Times Square and no place else from then on.

As the 14th Street subway station flashed by I made a sudden decision. Now was as good a time as any for me to try to be an actor. I would never have less to lose. I got off the train, threw the copy of the *Times,* with the marked want ads in it, onto the subway tracks and walked toward the steps that led up to Times Square.

I had an advantage now that I had not had two years before. I was no longer a theatrical innocent. I knew where theatrical offices were, what the lingo was, and I knew too how haphazardly most of the smaller parts were cast. All I needed was "beginner's luck." I straightened my tie, fixed the handkerchief in my breast pocket at a more jaunty angle and stole a glance at myself in the mirror of a chewing-gum machine. It seemed to me I already looked different. I had felt like a shipping clerk or an errand boy riding downtown on the subway this morning, but now I felt like an actor and it seemed to me I looked like one. I knew the look well. The too eager, too bright smile, the glint in the eye serving notice to the steely office boy of the implacable desire to wait, if need be, all afternoon; the knowing air of being conscious of some secret casting going on that the others in the already crowded office did not share. I practiced the look in the mirror for a moment and was satisfied with it. I had one other advantage as well, I reminded myself. I had, until very recently, been a theatrical office boy myself, and for a little while, at least, I thought I could count on my acquaintance among the enemy to get me in to see a casting director first.

Cannily, I chose an office boy who I knew had had the same difficulty saying "no" to actors that I had had and who also knew something of my ambitions to be an actor. Irving Morrison, George Tyler's office boy, was a kind and good-hearted fellow, and if I had to put a toe into the icy waters that actors daily swam in, Irving Morrison was by far the warmest way of making the plunge. It was a wise choice. He showed only a mild surprise at the news that I had turned actor, and though I suspected he knew I had been fired, he had the grace not to mention it and asked me to wait until he could get me in to see Mr. Tyler. There was nothing much going on, he informed me, but at least I could meet Mr. Tyler.

I turned around and tried to find an inconspicuous place among the others who were already waiting, and while I waited I listened to the easy bantering talk that flowed so effortlessly among them. Not enough has been said or written about the way actors talk among themselves. It is delicious, dim-witted and valiant talk, and since the bulk of it is based upon harmless little falsehoods which everyone accepts nonchalantly, it is also gay, sardonic and very often sprinkled with a nice edge of malice. It is valiant talk because part of an actor's equipment is a gallantry he must carry along daily like a shield; whatever despair he may feel as he faces himself in the mirror in the morning before he sets out on the daily round, he must learn to dissemble completely as he stands waiting in the outer office—not only must he look his best, but he must give no hint to the competitors who wait along with him to be interviewed for the same part, of how desperately he may need it or how slim the pickings have been up to now.

It is not always easy to look one's best on a meager breakfast and the knowledge that lunch must be skipped, or to chat lightly while one stands against the light so that the shine on the suit pressed too often does not show. But there is a quality of childlike innocence in most actors that manages somehow to suspend reality until to-morrow and along with it a *politesse de coeur* toward their fellow actors that I do not think exists in other professions.

[95]

One of the actors in the office turned to me now and asked politely, "What have you been doing lately?"

I knew the lingo well enough to shrug my shoulders and answer, "Nothing on Broadway," and let my voice trail off.

It was no doubt obvious to them all that I had never set foot on a stage but they included me in their chatter as though I were a veteran. I listened intently, for running through the conversation, hidden among the boasts and the lies that fooled nobody, were little nuggets of valuable information about what was going on in nearly every theatrical office in New York. When the bright-eyed girl in the freshly washed cotton gloves loftily announced that she had refused a part in the new Avery Hopwood play because the character did not appear until the third act, two other ingénues on the edge of the crowd left shortly afterward. It was as apparent to everyone in the office that the two ingénues were making a beeline for the A. H. Woods office as it was that the bright-eyed girl had applied for the part and been turned down cold, but the information that a part might still be open in the new Hopwood play was well worth a morning's wait.

The grapevine was apt to be hung with highly colored fruit of pure imagination, but to the initiate the leads it conveyed of what was going on were usually accurate. Another man was talking now and I pricked up my ears. "I don't know how they think they're going to cast it," he sniffed, "but they're offering twenty-five dollars for someone to play Smithers in a revival of *The Emperor Jones* over at the Mayfair Theatre. It's non-Equity, of course," he added contemptuously.

"Who's doing it?" someone asked.

"I didn't even bother to ask," the first man answered, and as a little chorus of appropriate laughter rewarded him for his sally, I got up and quietly made my way out. If they were having trouble casting it, this might be the beginner's luck I had been hoping for. And non-Equity or not, twenty-five dollars a week was ten dollars more than I had ever earned in my life. I motioned to Irving Morrison that I would be back and made my way to the Mayfair Theatre on 44th Street in no time flat. There was another hungry-looking actor in the Tyler office who had seemed about to make his way to the door just as I had.

The Mayfair Theatre was a tiny little affair of no more than two hundred seats that has long since been turned into a bus terminal, but it seemed big enough to me as I climbed the stairs to the manager's office. It was owned or leased, I never quite knew which, by two gentlemen whose connection with things theatrical seemed to hang by the proverbial shoestring; and one of the gentlemen was sitting in the office now, puffing contentedly on a cigar. A little breathlessly I told him what I had come for. He pushed a copy of the printed play across the desk toward me and said, "Read it."

It did not occur to me to hesitate or to be in the least nervous. I opened the book and plunged in. I had not seen the original production of the play at the Provincetown Playhouse five years before, but I had read it, and my English ancestry now stood me in good stead. The part of Smithers is that of a dissolute cockney trader and I could simulate the accent passably well. I had only to recall my father's accent, which was still pure Whitechapel, to make the words ring true, and my ear was a good one. The fact that I was eighteen years old and Smithers was supposed to be a drunken and battered sixty did not faze me at all nor did it seem to bother the man behind the desk. In some ways the theatre is marvelous— nothing is too preposterous not to at least be given a hearing. I finished the scene and handed the book back to him. The man behind the desk looked at me and relit his cigar before he spoke.

"It's not Equity and the salary is twenty dollars a week." He looked at me inquiringly, waiting for an answer.

"I thought the part paid twenty-five," I said hesitantly, and only because I was afraid of seeming too anxious—I suppose I would have taken twenty dollars or even fifteen!

"Well, if we're stuck, I guess it does," he answered pleasantly, and then added somewhat surprisingly, "Do you happen to know what time it is right now?"

"It's about one thirty," I replied.

"Good," he said. "Go downstairs and tell Gilpin you're Smithers They're rehearsing on the stage. I promised him I'd have a Smithers by two o'clock. If he says anything, tell him you're the best we can do for the money. Wait a minute," he called after me, for I was already out the door, "take this copy of the play down with you. I think we only bought two copies."

I grabbed the book and raced down the stairs. I was an actor on Broadway! I knew enough to know that the management and the production would probably be as shoddy and threadbare as it was possible to be, but what did it matter? What mattered was that I had had the unique experience of outwitting life, and it was a victory that would not diminish with the years. I would remember it long afterward when I needed to.

My first glimpse of Charles Gilpin, the great Negro actor, was a fairly typical one. He was not quite sober and he was in a smoldering rage. He was directing this revival of the play himself, for he had played the Emperor Jones over a thousand times. I waited until there was a pause in the rehearsal and presented myself to him. He did not seem surprised that Smithers was going to be played by a youth of eighteen—there was a timeless resignation and disenchantment about everything he did or said. He looked at me with a pair of somber eyes, which seemed to be burned into his face, and sighed softly. "All right," he said quietly, "wait."

I wandered over to a dark corner of the stage and watched him rehearse the others. He was walking through his own part, but every so often he would flash out and act for an isolated moment or two. The effect was shattering. He had an inner violence and a maniacal power that engulfed the spectator, and he and the Emperor Jones were a classic example of actor and part meeting to perfection.

Eugene O'Neill once said that Gilpin was the only actor in any of his plays that realized fully O'Neill's inner image of what the performance should be, and he was probably correct. Charles Gilpin was the greatest actor of his race. He was limited not by his own range as an actor, but by the limitations of the part the Negro could play in the theatre. Had he not been a Negro, there is no doubt that he would have been one of the great actors of his time, but other than the Emperor Jones, there were no parts of any stature that ever came his way. Not unnaturally, his success in *The Emperor Jones* and the probability that he would never play anything else worthy of his talent embittered an already violent and hostile nature, and he took what refuge and solace he could find in alcohol.

He signaled me now to come over—that he was ready to mark out the first act. Smithers is the only other speaking part in the play, and the entire first act is played by the Emperor and Smithers alone on the stage. I began to shake with nerves. All the bravado I had displayed in the office upstairs deserted me completely and I shook and stammered and constantly lost my place. Gilpin seemed to pay no attention whatever to the agony I was going through or to the fact that even to my own ears I sounded hollow and fake and incredibly young.

Stolidly and wearily he plodded on—mechanically he marked out the movement—"You stand there . . . now I come over to you . . . now I go back and sit on the throne . . . now you come over to me . . . when the drums start you walk to the door and listen . . . then you come back . . . no, no . . . just go back to where you were before."

Finally it was over. He looked at me and sighed. "Did they tell you when we open?" he asked. I shook my head. "Day after tomorrow—you better learn the words fast," he said and started to leave the stage.

I managed to gather up enough courage to go after him and tug at his sleeve. "Could you tell me how you want it played?" I stammered. For the first time he smiled. "You ain't as bad as you think you are." He chuckled. "You learn the words tonight and we'll have a hassle with it tomorrow." And he was on his way to his dressing room and the always-waiting bottle.

There was considerably less astonishment than I would have believed possible when I announced the news at home that evening that I was an actor. Perhaps everything else was overshadowed by the relief that though I had lost one job, I already had another at ten dollars more a week. There was not too much time for discussion, for I explained that I had to commit the part to memory that night, and once again my mother construed this to mean some sort of "homework" I had neglected during the day that might cost me the job tomorrow. Everyone was shooed away, just as years later, long after I had become an established playwright, she would say, "Don't go into the room now—he's doing homework," her tone implying that I was writing "I won't do it again" on the blackboard. My mother never quite believed that any work one could do at home was quite honest, and I think she remained firmly convinced that all the writing I did at home was some sort of well-merited punishment for neglecting my duties on the outside.

The part of Smithers is not a long one and I learned it with ease, and the next day, as he had promised, Mr. Gilpin gave me a "hassle" with it. He was not a good director, but he had one great virtue—he let an actor act and did not waste endless time in discussing motivation and inner orientation or indulge himself in any of the meaningless patois and sophistry that pass so often for the directorial touch. He was impatient, intolerant and somewhat inarticulate about what he wanted—but being a first-rate actor himself, he knew the folly of giving lessons in acting to anyone, and he did not permit himself the self-indulgence of showing off to impress the rest of the company, as well he might have done in my case.

I imagine he had made up his mind the day before that I could do it, and he talked to me now in a kind of shorthand—swift, unadorned and, when I could interpret him correctly, wonderfully precise and helpful, for like everything else connected with the theatre, where life moves only in long, arid stretches or sudden acute crises, my debut as an actor was being made under the pressure of a dress rehearsal that evening and an opening on the following night.

I had very little time for alarm as to how good or bad I might be, for my chief concern all through the afternoon was the fact that I did not know how to put make-up on my face and was too ashamed to admit it to anyone in the company. I solved this ignominious admission of my inexperience by hanging around the counter at Gray's drug store during the dinner hour until another actor came along to purchase some make-up for himself, and under the guise of being puzzled as to just how to get the effect I wanted, I let him suggest the proper crepe hair, the glue or spirit gum, the right shade of powder, and all the rest of the paraphernalia I needed to look the part of the disreputable Smithers.

He must have given me good advice, for I was a little staggered as I looked at myself in the dressing-room mirror later on that evening. The blacked-out teeth, the rusty gray stubble, the heavy dissipated drooping eyelids, the thin-lipped sneer that curled and aged the mouth into something evil and craven were decidedly right. I understood for the first time why it was more or less classic for young actors to start out in the theatre by playing old men, and I perceived how completely make-up depersonalizes the actor. I was so delighted with the effect I had produced that I sailed through the dress rehearsal absolutely nerveless, nor can I truthfully record the traditional case of stage fright the following evening when the play opened. I had a mild flutter of nerves as I stood in the wings waiting for the curtain to go up, for mine was the first entrance in the play; but I think I was rescued from anything approximating stage fright by a sudden image that flashed through my mind as the curtain hit the top. "Well, I'm not wrapping packages or delivering telegrams for Western Union," I thought happily as I heard a polite spatter of applause greet the set—and on I went.

Gilpin, who came on shortly afterward, received what I suppose was a thunderous reception in terms of the tiny Mayfair Theatre, and with nothing more than a pleasurable sense of excitement I played the rest of the act with him as though I had been playing it for months.

After the first act I did not come on again until the final few moments of the play and I took the opportunity of watching Gilpin play out the role in full from the side of the stage. At his best, which he was that night and not very often afterward, he was a spectacular and memorable Emperor Jones. Even on the wrong side of the proscenium, and pushed out of the way every so often by the stage manager, I was caught up and held by the majesty and grandeur of his performance.

At the end he received an ovation, and the next morning the notices were glowing for Gilpin and, to my intense surprise, excellent for me as well. The *Times* commented, "Moss Hart as Smithers is a delight both to the eye and the ear." And even the *World,* while complaining bitterly about the general sleaziness of the production, went on to say, "The fault is not Mr. Gilpin's, who can never lose the laurels he has gained in the part, nor is it the fault of his colleague, Moss Hart, who does the cheap cockney trader to perfection."

My surprise was genuine. In the hullabaloo of getting the job and opening two days afterward, I had literally had no time to speculate on what the critics would say. It was the first and last time I would be so blissfully oblivious of the critics, but now I was immoderately pleased by the notices—they confirmed my belief that I had nothing to do but to act from now on, and only glory lay ahead. I could hardly wait to get to the theatre that night and have the curtain go up.

Fortunately, I did not see Mr. Gilpin before the performance, for it took me a long time to put on the make-up and I was still quite awkward about it. I expected to see him during the intermission, congratulate him on his fine notices, and no doubt receive a few words of praise from him on my own sterling performance. I did not know, luckily, that Mr. Gilpin was a little less than sober that evening and that the management had decided that rather than refund the money they would get him into his costume, push him out on the stage, and take a chance on what would happen.

No doubt they needed every penny to keep going and no doubt they were right to take the gamble. I suppose, too, they were also correct in not warning me about his condition beforehand. I would have been too downright scared even to set foot on the stage. As it was, I was barely able to finish the first act and I think my very inexperience as an actor saved me at that.

Gilpin made his entrance stumblingly, quite as though he had been pushed out from the wings—which indeed he was—and made directly for the throne, where he sat down heavily and proceeded to go to sleep. The audience sensed nothing strange in this, for it was in keeping with the part that it be played that way. For myself, however, I was openly panic-stricken, and the stage manager, seeing the obvious panic on my face, hissed to me from the wings, "Shake him—go ahead and shake him. Keep playing."

Too frightened to do anything else, I did as I was told. I walked over to the throne and shook him as hard as I could. He opened his eyes and looked up at me wonderingly—he did not know where he was for a moment or two and looked around the stage and out at the audience in some bewilderment, as if trying to focus on what was going on. Again the stage manager hissed, "Keep shaking him—get him up on his feet."

And again I did as I was told. I pulled him to his feet, and hanging onto his arm to steady him, I yelled my first line into his ear. Astonishingly, he answered with the correct line. He shook his head a few times, like an old lion at bay, and to my horror thrust my hand roughly away and sat down on the throne again. I stood there frozen, not knowing what to do next and not even able to hear the words the stage manager was hissing at me from the wings.

Haltingly Gilpin began to play. His voice was thick, and he jumbled the cues, but he sat on the throne steadying himself until he regained something like control over his movements, and then he rose and as the act proceeded he even seemed to play with something of his old power, though every so often he would suddenly grab hold of me to stop himself from falling—each time, of course, scaring me out of my wits.

Throughout all this the audience seemed entirely unaware that anything other than the drama on the stage was being acted out before them, and when the curtain of the first act finally came down—a full ten years later, it seemed to me—a very good hand accompanied it. Gilpin left the stage without a word. I stood where I was, trembling. I was too shaken to even wipe away the perspiration, which was running down my face in all the colors of my make-up. The stage manager patted me on the shoulder and said, "I think we'll make it now—good boy!" and hurried down with a pot of steaming black coffee to Gilpin's dressing room.

I walked back to my own room and sat limply on a chair, recovering as best I could. I could not even summon up sufficient curiosity or strength to find out if the second act was going on, but apparently Gilpin, with the help of the black coffee, snapped back completely and was fine for the rest of the play. At the end, as we stood taking our bows, he whispered to me, his eyes twinkling, "You're learning to act fast, Smithers." And that was all he ever said about it, that night or any other night, for the same thing occurred not too often, but often enough to make the nights when it did happen real horrors. Only once did the management agree to cancel a performance; the rest of the time when they saw the danger signals flying as Gilpin arrived at the theatre, they would get him dressed, push him onto the stage, and take a chance that he would be able to play. How he managed to get through some of those performances I do not know; and he was able to do it, of course, only because the very nature of the part allowed the audience to believe that some of the reeling behavior going on on the stage was part and parcel of the play itself. But it left me terrorized and shaken each time it happened.

Nevertheless, I was learning to "act fast," as Gilpin so aptly put it. I learned one or two things about the craft of acting and its relation to the other arts of the theatre that I thought sound at the time, and I have seen no reason to change my mind since. There is no arrogance like the arrogance of the beginner, of course, and it almost goes without saying that no one ever knows as much about an art as the most inexperienced practitioner of it. But it seemed to me then, and it still does, that acting is more a fortunate quirk of the personality than it is anything else. Certainly, education, technical training and the finest of Stanislavskian theories have yet to produce the same effect as an actor walking out on the stage with a curious chemistry of his own that fastens every eye in the audience upon him and fades the other actors into the scenery.

All the techniques so painfully acquired, all the passionate dedication to the methods of the various schools of acting, go right down the drain when this happens. And it can happen with so trifling a facet of an actor's personality as an arresting quality of speech or voice. I have no wish to minimize this gift—it is equally as valid as the ability to write dialogue that actors can speak, a gift which also requires neither education nor technical training, but without which no play can be written, despite dedication, the best motives in the world, or all the courses in play-writing strung together. Yet, like the perennial effusions on the art of the director, more pure nonsense is written about the art of acting through the years than one would believe possible. The very same critical acumen that can be so acute and penetrating in evaluating the merits of a play seems to stop short of an ability to divorce personality from acting, or direction from playing.

I have worked intimately with two or three of the finest actors of our generation, and it seemed to me they achieved their effects with a minimum of help from me, just as I have received critical praise for the directorial touches that belonged more properly to the playwright. The great ones all have one thing in common—it is sometimes called "star quality," but among the learned it is more often discussed in terms of "level of emotion" or "playing in depth." To me the fact is inescapable that this magic of personal chemistry occurs at the moment of conception and is, as J. M. Barrie has said, like charm in a woman: "If you have it, you don't need to have anything else; and if you don't have it, it doesn't much matter what else you have." Certainly, no voodoo of acting method, however high-minded, can bring it about, nor is there any directorial sorcery that I have ever observed that can make it happen.

It was of some importance to me that I dimly perceived some of this early on, for while I do not pretend that I thought it out in any such clear-cut terms, I nevertheless had an inkling of part of it. It saved me from wasting some valuable years and perhaps from the greater misfortune of remaining emotionally trapped in a childlike idolatry of actors and acting until it was too late to do anything else. One can witness daily in the theatre the tragedy of those who did not turn away in time.

With my lucky beginning in *The Emperor Jones,* however, no such depressing thoughts ever crossed my mind. I smugly concluded that I had found my proper niche in life, had received only what was my just due as an actor, and as far as I could foresee after so auspicious a start, there could follow only good parts, good notices, and, in the very nature of things, featured billing and inevitable stardom. The one thing I could not foresee was that Smithers would be the first and last part I would ever play on the stage as a professional actor; it was the only major flaw in the otherwise glittering future I had forecast for myself. So, unknowing and thoroughly complacent, I began to plan the next step in my acting career as *The Emperor Jones* came to the end of its fifteen-week run.

Although I had received good notices, I knew that almost everyone connected with the theatre had seen the original production, so my performance in the revival would have remained largely unobserved by those who might have done me some good. Still, I was armed now with an answer to that traditional bugaboo of all beginners, "What have you done before?" and that was in itself a great asset. I decided not to be choosy in spite of my own high opinion of myself, but to take whatever came along, even a walk-on. The important thing was to be in back of that proscenium arch when the lights dimmed down, and not in front of it. Once again I turned to my mentor, Irving Morrison, and kindly as ever he obtained a letter of introduction for me signed by George Tyler himself.

Mr. Tyler had placed in rehearsal an English importation called *The Constant Nymph,* with Claude Rains and Beatrix Thomson, and since the play called for a number of extras in the crowd scene the letter was to the English director, Basil Dean, who like the stars and most of the rest of the company, had been brought over from England for the production.

On the morning after *The Emperor Jones* closed, I presented myself to the stage manager half an hour before the rehearsal began and waited for Mr. Dean to arrive. I was completely satisfied in my own mind that there would be no difficulty getting the job. Extras were usually hired by the stage manager sight unseen by the director, and with a letter from George Tyler to Basil Dean, I took it for granted I would be told that the job was mine and that meeting Mr. Dean was a formality. It was not much of a job to be sure, but it paid fifteen dollars a week, and I knew how vital it was for me to keep working until something better showed up.

The rehearsal hall was a rather small studio on West 57th Street, so that any exchange between actors, director or stage manager was highlighted by the very proximity of one person to another. Actors as a rule loathe rehearsing in so confined a space, for it makes them unnecessarily self-conscious and usually hamstrings a director from doing anything more than going over lines. I soon gathered that Mr. Dean was using this particular day to polish scenes with some minor members of the company and that the stars themselves would not appear. Mr. Dean himself appeared briskly enough, and with his appearance the atmosphere in the studio changed markedly. The tension that he brought with him and engendered throughout the day did not dissipate from the moment he appeared in the doorway until the rehearsal was over, and it gathered momentum with every look and with every word he uttered.

Mr. Dean was a famous director and undoubtedly a gifted one, but the one thing he did not do in spite of his gifts was to inspire a personal loyalty or liking from his cast. They were virtually frightened to death of him. As he walked to the stage manager's table all conversation ceased and there was a nervous coughing and clearing of throats all over the room. There was a soft-spoken colloquy between stage manager and director, during which I saw the stage manager hold up my letter of introduction from Mr. Tyler, but Mr. Dean waved the letter impatiently away and did not even glance in my direction.

Quite peremptorily, without a greeting of any kind to anyone, he began to rehearse. He was not rehearsing the play in any chronological sequence of scenes, but jumping from second act to first act, or from first to last, as he saw fit. He was fascinating to watch, though I was silently thankful as the morning wore on that I was going to be a walk-on in the play and not an actor with a speaking part.

I do not think it an unjust assessment of him to say that Mr. Dean may well have been the last of the directorial despots, for despot he was. I imagine there are still directors who indulge in one sort or another of tyranny over actors, but Mr. Dean had refined his own kind into a weapon which he used with surgical skill. He did not tolerate discussion and he was unflinching in his demand to get exactly what he wanted in the way of performance. He spoke quietly, but his words were edged with a marvelous spleen, and his silences were wonderful to watch. They could be withering. His displeasure could be felt like a living thing, and all morning the hapless actors perspired and struggled under that cold appraising eye and the acid tongue.

Shortly after one o'clock he told the stage manager to dismiss the company for lunch, and as he walked to the prompt table, again I saw the stage manager offer him my letter of introduction and point to me off in the corner. Again he glanced neither at the letter nor at myself, but simply walked out of the room. There was nothing to do but wait, the stage manager informed me—perhaps he would take a look at me before the afternoon rehearsal began. I was hungry but I decided I had better not leave, on the chance that I might miss the right moment when he returned. Actors are always coming back to rehearsal with containers of coffee and Hershey bars and I was offered some of both by two early returnees, who were talking over the morning rehearsal as the rest of the company straggled back. Mr. Dean was not mentioned. The actors talked freely of the play and of their parts in it, but no word was spoken of Mr. Dean. It was almost as though by the mere mention of his name the atmosphere of terror he created would come into being and put a stop to the conversation. And suddenly the conversation did stop. Innocent as it was, it stopped abruptly; and though my back was to the door, I knew that Mr. Dean had appeared.

I turned around and watched the stage manager go through the same pantomime of presenting the letter to Mr. Dean and pointing to me, and with the same results. So far as Mr. Dean was concerned, it was as though the stage manager had not spoken at all. Mr. Dean busied himself with the script for a few moments and then plunged headlong into the rehearsal. It was obviously going to be heavy weather, for he seemed to be, if such a thing were possible, even more testy than he had been at the morning rehearsal.

Nothing suited him, from the manner in which the stage manager placed the chairs and tables for the setting of a scene, to the way the actors stood or sat or listened or picked up a prop or entered or left. He was never openly ill-tempered. That was not his method. A healthy outburst of temper would somehow have been easier to bear for everyone concerned. Mr. Dean's irritation took the form of a savagely accurate appraisal of each actor's inadequacy at whatever he was being asked to do, and it was uttered in tones of biting contempt. He had a wonderful command of irony and a subtle awareness of the essential weakness in each actor's armor that enabled him to pierce whatever little self-confidence or security any of them may have had left and adroitly tear it to shreds.

His dislike and displeasure that afternoon seemed to focus especially on the character man. The character man was a fine-looking old fellow of about sixty, but he was not a very able actor and his knowledge that he was somehow the core of Mr. Dean's annoyance with the company made him less sure-footed than he might have been even with such limited talent as he possessed. He fumbled and stumbled and was obviously incapable of doing the simplest thing correctly, for the good enough reason that he was so frozen with fear that he did not even hear what was being said. What seemed to make matters worse for him was that Mr. Dean seemed to take special pains not to speak to him at all, so that the actor appeared to be waiting constantly for the blow to fall, and until it did, he could do nothing.

Late in the afternoon, just before the rehearsal ended, it did. Mr. Dean had apparently been saving the character man for dessert. After a particularly spectacular tirade at one of the ladies, Mr. Dean lapsed into one of his long silences, and then suddenly he spoke, quietly, evenly but with a deadly precision. "Would you mind doing that again?" he said, addressing the character man directly for the first time.

"Do what again, Mr. Dean?" asked the character man, flushing a deep red and then going rigid with the awareness that his moment had come at last.

"Why, that splendid bit of acting you were perpetrating just now," replied Mr. Dean with a sweetness that was almost purring.

The character man moved his tongue over his lips as though to unlock his jaws and then made the hideous mistake of trying a riposte. "I'm pleased you thought so, Mr. Dean," he said with a hollow little laugh. "I'm rather fond of that bit myself. I wondered if you would notice it."

"Notice it?" said Mr. Dean. "Indeed, indeed! I have been riveted." He smiled dangerously at the character man and addressed the rest of the company with a disarming frankness and charm that was only belied by the cruelty of the words he was uttering. "In my many years in the theatre, ladies and gentlemen," he said, "I have witnessed and been subjected to many kinds of acting, and, of course, styles in acting change. I do not cherish tradition and I welcome innovation, but I have been greatly puzzled this last few minutes. I've never seen anything quite like our colleague's performance before, and since I think it unlikely that we shall ever see anything like it again, I suggest that you all come here to the front with me and watch it. Baffling as it appears to me to be, we might all learn something."

The company stirred uneasily, but they were as helpless as the character man. Actors who need their jobs are defenseless against a director. They rose from their chairs all over the room and came to the front of the hall. Mr. Dean lit a cigarette carefully and settled back in his chair. "Do go ahead, old chap," he said amiably. "Do exactly what you did before. We are all agog."

There was a blood-curdling pause and for a moment or two it seemed as though the character man was going to protest, but actually I do not think he heard very much of what had been said, for his complexion was a dull gray now and his head suddenly bent over the script in his hands like some treed animal anxious to have the dogs called off and the killing over with. He had, of course, no idea of what he had been doing before, and under the circumstances he could not be blamed for the absurdity of what he was doing now—but it was acting of the most embarrassing kind.

Fortunately, it was soon over. Mr. Dean did not interrupt. He had made his point, sadistic as it was, and he did not comment afterward.

"Ten o'clock tomorrow morning, ladies and gentlemen," he said, and walked over to the stage manager's table.

The actors gathered up their things and filed silently out. I watched the stage manager, waiting for him to present my letter to Mr. Dean, but he had forgotten, as well he might have, all about me. Mr. Dean was already out the door by the time I grabbed up the letter from the table and ran after him. I overtook him in the corridor on the way to the elevator and silently held the letter out to him. Like the others, I was too plain scared to address him directly. He waved me away as though I were an insect buzzing about his head and strode on toward the elevator. He was trapped at the elevator doors, however, for though he pushed the button angrily the elevator did not appear, and he could no longer deny the fact of my presence or the letter I still mutely held before him. There was no one else in the corridor but myself and the terrible Mr. Dean. Without a word he took the letter from me, ripped it open, glanced at the contents, and for the first time I felt those glacial eyes turn directly upon me.

"We want only English actors for this play," he said coldly, crumpling the letter and letting it fall to the floor.

"But I just played an English part, Mr. Dean," I replied with a bravery I did not know I possessed.

"Well, you must have done it very badly," said Mr. Dean in the pleasantest tone I had heard him use all afternoon. And with that the elevator appeared and he stepped into it. I did not follow him in—my bravery did not extend quite that far. I waited for the next trip down.

It was beginning to grow dark as I started back to the New Amsterdam Theatre at 42nd Street to report to Irving Morrison. I walked slowly, the lights of Broadway coming alive all around me—and I came to a bitter conclusion. Mr. Dean's conduct had been inhuman, but he was right—the character man was an actor of little talent who long since should have faced up to that fact. Had he done so early enough, he would not have been exposed to the indignity and humiliation I had just watched him suffer. In terms of strict justice he deserved it.

Though I found it hard to excuse Mr. Dean's behavior, I could after a fashion understand it. There is something maddening about mediocrity that calls forth the worst in those who are forced to deal with it. What sort of brainless vanity had caused the character man to persist in a profession where his own limitations must have long since been apparent even to himself? Was it just plain indolence or was it the very haphazardness of an actor's life that had brought him in his sixties to the sorry moment I had just witnessed? With his good looks and commanding presence he might easily have done very well in some other field had he made the choice early enough. Why had he not done so? Or, like myself, had he had "beginner's luck," and with not much else than a desire to act and an adolescent infatuation for the theatre, had he set forth long ago on the path that had led to this afternoon's deplorable failure? Had it been as unthinking and foolish as that? For back of this afternoon lay the failure and waste of an entire life, and it was failure that lacked the redeeming quality or the saving grace of aspiration. Almost surely he must have known long ago that he was second-rate and that the shoddy rewards the theatre offers to the second-rate do not compensate for the humiliations that go along with it.

Somehow I made a complete and terrible identification with the character man. I do not know if it is true of others, but all my life I have been prey to this curious psychological quirk. If I am in the middle of writing a play and happen to attend the opening night of a play that has gone badly, I am likely to make a swift and thorough-going identification with both the author and the play, even though the playwright may be completely unknown to me. I have even made a melancholy identification with someone in a field quite unrelated to my own, and then spent a depressing few hours afterward bringing myself back to reality.

Now I made a complete identification with the character man, and in the immediacy of the fear that clutched my heart I felt an irrevocable "There but for the grace of God go I" and I could not shake that fear off. It took hold of me completely, and for the first time I faced up to the grim possibility that a passion for the theatre and a deep desire to be an actor might not be enough. I had taken both these things for granted for so long a time that to make a stern assessment of just how much talent I had for acting was almost more than I could bear to do. I do not think I could have done so at all without that pitiable figure of the character man still so clearly before me; but the truth I was resisting, the truth I was so reluctant to come to, the actual truth when I allowed myself to know it, was simply that, in spite of a lucky beginning, in spite of passion and dedication, I would never be more than a passable actor and at best an adequate one—and there is no more damning word to apply to acting than "adequate."

It was a conclusion I did not come to easily. I was wrestling with a dream that had satisfied the needs of my childhood, and the elements of fantasy attached to that dream ran deep and strong. To give it up, to let it go, was to relinquish a secret part of myself that had sustained me through the years. Without it a new fear settled over me. I felt suddenly more alone than I had ever felt before— without the theatre as the goal that gave direction and point to my days, I felt engulfed by a world that was alien to me, a world I felt I was unequal to cope with. All the anxieties and insecurities of my years and my nature seemed to rise up in defense of the dream I had cherished for so long and that must have been a substitute and a symbol for so much. But I suddenly and sharply knew once and for all that however I remained attached to the theatre, it would not be as an actor.

THERE ARE certain crucial moments in life when the emotions one feels come perilously close to the mawkish, but the pain of those moments is not any the less acute because the moment itself happens to be a small or an unexalted one. I walked on, overwhelmed by a sense of sorrow and personal loss, and by the time I reached the New Amsterdam Theatre I knew that the dream of being an actor was behind me—that if I was to be a part of the only world I cared anything about, I must find some other way. And I knew now how bleak those prospects were.

As I waited for the elevator to come down, I wondered if it would not be wiser to walk out of the lobby and get the smell of the theatre out of my nostrils for good and all. But I remained standing there, watching the indicator as it marked the slow downward count of the floors. The elevator doors opened and a young man stepped out into the lobby. His name was Edward Chodorov, and let no one say that luck does not play a large part in the fashioning of any career. There is not the faintest hint of the mystic in my nature, but I have seen the large role that coincidence and chance play in all of our lives too clearly demonstrated to reject as mere superstition that portion of our destiny or fate called luck. It is as inexplicable as fate itself and as inexorable.

Would I not have gone on to write plays if Chodorov had not stepped out of the elevator at that particular moment? Of course. I am not suggesting anything so foolish as that. But Chodorov walked into my life at a moment when a different corner turned, a chance meeting missed, might very well have changed the whole course my life was to take from that time on. It is a prime example of what I mean by luck, that I did not take the elevator up to see Irving Morrison that evening but instead walked out of the lobby with Edward Chodorov—and into six years of apprenticeship and work that I am convinced made a fundamental difference in all my years in the theatre that were to follow.

Edward Chodorov had drifted into the Pitou office during my days of glory as office boy and we had hit it off immediately. He was exactly my age but I had never met anyone like him before. Though he had presumably come into the office as an actor looking for a job, he did not talk like an actor and he certainly did not look like one. He had a copy of the *American Mercury* stuffed into his overcoat pocket, and under his arm he carried a large volume, in German, on the influence of Max Reinhardt on the world theatre. No actor I had ever seen before had carried such props, and from the moment he sauntered in, full of easy assurance and with a carefully tailored *avant-garde* manner, he made a formidable impression on me.

He talked of Meyerhold and Georg Kaiser and Jacques Copeau —names that were utterly new to my provincial ears—and in subsequent visits he demolished my own heroes of the day with a cascade of invective that was wonderful to listen to. His attitude toward the theatre was as unsentimental and cynical as mine was stage-struck and hero-worshipping, and when I had recovered from his monumental disdain of almost everything I had heretofore held sacred, it was as though a fresh gust of wind had blown through the musty pages of the theatre magazines I still pored over, and I could never look at them in the same way again.

He had taste and wit and a gift for exploding pretense in a quick, bold comic way that dissolved me into helpless laughter, and he dispensed these wonders before my newly opened eyes and ears with the expert ease of a circus barker performing in front of a country yokel. There is no doubt that I was a flattering audience and there is no question that he enjoyed showing off before me,

[115]

At the same time the narrow horizons that had constituted the theatre for me up until then were being widened and enlarged almost without my being aware of it.

We had not yet become close friends at that time for the reason that he had a faculty of suddenly appearing and then disappearing again quite as suddenly for months at a time, so that any kind of sustained relationship was impossible. But I always enjoyed his reappearance and the gallows humor with which he related some exploit or other of his own making that had turned out a shambles, as they invariably did. He had a wonderful Don Quixote quality about him always, and I fitted into the role of his Sancho Panza with no trouble at all. He had just returned from one of his periodic disappearances and had been up to the Pitou office to see me—unaware, of course, of *The Beloved Bandit* and all that had happened since. I filled in the details for him, including what had happened that afternoon and my present despair as to just what to do next.

He listened with an interested eagerness that was one of the unexpected charms of a man who liked to talk as much as he did, and when I had finished he said explosively, "Time! Time! That's what we need—*Time!* We need to escape being swallowed up. That's what we've got to fight for—*Time!*"

It was typical of him, and it was touching as well, that he should include me in this battle cry, for I knew that he rather looked down his nose at my own timid theatrical ambitions. His own ideas for himself were a good deal more grandiose. Though he had never spelled them out exactly, I had gathered that he was to be a combination of Max Reinhardt, Eugene O'Neill, Robert Edmond Jones and the Shuberts. The pivot on which his enthusiasms swung would vary from time to time, but there remained always the grand scale, the large canvas, and now as ever he was equal to the occasion.

Eddie's scheme of things invariably included biting off more than he could chew and a deep aversion to anything approximating logic. His appetite for the implausible and the audacious remained unchastened by experience, and what he was proposing now was quite in key with everything else about him.

[116]

"A man offered me a job yesterday," he was saying, "and I told him I'd let him know by tonight. It's to take over and direct a little-theatre group at the Labor Temple. It doesn't pay much, but this man owns a summer camp and he hinted if I made good he might consider me for the job as social director at his camp this summer. See what I mean?"

"No, I don't," I replied.

"You're not using your head," he said and shook an impatient finger under my nose. "We need time—*time!* Once you step out of the theatre you never get back inside—you mustn't step backward—there's no escape from the civilians—you know that. Now, we'll take over this little-theatre group together—do a group of one-act plays—you direct three and I'll direct three—and this summer I'll go to his camp as social director and you'll be my assistant. See? Three solid months in the country with a salary and all expenses paid. It'll give us time—time to think, to plan."

"But did you ever direct a little-theatre group before?" I asked a little breathlessly.

"No," he answered. "What's that got to do with it?" He looked at me eagerly, his eyes alight with pleasure at the prospects of wind-mills in the distance.

"Well, neither have I," I said. "I don't know any more about it than you do."

Again the impatient finger was being shaken under my nose. "You'll get nowhere with that attitude, my boy," he sighed, "in the theatre or out of it. We must improvise—improvise!—play it by ear. These people are amateurs."

"But so are we in that field, Eddie," I protested.

"And who's going to tell them *that*," he cried triumphantly, "unless *you* do. All you have to do tonight is to sit there and look bored. You can do *that,* can't you?"

"And what about afterward—what happens when we have to get up on our feet and put these plays on? Won't they catch on to us?"

He laughed aloud. "Right now," he said, "standing here unemployed on the corner of Forty-third Street and Sixth Avenue, either one of us is a better director than Philip Moeller or Robert Milton. Want me to prove it?"

"No, no," I said hastily, for I well knew he could convince me that the moon was green. "Just tell me what to do so I don't make a fool of myself. Perhaps if we told them the truth . . ."

"The first thing you've got to do," he said severely, "is to stop being so damned ethical. All right—we've never directed little theatres before. Well, we're doing it now. Why advertise it? We just go ahead and do it. The point is," he went on, "you can't hock moral scruples. If you could, we'd all be eating more regularly, and you're not exactly in a position to be this finicky, are you?"

That settled it. Actually, it was nothing so high-minded as moral scruples that held me back, but plain, ordinary cowardice. Though I vaguely knew the mechanics of directing, it was one thing to have observed Priestly Morrison directing but quite another to get up on my own feet and do it myself. Furthermore, I completely lacked Eddie's abiding faith that he could master whatever situation arose, or talk himself out of it—sideways, backward, or straight down the middle. Yet the point he made was unanswerable—time to avoid being swallowed up; time not to turn the wrong way and be unable to get back—that was the thing that mattered most now, and in spite of my fears, I knew that I must follow my friend Don Quixote toward the windmills.

I watched him take over the little-theatre group at the Labor Temple that evening, lost in admiration for the brilliant way in which he convinced not only everyone there but himself as well that he knew exactly what he was talking about, which of course he did not. Much of what he said lay well beyond the realm of common sense, but even I, who knew that most of the time he didn't have a clue as to what was going to come out next, was sometimes swept along by the authority with which he conveyed to the spellbound little group a skill and a knowledge he did not possess at all. It was a bravura performance of audaciousness and pure gall that made it very hard for me to keep looking bored as I had been instructed to do, and when at the end of a solid hour of talk he finally sat down, I was hard put not to join in the applause that followed.

He winked at me as he cupped his hands to light a cigarette, and if I had not actually known what frauds we were, I might almost have believed, as everyone else in the room seemed to, that two young Max Reinhardts had, by some miracle, come to take over their little-theatre group. This country has reason to be grateful that Chodorov's talents did not take a turn toward the career of revivalist preacher. Had they done so, our rivers, fields and streams would be full of his converts being baptized in a faith that he improvised as he led them to the river banks and that he knew no more about than he did little-theatre directing. He could hypnotize a group of people into believing almost anything he wanted them to believe, and more often than not, in the process of doing so, he also succeeded in completely hypnotizing himself.

As we walked back to the subway station later that evening, well satisfied with the way the first meeting had gone, I was a little startled to hear Eddie saying, "The impact on our culture of the little-theatre movement is very possibly the beginning of a renaissance in our literature as well."

I almost turned around to see whom he was talking to, for I could not believe he was addressing this balderdash to me, his friend and partner in crime. But he was. For the moment he had quite succeeded in believing what he was saying himself and he would go on believing it till the moment when, as it always did, his own sense of humor came to his rescue and unhypnotized him. Until then all I could do was nod and try not to get hypnotized myself.

Two evenings later I conducted my first rehearsal.

It was as ticklish a business as I figured it was going to be, not made any the easier by the group of sullen and rebellious faces that stared resentfully at me as I sat at a table in the front of a bare rehearsal room. I knew the cause of their bad temper and I did not blame them. Every single one of them had ardently wished to be with Eddie and not with me. There had been a great vying and jockeying the evening before, when the entire group had been split into two units, one to be directed by me and the other by Eddie, and though their conniving had been painfully obvious, I did not hold it against them.

Eddie had made a great impression. He had dash, color and an electrifying way with him, and the idea of being shunted off to what must have seemed to them no better than an assistant sat very badly indeed. There were sibilant whisperings (quite palpably meant to reach my ears) of possible withdrawals, some uncomplimentary references to myself, and even outright declarations of how unfair the choosing had been.

Actually, this was not true. Eddie had not selfishly or greedily chosen the best actors for his own unit, but had quite rightly cast the two groups of plays as he thought best for the plays and for the limitations of the people themselves. Though he had tried to make this clear, the impression remained that Eddie's was a superior group, and paramount in all of their minds right now was the fact that the favored group was to be directed by Eddie while they, the unlucky others, were to be directed by me.

Even had I been an experienced director and not a raw amateur, it would have been a difficult situation to handle. As it was, I simply sat stalling for time, and under the pretense of thumbing through the plays on the table before me, preparatory to starting the rehearsal, I kept nervously thinking of how best to get off on the right foot. I rejected a reiteration of what Eddie had told them the night before, knowing that would merely add to their annoyance. I decided quickly against a humorous approach, which, if it fell flat, as seemed likely in their present mood, would confirm their already low opinion of me; and something within me—perhaps my own sense of injured vanity—refused to make the effort to charm them. Instead, I decided to behave with an authority I certainly did not feel, but which I felt I must make them feel, and quickly, too!

I rapped on the table for silence, and when the room did not quiet immediately, I sent a withering glance at the offenders. I was not going to speak or make a move until there was absolute quiet, and I indicated my irritation by something that approximated a snort of disdain. Not for nothing had I watched Basil Dean use peevishness as a weapon! There was an unpleasant pause and it seemed likely that several of them were defiantly going to keep talking, but I held my ground and in a few moments I knew that my approach had been the right one. The room became surprisingly still and I had their attention, if nothing more. I had won the first round.

The real test would come when I distributed the parts. Amateur actors are notoriously petty and their malice toward a director is straightforward and unsubtle, for unlike professional actors, they are paying the director's fee out of their own pockets. And since they usually cannot be "sacked," they intrigue endlessly against the director as part of the pleasure of rehearsals and quickly sabotage any effort on his part that seems to them not to take into quick account their own estimation of their ability to play a particular part they have set their hearts on. At the time I knew little of this, of course; but I made an instantaneous and lucky guess about actors in general, whether amateur or professional, that was to serve me in good stead then and afterward.

In some measure an actor is rather like a thoroughbred horse— he knows at once if the rider is afraid of him, and immediately he senses this, he takes the bit in his teeth and the rider is never really in control of him again.

To gain control of a cast, to get control early and to keep this control in an iron grip, is essential to a director facing a new company for the first time. There will be times—even whole days, perhaps—when a director, if he is a good one, will not always know what he is doing or if what he is doing is actually right for the actors or the play. He must proceed to do it, nevertheless, with certainty and surety and never relax his control for a moment—the more uncertain he feels, the more sure-footed he must appear. He can always change everything he has done at the next rehearsal, but on the day that he is floundering and insecure himself, he must never allow the actors to know it. All is lost if he does.

Actually, the only bad behavior I have ever witnessed in the professional theatre was that ghastly moment when a star or a cast of actors became aware that their director was not in control of either the play or themselves. It is then that "temperament" sets in and makes rehearsals hideous, but it has always been my opinion that "temperament" is little else than a mask for panic, and when people are panic-stricken, they of course behave badly. Why should they not? Actors know that on a certain not too distant night they will be up there on a brilliantly lit stage, naked and exposed, and if they cannot trust, or have lost faith in, the man who is to guide them and see them through that moment, they strike out in fear and hide their panic in bursts of temper and impossible behavior.

Watch a cast of actors with a director they trust and who is in control of rehearsals every moment of the day or night, however, and you will observe the atmosphere and the discipline of a research laboratory. It has always seemed to me that the first necessity a director faces is the creation of a climate of security and peace, in which actors can do their best work. And he creates this most surely by assuming and maintaining an ironclad control of the proceedings from the moment the actors pass through the stage door on the first day of rehearsals until the curtain rises on the opening night in New York.

After all, actors are not acting machines. Rehearsals, and most particularly the early days of rehearsals, bring to the surface of each actor his own special insecurity about himself and the job he faces, and it is part of a director's task to perceive this weakness as quickly as he can and within the limits of the time at his disposal, to make each actor secure in himself and his part, and establish himself as the person around whom must flow all the hidden but vital mechanism of bringing a play to life on a stage.

I do not know how I knew any of this then, nor even how I glimpsed a small portion of it, sitting at that table with my knees knocking together with nervousness; but it was lucky for me that I sensed the essential part—to gain control early—for from down the hall came the sound of Eddie in rehearsal, and echoing into my own rehearsal room came his roars of anger, his crows of delight, and then the excited laughter of his group as they reveled in the pleasure of the electric personality who was directing them. It was lucky for me, too, that I had not chosen to compete with Eddie on his own terms, for I could only have emerged a miserable second best. Instead, I distributed the parts in the three plays in my best Basil Dean manner; and without taking any notice of the protest and outrage that was all too plain on several faces, I proceeded to plunge into the rehearsal of the first play.

The rest of that first evening was a grim business indeed. I matched their hostility with a sullenness of my own and I equaled their bad manners with a contempt for their behavior that I did not attempt to conceal. When the rehearsal ended at eleven o'clock, I was limp with exhaustion from the effort of imposing my will on a group of people resentful of my very presence; but I was determined to hold on to the job in spite of them.

Eddie was correct—a summer free with a salary and all expenses paid was a goal worth fighting for, and it would have taken a good deal more than one grisly evening to make me throw in the sponge. Nevertheless, when I met Eddie outside the building late that night and we walked toward the subway together, I could easily have punched him in the nose with a great deal of pleasure. He was fresh as a daisy—indeed, he was exhilarated enough to have conducted an all-night rehearsal then and there. And his first words to me were, "See? I told you how easy it would be. It's almost a shame to take the money, isn't it?"

I was too weary to answer. I grunted something in reply and listened to him hold forth above the clatter of the subway wheels on the Meyerhold theory of expressionism without saying a word until we changed trains at 149th Street and went our separate ways.

Rehearsals took place three times a week, and the next one, though not exactly pleasant or marked by any special *esprit de corps* flowing between director and cast, was at the same time less painful for me than that initial baptism of fire. For one thing, they had all turned up—a fact which I sharply noted as I walked into the room. I had actually expected several resignations and was quite prepared to deal with them; but apparently they had all gone out for coffee after that first rehearsal, talked me over among themselves, and

[123]

decided they were sufficiently intrigued to come back once more and see what would happen next.

The fact that they had all turned up gave me my cue. If anything, I was more high-handed and testy than I had been two evenings before. I must have been relaxed enough, however, shortly before the rehearsal ended, to have made an imaginative leap in the scene I was directing that ignited a spark of excited interest or grudging admiration among them. It is a lovely and rewarding moment when this happens. I could feel it happen with the actors I was talking to and in the rest of the group who were watching me from various parts of the room. Though there was nothing but silence in the room except for the sound of my own voice, it was almost as though applause had broken out—a special kind of applause that is reserved for unexpected victory. I was conscious of it almost immediately, but I was wise enough not to push the advantage. Though it was not yet quite eleven o'clock I said, "That's all for tonight," and picking up my hat and coat, put on my Basil Dean manner again along with my overcoat, and walked out.

I knew now that I could drop that fatuous pose whenever I saw fit to do so, but it had served me well enough. I had begun to weld them to me as a group and on my own terms. Though I might not teach them very much about acting, they would at least learn to mind their manners with the next hapless fellow who directed them and give him a decent chance. As it turned out, I think I learned a good deal more from them than they did from me. Although they were amateurs, and not very talented ones at that, it is almost impossible to direct a group of people for the stage without learning something valuable about the theatre somewhere along the line.

In my own case, I became aware almost for the first time of the inner structure of a play, for the good and simple reason that I had to. After a good many false starts and quite a bit of stumbling around, I was finally forced to go back to study the author's intent in each play I was directing—to gain a knowledge of how each play was built to achieve the effect the author wanted and to decide on how best to translate what I had learned into a performance that maintained an audience's interest without foreshadowing or destroying the climax, and at the same time preserving the entity of the play as a whole. This was a good deal more than just seeing to it that the actors did not bump into each other, which was more or less what I had been doing and which I soon discovered would not work.

I was directing three one-act plays—one by George Kelly, one by Lord Dunsany and one by Susan Glaspell. They were as unlike as three playwrights could possibly be and I began to be fascinated by the problems each play brought with it. The mechanism and construction of a play began to hold far more interest for me than the actual staging of it, and all through that winter I read every published play I could get my hands on. When my neighborhood library in the Bronx ran out of published plays, I went down to the main branch at 42nd Street and sat in the reading room all day long, completely and utterly absorbed. With my days free, I suppose I could have and should have taken a job during the day to supplement the paltry sum I was earning in the evenings, but I could not tear myself away from my obsession with the mechanics of play-writing.

I do not believe that play-writing can be taught any more than acting can be taught, and I am quite certain that I did not consciously think of play-writing seriously in relation to myself, for all during that time it never occurred to me to read a book on how plays are written. I simply read the plays themselves. I read the published version of plays that I had seen and then plays that I had never seen, sitting there day after day like a bacteriologist trying to isolate a strange germ under the beam of a new and more powerful microscope. Whether I was conscious or not that I wanted to write plays myself is perhaps academic, for there is no doubt that a good deal of this exploration rubbed off on me whether I knew it or not. I began to perceive and place in proper perspective the distinction between plot and character, the difference between tricks of the trade and honest craftsmanship, and though I was hardly aware of it, I began to discern the gradual steps by which a play is built and, in the really good plays, the wonderful economy with which each salient point is made and not a moment on the stage wasted.

Another thing I seemed to be unaware of, though it was taking place under my very nose, was that my group had made a complete reversal in their feelings about me. They liked me now! It was, as Eddie pointed out, shaking a finger at me, obvious to everyone but myself. I suppose I had become so absorbed in my daytime life of reading plays that I was hardly conscious of the three evenings each week I rehearsed with the group, except as a necessary interruption to earn money.

But as the days of the actual performance approached and we rehearsed four and sometimes five evenings a week, I could not help noticing how eagerly each word of mine was listened to and how highly charged the atmosphere had become with a kind of grave dedication on each actor's part to give me his best. Finally, on the evening of the first dress rehearsal I received what I suppose was the accolade of their change of heart—I was asked to go out for coffee with them after the rehearsal. I did not have sufficient character to refuse and it was too close to the actual performance to tamper with the fine ensemble spirit I had apparently engendered. I got a bit of my own back by having not just coffee but a full-sized meal and letting them pay for it. I felt I had earned it.

The performances, which took place on four successive nights, two evenings being allotted to my group and two to Eddie's, were an unqualified success. Though Eddie's group made by far the greater impression, my own acquitted itself quite well, and both groups were, we were assured on all sides, the best ever seen on the stage of the Labor Temple. We had hoped under the flush of such success that there would be immediate word forthcoming, from the gentleman who owned the summer camp, about our promised jobs for the summer; but he was wily enough to insist that we do another group of plays for the spring season before he made up his mind. There was nothing for us to do but continue; for in spite of Eddie's high opinion of himself, there was no great clamor for his services in the professional theatre, and certainly none for my own, but I was determined now to have that summer job.

A vague sort of plan, too hazy and unclear even in my own mind to discuss with Eddie, was beginning to formulate itself as a course of action whereby I could attach myself to the theatre again, and the first step was to make certain of landing that job for the summer. Perhaps it was a desperate effort to insure it that led me to so foolish an undertaking as I now embarked upon. I can think of no other reason compelling enough for me to make so complete a fool of myself. It is astonishing how wanting anything badly enough can invariably suspend judgment, intelligence or plain common sense, in all sorts of people, from those who want a job for the summer to those who want to be President.

A few evenings after the final performance, the group met as a whole to discuss the new series of plays to be done for the spring season. Eddie suggested, again unselfishly, that we switch groups, and I was touched and pleased to find that my group elected by unanimous consent to stay on with me. A little drunk with power at this obvious testament to my directorial charm, and overzealous now about protecting the summer job, I decided not to do another group of one-acters, but to do a three-act play instead. This was idiocy of an inspired kind, for neither the group nor I was ready to tackle a three-act play yet. To compound the felony, I chose, of all things, that most difficult of plays to do even for professional actors—Ibsen's *Ghosts*. The dour Norwegian and my inexperience as a director met head on and there was never any doubt as to who would emerge triumphant.

Rehearsals were a misery both for myself and the cast from the moment the first line was uttered, but I was either too stubborn or too cowardly to admit my mistake and switch to something more feasible. Instead, I bluffed and blundered and took refuge in displays of bad temper, thereby not only undoing all the good I had done, but making it altogether impossible for us to do anything but go steadily along to the disaster I had chosen.

I am certain, too, that it was no one's fault but my own that a week before the performance the leading man threw his part down on the floor, kicked it across the room, and walked out. It was far too late now to attempt to get anybody else up in the part and I decided in another moment of lunacy to play Oswald myself! There could be no question of calling the performance off—with my eyes fixed on that summer job, I would have played Camille if necessary. I doubt if I or the audience would have fared much worse had I done so. I suppose I secretly felt that a brilliant performance of Oswald by myself would save the day; but Eddie, attending the first dress rehearsal at my request, soon dispelled that illusion. He came backstage shaking with helpless laughter. "I'm sorry," he said, "but the whole thing is ridiculous, and you, my boy—to put it in the kindest fashion possible—are ludicrous."

"I don't care about that," I said miserably. "Is it bad enough to make us lose that job?"

"It's bad enough, all right," he replied, "but it's too late to do anything about it now." He shrugged his shoulders. "I've got something else in mind, anyway—even better. So don't worry. But for God's sake," he went on, "as long as you've got to go through with it, can't you do something about making that final moment when Oswald says, 'The sun, Mother, I want the sun,' sound a little less like you were asking for Grape Nuts for breakfast? It's bloody awful." And he went off into gales of laughter again.

I have not entirely forgotten to this very day the agony of having to walk out onto a stage and play for an entire evening a part that, as Eddie quite properly said, I was ludicrous in. It has made me suffer and sympathize with actors who are miscast in a play, for they invariably know it, and it can only be the urgency of meeting the rent and telephone bills that enables them to do it for more than the two performances which were all that I had to suffer through.

Nevertheless, by some miracle of unknowingness, even by amateur standards, the audience sat solemn and polite throughout the two evenings we performed *Ghosts,* and though very little applause greeted the final curtain, at least laughter, that nightmare sound to even amateur actors' ears, did not punctuate the proceedings. At the end of the second and last performance, I sat wiping the make-up off my face with so great a sense of relief that even the thought of the summer job, which was never very far out of my mind, was momentarily gone in the pleasure of knowing that Ibsen and I had parted company forever.

[128]

One thing was clear at any rate. I had evidently been wise to put the idea of acting behind me—to fail as dismally as I had failed these past two nights was a depressing enough proof that I had been right—but it was a small consolation. Wiping the marks of the wretched Oswald off my face, I could see the want ads of the *New York Times* in front of my eyes, and once more I decided *no*—there would be no turning back, whatever happened. Though exactly what would happen, except simple starvation, I failed to see.

I was suddenly aware of Eddie's grinning face in the mirror in front of me and I felt his hand fall heavily on my shoulder. "I bring you incontrovertible proof that He who watches over Israel does not slumber," he said, talking into the mirror. And as I turned around to look up at him he whispered, "We got the job!"

Sure enough, the gentleman who owned the summer camp was coming into the room smiling, not glowering. "You liked it?" I asked ingenuously.

"It was hopeless," he replied, still smiling, "but it was Ibsen, that's the point. I like a young fellow who makes this kind of mistake— that's the kind of fellow we want on the staff at Camp Utopia." And he held out his hand to me.

This somewhat enigmatic compliment was an excellent clue to the character of my future employer. William J. Perleman was a would-be playwright, not yet produced, and part owner of a summer camp, to both of which endeavors he brought artistic and intellectual pretensions, and no talent of any kind whatever for either enterprise. Yet in his bumbling way he was a sweet-tempered man and certainly a most forgiving one, considering the travail Eddie's inexperience as a social director was to put him through. He shook my hand again warmly, and after another complimentary word or two to the effect that "large mistakes were the only kind to make," he smiled his way out.

Almost before I could realize the wonderful turn for the better my fortunes had taken, I became aware that I was suddenly ravenously, wolfishly hungry. As always, at a moment of triumph or disaster, the first return to reality was announced by my stomach. "How much money have you got?" I asked Eddie.

"Three dollars," he answered.

"I've got two," I said, throwing caution to the winds. "Let's go out and eat all we can get for five dollars."

"Get the rest of Oswald off your face," said Eddie, "I'm going to treat you to a bottle of wine."

Jubilant, I made short work of the last traces of Oswald and I was even a little more than jubilant very shortly afterward, since Eddie's idea of a bottle of wine was changed to straight gin by the time we sat down in the speakeasy around the corner from the Labor Temple.

By the third gin I was so murderously hungry and riotously drunk that in order to get the food on the table as quickly as possible, I cheerfully agreed to all the lunatic plans Eddie was suggesting for our debut as social directors. At that time, one could get a really mountainous amount of food for very little money, and I ate the greater portion of it myself, hardly stopping to interject a word or to object to the utter nonsense that Eddie was spouting. By the end of the meal we were both sufficiently sober for Eddie to discuss in more sensible and less grandiose terms our plans for the summer, which was actually then only about six weeks away.

"The greatest asset a social director can have," he said, "is a stock-pile of special material . . . comedy skits, songs . . . especially the newest stuff from the musical comedies. It's a *must*, we've got to have it!"

"How do you get it?" I asked. "We can't afford to go and see the shows."

"There are ways," he answered mysteriously.

"How?" I demanded. "If we can't get to see the shows, how do we get it?"

"Go home and get some sleep," he answered, still with an air of mystery. "Get some sleep and I'll show you how we get it. We'll start collecting the stuff tomorrow night." And that was all I was able to make him say on the subject the rest of the evening.

There were indeed ways, as I was to learn in the following weeks, or at least Eddie's ways, of collecting the necessary material for a

[130]

social director's portfolio. One of them was for us to arrive on the sidewalk in front of the theatre of a reigning musical comedy hit just before intermission time. We then mingled with the audience as they emerged into the lobby at the end of the first act, picked up a program that someone inevitably dropped and left on the lobby floor, and brandishing the program conspicuously in front of us, walked back into the theatre with the audience to see the second act.

Though this system restricted the amount of material we could steal, the authors of musical comedies and revues invariably save some of their heavy ammunition for the second act, and there were always reprises of songs from the first act. There were a few theatres, of course, that issued intermission checks to the audience to stop just such banditry, but there were not many of these. The New Amsterdam Theatre, where the *Follies* was playing, issued these checks and moreover kept a sharp lookout for intermission crashers, but I knew the ticket taker and he allowed us to pass through not once but several times. The *Follies* was very necessary for us to see, for it contained not only a large amount of special material in skits, but Fanny Brice as well, of whom I was to do an impersonation for several summers thereafter.

After each show, it was our practice to go straight to Eddie's house and between us piece together all the material we had stolen from the show with the help of a pocket flashlight and notes scribbled on the program. It was quite astonishing how accurate our thievery became after a time. We were very often able to piece together whole sketches word for word, and what we couldn't remember we wrote ourselves.

There were three new musicals opening that spring just before we were to leave for the camp, and to pilfer from these in their entirety Eddie had an even more ingenious scheme, for he felt it was vital to his prestige as social director to be able to present material from the newer shows on Broadway.

His theory was that on an opening night the stage doorman could not yet possibly know the chorus boys by sight, since the show itself was but barely installed in the theatre. Therefore, just before the half-hour was called on the opening night we were to brush past the doorman with a hurried and excited "hello" or "good luck" as though we were part of the chorus, cross the stage, and go out the pass door from the stage into the theatre. We were then to hurry down to the men's room, lock ourselves in a booth, and remain there until we heard the overture begin, when we would walk upstairs and stand at the back and see the entire show. Eddie's other contention was that there was always so much excitement on an opening night and so many hangers-on standing about in the back of the orchestra that we would never be noticed.

He turned out to be correct on both counts: the stage doorman grunted a hello as we brushed past him, and no one paid the slightest attention to us as we stood in the back—but it took a good deal of passionate argument to overcome my initial timidity and even outright threats on Eddie's part to get me to screw up my courage sufficiently to brush past the first doorman. It all worked like a charm, however, and was well worth the anguish I went through.

I was greatly surprised all those hectic few weeks by the industry and concentration Eddie showed in scrupulously planning each week of the camp season, which was to last from Decoration Day until Labor Day. It was unlike him to maintain a pitch of excitement about anything once the windmill had been tilted at, and I was immensely relieved to see him buckle down and set a definite schedule for each play and each musical we were to do.

This singular enthusiasm and industry did not, regrettably, persist past Decoration Day; for just before we were to leave, Eddie received an offer to join a company that was to make a tour of South Africa in the fall. The appeal to his sense of the spectacular that the very words "South Africa" made was immediate and profound. He promptly lost all interest in the summer job and went through with it, I believe, only because it was a way of marking time until the fall.

Moreover, with the usual theatrical nepotism, he had engaged as other members of our social staff his sister Belle, a cousin, Eleanor Audley, and three of the members of his group from the Labor Temple. All of them were not only as inexperienced as we ourselves, but were to remain throughout the summer his willing and adoring slaves, taking his indolence for the musings of an artist and his pulverizing lack of organization as the unmistakable mark of genius.

It had been a necessity between the end of my employment at the Labor Temple and the beginning of the camp season to take a temporary job of any sort to fill in the time and earn some money, and I took the first job that came along. It was not a very likely job and I lasted exactly a week at it. I was no better at being a floor-walker at Macy's than I had been at playing Oswald. Not only did my mind wander alarmingly, so that I found myself walking out into 34th Street one afternoon for a breath of air (an unheard-of thing for a floorwalker to do while on duty, I was told), but the collecting and writing up of the material we were gathering was spilling over into the days as well as the nights.

Very often we were unable to finish setting down at night all that might be useful to us from the show we had seen that evening, and it was the kind of work that had to be done by both of us to-gether, for what one of us failed to remember, the other always did. Macy's solved the difficulty for us by firing me at the end of the first week, and I then conceived the bright idea of getting a job that required only night work, sleeping a few hours during the day and having the rest of the day and evening free. Eddie was skeptical, but it turned out there was plenty of night work to be had.

One of the astonishing things about the astounding City of New York is that it contains a large population of people who work only at night. A great portion of the city's daytime life is supported by these night people, who keep the necessary circulation flowing through the city's hidden veins at night, so that it comes alive each dawn when other millions of day people continue the city's life, largely unaware of those others who all through the night have made ready for them.

The job I selected was at the *New York Times,* classifying and routing to their proper departments the handwritten want ads that had passed over the *Times'* counter during the day. The hours, from eleven P.M. until seven A.M., fitted our requirements perfectly, allowing me to go straight to the *Times* from the theatre, be home by eight thirty in the morning, sleep until one or two in the afternoon, and be at Eddie's house by three o'clock to start correlating the material, until it was time to be in front of whatever theatre we were crashing at intermission time that evening.

After two or three weeks of this I found myself falling asleep in the subway and riding past my station almost every morning, leaning against whatever I could find that was fairly soft and falling promptly to sleep. Strangely enough, I found this rather rugged schedule no hardship at all. For one thing, there was something poetic and quite magical about the city at night which I deeply enjoyed being part of. Our lunch or supper hour at the *Times* was between the hours of three and four o'clock in the morning. I would eat as quickly as possible, and with another fellow who worked beside me, walk the streets until it was time to get back to work. I have no gift for describing the peculiar quality of magic the city possesses at that hour of the night; but it contains an elusive magic and wonder of its own that is never glimpsed, I am certain, except by night people such as I was then myself.

Though my eyes kept closing constantly, almost without my being aware of it, so that I sometimes would go to sleep in the middle of a sentence, I felt not in the least tired, but on the contrary remarkably fresh and alive. The prospect of getting away completely for three whole months from the surroundings I had lived in all of my life kept me buoyed up and keyed to a feverish pitch of excitement that seemed to banish fatigue or exhaustion.

The mere idea, little enough in itself, of not returning home each evening and walking those four flights up the grimy stairway to our apartment, filled me with an almost unbearable sense of exhilaration and freedom such as I had never before known. It is hard to describe or to explain concisely the overwhelming and suffocating boredom that is the essence of being poor. A great deal has been written about the barren drudgery of poverty; but I do not recall that the numbing effect of its boredom has been much written or talked about. Yet boredom is the keynote of poverty— of all its indignities, it is perhaps the hardest of all to live with—

[134]

for where there is no money there is no change of any kind, not of scene or of routine. To be able to break out of its dark brown sameness, out of the boredom of a world without movement or change, filled me with a deep excitement. The thought of escaping from another city summer, with its front stoops and fire escapes filled with tired, sweating adults and squalling children, into a world of green lawns and shady trees made sleep an unnecessary indulgence, and seemed to give me the energy of ten men my size and weight.

I realized suddenly and acutely that the summers had always been the worst time of all for me: the season of the year that I hated the most. There is anonymity about poverty in the wintertime; it remains hidden behind drawn curtains or blinds. But in the summer the choking heat of the tenements sends it sprawling out onto the stoops and fire escapes and sidewalks, to be nakedly exposed for the offense and the ugliness that it is. I knew now why I had always dreaded the approach of warm weather, but as this particular spring deepened into early summer, I could almost sniff the aroma of country meadows even in the bowels of the subway or in my cubbyhole at the *New York Times*.

When the great day arrived at last for us to leave for Camp Utopia, the moisture in my eyes which my mother mistook for filial sentiment (it was to be my first long absence away from the family) was, I suppose, actually something akin to tears of joy at getting the hell out.

Rarely have I set forth on a journey with such a lift of the heart. Innocence, however, always carries the seeds of its own destruction and I carried mine to Camp Utopia that glistening summer's day, like Dick Whittington approaching London with his heart on his sleeve and his possessions on his back, hearing nothing but the lovely sound of Bow bells in the distance.

CAMP UTOPIA was a fair enough sample of summer camps in general to give me a rough idea of what life as a social director was going to be like.

The camp nestled beside a pretty pine-wooded lake in the foothills of the Poconos in Pennsylvania; it consisted of a large central building, which housed the dining room, and cabins built along opposite sides of the lake, the lake itself supposedly keeping the men and women apart at night—a remarkably naïve assumption, as though a body of water or even a ring of fire could accomplish the impossible! There were tennis courts, a swimming dock, canoes and rowboats, and a social hall with dance floor and stage, which was the hub and core and heartbeat of everything that took place in camp in the evenings—at least until the lights were turned out, at which time traffic on both sides of the lake front took on the proportions of a rush hour at Times Square.

Camp Utopia was neither the largest nor the smallest of the camps I was to work at in the five years that followed, some of which ranged in accommodations for guests from two hundred to fifteen hundred on crowded weekends. But I remember it kindly, for it had the virtue at that time of being almost brand-new—I believe this was its second summer of operation—so that the clientele was not sufficiently incrusted in its folklore to immediately complain almost before they had unpacked their suitcases that last year's social staff was infinitely superior to this year's—a complaint I was

[136]

to run into with infuriating regularity at every camp I worked at thereafter.

The world of summer camps, and a very definite world it was, was entirely new to me, of course; and since that world no longer exists as it did in those days, I think it is of some interest, quite apart from myself, as a curious kind of Americana that blossomed and flourished in the 1920's, for it is unlikely to appear in the same form again. Adult summer camps at that time represented quite a new way of summer vacationing for thousands of young people of ages ranging from twenty to thirty, marking as it did the first breaking away from the old regulation summer hotel, with its standard long front porch where fond mamas rigidly chaperoned demure young daughters, and circumspect young men carefully carried their mandolins along on hayrides and thought twice about asking a girl for a good-night kiss.

When the first summer-camp owner, whoever he was, hit upon the idea of banishing the front porch and fond mamas in one fell swoop and substituting rustic cabins along a lake front instead, he struck a responsive chord in thousands of rebellious young breasts that beat furiously with the new-found sexual freedom of the early twenties, and they flocked in ever-increasing numbers to sample the particular mixture of free-wheeling camaraderie that each camp cannily offered. I do not mean to suggest that these camps were simply carnal spots set in sylvan glades, and certainly a great show was made of sternly patrolling the cabins; but there can be no question that the firm rock on which the great popularity of summer camps rested was the ageless Gibraltar of sex.

Summer camps still exist today, of course; but they are a far cry from the uninhibited ones of my own apprenticeship. Indeed, the camps of today would be almost unrecognizable to a guest or to a social director of those days. Today, the entertainment programs are completely professional and booked into the camp by Broadway agents, and the larger camps frequently have well-known names at large salaries perform for its guests on weekends. The golf course employs not one but usually three golf pros, and the tennis courts and swimming activities are likely to be in the charge of a former college or Olympic champion.

At the time I am speaking of, however, the entertainment *in toto* was provided by the social director and his staff—every item of every day and evening was devised, rehearsed and presented by him and his assistant, and a back-breaking job it was! Out of the summer camps of those early days emerged such figures as Danny Kaye, Don Hartman, Dore Schary, Lorenz Hart, Garson Kanin, Arthur Kober, Phil Silvers, and countless others. It is constantly suggested in well-meaning press interviews that the summer camps provided the training ground or springboard that enabled these talented gentlemen to make the leap to Broadway and Hollywood. It may be so, and I am not prepared to argue for anyone but myself, but in my own case, social directing provided me with a lifelong disdain for the incredible contortions of the human spirit at play, and a lasting horror of people in the mass seeking pleasure and release in packaged doses. Perhaps the real triumph of those summers was the fact that I survived them at all; not so much in terms of emerging with whatever creative faculties I possess unimpaired, but in the sense that my physical constitution withstood the strain, for at the end of each camp season I was always fifteen to twenty pounds lighter and my outlook on life just about that much more heavily misanthropic.

To understand the stresses and strains a camp season entailed, and which a social director of those days labored under, it is necessary, I think, to set down an actual week's schedule of camp activity, which was repeated, though with different material of course, every week of the entire camp season.

Monday was campfire night. This was presumably an informal get-together, for the new guests usually arrived on Sunday; and a campfire in the woods, with entertainment provided while marshmallows and hot dogs were being roasted over the fire, was supposed to initiate the new arrival into the carefree camp spirit. I suppose it did—but since the wood for the fire, as well as the hot dogs, marshmallows and the blankets to sit on, had to be dragged out into the woods by the social director and his staff, it did not hold quite the same easygoing informality and gaiety for us that it did for the guests, to say nothing of the fact that the entertainment around the fire had to be devised and rehearsed, and was not informal at all.

Campfire night always held a special kind of torment for me, for Eddie had delegated to me at the beginning of the season the task of leading the community singing that opened the festivities as the campfire was lit, a job that I was unfortunately good at and which I whole-heartedly loathed. There was always a good deal of heckling, actually quite good-natured, as I stood up in front of the fire to start the singing off, and it had to be answered with equally good-natured banter in return on my part. It was a rare campfire night that I did not devoutly wish that I could disappear into the air or sink into the earth.

I had two other regular spots in the campfire programs. One, a Shakespearean recitation, usually a soliloquy out of *Hamlet, Macbeth* or *Romeo and Juliet,* and a "boy and girl" number complete with ukulele, which I strummed and sang to while a female guest, carefully selected that afternoon as the best of a bad lot, sat on my knee and sang along with me. The fact that the crowd was usually insistent that we encore the number by doing the Charleston together did nothing to minimize the deep hatred I held for each Monday night that stretched from June to September.

Tuesday night was costume or dress-up night. Depending upon the whim of the social director and the kind of costumes at hand, the night was designated and proclaimed as "Greenwich Village Night," "A Night in Old Montmartre" or "The Beaux Arts Ball." The social hall had to be decorated by the staff to simulate old Montmartre or Greenwich Village, and tables and chairs were set around the hall in night-club fashion. It was imperative, moreover, that the guests, both male and female, turn out in appropriate costumes, for the evening was a failure if they did not; so most of Tuesday afternoon from after lunchtime on was spent in going from cabin to cabin and helping guests prepare their costumes or cajoling them into getting themselves up in one if they showed a disinclination to do so.

Most girls arrived in camp with some sort of catch-all costume for dress-up night, as advised in the camp brochure; but the men usually brought along nothing but the inevitable white flannel trousers and blue sport jackets. We had a supply of costumes in the camp wardrobe that could be used for just such emergencies week after week, and I have yet to see a figure of a French apache on the stage or in the movies that does not give me a shudder as I recall how many unwilling male guests I badgered into being an apache from old Montmartre. We seemed always to have had more apache costumes in the wardrobe trunk than any other kind, though "A Night in Old Japan" was a close runner-up for the male contingent for reasons that now escape me.

For "A Night in Old Montmartre" one or possibly two Grand Guignol sketches were usually presented—with the result that there was almost never any catsup to be had in camp the next day because we used it to simulate the streams of blood always necessary in the Guignol sketches, and the social staff's hair was usually matted or streaked with catsup that would not come out for the next two days.

On "Greenwich Village Night" there was a good deal of candle-lit free-verse poetry reading, usually done by Eddie, and a good deal of Edna St. Vincent Millay usually read by me. No one was ever more weary of hearing, "My candle burns at both ends, it will not last the night" than I was by the end of that first summer. And there were quite a few evenings when I was not quite sure that I would last the night myself, Edna St. Vincent Millay or no Edna St. Vincent Millay!

For "A Night in Old Japan" we presented our own version, complete with local jokes and lyrics, of *The Mikado,* and for "Beaux Arts Night" there were tableaux of guests, decked out in silver and gold gilt paint, gilded and arranged, of course, by a sweating and cursing social staff.

Wednesday evening was "Games Night," and between dances, potato races, sack races, one-legged races and peanut relay races were run off for prizes, and though no entertainment was deemed necessary by the management for this carefree evening, it was thought essential, nevertheless, for the social staff to encourage participation in the games by setting the example of being the first ones out on the floor for each game and seeing to it that the shy or unattractive girls in particular were included in at least one game during the evening. It is not easy to feel the proper compassion for a shy girl or an ugly duckling when you are tied into a sack with her and are hobbling down the social hall to the finish line. On the contrary, rolling a peanut along the floor side by side with a bad-complexioned girl with thick glasses and unfortunate front teeth does nothing to kindle the fires of pity within you, but instead makes you want to kick her right in her unfortunate teeth.

There was no escape possible from this nightly gallantry, however, for the one camp rule that was inviolate—that could never be broken under any consideration—was that the male members of the social staff dance only with the girls who were not being danced with, and that the shy and ugly ones be "socialized" with first. It was up to the social staff and to the social director and his assistant to set the example for this, not only so far as dancing was concerned, but in every other aspect of camp activity.

There was actually a sound reason for this. The population of every summer camp was always predominantly female—the girls sometimes outnumbering the men two to one—and this thorny problem the wily camp owners met by hiring college boys instead of professional waiters to wait on tables, for these college boys were part of the social staff after their duties in the dining room were finished.

Indeed, it mattered very little how sloppy a waiter a young medical or legal student might be if he was a good dancer and "mixed and mingled" well in the social hall. The trouble, of course, lay in the fact that the college boys disliked dancing with "the pots," as they called them, quite as much as we did, and devised all sorts of stratagems to be out on the floor with an attractive girl in their arms almost before the first note of each dance number sounded from the orchestra. It was always necessary to make a blanket rule at the beginning of each season that if a girl was not dancing after the first sixteen bars of music, she must be danced with forthwith. And there was a further ironclad rule that no one girl was to be danced with more than once in an evening, for it was the boys' practice to latch onto a pretty girl and dance every dance with her, proclaiming loudly and innocently that they had danced every dance that evening and had not sat out one!

By the middle of July in every season, it was always necessary to ship one or two insubordinate waiters home for flouting this rule, for inevitably love blossomed between a waiter and a guest, and when that happened, he would defiantly dance every dance with his beloved. There was nothing to do but ship him home as a stern example to the others. I was not always certain that it was exactly love that blossomed in a waiter's bosom, for once a waiter glimpsed that unmistakable light in a girl's eyes, it almost inevitably followed that the hapless girl, for the entire span of her two weeks' vacation, barely saw the sunlight from then on. Instead, she was in the kitchen most of the time helping him polish silver and make salads, and then setting his tables for him. These poor creatures would arrive in camp with a decent glow of health on their cheeks and leave two weeks later hollow-eyed wrecks.

Curiously enough, this practice of guests' helping waiters in their work was not frowned upon by camp owners, but in a way had their blessing, for I don't suppose the waiters could have gone on moonlight canoe rides night after night and been up at six thirty every morning to prepare for breakfast without some sort of unpaid slave labor to help them. And I am certain it was love by and large that kept the camp silverware as clean as it generally was. Week by week one could very often tell whether or not love was rampant among the waiters by the way the tables were set or how the salads were decorated, and when love ran riot in the kitchen, it played hell with the dancing in the social hall at night.

I am certain, too, those camp years ruined the pleasure of dancing for me forever. It is seldom now that I will venture out onto a dance floor. For six whole years I danced with nothing but "the pots," and that was enough to make me welcome the glorious choice of sitting down for the rest of my life.

The one night in camp when there was no dancing at all was Thursday night, and it may be imagined that sometimes it seemed to the social staff that Thursday was terribly slow in arriving or had disappeared out of the week entirely. That was the night for basketball, played by a team of our own waiters against a team of waiters from a neighboring camp, sometimes in our own social hall and sometimes in theirs.

This night was always held up with a great show of largesse by camp owners as the night that the social staff was entirely free to rehearse the weekend's play and musical, but it was not entirely as generous as it sounded. Thursday night after the game was the night that the owners always chose to give a party in their own quarters for specially selected guests, and to this party the social staff was not only invited but more or less *ordered* to appear, for they were expected to supply the necessary entertainment for the festivities. The idea was, I suppose, that since the social staff had not entertained guests for the entire evening, they must now be panting to do so, beginning at midnight.

Another occupational hazard of camp life, and a dire hazard it was, was the parties tossed two or three times each week by the guests themselves in their own cabins after the social hall closed, and to which the social staff was always bidden. It seemed to be taken for granted by any and every guest that included in his weekly rate, was the right to the private as well as the public services of the social staff, a conclusion that most camp owners concurred in, and if you refused to appear at parties, either in self-defense or out of sheer exhaustion, there were always loud and long protests the next morning that the social staff refused to "socialize" and that next summer they would certainly go to a camp that had a social staff that did.

We could escape only some of the parties and the others we suffered through as best we could, for if there was one thing worse than entertaining the guests ourselves, it was being entertained by them at their own parties. Almost every guest who gave parties had a sneaking suspicion that he or she was equally as talented as the social staff. This was their chance to prove it—and the remembrance of various young men, a salami sandwich in one hand and a glass of celery tonic in the other, bellowing out "I'm the Sheik of

Araby" can still chill my blood; or the recollection of countless ill-advised girls giving their own rendition of "Dardanella" is enough even now to make me wonder how I lived through six solid years of it, without entering the realm of the demented.

There was one hazard of camp life, however, that the social staff did not share. It was faced exclusively by the guests themselves, and it provided the staff with an endless source of entertainment and pleasure. The hazard was a simple one, but it was unfailing and constant in every camp I ever worked at. Both male and female guests always arrived in complete anonymity except for the initials on their luggage; and when they decked themselves out in their summer finery for their first appearance in the social hall or the dining room, it was impossible to tell whether a shipping clerk or the boss's son had arrived in camp. By the same token, it was impossible to tell whether a private secretary to a Wall Street broker or a steel executive was making her first appearance, or, what was more likely, a salesgirl from behind the glove counter at Bloomingdale's was beginning her two-week vacation.

Each suitcase bulged with a hard winter's saving of every penny that could be spared and strategically spent on a series of flamboyant sport shirts and doeskin trousers, or flowered prints and organdy dresses, to say nothing of the very latest in the way of bathing suits and costumes *pour le sport* for every hour of the day that might dazzle and titillate a member of the opposite sex. There were, of course, some well-heeled boys and girls among the guests, and I suppose even a boss's son or a private secretary to a Wall Street broker occasionally turned up. But in the main, the bulk of the contingent that descended on the camps every summer was composed largely of shipping clerks, bookkeepers, law clerks, receptionists, and what-not, who spill out of New York City and it environs for their annual two-week vacation.

And since part of that vacation at camp had as its goal sex on the part of the boys and marriage on the part of the girls, there was a better chance for the achievement of these goals if both partners gave no hint of their true status while in camp, but played the game of letting the other one assume that each was heir to a junior executive's job or a wealthy father. It was a game of endless variations—a stately minuet of lying and pretense, and the social staff watched it flower and blossom every two weeks with no little delight and a good deal of malice.

We even aided and abetted the masquerade whenever we could, not only as a method of revenge against our mortal enemies—the guests—but because it was uncommonly instructive and somehow wonderfully comic to see the citadel of virginity being stormed each day and wavering uncertainly every evening before a pair of white flannel trousers. It was impossible to tell, of course, if those trousers encased a young man on his way up the executive ladder, or a packer who worked in Gimbel's basement. Nor could the white flannel trousers themselves tell if the girl beneath the flowered chiffon he held in his arms as he danced around the social-hall floor was really the young lady of means she seemed to be.

We made bets on the outcome of the more spectacular stormings of the fort and we listened with unending pleasure to the lies that blew through camp like thistledown in a field of clover. It was one of the few outlets we had for anything approximating glee as the camp season rolled on. Even this source of amusement was apt to wear a little thin by the time Friday morning came around, for Friday evening was "Drama Night"; and with Eddie's staggering lack of organization, both Friday and Saturday nights—Saturday being "Musical Comedy Night"—were always torturous and exhausting beyond belief or necessity. It was, of course, no easy task to present two one-act plays each week, as well as what we called "An Original Musical Comedy" on the following night, in addition to all our other activities.

Nevertheless, it could have been done without the back-breaking, brain-fagging effort it always was, if Eddie had made the slightest effort to organize his work at the beginning of the week in even the mildest degree. This, however, he would not or could not do. Parts for the plays would not be distributed until late Tuesday afternoon, and on Wednesday night Eddie would quite likely change his mind and decide to do two other one-acters instead. We almost never got the script of the musical comedy until Thursday afternoon, and since songs and dance routines had to be learned for this, in addition to the script itself, by Friday morning, rehearsals for both shows were usually shambles.

Invariably, if Eddie switched plays in the middle of the week, the entire staff would have to heave to and help repaint the scenery, to say nothing of the fact that ingenious ways had to be devised to distribute small slips of paper with key speeches typed on them among the props and furniture so that we could have a glance at them occasionally and know what, if anything, we were going to say next. It was somewhat easier to arrange this if the plays called for an exterior set, for the slips could be pinned on the backs of bushes or even pasted unobtrusively on the top of a stone wall or fence. In the interiors, Eddie's wizardry at devising bits of business that allowed us to walk to a spot that held a piece of paper concealed from the audience's view, and that seemed part and parcel of the rightful movement of the play, was unparalleled. His genius for this sort of thing reached a new height even for him, when in one particular play which called for an outdoor set, but which had of necessity to be played throughout in extremely dim lighting, he put the typed slips of paper behind rocks and next to each slip of paper a small flashlight. As we switched on the flashlights for a quick glance at the speech coming up, he had one of the characters in the play remark, "An unusual amount of fireflies about for this time of year, aren't there?" Considering the fact that the play took place in the dead of winter and we were bundled up in coats and mufflers, there were indeed an unusual number of fireflies about. The audience never even sniggered—which was, I chose to think, a rare tribute to the high caliber of our acting.

By Thursday evening of almost every week, all-night rehearsals after the camp owner's party was over were usually an absolute necessity. We would begin rehearsals at about one and continue through in the darkened hall until six or seven o'clock in the morning, and it was under these conditions that Eddie was always at his best. Indeed, it occurred to me more than once that a goodly portion of his disorganized behavior was perhaps an unconscious arranging of just such tension and pressure to allow him to work in the way he enjoyed most. There are a good many theatre people whom I suspect of arranging just a shade more than is absolutely necessary to be under constant fire, merely to indulge themselves in a public exhibition of their innate grace under pressure. Whether Eddie did this unconsciously or not is perhaps beside the point, for it was on these nights, as the hours wore on and everyone else approached the threshold of exhaustion, that Eddie was at the top of his form.

He drank countless cups of black coffee to keep himself awake, ate innumerable Hershey bars to give himself energy, and was capable of quite brilliant bits of invention as the night wore on and he drove the rest of us unmercifully, achieving in one compressed, agonizing rehearsal what might have been easily and just as well accomplished in four leisurely and sensible ones. But that was not his way, and perhaps it was his strength as well as his weakness. Hollow-eyed, we would stagger out of the social hall to get what sleep we could until nine o'clock, when we had to appear in the dining hall for breakfast, ready to joke and "socialize" with the guests and pick up the day's activities.

At four o'clock that afternoon the doors of the social hall were again closed for our dress rehearsal, and there we stayed until eleven, when the show was over. Then, good or bad, applause or no applause, we scrambled up the hill to the dining hall and ate an enormous meal in the kitchen. Then back down the hill again to the social hall at midnight to go through the same procedure as on the night before. Only this time, since it was the first complete run-through of the "Original Musical Comedy" and the chorus line was made up of guests who had volunteered to be in the show, tempers ran extremely short as the rehearsal veered toward five A.M.

Saturday was a complete repetition of Friday—up at nine and the daytime activities until the dress rehearsal at four; only at this dress rehearsal fulminating pandemonium was the rule. These weekly musicals—stolen, slapdash and amateur though they were —were elaborate and difficult in terms of light cues, props and quick changes of costume and scenery. Since the general level of weariness and irritability was pretty high by Saturday afternoon, the dress rehearsals of the musicals were major horrors that went on until we could see the audience coming down the hill to the social hall. We then drew the curtains and prayed for the best, the hammering and setting up of the scenery sometimes drowning out the overture being played by the six-piece orchestra.

The members of the social staff were barely on speaking terms with the social director or even with each other by the time those curtains drew apart again on the opening number. What usually saved whatever remained of the staff morale by the end of Saturday night was the fact that we were all far too exhausted to remember what the bitter quarrels of the afternoon had been about.

There was always after the Saturday night show the inevitable farewell party of a guest who was leaving the next day, but we were allowed to skip breakfast on Sunday morning and were not expected to make an appearance until the two o'clock buses arrived to take the departing guests to the train. There, standing on the steps of the dining hall, the social staff en masse sang camp songs and parodies of popular songs of the day, with guests' names and camp catch-phrases scattered through them, and clowned and cavorted and created a general bruhaha until the buses and cars left.

We returned to the steps at three thirty, when the same buses came back from the station with a new load of camp guests for the next two weeks, and a group of welcoming camp songs was then sung for the new arrivals. Here a peak of hilarity was reached by Eddie or myself, pretending to be a dumb bellboy and mixing up the new guests' luggage, or opening a girl's suitcase and letting her underthings spill out and then conducting a mock auction of her effects. There was always a large audience for this ridiculous ritual, for the guests remaining in camp always assembled around the steps not only to see the social staff "make fun" but to inspect the new prospects for the two weeks coming up.

Sunday evening was a fairly easy night for the social staff, as a movie was always shown in the social hall. But it was preceded by a "Roxy Presentation," which served to introduce and show off the social staff individually to the new guests and in which we each did a number, musical or dramatic. Then, sometimes even as the movie screen was being lowered, the social staff was on its way to bed, bone-weary and almost mindless, as another week of camp life dropped behind us. I sometimes fell asleep on the edge of the bed half undressed on Sunday night, only to awake an hour or so later with a groan of recollection, that this time tomorrow night I would be standing in front of the campfire and leading the community singing, and that another week would be starting all over again.

Thus, in somewhat formidable but necessary detail, a social director's week in camp.

It must not be supposed, however, that life at camp was completely without its compensations or even actual rewards and enjoyments. For one thing, it was the first time I had ever actually lived in a realm of trees and lawns and flower beds, and the pleasure of awakening in the morning and glimpsing a pine-fringed lake outside the window as I opened my eyes, instead of grimy courtyards and a network of clotheslines, was considerable. Each morning it gave me a moment of undiluted pleasure, and it was a moment that remained undimmed, no matter what other ignominious hours the rest of the day held.

For another thing, the food at camp, while actually no great shakes by gourmet standards, was at least varied, well prepared and decently served, and the fact that I had a choice of what to eat was a special kind of enjoyment. I had not realized how weary I had become of the unending stream of stews and hamburgers which was the general family fare at home, until I sat down to the first three or four meals at camp—each meal different. I ate prodigiously all summer, as though I could see, as each meal slipped by, the slew of stews and hamburgers that was going to face me again all winter.

Perhaps the greatest reward that first summer in camp offered was the fact that I learned how to swim—thanks to being unceremoniously dumped in the lake by a group of waiters that I had penalized the night before for sneaking out of the social hall and skipping the last three sets of dances. Like most city-bred children whose summers have been spent on the curbstone in front of the house or hanging around the candy store on the corner, I was deathly afraid of the water. While I stoutly maintained those first few weeks at camp that I had no time free for anything but a quick shower, secretly I longed to be able to paddle a canoe and get out to the middle of the lake and even hide away alone for a half-hour or so from the hubbub of camp in one of the bends of the shoreline, but non-swimmers were strictly forbidden to use the canoes and a rowboat somehow negated the whole idea of escape. Actually, I was even frightened of being out in a rowboat alone, and so I gave the lake as wide a berth as possible.

After that initial toss into the water, however, and the knowledge that I would not immediately sink and drown, I got up at dawn the following morning and began two weeks of swimming lessons with the lifeguard—a young fellow who rather fancied himself as an actor, but whose pleadings had received short shrift from Eddie. In return for promising him a part in a play to be put on the weekend his girl friend was to be at camp, he used his proper talents and taught me how to swim—not too well, perhaps, for my timidity was still great, but well enough to be able to take out a canoe.

From the moment I pushed that first canoe away from the dock and paddled awkwardly toward the center of the lake, I experienced a lift of the heart that more than made up for all the brainless boy-and-girl numbers I had to sing with girl guests, or all the Japanese costumes I draped around the men's unwilling shoulders. It made a vast difference, my being able to swim that first year and all the years thereafter that I spent at camps.

The lifeguard could barely walk across the stage, much less act, but I kept my promise and got him a part the week his girl came to camp, for I knew I was greatly indebted to him. Almost every day after that first canoe ride I managed to steal away for a half-hour and paddle swiftly to the middle of the lake, where the sounds of camp were not only muffled but somehow not unpleasant; I would drift idly, letting the clup-clup of the water against the sides of the canoe lull me into a peaceful ignorance of the fact that in an hour or so I would be doing my impersonation of Fanny Brice as "Mrs. Cohen at the Beach" or leading the Charleston Contest.

[150]

Every so often I would manage to skip dinner, and with a couple of bottles of Coca-Cola and some cookies and boxes of raisins in the bottom of the canoe, I would make straight for a little island at the far end of the lake and have as much as two glorious hours all to myself. It was in these hours, as I lay naked on the grass, letting the late afternoon sun dry off the best swim of the day, that I would plan the campaign that was to get me back into the theatre again. This time it was not just dreams of glory or any one grandiose plan, but a slow strategy of gaining a foothold that, if it worked, might fix my feet firmly in the theatre. I did not mention these schemes even to Eddie, for I could not bear to have the fantasy I was building punctured or exploded—at least, not just then. These hours that I managed alone on that island at the end of the lake were a necessary oasis, a refreshment of the spirit, that I needed to see me through that first summer, for I loathed much of what I was doing and the desire to pack up and go home was an almost daily temptation.

I hated being pleasant to large numbers of people, the majority of whom I despised. I resented the meaningless impudence of being on tap as extra entertainment for the bunk parties we were forced to attend, and most of all I hated the ridiculous, clownish figure I was in my own eyes as I capered around the campfire or "made fun" on the dining-room steps. Had I not learned to swim and contrived those occasional hours alone, I very much doubt if I could have lasted out that first season, for I could not shake the inner picture I had of myself that made my days and nights in the social hall acutely painful.

Lying alone on the little island, I was able not only to make peace with the repugnant tasks I was called upon to do each day, but even to see how summers at camp fitted in perfectly with the plan I was weaving to take me back to the theatre. Anything that served that purpose was endurable, humiliating or not! Also, the moment I was out on the lake, however briefly, I began to see that in spite of the crudity of most of the plays and musicals we did, they were nevertheless pieces of theatre put on behind footlights for an audience's approval, and as always, the moment one draws a curtain and dims the lights, one begins to learn something of value about the theatre itself. Some of the lessons I learned at camp served me very well later on in the professional theatre, for certain absolutes obtain in the amateur as well as in the professional theatre.

For one thing, I became convinced that talent by itself is not enough, even an authentic and first-rate talent is not enough, nor are brilliance and audacity in themselves sufficient. There remains the ability to translate that talent, whether it be for acting or play-writing, into terms that fulfill the promise of a play so that the performance succeeds in realizing the full measure of its potential. Too many plays emerge better on the printed page than they do behind the footlights. For in the workaday theatre there seems to be a hidden conspiracy to defeat a play the moment "End of Act Three" is typed on the author's typewriter, and it moves into inexorable operation the day rehearsals begin. The rocky shoals that beset a play's wavering course to the tempestuous shores of Broadway are strewn with the wreckage of good plays and good actors whose authors or directors grew tired just a trifle too soon in Boston or Philadelphia, or failed to withstand the hurricane blows of New Haven.

In those summers at camp I began to learn to push past exhaustion and to think on my feet, and to become slowly aware that weariness and exhaustion were the twin sirens of the theatrical deep. Let them take over and they will rob one of courage and the ability to improvise in a crisis, for stamina in the long run is as necessary an adjunct to success in the theatre as talent itself. Time after time at camp that first year, I watched Eddie bring order out of chaos and turn a dress rehearsal that was a shambles into a show of considerable merit by the sheer dint of a kind of buoyant and contagious courage that made him deaf to the babble of defeat going on about him, and by an ability to remain untired at all costs. These two priceless assets—qualities that seem to stem one from the other— were as valuable as any talent for the theatre that he possessed, and its lesson was not lost upon me. Years afterwards, both in camp and in the professional theatre, weariness was the villain I fought and wrestled with, much as a revivalist preacher casts out the devil, and three-o'clock-in-the-morning courage was what I prayed for far more than for inspiration or an ingenious device to bring the second-act curtain down.

It was lucky that I made my peace with the camp routine when I did, for as the season rolled on into August, each day's and night's activities became doubly difficult. August, and not April, to paraphrase T. S. Eliot, was the cruelest month. By August the camp was at its most crowded and noisome, the staff at its lowest ebb in both body and mind, and the petty quarrels that could be smoothed over and forgotten in a day in June or July now flared into bitter open enmity. The social staff barely spoke to one another. Even the waiters risked open rebellion, for they knew they would not be fired in August when the dining room was filled to overflowing and guests were sleeping six to eight in cabins meant to accommodate only four.

To add to our woes, that nightmare of all social directors, a rainy spell, began in the middle of August that year and continued for nine solid days.

The few daytime activities the social staff could take advantage of to give them time to rehearse in order to prepare for the evening's activities were the tennis tournaments, the swimming meets and the golf matches—and we went to great pains to see that they took place almost daily. Now, with all outdoor activities cut off and the social hall thrown open from ten in the morning until midnight, we were at our wits' end trying to fill the days as well as the nights of eight hundred sodden, disgruntled and increasingly furious guests.

At nine thirty in the morning, Eddie and I would look out of one of the rain-splashed windows of the social hall and see a long line of yellow raincoats and black umbrellas streaming down the hill toward the social hall—and groan out loud. They had no place else to go, of course; and when they got there they sat in maddened, steaming heaps, smelling of overshoes and mud, and glared balefully at the social staff, daring us to amuse them. Their hard-earned vacations were being hopelessly ruined, but any compassion we may have felt for them was extremely short-lived, for in some inexplicable way they seemed to blame the social staff not only for our inability to keep them entertained fourteen hours a day but for the rain as well.

They complained bitterly to William J. Perleman. By the fifth day of the downpour they checked out of camp in droves, and as the sky showed no signs of turning off its seemingly inexhaustible water tap, Mr. Perleman, driven frantic himself by a mass exodus in the height of the season, lost his proverbial sunny disposition and gave way to immoderate fury, castigated the social staff as slovenly and lazy, and screamed that they were ruining the good reputation of his camp for superior entertainment in good weather or bad. Actually, this was highly unjust, for we were not only doing everything possible to keep the angry guests occupied and amused, but several highly improbable things as well. In addition to treasure hunts, square dances, spelling bees, and a county fair set up inside the social hall, complete with barkers and booths, and a musician dressed up as William Jennings Bryan who fell into a tub of water when a baseball hit the plank under him, Eddie gave tango lessons and I held symposiums on "Companionate Marriage" and gave character analyses by handwriting. I knew as little of handwriting analysis as Eddie did of the intricacies of the tango, but by the eighth day of rain we were performing in a kind of stupor and not quite in full command of our senses.

On the evening of the ninth day we held our breath as we saw the sun manfully trying to arrange a sunset through the still-lowering clouds, and at that first glimpse of pale sunlight, Eddie, a little hysterical, took a spoonful of mustard he was about to dab on a frankfurter and splashed it across the table at me. I took a spoonful of mustard and returned the same in kind to him. And suddenly, as though at an awaited signal, mustard and chili sauce were being tossed all over the dining room onto faces, dresses, walls and ceiling. It was known as the Great Mustard Fight—and why some four hundred people splashing mustard at each other and screaming with laughter should have considered it hilarious, I cannot explain; but eight days of rain in camp can bring one perilously close to the threshold of insanity. There was a limit, apparently, to what even our healthy young nervous systems could stand, and eight days was that limit. In the years to follow, I went through other rainy spells at other camps and they were always horrors; but nothing ever matched the unremitting downpour at Camp Utopia.

With the sun overhead once more, we managed to achieve a second wind, somehow, and plowed through the rest of the season, not without a few stern measures being taken by W. J. Perleman, for Eddie's eyes were turned toward the upcoming South African tour, and his lack of interest in what went on on the stage of the social hall of Camp Utopia was painfully obvious and his rehearsals increasingly disorganized, even for Eddie.

One historic Saturday night's musical comedy was improvised right on the stage after the curtains parted, with Eddie shouting from the wings what to do next, no rehearsal of any kind having been held beforehand. The audience howled and jeered, and that Sunday we did not appear on the dining-room steps to sing farewell songs to the departing guests. We were right back on the steps, however, to sing welcoming songs to the new batch of guests that arrived from the station, on the shaky assumption that the new arrivals would not have had time to compare notes with our audience of the night before.

And then, suddenly, it was Labor Day—and my first season in camp was over.

I was fifteen pounds lighter. My face was pallid; those nine days of rain and the subsequent all-day rehearsals in the social hall in preparation for the Labor Day weekend had robbed it of the last bit of tan, and my eyes seemed to have sunk far back in their sockets. It was too bad that we had not scheduled some scenes from *Julius Caesar,* for though I had eaten like a horse all summer, I had the lean and hungry look that Cassius is supposed to have and could have played him without any make-up at all.

By the afternoon of the day after Labor Day, the camp was empty of guests, waiters and social staff—not a single remnant remained of the summer except myself. It was as though a sudden outbreak of cholera had emptied the place of all humankind, and only the trees and the cloudless sky looked down on what had been, just the day before, a teeming, roiling mass of humanity that overflowed the lawns and walks and dotted the lake with every available canoe and rowboat. I was staying on for three or four days by permission of William J. Perleman, while the local workmen closed up the camp for the winter.

Eddie had left on the early-morning train for New York, his nose pointing straight to South Africa, where indeed it took him in company with a troupe that included Luther Adler and Harry Green, and I did not set eyes on him again for over two years. The rest of the staff, still barely speaking to each other now, became as one with the last of the departing guests and cluttered around the buses, cars and piled-up luggage, and it was I alone who stood on the dining-room steps and waved them off.

I stood on the steps and looked down the cabin-lined paths toward the lake. There was not a soul to be seen—not a single girl drying her hair in the sun, her shoulder straps pushed down as far as the law would allow; not a single boy doing push-ups in front of his cabin, showing off his muscles to the girl. The silence of a lovely September day was unmarred by wolf calls, whistles, or the shrieks of girls being pinched on their bottoms through a bath towel as they ran toward the showers. Not one ukulele strummed, not one record played "Indian Love Call," while another record drowned it out with "The Japanese Sandman." And the dining room, a roaring boiler factory at each mealtime, was empty and silent behind me.

I strolled down to the social hall and peered in; the litter of the farewell Labor Day Carnival still strewed the floors and walls. On the empty stage lay the tin shovels and pails I had used the night before in my impersonation of Fanny Brice as "Mrs. Cohen at the Beach." Two straw hats, kicked clean through the center now, that Eddie and I had used for our Gallagher and Shean number, rested on the footlights, and tossed heedlessly over one of the musician's stands was the black cape I had used for my Hamlet soliloquy at the last campfire. I smiled benignly on it all and strolled on down to the lake. Next Monday morning I could awake without the knowledge that I would have to do a Charleston encore that evening—and next Monday was what I wanted to think about.

It was to have time to think that I had asked permission to remain these three extra days in camp alone. I took my favorite canoe and paddled straight out toward the island. Never had camp seemed so pleasant, and I knew that never again would it be like this. But summers in camp were part of my plan now, and they would remain part of my life until I was permanently attached to the theatre.

It had become clear to me, or so it seemed in those hours I had managed to snatch away on this island, that only by a process of ruthless elimination and no daydreaming whatsoever would I find a path of re-entry into the theatre. Acting was out of the question. That I already knew, for even my success as an actor in certain parts in the plays we had done this summer had not changed my mind on that score. I had ruled out very quickly the possibility of getting another job as a theatrical office boy, for if I was going to have to swallow being a social director every summer far into the unforeseeable future, I wanted a good deal more than just free theatre tickets and the smell of a theatrical office. I wanted nothing less than to be an active part of the theatre itself.

I thought long and hard and from every conceivable angle, including that of lying about my inexperience and trying for a job as a stage manager, but I felt that even if I were not quickly found out, I might very well starve in the process of trying, for stage manager jobs were almost the hardest to come by. I had even, in a wild moment or two, considered writing a letter to Edgar C. Davis—a credulous and seemingly demented Texan, who poured thousands of dollars into a play called *The Ladder,* giving the tickets away free—and asking him to subsidize me until I found my place in the theatre. But subsidize me for what? I had composed half the letter in my mind when I stopped. Even a crazy Texan did not dish out money to an unknown youth from the Bronx simply because he was stage-struck! I made a list of other possible and perhaps saner benefactors of the theatre, including Otto Kahn, and then tore it up. My own sense of reality set me to laughing even as I put down the names.

Finally, I came to the conclusion—and so simple it seemed that I wondered why I had not hit upon it right off—that the only way for me to get past a stage door again was to write a play.

Nothing short of that would bring me within sniffing distance of the grizzled old doormen that guarded the backstage portals. There was no hesitation once I thought of it—it was as though another apple had dropped on Newton's head and my own theatrical law of gravity established once and for all. I knew instantly that I was right. It struck me even then how downright accidentally a life-long vocation can be come upon. I have wondered since if others have experienced the same strange difficulty of perceiving where they really belong.

Having stumbled dim-wittedly upon the correct choice, however, I proceeded to plan as carefully as I could for its achievement. I was not fool enough to think that plays were easily written, or even if they were, that they had any certainty of success or of production. A number of years might pass and a number of plays might have to be written before one even received production, let alone achieved success. The question was, how to exist and earn a living in the meantime? I dismissed the facility with which I had tossed off *The Beloved Bandit* as a snare for claptrap writing—indeed, some of its shoddy dialogue still echoed embarrassingly in my ears. Even if I could quickly write another play on the kitchen table at night after a day of work as a shipping clerk or an office boy, the chances of its being any good were highly unlikely.

Instinctively I knew that I would need a certain sense of composure, a time to work when my mind was fresh and all my senses alert, if I was to have a fair shake of the dice for the high stakes of the game I was going to play. If I was going to attempt to be a playwright, the first necessity was to arrange to have my days free, and Eddie and this past spring and summer had shown me a heaven-sent way. If I could convince William J. Perleman to let me continue directing plays at the Labor Temple and also get one or two other little-theatre groups to direct (for one group alone would not pay enough for food and the roof over our heads), social directing during the summer would see me through the year until the little-theatre groups picked up again in the fall. Except for the summers, only my evenings would be taken up with work and I would have the days free to write plays. It seemed simple, conclusive, almost an

[158]

accomplished fact. All I would have to do from here on in, as a famous playwright once fatuously remarked when asked how a play of his was coming along, was to "dialogue it." "It's all right here in my head," said this fool, tapping his brow. "All I have to do now is dialogue it."

Paddling back across the lake in the twilight, "dialoguing it" seemed the easiest thing in the world to do. The hammer blows of the workmen boarding up the dining-room windows echoed softly across the water and seemed like the gentle tap-tap of fame already knocking at my door.

Three days later I was home once again, ringing the doorbell I had rung for so many years and waiting for the door to open.

I T WAS A CURIOUS homecoming. I don't know quite what I expected after this, my longest absence from home. I suppose I had carried back from camp with me a fantasy of change—that somehow my mother and father and brother would be "different," that even the dingy rooms and the threadbare furniture would be less ugly.

Nothing, of course, had changed. Pleased though they were to see me, my mother and father were utterly incurious as to what the summer had been like or even what I did at camp, and my brother Bernie as usual ignored me, speaking only when I pointedly asked him a direct question. Almost before I sat down, the litany of unpaid grocers' and butcher bills, the two boarders' rooms unrented, and the rent three months overdue now that must somehow be paid by the first of the month, began as though I had never been away. In less than half an hour I settled back into the old thralldom; it was as though not a day had passed since last spring and I had simply emerged from the subway that evening as usual.

But there *was* a difference in this homecoming—a very significant difference. And I wonder if a first absence away from home marks for others the same curious emotional change in family orientation that this absence did for me in my relationship with my mother and father, and most of all with my brother. Is there a precise moment when we see our parents as though for the first time— look upon them with eyes that seem to see them as strangers see them?

I think there is such a moment—a moment when we see our parents plain, not when they are grown old and are a symbol of ancestry to be honored or tolerated and when we can no longer know what they were like, but a moment when we see them suddenly for the first time as people. It is a fleeting moment and it passes, to be quickly replaced with the usual façade of filial devotion—that coin of the realm that passes for affection between the generations—but when this moment occurs, it seems to cut through a lifelong incrustation of love and hate, and for however brief a time it lasts, we see our parents as the fallible human beings they are and for a little while we hold them blameless.

The precise moment happened for me as I stood in the hallway in front of our flat, pressing the doorbell and waiting for the door to be opened. When my mother opened the door, I stood blinking at her as though it were an unexpected and surprising stranger I was seeing, instead of the face of my earliest memories, the face and eyes I had looked up into from the time my own eyes had sight in them. But in a very real sense, or so it seemed to me, I was gazing at a stranger—for the first time I was seeing my mother as the person she was. Even as we threw our arms around each other and embraced, and her first words of greeting reached my ears, I was conscious of hearing her voice as a stranger might hear it—not as her son—without the clatter of a thousand admonitions, beseechings and warnings echoing in my ears. It was a young voice with music in it—not the voice whose every nuance I thought I knew so well; nor was it the face I carried in my mind's eye, lined and careworn, a face twisted by a thousand demands—so that I was impelled to look at her before I kissed her, and I was surprised to find her face still young and unmarked.

Behind her my father stood waiting, a stranger, too. In back of him my brother stood, grave and unsmiling—all three of them as curiously removed and remote from myself as figures glimpsed in a distant landscape. In these first few hours at home, I moved through the familiar rooms a stranger myself—almost an observer —seeing clearly my father's corrosive sadness and defeat, understanding for a little while, and able to forgive, my mother's tyranny.

[161]

But my thoughts turned mainly to my brother and myself. We had lived all of our lives together, he and I, yet between us there existed only the slimmest line of communication and not the slightest awareness of each other—of what we might be like as human beings. We were more than strangers—we were alien figures who slept in the same bed together each night, the breach between us widening as we awoke each morning and, almost without speaking, went our separate ways.

Why could we find no words for each other? Was it the seven-year difference in age that separated us? Was it simply the years that kept us locked mutely apart? I did not think so. The age span narrows as one grows older, and a boy of twelve is already an individual, he has tastes and strong judgments and a temperament already formed—and of these things in my brother Bernie I knew nothing. In the uncomfortable and uneasy silence that had become a way of life between us, I could discover not the slightest clue to the kind of person who was growing up beside me, and now for the first time I felt the need to know.

Puzzling it out, trying to fit the separate pieces of our lives together, I thought I could understand why we had had almost no chance to know each other, or even feel the lack of a normal relationship between us. After all, he had been only five years old when I was working in the music store afternoons after school, a bare seven when I was first locked away in the fur vault, and hardly eleven years old when I returned from Chicago after *The Beloved Bandit,* a full-fledged failure at eighteen. I had been out of the house and into the world almost before he could put words together; but now he was twelve and I was nineteen, and I was puzzled by and resentful of this total stranger who slept beside me. Perhaps for the first time, in these months away, I had felt an unconscious need for the brother I had never had, or a desperate want of someone to confide in. Whatever it was, I felt a compelling need to try and bridge the gap between us.

In the first day or two at home I became sharply aware of something that I had not been fully conscious of before. The major decisions of family life were left to me, and it was taken for granted not only by my mother but by my father as well that I, and I alone, should make them. My mother turned to me and not to my father, even in the smallest crises of daily living, and with a somewhat late and guilty clarity I realized that in these last few years my father had receded more and more into the dim background and I had replaced him, as husband and father. This is not an unusual occurrence in families of our circumstance. The breadwinner, whether he likes it or not, and sometimes unbeknownst to himself, gradually assumes a role that is not rightly his, and should not be. And when this happens there is a displacement in the family picture, a twisting and disorientation of family relationships that the years afterward fail to make whole again. It is not surprising that my brother should have rejected a brother he had never known or refused to accept the substitute father I had become.

Poverty does more than rob one of creature comforts and the right to live with dignity—its thievery can encompass the loss of a brother and father as well. Shaw was correct when he declared that poverty was a sin against God and man alike, and he might have added that ugliness, which is a concomitant of poverty, can be equated with evil. I resolved to do something about both.

I looked around me at the ugliness in which I had spent the first nineteen years of my life. I watched my brother, more withdrawn and distant than ever, and I decided that somehow or other I must manage to take him away with me to camp the following summer. He would be almost thirteen by then and a job as busboy in the dining room would not be impossible for him to handle. If I could also contrive to get my father a job in the canteen that dispensed cigarettes and soft drinks in the social hall, our combined salaries, if we watched every penny during the summer, might enable us to move to a different flat in a different place—as far away as possible from this present ugliness which was choking us all. If it did nothing more than serve to bring Bernie and me a little closer, it was worth the try.

It did not. It was a long time before we reached each other unencumbered by the past, and those lost years I still hold guilty of

[163]

denying me the companionship of the witty, beguiling, sweet-natured human being to whom I am now devoted.

I hated to let a moment of time slip away now, but I let almost a week go by after my return to the city before I called on William J. Perleman and asked to take over the little-theatre group at the Labor Temple again for the new winter season. I thought it wiser to allow a little time to elapse before we met again, for I was certain that his memory of that last unrehearsed musical at camp was still green. It was indeed, and he grumbled and harumphed a good deal about Eddie's disorderliness, of which he held me a part. But he was surprisingly sympathetic to my aspirations as a playwright and willingly gave me the job. He even suggested another little-theatre group —flourishing, or rather, withering away—in the far reaches of the Bronx, which was in need of a director, and gave me a letter to them.

I was launched even more quickly than I had dared hope. By mid-October I was commuting every other evening between the Upper Bronx and 14th Street, and by November I had already started a play. Even with two groups to direct, the combined fees amounted to less than twenty-eight dollars a week, but it was enough to get thinly by on. The important thing was that I had my days free to write now, and I plunged ahead with a supreme inner confidence and a pencil that never seemed to hesitate above the paper. It had not taken me long to come upon an idea for a play, since I had hit upon, unsurprisingly enough, that most cliché of all play ideas—the boarding house, with each lodger having his own separate dramatic and soul-searing story. It had seemed to me, of course, like an utterly new and God-given inspiration, happily fresh and untouched as a source of stage material.

All winter long I wrote slowly and carefully each and every day, unconsciously using every timeworn device and cliché-ridden bit of stagecraft I had ever seen, blithely convinced all the while that what I was setting down was completely new and even daring! I wrote happily on, blind to the fact that the dialogue was turgid, the invention imitative, and the style an unholy mélange of Eugene O'Neill and George Kelly.

Furthermore, in the true classical tradition of a first attempt, it was to be a deeply serious and startlingly candid examination of life's bitterness and ironies, told with unrelenting rectitude, and making no concessions to the popular taste of the day. It contained among other things my mother as the chief character who ran the boarding house, my father as the janitor and handy man, two immensely talented but unlucky actors easily identifiable as Eddie and myself, and a composite portrait of my aunt and my grandfather embodied in the character of a Southern lady of vanished grandeur around whom the Furies played and whose tragic death gave the play its final curtain, as well as a resounding speech of wisdom and compassion by the author. It was a perfectly terrible play in every respect, but this I did not know—not, at least, immediately.

I finished the play in mid-February on a note of triumph and with exultant admiration for my own rare gifts as a playwright. But I made myself keep, not without some difficulty, my promise to put the manuscript away for a week and not look at it. Somewhere or other I had picked up the information that veteran playwrights always let a play cool off, so to speak, before they read it through again for a cold, unemotional appraisal. This had struck me as a wonderfully professional custom, and since I considered myself a professional now—though an unproduced Bronx one, to be sure—I was pathetically eager to use every professional trick that came to my attention.

Accordingly, on a bright February morning a week after I had written *The Curtain Slowly Falls,* I went into the bathroom, locked the door, and settling myself with a pillow behind me in the empty bathtub, I opened the closely written pages. The play's awfulness did not dawn on me slowly—the full impact of its hackneyed dreariness hit me by the sixth page. I was hard put to finish it without getting out of the bathtub and flushing it down the toilet, and it was difficult by the second act for me to believe that I had written it at all. I lay there afterward for a long while—wondering at my own naïveté of a week before and marveling at the self-delusion that seems to impose itself on a writer's senses, even such a neophyte as myself, the moment he picks up a pencil and starts to write. How could I have gone so miserably wrong? Amateur though I was, I should have known better. At least I'd been exposed to enough decently written plays to make the mound of paper lying in the bathtub beside me seem incredibly inept. Not one line of it seemed to me to give the slightest indication that I could write postcards, let alone a play.

I suspected one way I had gone wrong from the start; and forever afterward it made me more than a little leery of those golden nuggets of advice so capriciously tossed out by elder statesmen of the theatre to credulous beginners, one of which I must have stumbled across and taken to heart: "Begin by writing of what you know best —do not wander off in fields that are strange to you. Take for your setting and characters only the places and people you know and stick to them." So went this preposterous bit of dramatic wisdom, thereby discounting the vital and immeasurable quality that imagination gives to all writing, whether it be for the stage or anything else. Since this bit of nonsense had issued from the lips of a quite famous playwright, I had slavishly followed it, writing of a place and people I knew, but completely failing to allow imagination to riffle through the pages as it might have done had I chosen a setting and characters not so highly colored by my own attitudes and prejudices. I had simply set down what I knew best, and stuck to it. The play had verity; what it lacked was the breath of life and imagination —two necessary ingredients for what is usually called creative writing.

Well, the time had not been wasted. To be aware is to be fore-warned. I would not, I thought, make the same error again. Yet despite the force with which this simple truth struck me, I kept making this identical mistake for years afterward. Play-writing is a most devilish profession. It is not only the most difficult of literary forms to master—one of the reasons, I suppose, that it pays so handsomely—but it is a craft one never seems to truly learn anything about from one's past mistakes.

It is taken for granted that a cabinetmaker or a shoemaker, or a lawyer or a doctor, for that matter, starting with a certain degree of talent for his profession, does, after the practice of that profession for ten or twenty years, learn how to make a good cabinet or a decent pair of shoes, or plead a case or diagnose an illness correctly. Not so the playwright. He is quite capable after twenty years of practice of having a left shoe for the second act when a right shoe is obviously called for, and is as unable to perceive the tumor in the third act that stares him in the face as the merest beginner or even someone who has never written a line for the stage.

If it maddens and seems inexplicable to the critics and public that a playwright of standing and success should be represented one season by a mature and sure-footed work, and the following season by a most barbarous bit of stagecraft that does not seem to have been written by the same fellow, it frustrates and bewilders the playwright also. He then bitterly asks himself, "Do I know nothing at all about my profession? Is it possible to write a success one season and an abysmal failure the next? Am I never going to learn anything about this craft I practice?"

The answer I suspect is, "Yes and no." One does learn a little through the years, of course, but what one learns is the surface tricks of play-writing, never how to avoid the major errors. Perhaps the reason that one can never practice the art of play-writing with any degree of sureness or security is that each play has a peculiar and separate life of its own. The problems of one play are not the problems of another, and the very mistakes that have been avoided in the previous play bear no relationship to mistakes that must be side-stepped in this present one. Unlike the surgeon who knows exactly where he must make the incision and tie off the blood vessels, or the lawyer who has legal precedents on which to base his case, the playwright confronts in each new play an operation that has never been performed before, or a brief that is being written for the first time in the history of legal annals.

With each new play the playwright is a Columbus sailing uncharted seas, with the unhappy knowledge that those unfriendly Indian tribes—the critics and the public—will be lining the shores at the end of the voyage waiting to scalp him, even if he survives the mutiny. Little wonder that he shivers and shakes and groans too loudly in the public prints and into the ears of his forbearing friends when he writes "Act I" anew. For if he is a man who respects his craft and not merely a dealer in theatrical merchandise, he very well knows that no matter how skillful or successful he may be, each time he scribbles "Act One" on a blank piece of paper he is starting afresh, and, if he will allow himself the full and bitter truth, he is writing a play for the first time. His years of experience and his past successes count for nothing. Each time, if he is honest, he must face his own inadequacy and come to terms with it, for he has learned almost nothing about his profession in the meantime.

There have been times, not unfew, when I considered that I had done neither myself nor the theatre any great service by getting out of that bathtub, tossing the manuscript into a bureau drawer, and resolving to go on being a playwright. At that moment of bright illumination, however, I was so fired with my discovery of what I thought had led me astray and so keen to put my conclusions to the test, that I was ready to begin another play immediately. But I knew that would have to wait.

Late February and early March were the times when all camps engaged their social directors for the coming summer, and getting a job that would include my father and my brother Bernie was not going to be quite as easy as getting a job alone. But on that score I was determined, no matter what sort of job I had to take or in what kind of place. I ruled out even trying for the big camps or hotels in the Catskills—the area that later became known as the "Borscht Circuit"—on the grounds that my experience of only one summer as an assistant director would preclude my landing a social director's job, for I knew that only if I were hired as social director could I insist on having my father and brother with me. There would be plenty of other places to pick and choose from, I decided, even without the Catskills. I was wrong.

Not only were most camps unwilling to take the chance of making a social director out of someone with one summer's experience as an assistant, and including two members of his family in the contract as well; but the majority of camp owners, unlike the bemused

William J. Perleman, were aghast at my suave patter of doing Kelly, Shaw and O'Neill on the stages of their social halls. They were, in fact, appalled at the mere suggestion of such a thing. Too late did I discover that my unquestionably high-falutin' and foolish approach sent them hurrying to the telephone to call back their old social director of the previous summer, good or bad! I frightened them off one by one by my stupid emphasis on "art and uplift" in the summertime. How could they know I did a wonderful Fanny Brice, an impeccable Charleston, played the ukulele and "made fun" on the dining-room steps, when I talked only of Edna St. Vincent Millay and Lord Dunsany? I ruined every good lead and chance I had, and by the end of March I was desperate. By April, I knew, only the dregs were left, the jobs that no self-respecting social director would even consider taking, since they not only paid the lowest salaries but they no doubt offered the foulest working conditions.

The owners of these ramshackle resorts, however, no doubt counted on and patiently waited for just such fools as myself to turn up in April, when there was no choice of anything better, and on an unlucky April day I arrived for a fatal interview with Mr. Axeler, the owner and guiding spirit of a summer camp called not "The Dregs," as it might rightfully have been labeled, but the "Half Moon Country Club." He was a short and stocky little man with a bright and metallic eye and the mark of a crank stamped clearly all over him.

I was not especially put off, however, by this, my first impression of him. All camp owners, of course, had something of the crank in their make-up, since no man in his right mind would choose to run a camp as a way of life in the first place. There was money in it, of course, but not enough money to warrant the wear and tear which running a camp entailed, and in point of fact camp owners were not, almost without exception, actually much interested in making money. It was the life itself, the idea of running a summer camp, that they deeply relished.

They were a special breed of men, these fellows, with the flush of megalomania on their cheeks, the glint of the true hysteric in their eyes; and their camps were their overpowering obsession. They came truly alive only in the summers, and then not with a whimper, but with a great bang. They seemed to hibernate in the winter months, half-heartedly pursuing some trumped-up profession, but it was the happy megalomaniacal summers they waited for, marking time till they could reign as the unrivaled monarchs of all they surveyed.

They thought of their camps as little kingdoms, where they indeed reigned supreme, and depending upon their inner picture of themselves, which usually resembled Napoleon, they issued their own codes and edicts all summer long in the most regal fashion and their wives and children reigned as the royal family, with a ready-made retinue of poor relations who were being given a two-week vacation free of charge as part of the emperor's largesse. Their prime minister, of course, was the social director, and woe betide him if he did not stand in well at court, poor relations included!

I played Disraeli to these idiot Victorias for six damnable years, and it is no small accolade I bestow on Mr. Axeler as the worst by far of them all. In a wide choice of egomaniacal cranks, the laurel wreath is unquestionably his and his alone. For one thing he had charm, which most of the others did not; and for another, he was a pathological liar, and in the end I don't know which I held most against him, his charm or his lying.

I sat across the desk from him, carefully screening my answers to his questions; but so genuine was his interest and so refreshing his candor compared with the others I had interviewed, that very soon I was disarmed sufficiently to fall back into my plea for Kelly, Shaw and O'Neill as part of the summer's dramatic program, in spite of the fact that I had privately sworn to stay clear of these names that had already proven anathema everywhere else.

Far from being put off, Mr. Axeler seemed quite intrigued. He admitted that the level of entertainment in the social hall of the Half Moon Country Club had not been on so high a plane heretofore, but he saw no reason whatever for not trying to raise that level. He deftly suggested that audiences, even in summer camps, invariably rose to an appreciation of what was offered them if it was properly presented, and moreover, he announced, he would enjoy taking the gamble of doing some of the things other camps had not the courage or the gumption even to try.

I could hardly believe my ears! I had sat down opposite him with a heavy heart, convinced that I must take this job, if I could get it, under any conditions that were set down, and my first look at him and the fact that at the end of April the Half Moon Country Club was still without a social director, gave me every reason to suppose that this was a camp and a job too shoddy for anyone else to consider. After fifteen minutes of listening to Mr. Axeler talk, I was quite oppositely convinced that I had fallen into a tub of honey—that my luck in being turned down by all the other camps was almost too good to be true. This of all jobs seemed to be the one made to order for me.

I hesitated and stalled for as long as I dared before I came point-blank to the question of my father and Bernie. With as much bravery as I could summon, for I was not at all certain that I could bear to give the job up if he refused my request, I told Mr. Axeler it would be impossible for me to accept an offer that did not include my father and brother. Again Mr. Axeler astonished me. He would be glad to find a job for my brother in the kitchen and place my father in charge of the canteen in the social hall, in return for a small concession on my part. Would I be willing to go up to camp two weeks earlier than usual and get the social hall in readiness for the Decoration Day weekend?

The Half Moon Country Club was in Vermont and it was a little more difficult to get everything in order there than it was in camps closer to New York. Of course I would, I assured him immediately; but since next week would be the first of May, how would it be possible to engage a social staff and an orchestra in the short time that remained? All that was already done, he airily explained. The country club was run in conjunction with a boys' camp on the shores of Lake Champlain, just down the hill from the club itself; and the camp counselors were all young men carefully selected with an eye to their previous dramatic training; they were eager and available at all times to do anything I needed them for. Even the camp nurse was studying to be an opera singer on the side and she, too, was to be considered part of the social staff. An orchestra of six pieces had already been engaged and they also, it seemed, were not only first-rate musicians but had fine singing voices and doubled as actors as well.

Much as I wanted and needed the job I hesitated. It was unorthodox, to say the least, for a social director not to engage his own social staff—the staff he selected during the winter and the luck or good sense he had in choosing the right one made the difference between a good summer or a terrible one. I had never before heard of a staff being engaged before the social director, and noticing my flicker of hesitation and doubt, Mr. Axeler opened a drawer of his desk and drew out a legal-looking bit of paper.

"I'm fixing the contract to include your father and brother," he said, "and don't worry about the staff—take my word for it. I'm taking a gamble on you—you take a gamble on me. Here—just fill in your father's and brother's names and sign it."

He smiled that wonderfully candid and honest smile of his and pushed the paper across the desk toward me. I returned his smile even though, as I had suspected, the salary was ridiculously small and my father and brother were to get nothing at all but board and lodging—their salary was to come out of a common pool of tips from the guests, that was divided up among the waiters and other help at the end of the season.

"Maybe we don't pay as much as some other camps do," said Mr. Axeler as I sat staring at the contract in front of me, "but we make up for it in a lot of other ways." He rose and came from behind the desk, a pen in hand. "By the end of the summer you'll want to pay *us* for giving you such a fine vacation." He chuckled. "Here— sign it—so I can officially welcome the newest member of our Half Moon family."

He smiled even more winningly and offered me the pen, his other hand resting paternally on my shoulder. His hand remained on my shoulder while I signed my name in the two spaces indicated, and before I even had time to blot the signatures, he had somehow whisked it from the desk and was escorting me to the door. He stood cordially shaking my hand at the doorway and beaming good will all the way down the corridor.

"Anything you need—anything you want—drop in any time and just ask me for it. I'll have the train tickets for you and your father and brother for May fifteenth, and I'll be up at camp a day or two before you arrive waiting for you. You've done a very good thing for yourself today," he called jocularly over his shoulder as the door closed behind him, that forthright smile still lingering on his lips. Basking in the security of a job at last and the warmth of that smile, I whole-heartedly agreed with him, having no inkling whatever that I had just signed a contract with one of the most thorough-going rascals I was likely to meet for quite a while.

That evening, hesitantly and using all the powers of persuasion at my command, I outlined to my mother and father and brother the change I contemplated making in their lives. I was quite prepared to argue all night and if necessary until an hour before the train left for Vermont, for I knew how big a change I was asking them to make. I was prepared to argue interminably, but I was by no means certain I could make them accept it, for to separate my mother and father for the first time in their married life, to put all our belongings in storage, to send my mother off to live alone in a furnished room for the next four months, was no small thing to ask.

I well knew my mother's intense and fierce feeling for the tiny world of her family and the grim battle she waged against any part of it being separated from herself. Only bleak necessity had allowed me to escape for so small a time as I had. To my complete surprise, it was she who was the first to agree—the first to see the wisdom of the move—the first to declare herself in favor of the whole idea of change. To this day I do not understand why. It was opposed to her every trait of character—to everything she seemed to hold inviolable.

The simple truth perhaps was that she, too, may have come to the end of her rope in the ceaseless struggle of staving off day after day the butcher, grocer, milkman and landlord. She would have to do it still, of course, wherever we moved, but at least the old pleas and lies would not seem so worn and threadbare with a new butcher and landlord to tell them to. It may have been quite as simple as that. I cannot otherwise explain her immediate and delighted welcome of a change to which I had expected to find her in bitter and implacable opposition. I was a trifle stunned, in fact, by my almost too easy victory, but my mother's quick and unexpected agreement had an electrifying effect on all of us.

We talked and shouted and interrupted each other and began to plan immediately on where we would go—even of the possibility of finding a small flat and doing without boarders to help pay the rent, an idea that had not occurred to me but which delighted us all, for we shared an equal distaste for the dismal people who seemed forever to be moving among us.

The prospect of sitting down to a meal by ourselves and not having to share the rooms we lived in with others was something to savor and relish, even in anticipation. We became, all of us, a little intoxicated with the excitement of the great change to come, and by the time we went to bed that evening my brother spoke to me not as a stranger, I thought, for almost the first time.

"What's camp like?" he asked, as we lay side by side in the dark.

I tried to tell him and I spoke also of the good times I hoped we would have together, rushing headlong and too fast into an intimacy that he was not yet prepared to give, and he relapsed back into silence. But I was well content. It had been a remarkable and lucky day, and whatever misgivings I had about going to camp with a staff I had never laid eyes on, I brushed aside as the usual twinges of my overcautious nature and refused to be deviled by them. It was enough to fall asleep with a job safely tucked under the pillow and the knowledge that come fall, my eyes would not open each morning on that same grimy courtyard.

The next two weeks seemed to fly by with an unholy speed. There did not seem to be quite enough hours in the day for all that had to be done in the time that remained. The little-theatre group at the Labor Temple and the group in the Bronx were winding up the year with public demonstrations of their art. My days were filled with dress rehearsals and my evenings with the performances. The clutter of more than nineteen years of living had to be gone through and some of it discarded before our belongings could be put in storage, a task complicated by my mother's desire to hold on to every scrap. A place had to be found for her to live in while we were away and, if possible, a new flat spotted for our return. And endless hours on my own part were devoted to reassembling all the material Eddie and I had used at camp the previous summer, a good deal of which I had thoughtlessly mislaid and now could not find in the welter of furniture and boxes piled in every room.

In the midst of these last hectic days I made the unpleasant discovery that I possessed no summer clothes at all other than two pairs of bathing trunks faded green by the sun and a couple of sport shirts rather badly frayed around the collars. At Camp Utopia I had filled in my scant wardrobe by liberally borrowing whatever I needed from Eddie. All I had with which to make my debut as a full-fledged social director at the Half Moon Country Club, except for those bathing trunks and two bedraggled shirts, was the blue serge suit I walked around in every day.

Now, a sport coat and white flannel trousers were as necessary to a social director as a suit of armor to a Knight of the Round Table—perhaps a little more necessary, for a Knight without armor at King Arthur's Court would appear less foolish somehow than a social director making announcements in front of the curtain on show night, or appearing in the dining room and on the dance floor of the social hall, in a blue serge suit.

He need not outdress the Beau Brummells who arrived in camp every two weeks with wardrobes whose colors put the Japanese night moth to shame, but whatever else his wardrobe lacked, however sparse it might be, a sport coat and a pair of white flannel trousers were the dead rock bottom he could get by on. Those he had to have. I knew I could not go to camp without them, yet I doubted, in fact I knew, that by the time we paid the necessary deposit to the storage and moving people and left enough for my mother to live on until I could send her some money from camp, there would be nothing at all left to buy a handkerchief with, let alone a sport coat and a pair of white flannel trousers.

It was going to be embarrassing, but I would have to ask Mr. Axeler for a small advance. After all, he had said, "Anything you want, anything you need, just ask for it"—and this request after all was as much for his sake as for mine. He would certainly understand that a social director in a blue serge suit was a downright impossibility. Mr. Axeler did understand. Quickly and sympathetically he proved to be as charming, as forthright and as good-humored as he had been at our first meeting. Of course I must have the sport coat and the white flannels. He saw that at once. And perhaps even a change of sport coats and a pair of gray flannels as well.

There was one little hitch, however. He had partners, and one of the strict rules between his partners and himself was that no one of them was ever to advance any sum whatever to any of the employees no matter what the circumstances. He must have seen my face fall, for the smile came brightly on as though he had touched a switch under his desk, and his voice grew cheerful again. He had a solution, never fear. A dear friend of his owned a haberdashery store on Eighth Avenue. I was to go there, mention his name, select whatever I needed or wanted and have it all sent direct to the Half Moon Country Club and charged to him personally. Wouldn't that solve the difficulty? It would indeed. I thanked him profusely. We talked for a few minutes more, but now I could hardly wait to get out of the office and over to that haberdashery store.

Though I had never had the wherewithal with which to indulge myself, I was at that time and for a long time afterward absolutely clothes crazy. It amounted to a hunger for clothes I could never seem to satisfy. I professed to scorn the high-style outfits most male guests paraded around camp in, but secretly I envied them. I craved and coveted the sky-blue turtleneck sweaters and the striped jackets with brass buttons, with a multicolored handkerchief peeking discreetly out of the breast pocket, and a tie that matched, and white suede shoes with patent leather tops. I craved those absurd getups with a real passion.

It may be imagined, then, with what haste and urgency I made my way over to Eighth Avenue and that haberdashery store. I stood outside the shop admiring the display of shirts and coats and trousers in the windows for a full five minutes, and when I opened the door to step inside, it seemed as though every article of apparel on the shelves and hangers trembled with pleasure in anticipation of being on my person. I could hardly see anything at all at first, not because I had been standing in the bright sunlight outside, but because my eyes seemed blinded by the dazzling array of rainbow-hued wonders that might soon be mine.

I could hardly speak for a minute or two. Never before had I been in a clothing store with the opportunity of saying, "I'll take this—and give me two of those—" no one who has cared about clothes as I did, and who has never experienced the joy of being able to buy clothes for the very first time, can know or understand the almost sensual pleasure this can be. I proceeded to go on what can best be described as a "clothes drunk." I bought and bought the way a man, about to fall off the wagon, blindly and blithely starts on a lost weekend. I went a little berserk. The sport coat and the white flannel trousers were bought almost without looking at them, and I went on to splurge in sweaters, shirts, socks, ties and what is known in haberdashery circles as "novelties"—kerchiefs to wear twisted around the neck instead of ties, reversible two-toned pullovers, a beach jacket and sandals with flying fish all over them, and the crowning purchase of all, an utterly useless but completely irresistible smoking jacket with what appeared to be a coat of arms embroidered in silk thread-of-gold on the breast pocket. I stood in front of the mirror in it, staring at myself absolutely enraptured. Where or how or under what circumstances I expected to wear this thing of glory, even I could not have explained; but I knew that I was incapable of not buying it. Even the clerk who was waiting on me demurred at this obvious bit of folly and suggested I think it over and come in and try it on again when the owner of the shop, Mr. Axeler's friend, would be there himself to advise me, but I could not be dissuaded. Think it over indeed! I could almost not bear to take it off and hand it back to him to wrap.

By the time I finished, I had bought in all about $135 worth of clothes—an amount of money that in those days could have outfitted at least three people for two summers. The clerk, himself a little flushed at so large a sale, shook my hand and promised faithfully to explain everything to Mr. Axeler's friend and have it all charged and shipped immediately to Mr. Axeler in Vermont. I think he understood in a dim way the extent of my passion. I staggered out of the store as a drunk might stagger into the dawn from an all-night bar, wonderfully warm inside and satisfied to the core, my thirst quenched at long last. I well knew that I had bought foolishly and wildly, that I could not afford any of it, that I did not even know how it could be paid for. But for once, none of that seemed to matter in the least, any more than tomorrow's hangover seems to bother a man at the height of a wonderful jag; and trancelike I moved through the remaining days until we left, thinking of practically nothing but those clothes.

I opened each package over and over in my mind, I saw myself entering the dining room or social hall in one of the two-tone pullovers with a yellow kerchief tied around my neck. I even found a one-act play to do that would give me a chance to wear the smoking jacket on the stage. I might even, I thought, give a select party or two in my own cabin and as host wear the smoking jacket. I could barely wait for the sun to go down each evening and to come up again the next morning. My impatience to be off was doubled by the fact that each day that passed was one day less we would have to spend in that hated flat.

Yet when the day at last arrived and I opened my eyes to look for the last time at the streaked wallpaper on the bedroom walls, the elation that I had expected to feel was strangely missing. I could not think why. Perhaps the end of anything is somehow a little sad. Perhaps it seemed the final erasure of my aunt and my grandfather, whose living presence these rooms had known; or it may be that my feeling of abhorrence for the place was already expended, now that we were to leave it forever.

We must all have felt something of the sort, each one in his own way, for we walked down the four flights of stairs to the street soberly and without speaking, and stood, still silent, on the stoop in front of the house. To my mother's credit, she was for once untearful. Now that she might have rightly shed a tear or two, watching her family leave her and going off while she was to live alone in a furnished room, she was dry-eyed and cheerful. There was, as a matter of fact, no time for much of anything in the way of emotion. The moving van was at the curb, the men already clambering down from the truck, mercifully cutting short the good-byes. There was time for nothing but a quick kiss to each of us before she had to return upstairs with the moving men. She waved again from the front window as we got to the corner, and then we climbed the subway steps and were on our way.

THE RIDE to Vermont was an overnight one; and by coach, as we were going, it was long, hot and uncomfortable. The train seemed to make endless little stops, so that it was impossible to sleep except in fits and starts along with the train. Even if we could have slept, hunched up in the seats as we were, we gave up the pretense long before the train pulled into our station at six o'clock in the morning.

We scrambled onto the platform with our suitcases and bundles, unwashed, unkempt and hungry, and stood blinking in the uncertain light for a glimpse of the car that was supposed to meet us. It was nowhere in sight, nor was there anything to be seen that looked like a diner or restaurant. Quite some distance across the tracks there seemed to be a place with a light still on that looked like an all-night coffee shop or a bar and grill, but it was too far away to go and run the risk of missing the car. There was not even a ticket taker to ask a question or leave a message with. The ticket window was shut tight.

We sat down on our suitcases in the empty station and waited, shivering a little with sleepiness and hunger. "They must have had a flat tire," I said cheerfully, and then with a further attempt at cheerfulness, rendered quite hollow by the fact that my teeth were chattering, I spoke again. "Bad beginning, good ending. Isn't that what you always say, Pop?" I asked. He did not answer and I did not speak again. We just sat—staring miserably up the one road leading to the station that the car might appear on. Finally I got up and walked over to a door marked "Gentlemen." Inside, the washbasin was filled with cigar butts and what appeared to be a sodden remnant of the *Police Gazette*. The floor was littered with cigarette ends and toilet paper that had been used in lieu of towels—though how anyone could have washed his hands in that basin escaped me.

I let quite some time go by before I emerged from the washroom, because I was shaking with rage and a strange kind of panic. Our arrival seemed to me (who was forever on the lookout for omens, good or bad) to be an omen that foretold the whole horrible summer that lay ahead—I seemed to know at that instant that something was rotten in both Denmark and Vermont. I stood in that filthy washroom in a morass of indecision, unsure of whether to wait right there in the station for the next train out and go back to New York, or to go on. But where was the train fare to come from? And go back to what? Our furniture was in storage, my mother was in a furnished room; and outside my father and brother sat on two suitcases waiting for me to lead them on to the summer of milk and honey I had promised.

When I rejoined them, and sat down on my suitcase again, I knew we must go on, for there was no place else for us to go.

At eight thirty or thereabouts, some two and one-half hours late, a car drew up to the station with a fearful grinding of brakes. The driver, a grizzled, taciturn, unpleasant man, did not even bother to get out, but called out of the side of his mouth, "You the social director? Get in." I stared at him for a long moment. In some fatheaded way I had half expected Mr. Axeler himself to be in the car, to welcome us and smooth everything over with his easy charm and ready smile. Now there was not even a word of apology or regret for the two and one-half hours we had sat there waiting.

"Could we get a cup of coffee before we start?" I asked. "We've been sitting here a long time."

"You can get coffee at camp," he replied disagreeably, still talking out of the side of his mouth and making no move to help us load our suitcases and bundles into the car. He barely waited until we were seated, and then he slammed away from the station with the same grinding of brakes and squealing of tires. It did not occur to me until we were already under way to ask, "How far is it to camp?"

His reply, and he addressed no further words to us the rest of the trip, was, "Forty-five miles. And it'll take just as long as it takes me to get there," he added, just in case I might ask him a further question.

We rode in silence, too dispirited to talk among ourselves, but as I stared at the Vermont countryside whipping by, my spirits rose in spite of myself. One could not remain low in mind for long in the face of those beautiful hills and the fresh, clean fields dotted with trim farmhouses and grazing herds. Vermont is a feast to the eye, and a first glimpse of it on an early spring morning is enough to lift the heaviest heart or the lowest of spirits. I felt the weight on my chest begin to lighten. Things may not be as bad as you think, I told myself reassuringly. Everything was bound to take on a sinister look in that dark, depressing station, with no breakfast and that long, long wait. Anyway, why not wait and see? How could anything be really bad in this beautiful setting? My spirits shifted suddenly from low to high and I began to sing, partly out of relief but mainly, I think, because I was so pleased to feel my confidence returning.

Long before we reached the road that led into the club itself, the surrounding countryside suddenly changed for the worst. The hills and green fields stopped abruptly, as though a stage manager had called out, "Strike the set," to a crew of stagehands, and in place of the shimmering hills and lush green fields came a barren reach of flat, stony land with stunted trees and great rolling beds of poison ivy stretching away as far as the eye could see. There seemed to be nothing else on either side of the car for miles and miles, though I knew we must surely be approaching Lake Champlain itself and I had heard of its beauty and had seen photographs of it. Indeed, the Half Moon Country Club featured a stunning picture of the lake on the cover of its booklet.

Suddenly the car made a sharp turn around a bend and I saw a sign, hanging crookedly between two entrance posts, proclaiming,

"Entrance Half Moon Country Club." I stared hard at the sign, its painted letters peeling and flaking off, and I felt that tight knot beginning to form in my chest again. First impressions are likely to be true ones, and the first impression one received of the Half Moon Country Club even as one approached it was one of slovenliness. It was not really dirt that one was conscious of, for dirtiness is not always immediately visible to the naked eye; but slovenliness and loose management are somehow instantly and unpleasantly apparent, even as one drives through an entrance gate.

The crooked sign that swung lopsidedly in the breeze swung from chains that had the rust of years on them, and the boulders that lined each side of the dusty road had not seen a coat of white paint since they had first been put in as markers. What had once been a sorry attempt at flower beds between the boulders was now just weeds and poison ivy, and the road itself had large holes in it, still filled with rain puddles, so that the car had to twist and turn to escape the deepest ones. The very last hole, and the largest of all, the driver did not see or did not bother to by-pass, so that a wave of stagnant water swept over the car and drenched us all. The car had come to a stop in front of the main building of the Half Moon Country Club, and it seems quite fitting to me now that for the first moment or two after we got out of the car we actually could not see the building, or anything else, for that matter. Our faces, our hair and clothing streamed muddy water.

We stood there sopping wet—wiping the mud from our faces and eyes, and trying to look about us. The driver of the car had dumped our sodden suitcases and paper bundles on the ground beside us and rattled off without so much as a word of apology for the soaking. There was no one in sight, nor was there any sign of life within the building itself. I looked up at it and my heart sank. It was badly in need of a fresh coat of paint and its roof was pockmarked all over with sunbaked brown spots where the shingles had fallen off and had not been replaced. The middle section looked like nothing so much as an abandoned old shack—such as a fishing club might have put up to spend a few uncomfortable nights in— that had been added to in haphazard fashion until it had grown to be the ugly mass of wood and dented fly screens we now stood in front of. Torn yellow shades hung askew from the upstairs windows, and some badly worn and rapidly unraveling wicker furniture stood ghostlike on the porch.

My brother shot me a look. No words were needed for me to know what he was thinking. I looked away and spoke with an irritable assurance that could have fooled nobody.

"All camps look like this before they open," I said. "They're getting everything ready for Decoration Day. Don't let's just stand here looking—let's go find somebody."

I led the way inside and they followed, our shoes sloshing over the empty porch. There was a tiny lobby and registration desk just inside the door, and beyond this a rather large lounge or sitting room, with a sagging ceiling and enormous overstuffed chairs all garishly slip-covered and stiffly set out to face what appeared to be the dining room beyond, since we could see tables and chairs stacked high against one wall.

We proceeded on through, and since there seemed to be no sign of life in the dining room either, we went on in to the kitchen, a smoke-blackened cavern whose walls and cupboards suggested that the fire department had just left and there had not yet been time to wash away the soot and grime. The stove was thickly caked with last year's grease; a pile of dirty cups and saucers lay in the sink, a filthy dishrag flung over them. But an unmistakable coffee pot stood on the stove. It was a badly battered and dented old-fashioned enamel coffee pot, but I have never seen a more welcome sight in a kitchen anywhere. We made straight for it like lost souls. Holding my breath I shook it, then sighed with relief to find it half full and still warm. There was not a scrap of food to be found anywhere —at least none that had been left out in the open. A starving mouse would have headed back to the hills after one foray around that kitchen!

The icebox and one cupboard, however, had shining new padlocks on them—a pretty good hint of where the food was hidden —and probably the only new things in the whole damn place, I thought bitterly, as I walked back to the stove. "At least let's get warm and dry off," I called to my father and brother. "There's no food any place except what's locked up."

But my brother let out a sudden shout of victory. Rummaging around in the back of one of the cupboards he had come up with a box of Fig Newtons, obviously left over from last summer. They were hard as rocks, of course, but not moldy, and after submerging them in the boiling coffee for a while we stood by the stove fishing them out with spoons, downing the first food that had passed our lips in over fourteen hours.

It was while we stood by the stove gulping the last mouthfuls of the coffee and scooping up the fast disintegrating Fig Newtons, that the first sign of life at the Half Moon Country Club came in through the screen door that led out of the kitchen. He was a young man, a few years older than myself, with a fat, good-natured face covered at the moment with a thick layer of dust and wisps of straw and sawdust sticking to it, and he seemed totally unsurprised to see us standing around the stove, our damp clothes sending up little clouds of steam around our heads.

"So you got here," he said, addressing me directly. "The new social director, huh?"

I nodded. "I was beginning to think we had made a mistake— that we got here on the wrong day."

"Oh, no," he answered, "it's the right day. Mr. Axeler expected you all right. This your father and brother?" He evidently knew all about us. "My name's Herb Morris," he added, as we shook hands all around. "I'm the desk clerk when the season begins. Right now I'm unpacking new crockery and putting mattresses on the beds. Want me to take you to your bunks?"

"Thanks," I replied. "But where is Mr. Axeler?"

He gestured vaguely toward the outdoors. "Out there some place," he said.

"We didn't see him any place around when we drove up," I said. "I'd like to get to him."

"Oh, you'll see him," said Herb, smiling, "you can't miss him. He's on a horse."

I looked at him, for the smile apparently meant to convey something. "On a horse?" I asked.

"Never gets off it all summer," said Herb, and smiled broadly, "except to eat and sleep and go to the bathroom. He runs the whole place from that damn horse. We call him the Mad Cossack. You'll catch onto things soon enough. Want me to help you with your stuff?" He moved toward our suitcases and bundles.

"Thanks, Herb," I said gratefully. "That's about the first kind word we've had since we got off the train."

Herb grinned. "A kind word is what everybody needs the first time they get a look at this place. This way to the slave quarters, folks. Follow me. Your father's bunking in the main house, so I'll take him upstairs first."

We followed him up the stairs to a series of cubbyholes under the roof. There were four of these cubicles, each with walls and a door, but they could hardly be called rooms. There was no window, only a skylight, and though it was a cool spring morning outside, the airless, sun-baked room was already sweltering.

"Who else sleeps up here, Herb?" I asked, looking around the place in dismay.

"The baker and his two helpers," he replied. "They think it's cool up here, I guess, after standing in front of an oven all day. Here, let me open the skylight for you. I had to close it on account of the rain yesterday. It's not so terrible when it's open, but you're a dead duck if it rains during the night and the damn thing won't shut."

I hardly dared look at my father. He was sitting on the edge of the uncovered mattress, staring about him. He was not used to luxury in his surroundings, God knows; but he was shaken, I could see, by the utter squalor of this miserable hole under the roof. There was nothing I could find to say to him. I dared not try to explain away this new catastrophe. My brother was looking directly at me again and saying nothing.

"Why don't you unpack your stuff, Pop," I said instead. "I'll go find Mr. Axeler and come back for you." I turned to Herb again.

"Where do my brother and myself sleep?" I said, so inaudibly that he had to ask me to repeat it.

"Oh," he answered, "your brother bunks in Buckingham Palace with the rest of the kitchen help, the waiters and me, and you're all by yourself in the Bastille, over by the social hall. Come on," he yelled cheerfully, "this way to Buckingham Palace."

Buckingham Palace turned out to be a converted chicken house some hundred yards back of the kitchen, set tastefully between the cesspool and the incinerator, and landscaped at its entrance by uncovered garbage pails. One had to stoop to enter it and stay bent over until one stood in the middle under its V-shaped ceiling. It had been turned into a kind of army barracks, with two long rows of army cots lined up against both walls, foot lockers under the cots, and hooks in the wall above each cot to hang clothing from. There was an open shower and toilet at the far end of the room, uninhibitedly free of either shower curtain or door. Some naked electric light bulbs hung from the ceiling, last year's flypaper and dead flies still sticking to the cords.

Herbert bustled about seemingly oblivious of what we were thinking and feeling, which must have been all too clear from the stricken looks on our faces.

"Take this bed here next to mine, Bernie," he said. "These are the only two beds in the whole place that don't get the smell from the kitchen, the cesspool or the garbage. That's the one good thing about being up here first. Last year I had that bed over there, and half the nights I slept outside and let the bugs eat me, because I could stand the bugs better than the smell. Ready for a look at the Bastille?" he finished brightly, turning back to me.

"I think," I said darkly, "I think I'm ready for anything now."

I followed him out without looking back at my brother. What was there to do or say until I could think of a way out? I walked along with Herb, seemingly incapable of thinking of anything but finding Mr. Axeler and demanding our fare back home, contract or no contract, furniture in storage or no. Herb whistled cheerfully beside me.

"It's pretty crummy all right," he said blithely, "but what the hell?

Once you're here you're stuck good. It's too late to find another job for the summer. That's how he hooks everybody and keeps you here. If you need to make your tuition for the fall term in school, like me and the waiters and the rest, why once he's got you up this far away, what can you do?"

"But you were here last year, Herb," I said. "Why in the world did you come back?"

He shrugged. "Bad timing. My uncle promised me a job in his store and went back on his word. I waited just too long, so I had to run back to the Mad Cossack. It was the only summer job I could be sure of getting, and I need that tuition money. You'll get used to it. You get used to anything if you need the dough bad enough." He chuckled. "But I'll bet I'm the only one here from last year at that. He never gets the same dopes here twice."

"But how does he get guests to come to this place, Herb?" I asked. "They don't have to come up here—they can go to some decent place."

"Oh, it doesn't look as bad as this when it gets fixed up. He sprays some paint around and spreads some gravel, and puts some lousy geraniums on the porch and in the dining room." He grinned. "The slave quarters remain the same, though—just the way you saw. He gets away with it because the guests who come here are mostly the parents of the kids in his camp down by the lake. They only stay three or four days at best and they don't care much. They don't give a damn about having any fun—they don't expect to enjoy themselves. They just come up to see their kids swim around or get a medal for archery, and then get the hell out. He's got *them* hooked because it's the only place they can stay that's near the kids' camp. But last year he decided he wanted to attract a young crowd, so he built a social hall and hired a five-piece band and a social director." He stopped and laughed aloud. "That poor bastard social director! I bet he won't forget last summer for the rest of his life —that is, if he isn't in the booby hatch right now." He looked at me sideways. "How did you get hooked into this, by the way? From the guff he hands out in the office?"

I nodded.

"Yeah, he can sure make it dreamy," he went on. "I thought I was coming up to the Waldorf last year. I couldn't believe my eyes when I got here."

"Well, I'm not going to stay here," I said hotly, "I can tell you that."

He seemed genuinely surprised. "You're not?" he asked. "You've got something to go back to?"

"No," I admitted, "but I'm not going to stay here."

"I see," said Herb politely, immediately discerning the emptiness of the threat. "Well, in case you do stay, there's your cathedral. That's the social hall." He pointed to an unpainted building a few hundred yards ahead.

I followed his finger and stared at a small unpainted structure open on three sides and festooned across the front end with a score of what had once been Japanese lanterns and which now hung in ribbons, swaying limply in the breeze.

"Not exactly the Palace," said Herb, watching me stare. "Better come inside and have a look, anyway," he added. "If you do decide to stay, there's a hell of a lot to do."

Silently, I followed him across the field into the social hall. It was unpainted inside, as well as out, and had been constructed in the cheapest possible fashion. One good Vermont storm would have smashed it to smithereens, and I wondered how it had survived the winter winds. There were some non-survivors of the winter littering the floor—a chipmunk, several field mice, and a number of bats that had perished, I thought bitterly as I stepped over them, in a search for either entertainment or food. I stood staring up at the tiny stage. The curtain, half drawn, had a great hole in it, and what I at first took to be some sort of free-hand design across its center was merely bird droppings. The one trough of footlights had been viciously kicked in, a farewell gesture, I had no doubt, of that "poor bastard social director." I kicked at it myself and two beer cans rolled slowly out.

The floor of the stage itself was carpeted with the glass of broken light bulbs, and directly in the center stood a great mound of empty Coca-Cola bottles, at the top of which was a stick with a pair of torn lady's underpants hanging from it—a forlorn token of one of last summer's victories. I walked up onto the stage and peered into the one dressing room. Some animal had also died there, and although its remains were nowhere to be seen, the stench was deadly. I held my nose and walked over to read some words that were scrawled across the make-up table mirror. It was one succinct sentence consisting mainly of four-letter words and it suggested what Mr. Axeler could do with himself, his social hall, his guests and his camp—and it did not lean heavily on innuendo. I was glad I had braved the smell and walked over to the mirror. I felt better somehow for having read that message.

A large wardrobe trunk stood in one corner of the dressing room; I wanted to inspect it, but Herb's voice was calling to me from outside the social hall. "Hey, come on," he was shouting, "let's get going. I've got to get back to the mattresses."

I went out the back way and joined him. "All right," I said, "just show me where I bunk. I'll have to stay here for tonight anyway."

Silently he pointed to a tin-roofed shack almost directly in front of us. He sighed. "That's it," he said, "that's the Bastille. It's all yours."

I stared at it incredulously. "But that's a tool shed, isn't it?" I asked, still unable to believe what my eyes were seeing.

"It was a tool shed until last year," said Herb. "You hit it right on the nose. I guess the Mad Cossack ran out of lumber when the social hall was finished, so that's where the social director bunks."

He walked ahead of me and pushed open the door. "Phew," he exclaimed as a burst of fetid air rushed to meet him. "They ought to keep this door open. You could fry eggs in here with that tin roof." He stood aside to let me enter. Even Herb preferred to stay outside and let me look around alone.

I did not linger long. Rust-colored water, dripping slowly from the tin roof, had run down the discolored walls and formed little pools on the earthen floor which was rudely covered with wooden slats set fairly wide apart. One good rain could set the whole place awash, it seemed, for the ground under the slats was pure mud. Old toothpaste tubes, bottle caps, a shredded athletic supporter, and some rusted sardine cans lay scattered underneath the slats, just where they had been tossed the summer before. Whatever else he may have been, my predecessor was not a neat man, a fellow who could have believed that cleanliness had anything to do with godliness, and he had been richly free of the phobia that dirt breeds disease, for that room was as dirty per square inch as anything I have ever seen.

The temperature must have been somewhere in the high nineties and the air was as rank as the Jersey flats at the end of a heat wave. I began to feel a little queasy. I looked briefly at the army cot, its uncovered mattress darkly stained with spilled beer and coffee, and quickly rejoined Herb outside. I took a great lungful of fresh air, walked past him, and then threw myself full length down onto the ground.

Herb kneeled down beside me solicitously. "You all right," he inquired, "you feel sick?"

"No," I said. "I just had to lie down some place. I'm dead tired." It was true. The full flavor and scope of the morning's disasters seemed to have swept over me as I stood in that sweltering, filthy room, and I was suddenly desperately, deeply tired. I doubt if I could have walked another hundred yards.

Herb sat down beside me and chewed on a blade of grass for a while without speaking. "It won't be easy to get that fare back to New York out of him," he finally said. "That's been tried before."

I lay face down for another moment or two without answering. Then I sat up and looked back at the tool shed and the social hall. "No, I'm going to stay, Herb," I said. "I've got no choice—I've got to." I told him briefly of our plight, of our stuff in storage and no place to go back to, even if I could find another job in the city quickly, which I very much doubted.

"Yeah, I guess you're stuck," he said. "But you know something?" he went on. "Now that you know you're hooked and you've seen it, crummy as it is, it won't seem so terrible now. You'll see—that's the way it was with me."

He rose and stood peering down at me. "Anything else I can do or tell you about before I kick off? I've got to be getting back."

"No, thanks, Herb," I answered gratefully. "You've helped a lot just being around. Just tell me where I go to get my mail. I'm expecting some."

"There's no mail here for you yet," he said. "I'm in charge of the mail. No letters came for you at all."

"Not letters," I said, "packages. Some large packages. They must be here some place. They were sent up over two weeks ago."

He shook his head. "Haven't seen a sign of 'em," he said. "Did you send 'em c.o.d. or express collect? Because if you did, they won't deliver them up here—you got to go down into town and claim them at the post office."

"Oh, no," I answered, "they weren't shipped c.o.d. They were charged to Mr. Axeler personally but shipped direct."

Herb stared at me wide-eyed. "Charged to Mr. Axeler personally," he said.

"That's right," I replied. "He told me to charge it. I needed some clothes and he sent me to a friend of his and told me to charge anything I wanted to him and have it sent up."

Herb continued to stare. "And the man said he would?" he asked.

"No," I said, "the owner of the store wasn't there when I went, but the clerk who waited on me said he would tell him and send it up the next day. That was over two weeks ago," I added, "they must be here some place. You're sure they're not, Herb?"

Herb gave me a slow, patient smile, the smile of forbearance one gives to a not too bright child. "Yes, I'm sure they're not," he said. "How much did the bill come to?"

"It was quite a lot," I admitted. "I went a little crazy. I bought a hundred and thirty-five dollars' worth of clothes."

He burst into laughter and flopped down on the ground beside me, still laughing. "You're crazy, all right," he said. "Not because you bought that many clothes, but because you believed anybody who knew Mr. Axeler more than five minutes would let him charge a package of spearmint gum. Why, they won't trust him for a nickel around here. He has to pay cash before they even take a bunch of celery off the truck. You've got about as much chance of seeing those clothes up here as I have of flying over the lake by waving my arms up and down." He waved his arms up and down and fell to laughing again.

"But why would he send me there, Herb?" I protested. "Why would he do a thing like that if he knew the man would never send them?"

"Search me, brother." Herb shrugged. "He'll do anything or say anything to get out of a tight spot or to get you up here. The first time I walked out of that office he had me believing I was like his son and that by the end of the summer he might make me a partner in the damn place. He can make you believe the moon is green if he wants to. Those clothes are still right in that store where you bought them, boy, believe me!"

I looked at Herb and drew a deep breath. There was no question that what he was saying was true. I knew those clothes would never arrive now, and it was almost the cruelest disappointment of all. In some ridiculous fashion those clothes had remained at the forefront of my mind all through this horrible morning, and my first thought, once I knew that I would have to stay, had been of those packages waiting to be opened. They would have made up for a great deal.

For the second time in my adult life I felt like crying, and almost did. I was silent for so long a time that Herb finally turned to me and said, "What the hell? It's only clothes, and you won't have to pay for them now. Just wear what you've got."

"That's the trouble," I said bitterly. "*This* is what I've got." I gestured to the badly rumpled blue serge suit on my person.

"You mean that's *all* you've got?" asked Herb. "You came up here with that and nothing else?"

"That's all," I replied, "except for some bathing trunks and two sport shirts. What am I going to do, Herb?" I went on anxiously. "I can't walk around like this all summer."

"Gee, you can have anything I've got," he answered, quickly sympathetic, "but my stuff won't fit you. I'm too fat. Maybe when the waiters get up here you can borrow some things from them. They're a nice bunch, but they don't usually have too much in the way of clothes, I can tell you." He sighed. "You'll just have to hit him for some dough and go into town and buy some stuff, I guess," he said doubtfully.

"But will he give it to me?" I persisted. "That's what I did before and that's why he sent me to that store. He wouldn't advance me a cent."

"Oh, that's why he did it," said Herb. "Now I begin to see the light! Yes, sir, he parts from a dollar very slowly, I can tell you. You'll just have to keep after him till you get it, I suppose. Wait till he gets off that horse to go to the bathroom or something, then hit him over the head. Hey, lookit," he suddenly exclaimed, "over there." He leapt to his feet and pointed to a small building some distance away across the field. Two men, arms waving wildly above their heads, were running around the building and looking over their shoulders as they ran.

Herb squealed and jumped up and down with pleasure. "You'll see the Mad Cossack and his horse in a minute now," he yelled. "He's chasing 'em back inside."

"What is it?" I shouted back at him. "What's happening? Who are those men?"

"That's the bake shop," said Herb, "and those poor jerks are two Hunkies or Poles—they don't speak hardly any English—that he got up here as bakers. They took one look at the Iron Maiden they were supposed to work in and decided to quit beginning yesterday morning. He's been chasing 'em back in ever since with a whip. Yep, here he comes!"

With a wild Cossack yell, or what I took to be a wild Cossack yell, Mr. Axeler rounded the corner of the building on his horse. It was a large black animal and he rode it well. He was dressed in riding breeches and puttees and a glaring red shirt, his uniform for the summer, I was to learn. And sure enough he carried a long black whip, which he used with extreme skill and dexterity.

At sight of him the two men fled around the corner of the building, arms still waving, only to come back into sight a moment later with Mr. Axeler close at their heels and snapping the whip around their feet, so that blobs of mud spattered over their clothes. I watched, dumfounded. He was obviously not trying to hit them with the whip, for he could have easily sliced them to shreds, but only to frighten them back into the bake shop. They all circled the building two or three times more, the two men running wildly in front of the horse, the whip slashing the ground all around them, until finally the poor creatures gave up and retreated to the doorway where they stood shaking their fists at Mr. Axeler. He motioned them back into the bake shop with the butt end of the whip, and with a last shaking of fists, they went in and closed the door behind them.

Herb was still hopping up and down beside me. "Hey, you Mad Cossack you," he now yelled across the fields, knowing full well Mr. Axeler could not hear the words, "hey, you son-of-a-bitch you, your poor bastard social director is here. Come on over, you son-of-a-bitch Cossack, and say hello."

Mr. Axeler, conscious of someone yelling across the fields, turned the horse around and looked in our direction. Herb waved cordially at him. "You stink on ice, you Mad Cossack you," he yelled exuberantly and waved him toward us.

Mr. Axeler nudged the horse and galloped quickly over. He reined the horse to a circus-like stop directly in front of me and smiled down. It was the same candid, forthright smile, a little more dazzling in fact now that he was seated on a horse.

"Welcome, welcome," he said, "welcome to our Half Moon family."

I looked up at him and opened my mouth to speak. Before I could get a word out, he had reined the horse around and was galloping off, calling back over his shoulder, "We'll talk, we'll talk. Lots to do first; lots to do. Anything you want, anything you need, just ask."

We watched in silence until he disappeared over the horizon. "Yeah," said Herb sourly, breaking the silence, "anything you want, just ask. Some fat chance . . . and first you gotta catch him. Now you see what I mean, don't you?"

"Yes," I answered heavily, "now I see. Thanks for everything, Herb." I held out my hand to him and we shook hands rather solemnly. His unfailing good spirits seemed to have deserted him momentarily and he walked away dispiritedly without another word. I stood for a moment longer in the open field, then I moved slowly toward the Bastille. If I was going to sleep there tonight, there was certainly, as Mr. Axeler phrased it, lots to do, lots to do.

I kicked open the door and walked in. There flashed to my mind the fantasy I had concocted back in New York of playing host to a select party and wearing that glorious but now non-existent smoking jacket, and I laughed aloud as I looked around me. My second season at camp and my first as a full-fledged social director has officially begun, I thought bitterly, as I reached down and began to gather up the mess from beneath the slats of the floor. I wondered ruefully if the theatre was really worth it!

SOME TEN days later, the weekend before Decoration Day, the first guests began to arrive, and the summer of my discontent swung into full gear. It was not, I must record truthfully, a summer of complete, unrelieved misery. At twenty one does not remain utterly miserable for long stretches of time, no matter how bad the conditions may be under which one lives and works. At twenty one awakes every morning with the dewy-eyed illusion that this day cannot be as bad as the day before, and the resilience of twenty—the ability to bounce back in spite of bad food, long hours and sleeping in a wet, airless hole—is prodigious. Until the very end of the summer I was never quite as miserable as I had been the day of our arrival, because there was literally never any time after that to stop and think of how miserable one was. The small daily miseries of the Half Moon Country Club faded into the large catastrophes that came along one by one and reached a climax at the end of the summer in a disaster of Götterdämmerung dimensions. These recurrent catastrophes were the peaks of the icebergs that dotted the journey across the sodden sea of that summer, and one or two of them, I must admit, were of my own making.

The first one came with the very first show and on that Decoration Day weekend. Pigheadedly, I had chosen to go ahead with my program of O'Neill, Shaw and Kelly, despite the pathetically inadequate facilities of the Half Moon's social-hall stage, and for the big Decoration Day splash I elected to put on *The Emperor Jones* and play the leading role myself. This was stubbornness of a very tall order indeed, particularly since those sterling actors I had been promised, the counselors of the children's camp, had not yet arrived and I was left with only the six musicians and the operatic nurse to help me put on the play.

Doggedly, almost revengefully, I went ahead nevertheless; mainly I think as a just punishment for Mr. Axeler, for from the very beginning it was easily apparent how bad it was going to be and I could certainly have switched to something else. But I suppose it must have given me some sort of grim satisfaction to know that the first and one of the most important shows of the season was going to be a fiasco, for this was one of the few ways I had of getting back at Mr. Axeler.

The Decoration Day show, the July Fourth show and the Labor Day show were the high-water marks of the camp season that a social director tried to make as good as possible—presenting himself and his staff as contenders for the laurels of the competitive camp circuit and trying to insure a better job for himself the following season. Not only was his own reputation as a social director at stake with these three shows, but the reputation of the camp as well. For on those weekends the camp was at its most crowded, and on the Decoration Day weekend especially, the guests who saw the first show of the season were the ones most likely to go back to the city and spread the word that Camp So-and-So had a fine social director that summer. Moreover, a good report spread by the guest grapevine after the Decoration Day weekend could easily help to keep the camp filled for the rest of the summer.

I was thoroughly aware of this, and of the fact that I was quite likely digging my own grave as well as burying Mr. Axeler, since other camp owners kept an up-to-the-minute check on what was going on in rival camps and which social directors were doing the best shows. But my fury and resentment at Mr. Axeler were such that I was perfectly willing to foul my own nest if I succeeded in unfeathering his. For one thing, I still smoldered and smarted over the slick way I had been completely hoodwinked and trapped, and

[198]

for another, my clothes problem, with the arrival of the first guests, had become suddenly and painfully acute. It was the clothes, I think, more than anything else that made me plunge implacably and vengefully ahead with *The Emperor Jones*. For though I had caught Mr. Axeler unhorsed two or three times, my pleading had got me exactly nowhere. He feigned astonishment at his friend the haberdasher's failure to send up the clothes and blandly suggested I drive into the village, get what I needed and charge it to him. But not one cent of hard cash could he be pried loose from.

When I taxed him with downright dishonesty and refused to go on another fool's errand, far from being outraged, he was charm and urbanity itself. "Maybe you're right," he admitted, "these Vermont shopkeepers are funny about money."

"Everyone's funny about money," I said acidly, "especially when they don't get paid."

He laughed delightedly, as though I had just made a quip of Oscar Wildeian flavor. "Money, money, money," he chortled. "It's good I don't think about it too much—I wouldn't sleep nights. Come," he added, smiling that damnably honest smile of his, "I'll show you the books—I'll open the safe in the office. Any money you find there, you take and go buy the clothes. Every cent of ready cash we have we use to get the camp open every year, and until the guests start to pay there's not a penny left over. The cupboard is bare, my boy," he sighed, "but come around and ask me again next week and you won't go away empty-handed."

As usual he was lying. It was not until the end of June, some five weeks later, that I was able to gouge twenty-five dollars out of him and finally buy that pair of white flannel trousers and a blue sport coat with brass buttons. Meanwhile, it was necessary to come to terms and quickly with my lack of wearing apparel. I knew I couldn't appear in the dining room for all three meals in the same blue serge suit without advertising my plight, and while I could walk around camp during the day in bathing trunks and a shirt, a jacket was demanded in the dining room for all meals, and I could not forever continue to wear bathing trunks at night in order to

[199]

preserve for the shows the one good pair of pants I possessed, even if that were feasible.

I solved the problem ingeniously enough, since it had to be solved, but it was a painful and humiliating solution that I came up with. To this very day I can still feel a flush of embarrassment when I think of the absurd spectacle I must have presented for five solid weeks, and for years afterward I would cross to the other side of the street if I recognized a guest of that summer who had seen me in one of the grotesque getups I affected, for I used the costumes in the camp wardrobe trunk and pretended that my comic appearance was part of a social director's job of "making fun" for the customers.

Actually, I suppose, I was lucky to find even a wardrobe trunk at the Half Moon Country Club, though every camp no matter how small possessed a costume trunk which was replenished from year to year by purchasing cheap castoff outfits of any description from the big Broadway costume companies, Eaves and Brooks. For a hundred dollars or so, Eaves and Brooks would ship to camps a conglomerate assortment of costumes that were too threadbare for further rentals, but which might still be usable in camp shows, and the wardrobe trunk was considered as necessary a part of social-hall equipment as the front curtain.

The costumes, needless to say, were discolored and musty, and sometimes almost in shreds, but by switching them around with a redoing here and there, they could be made to serve well enough for a season and were invaluable if one were doing a play or skit that called for a military uniform or a Spanish dancer's outfit or the inevitable Indian chief's headdress.

Once my mind was made up as to what I had to do, and that appearing in the costumes was the only way out, I took the stuff out of the trunk in the dressing room and spread them about me on the stage. True to form, Mr. Axeler had purchased the cheapest and oldest rags that could be bought, and most of them were stiff not only with the sweat of last summer, but with the perspiration of the hundreds of panic-stricken amateurs who had worn them all across the country and sweated off their stagefright in them.

I selected the least smelly and disreputable of the lot, then summoned the six musicians, who were at the moment my complete social staff. "I'm going to pep things up a little in the dining room and the social hall," I announced. "I'm going to come in in a different costume for each meal and also in the social hall at night, and whatever I wear I want the trumpet and the sax to give me an appropriate fanfare before I appear. See?"

They did not see. They looked at me as though I had taken sudden leave of my wits.

"It's simple enough," I went on. "For instance, I'm going to come in to lunch today as a Confederate general." I held up a bedraggled uniform, its epaulettes hanging over the shoulders in shreds, for illustration. "Get it? Well, you precede me and play 'Dixie'—play it twice, walking in and out among the tables. Then I'll make an entrance. And if I come in tonight as Paul Revere, you play 'Yankee Doodle.' I'll always let you know beforehand what I'll be wearing. It's a good stunt and it works fine," I added, with a certainty I was far from feeling as they continued to stare at me.

"Well, it's 'Dixie' for lunch," I said irritably. "I did this last year at Camp Utopia and it was a big hit, so just do it," I lied.

"Okay," said the piano player resentfully, "I guess we have to do it." They shuffled off, muttering among themselves. This was their usual display of enthusiasm for anything they were asked to do, particularly if the request came from me. They took very little pains to hide their dislike and resentment of me, and I in turn made no bones about how I felt about them. They were a sorry, pimply-faced lot and from my first glimpse of them I had known what to expect in the way of help. It came as no surprise to me that they would not take kindly to the idea of being impressed into *The Emperor Jones* as jungle natives, of having to black up, not just their faces, but their entire bodies as well; but there was nothing they could do about it.

They walked through the days in a stunned, somnambulistic fashion, as if they had never quite recovered from the initial shock of finding themselves where they were. They had been as stunned, in fact, as I had been by their first look at the Half Moon Country

Club, but they played each of their musical instruments so horribly that I could feel no sympathy for any of them, and they had been remarkably lazy and unco-operative in helping to clean out the social hall, and even their own quarters, which were even filthier than mine were.

I watched the trumpet player and the saxophonist take their instruments and walk out of the social hall, and I looked down at the uniform I still held in my hand. It was almost lunchtime, and if I was going to do it, I must do it now, or I knew I might not have the courage to do it at all. I got into the trousers and coat, tied the sash around the middle and placed the hat (at least a size too small for me) on my head. I tried not to look into the mirror but I could not refrain. I looked ridiculous. The effect was lugubrious and sad, somehow, not comic. I looked woebegone and foolish, like a child caught in the act of trying on his father's clothes, and the expression of exasperated martyrdom on my face added to the impression that someone had just shouted, "Take those things off right away and put them back."

But I had gone too far now, with both the musicians and myself, to back down, in spite of my image in the mirror; and the effect would be even more ridiculous, I told myself, if I walked into the dining room in a blue serge suit while the trumpet and saxophone played "Dixie." I grimly glued on a mustache, then watched from the window until I was sure that the last guest had entered the dining room. Then I ran as fast as I could across the fields until I reached the porch of the main building. Being caught in the open sunlight in that outfit, and having to explain why I was got up in such fashion, would have robbed me of whatever little courage I had left.

The two musicians stood waiting sullenly inside the doorway. "All right," I said, "go on in and play." They put the horns to their lips and blasted into the opening bars of "Dixie." From the porch outside I could see every head in the dining room turn. I watched the two musicians march amongst the tables, blaring away, and took a deep breath—they were almost through the second chorus. I had to get in while the music still played or I knew I might turn tail and run.

I took another deep breath and stalked into the dining room, pausing dramatically in the doorway. "General Nuisance of the Deep South," I announced in a billowing Southern accent, "is up North here in your midst for a short stay to see how you damn Yankees socialize in the hot summer weather, and has been delegated by your social director to make the following announcements of the events of the afternoon." I stopped and gave what I presumed sounded like a rebel yell. The entire dining room broke into delighted laughter and applause. They had listened thunderstruck for a moment, as well they might have, in stony silence, not knowing quite what was going on; but now they realized that it was the social director "making fun" in the dining room.

They greeted the announcements I made of the afternoon's events with more shouts of laughter and applause, and I finally sat down at my table to eat lunch, dripping wet and throbbing with embarrassment and rage. The rage was directed at Mr. Axeler, who had appeared in the dining room in the middle of all this and was now moving among the tables and beamingly accepting compliments on how well the new social director "made fun." He even had the gall some weeks later to suggest that I keep on with it, even after I finally had some clothes of my own, and I strongly suspected him of holding back the twenty-five dollars he grudgingly gave me until the very last moment, for there could be no doubt that the guests liked it. Too well. To my horror they looked forward to these appearances and even tried to guess what disguise I would turn up in next.

That evening I appeared in the social hall as Tecumseh, an old Indian scout, and was greeted by shrieks of appropriate laughter and applause, and the following day at lunch, to the tune of "Turkey in the Straw," I walked in as Daniel Boone, coonskin cap and all, thereby anticipating the Davy Crockett craze by some twenty-five years. But the more they laughed and applauded, the more I loathed them, myself and my employer. And every time I entered the dining room or social hall in some ridiculous getup

[203]

I had to take a deep breath the moment before, because I trembled for fear that somehow a stream of filthy epithets would, in spite of myself, issue from my lips, instead of the announcements of the afternoon's or evening's activities.

It was in this actively vengeful mood that I went through with the rehearsals of *The Emperor Jones*, knowing full well it was going to be bad, but never, even in my wildest fantasies of evening the score with Mr. Axeler, imagining just how much of a nightmare that evening was going to turn out to be. It may well be that my appearances as Long John Silver, Louis XIV and Abraham Lincoln during the days preceding the show had ill prepared the audience for my appearance as the Emperor Jones on the social-hall stage that Saturday night. The clientele of the Half Moon Country Club were ill-prepared enough, of course, in quite another way, to witness the O'Neill tragedy. I doubt if ten persons among them had ever heard of O'Neill at that time, and their expectation of the big Saturday night show on the Decoration Day weekend was always of a musical potpourri of some sort, full of topical allusions and camp jokes.

It could have been predicted, I suppose, but it had not occurred to me, that when I came onto the stage as the drunken, tragic emperor, they took it for granted that this was a skit satirizing my own comic getups, and they roared with laughter. The fact that I was in blackface seemed to make it even funnier, and they applauded generously and patiently waited for me to burst forth in song or go into a soft-shoe routine. When it slowly dawned upon them that they were being asked to sit through a serious and tragic play, I could feel them settle back, angry and disappointed. A few people in the front row got up from their seats and walked out, raising their voices above mine on the stage to announce they were going to play cards.

I had other things to worry about, however, than a disgruntled audience and a few walkouts at that moment. Even nature herself, it seemed, had chosen to conspire against me this terrible evening. The day had dawned bright and hot, but suddenly in mid-afternoon the sun had disappeared and a mass of freezing air had settled over the countryside. I learned later that this brief cold spell is something of a Vermont phenomenon, appearing sometimes in late spring or even early summer. An actual frost could make a sudden quick havoc of the Vermont countryside and damage crops and flowers in its brief overnight stay.

This fiendish cold spell had chosen to make its appearance on the afternoon of the day I was doing *The Emperor Jones,* the greater portion of which is played by the emperor stumbling through the steaming jungle clad in nothing but a loincloth. I had shivered with more than the cold as I made up, for hailstones as large as marbles had fallen over the camp at dinnertime and immediately afterward the sharp stinging cold of a winter evening had settled in.

The audience had arrived wrapped in sweaters, raincoats and blankets they had taken from the beds, and a biting wind whistled through the open social hall. I was all right, of course, during the first scene, where the emperor makes his appearance in uniform before he flees the palace to the jungle. But what would happen when I appeared in a loincloth and had to speak the recurrent line, "I'se meltin' wid de heat," I did not choose to think about.

Sure enough, at my first appearance in the second scene, naked except for the loincloth, and my first cry of "I'se meltin' wid de heat," an irrepressible giggle escaped from the darkened hall and swept over the footlights. I quaked inwardly and waited for the worst to happen. The worst was not long in coming.

There were a few "ssh-sshes" from the more well-mannered and sympathetic of the audience; but when the skinny, silly-looking and easily recognizable musicians stepped out from behind the cardboard palm trees and stood there shivering, the entire social hall broke into a gale of uncontainable laughter. They were funny-looking enough, God knows, without their teeth chattering and their legs shaking from the cold, but they had so resented having to put on the black body make-up that they had applied it to themselves in streaks and patches. They looked now like nothing so much as six refugees from a leper colony or the victims of some virulent skin disease.

Moreover, the drummer, who had rather a large pot belly for

one of his tender years, had chosen out of some ostrich-like vanity not to apply the black make-up to this portion of his anatomy at all, so that a round white globe swung gently above his loincloth and made him appear about to give birth at any moment. I dared not steal more than a glance at him myself, for shivering and miserable though I was, I would have been hard put not to have joined in the uncontrollable laughter that greeted his every movement across the stage. Not unnaturally he thought his loincloth had come unstuck, and the more frantically he tugged at it and tried to cover himself, the more the audience howled.

To make matters worse, when the tom-toms started, two or three of the musicians gave a terrible start, quite as though they had not heard the drums all through rehearsals, and one of the loincloths actually did come unstuck on one of them. He made a tremendous grab and retrieved it just in the nick of time, but not before the audience had given him a round of applause and shrieked with glee.

My own teeth were chattering now, not only with the cold but with the agony of knowing that I must play it through to the end somehow, for *The Emperor Jones* is really a lengthy one-act play and is played in its entirety without intermission. There was no chance for me to get off the stage, for either me or the audience to recover ourselves, and I could tell they were now in a state approaching hysteria. They could not help themselves by this time, and laughed at nothing and everything. When this kind of laughter sweeps through an audience it is a kind of mass hysteria.

They laughed in that social hall when there was seemingly nothing whatever to laugh at. Even the recollection of something earlier would send someone in the social hall off into a peal of laughter on his own, and the rest of the audience would helplessly join in. They stamped their feet and banged on the chairs and whistled each time that idiot musician with the pot belly had to cross the stage, exactly as though he were Gypsy Rose Lee doing a strip-tease, and finally they began to beat time with the tom-toms, drowning me out altogether. I was beyond caring now, however. I doggedly mouthed lines and kept thinking of standing under a hot shower and drinking some boiling coffee to get warm again, if ever I could. I seemed to be aching cold in every joint.

At the final moment of the play, when I lifted the revolver to my temple and shouted, "The silver bullet!" and pressed the trigger and the off-stage revolver did not go off, it mattered very little. In an evening of such glorious failure, the traditional blank cartridge failing to go off seemed no more than a slight mistake. Even the audience was too exhausted from laughing to do more than send up a token roar at this ultimate fiasco. I dropped down to the stage anyway, dead in more ways than just play-acting, and waited for the curtains to close. They slowly drew together, and to my amazement the closing was greeted with a tremendous salvo of applause and cheers.

I could not understand the applause at first, until I realized I had evidently given them as good a time for the wrong reasons as if I had put on a funny, regulation Decoration Day show. I took one half-hearted bow and marched wearily off to the showers, the still shivering musicians trailing silently after me. It was over, at any rate, and I could even feel a kind of comradeship for those hapless musicians who had suffered through it with me.

It was not quite over, however. What we did not know until we stood under the showers was that the end of *The Emperor Jones* was not yet, and that its marks would remain, like the Scarlet Letter, to brand us for quite a while. At first we thought that the black body make-up would not come off our bodies no matter how hard we scrubbed because the water trickling thinly out of the nozzle was, as usual, barely warm. But as we scrubbed and scrubbed each other until our bodies grew red and burning, it became apparent that the body make-up I had found in the make-up box in the dressing room must have been purchased by Mr. Axeler from the leftover stock of some store in the village and had probably been lying on the shelves ever since local minstrel shows had gone out of style in the State of Vermont. Whatever ingredient it originally contained to make it wash off with soap and water had long since evaporated along with minstrel shows.

I dispatched one of the musicians for a can of kerosene and we doused ourselves with it, but the stuff still clung in large black spots to various portions of our bodies and faces with octopus-like tenacity. It did not come off that night or the next morning, or for some weeks following.

The musicians went off the following day and among some secluded rocks began to acquire an all-over tan; this helped somewhat, in the sense that they finally achieved one color all over, with what appeared to be black polka dots underneath. But since I could not take the time out for a suntan, I walked around with my black spots open to view in all sorts of untoward places until the beginning of August. All that finally served to remind me of that night was the mustache I grew to hide an upper lip that still looked as though I might plunge into an imitation of Charlie Chaplin at any moment.

But there was one figure of that summer that was to remain with me for thirty years afterward. His name was Joseph M. Hyman and he was a paying guest of the Half Moon Country Club. He had wandered into one of the last rehearsals of *The Emperor Jones* and had stood at the back for almost two hours quietly watching us. Now, a social director did not take kindly to guests wandering into the social hall during a rehearsal, but there was not much he or his staff could do about it. Since we could not order a guest out of the hall, our only defense against guests who plunked themselves down on chairs directly in front of the stage and stared at us while we rehearsed, was to give cues to each other in absolute whispers the moment any guests appeared. It always worked well. The starers and gapers, unable to hear anything of the rehearsal, grew bored quickly and usually wandered out of the hall in very short order. This particular guest, however, whom I had glimpsed out of the corner of my eye as he came into the social hall, did not plump himself down into a chair in front of the stage, but remained where he was at the far end of the hall, watching and smoking one cigarette after the other until the rehearsal ended some two hours later.

This was such strange behavior for a guest that I was sufficiently intrigued to come down from the stage, instead of leaving by the back door, and cross the length of the hall to where he still stood.

"You're a bitter-ender," I said. "Like what you saw?"

He did not reply, but offered me a cigarette instead. "How did you happen to get to a place like this?" he asked. "You deserve something better."

"It's a long story," I replied. "I'm trapped like a rat for the summer anyway. You interested in the theatre?" I asked.

Again he did not reply directly. "You seem to be pretty short-handed," he said. "If you need someone to work the lights and the curtain I'll be glad to help out. I'll make myself available for all the rest of the rehearsals whenever you need me."

I looked at him, for he was obviously dead serious and the offer was a kind one—there was no doubt about how short-handed I was and how desperately I needed someone I could depend on to work the light cues and curtains.

"You mean it?" I asked. "You have to stick around here a good many hours and maybe all night long on Friday. You won't get much chance to do anything else, you know."

"I know," he replied, "but if you want me to, I'll do it. It's not such a big favor," he grinned. "From what I've seen of the other guests I won't be missing much!"

"It's a big favor to me," I said gratefully. "Can you meet me back here about five o'clock? I'll have the light cues all written down for you and we can go over them together."

"Sure," he answered, and held out his hand. "My name is Joe Hyman, by the way."

It was the first time I heard the name of the man that I was to turn to so many times afterward in time of distress or decision. We shook hands and walked down toward the lake together, neither one of us having the faintest awareness that at every critical moment of my life from that time onward Joe Hyman would always be at my side. He was then a man in his middle or late twenties, his gaunt and saturnine features indelibly trademarked by a smile of derision and disbelief that seemed to hover forever about his lips. In spite of his misanthropic mien, however, there was about him an aura of innate goodness that belied the cynical gleam in his eyes. He was stubborn, tactless, outrageously certain of his opinions, anti-social, and chronically unenthusiastic about life in general and people in particular, to almost the same extent that I was opposite in all these things. Two more diverse people in temperament and character would be hard to place side by side in enduring friendship.

Yet out of this first meeting came one of the most rewarding relationships of my life. I suppose his passion for the theatre was the bond that initially sealed the friendship between us, for he was a businessman who hated business, and he was in fact as wide-eyed and stage-struck about the theatre as I was. For some reason, and it must have been a twisted reason of his own for he had a maddeningly perverse turn of mind, he believed in me immediately, and luckily for me he was a man of incorruptible honesty and steadfastness.

My CHIEF CONCERN, now that the opening show and the opening week of camp were over, was for my father and brother. I had had no choice but to let them survive as best they could through these first two weeks, for I was having some difficulty in surviving them myself. I suspected, however, that whatever hopes I may have had of bridging the gap between my brother and myself had now grown slimmer, if indeed they had not vanished altogether.

He had had, of course, no actual knowledge of what my duties as a social director would entail; but I knew that some of the posturings and foolishness he would see me engaged in would come as something of a shock to him, for he had never before seen this side of me; he was then, as now, a shy, private and intensely conventional fellow, but I took it for granted that in the loose and silly climate of camp he would accept my sometimes embarrassing behavior as a necessary part of my job. Unfortunately, he did not. Whatever hope there may have been for any kind of intimacy between us that summer vanished the day I stood in the doorway of the dining room dressed in that first ridiculous getup.

He had a tray full of dirty dishes in his hands when I made my appearance as a Confederate general—and for a moment I thought he was going to let the tray drop to the floor. Instead, he stood staring at me as though he were looking into a distorting mirror in some nightmare amusement park, and then dashed out red-faced and indignant. At my subsequent appearances he scurried out of the dining room as fast as possible, as if to disclaim any part of family relationship between us, and he avoided me as much as possible—not without, however, casting a malevolent glance in my direction if our paths happened to cross.

My father was an altogether different story—my father, in fact, turned out to be the surprise of the summer, for if my brother was seeing a side of me that he had never known before, I was seeing my father in an altogether new and quite astonishing way. From the night the canteen in the social hall opened and he stood behind the counter dispensing soft drinks, cigarettes and cigars, ten years seemed to drop from his shoulders and he became a loquacious, merry and delightful human being. He quickly established himself as a camp favorite, and he knew it and enjoyed every moment of his popularity.

Though neither his sons nor his wife seemed to have been aware of it, the simple fact was that my father had grown increasingly lonely as his role in the family circle grew dimmer and as my mother's dominant personality gradually rubbed out his own more gentle one. He had withdrawn more and more silently into himself. As I returned home each evening, I had grown used to seeing him sitting at the window, wrapped in an old gray sweater. Now he blossomed in a hundred different enjoyable ways. There was something heart-warming as well as faintly comic in seeing him hurrying all over camp at a fast clip, with never the slightest reference to the hacking cough that had seemed as much a part of him as the old gray sweater and his silence.

The cough and the sweater and the silence disappeared forever, as his loneliness was replaced by the newly discovered pleasure of being accepted for the sunny creature he really was, now that he was at last relieved of the role of husband and provider, and there was never the slightest complaint about the terrible cubbyhole he slept in or the long hours he worked. I doubt if he noticed either one, so heartily did he continue to revel in and enjoy every moment of what was to me this most miserable of summers.

I was grateful enough that this should be so, not only for his sake but for my own, for there was little I could have done about it in the way of help. The daily routine of camp activities was now in full swing, and as they ground steadily along I had time for little else but to grind ponderously along with them and to fall heavily into bed in the Bastille each night, trying not to lie too long awake in contemplation of the next day's program.

After a few weeks I settled into a lengthy siege of melancholia, from which I could not seem to rouse myself and on which outward events, including the ever-recurring camp crises, major or minor, seemingly made no impression whatever. There is a point where bottled-up rage, combined with the continuous and unending drudgery of a job that one hates, can give rise to a kind of homicidal mania. By the end of July, when campfire nights, dress-up nights, games nights, Saturday night shows and guest parties all seemed to blur together in a stream of deadly tedium, I began to indulge in a series of conscious daytime fantasies that had a touch of the paranoiac in them. I would "fantasy" myself setting fire first to the social hall and then to the main building, and these fantasies were not merely simple instantaneous bursts of psychic satisfaction that flashed through my mind, but hour-long, consciously induced daydreams filled with minute and scrupulous detail, all constructed anew each day, with a beginning, a middle and an end. The end was always, of course, the gratifying picture of the charred remains of the Half Moon Country Club still smoking behind me as I took off down the road to the railroad station to catch the train for New York.

Another manifestation of my sickly state of mind at this time was my deep and obsessive concern with money. I not only literally counted out every penny I spent, I grew incapable of spending the most trifling sum without experiencing a real and sharp stab of pain at the pit of my stomach, and almost without being aware that I was doing so, I gradually began spending less and less, until I had stopped using my money completely. Instead, I would stand by the canteen in the social hall of an evening and cadge cigarettes and Coca-Colas from the guests. I was open and shameless and compulsively driven into what was little short of outright begging night after night, and though I understood very well what I was doing, I could not stop. I would stand at a guest's elbow, staring hungrily at him as he smoked or drank, until he was sufficiently embarrassed to offer me a cigarette or a Coke, and for the space of six weeks I drew not one penny of my salary except the ten dollars I sent to my mother every Monday morning to pay for her room and board.

For the last two weeks of this curious period I would not even buy toothpaste and did not brush my teeth at all, nor would I send out any laundry, since we had to pay for laundering ourselves, and I grew a sparse and scraggly beard in order not to buy razor blades and shaving cream. I was not only unshaven, but unwashed and dirty as well. Then, as strangely as it had begun, this obsession about money completely disappeared. With it a large portion of the melancholy and despair seemed to lift also, and I shaved off the beard and was clean once more.

It was not that life in camp grew any more pleasant, for as the season rounded into August, the guests came in ever-increasing numbers, and the social activities pulsed and throbbed through every hour of the day and evening at a constantly accelerated pace. I think I finally was beginning to realize that the summer was coming to an end, a fact that had seemed to hold no reality at all for me during the endless month of July. Now that I believed it with some degree of inner conviction, I began to mark off the days remaining until Labor Day as I dropped off to sleep each night, much as prisoners are supposed to mark off a calendar as they await the end of their prison term, and the last two weeks of camp rushed headlong into the big Labor Day weekend almost without my being aware of it.

On Labor Day night, as the curtains closed on the final show of the season, I stood on the stage stock-still for a long moment, waiting to have the realization that it was over and done with at last flood through every particle of my being—but nothing happened. I could feel nothing at all but the same dull insensibility with which I had managed to blot out so much of the summer. What we badly needed at this moment—waiters, musicians and all—was an innocent relief of some sort to snap the tension, such as the Great Mustard Fight at Camp Utopia. But we were all too weary, and desperately sick of each other and of the Half Moon Country Club, to do anything more than apathetically kick the footlights in, half-heartedly pile a mound of Coca-Cola bottles in the center of the stage for the social director of next summer to clean up, and then trudge silently off to bed.

I looked around the Bastille for the last time and remembered my first horrified glimpse of it—it seemed years ago now—and tired as I was, I walked over to the garbage pails in back of the kitchen and came back with two paper bags full of garbage. It was a silly and mean thing to do, but I carefully placed the bags outside the door to be distributed the next morning under the wooden slats. Then, deeply satisfied and strangely wide-awake after this gratifying bit of malice, I began to pack. There was an early-morning train out, and what I now wanted more than anything else in the world was to collect my salary from Mr. Axeler and get my father, my brother and myself on that train.

There was not going to be a moment wasted, if I could help it, in putting Mr. Axeler, his horse, his smile and his damnable environs behind us. I dropped off to sleep finally, allowing myself the last indulgence of a fantasy that consisted of returning to New York, forming an Association or Union of Social Directors, and black-listing Mr. Axeler and the Half Moon Country Club right off the summer-camp circuit forever.

How absurd it was to dream of triumphing over Mr. Axeler in terms of anything except fantasy was exquisitely demonstrated the next morning in very short order. I had grown so used to accepting the unmistakable figure on horseback on some corner of the horizon as the first sight that greeted my eyes as I left the Bastille in the morning, that I was immediately conscious that something was amiss when I stepped out of the doorway for the last time and the horse and rider were nowhere to be seen. I was uneasily aware that the landscape lacked an unmistakable trademark, much as a sailor might be made uneasy if he were to sail into the Strait of Gibraltar and the Rock did not loom slowly out of the mist. My disquiet was heightened by an unusual amount of activity which could be heard going on in the office behind closed doors as I passed it on my way into the dining room, and I hurried through breakfast and came out to the desk to have a talk with Herb Morris. He, too, was nowhere to be seen, but I hung about a bit and finally the door to the office opened slightly and he emerged looking white-faced and shaken.

A premonition of the disaster about to befall us swept over me, but I dismissed it instantly as being too macabre for even my active imagination to accept. "What's up?" I said to Herb. "What's going on in there? Where is Mr. Axeler? What's all the mystery about?"

He shook his head and motioned me closer to the desk, his eyes large and solemn. "There's going to be a meeting of all the employees—counselors, waiters, kitchen help, everybody—in the dining room at eleven o'clock," he whispered.

"What for?" I whispered back. "What's happening?"

"Mr. Axeler took the late train out of here for New York last night," he replied. "He left a letter. The partners got it this morning. There's only enough dough to get the kids and the counselors home by train. Nobody's going to get paid, not a cent. They're in there now trying to scare up enough money between them to get the rest of us home somehow. Even the waiters' pool of tips is gone."

I stared at him stupidly, too stunned to take in quite everything he was saying. "I don't know what most of us are going to do for tuition money for the fall term," he went on. "It has to be paid by the fifteenth of September. Almost everyone let their salary accumulate so they could use it for school." He looked at me sharply. "You drew most of yours during the summer, didn't you, to send home? You're lucky, brother."

I shook my head at him, still unable to speak. He whistled softly and then sighed. "Well, we'll all get the glad news in a few minutes. I'll see you at the meeting—I gotta get back inside." He grabbed some ledgers from under the desk and disappeared into the office again. I stood where I was for a moment or so more, and then walked outside and wandered off into a field, avoiding everyone I saw. I did not want to be the bearer of this news or discuss it with anyone. I wanted time to think, but I could not seem to think clearly of what had to be faced now, and quickly, too; nor could I bear to try to find my father and brother and break the news to them myself

I could think only of the boils I had suffered, the filth I had slept in, the sweat and loathing I had poured into every moment of this horrible summer; and I reflected bitterly that in some way I should have known this would happen and been smart enough to have withdrawn my full salary week by week. Of course, this was sheer nonsense, for there was no way I could have foreseen this ultimate disaster. But the more I thought of it, the more insanely sensible it seemed that I should have known it, and I wandered over the fields in a torment of self-contempt at my brainlessness and a blazing fury at Mr. Axeler. Had that horse of his turned up at that moment I would have tossed rocks at the poor animal.

At eleven o'clock I joined the employees' meeting in the dining room. They all knew the worst now and sat in grim silence as one of the two partners spelled out the extent of the carnage and what little they could do about it. We were all to be given notes for our salary, which were to be paid in full as soon as possible in the fall— a grandiose promise that fooled nobody; and the waiters' pool of tips was to be figured on the basis of other years' pools, and that, too, was to be paid in full. And since the children were of first consideration and would have to be sent back by train, the counselors would accompany them; and all the others would be given an equal amount for railroad fare that would take them as close to where they were going as the sum allowed. The rest of the way they would have to hitchhike.

As far as I could make out then and afterward, Mr. Axeler had not actually absconded with any money, but had simply not kept his partners directly informed as to the true state of the camp's income and outgo—not unnaturally a somewhat difficult job to perform while in the saddle. And since his partners had been no more successful in catching him unhorsed than the rest of us, he had smiled his way through the summer and only dismounted long enough to write them the letter they had found in the safe this morning instead of the money.

We lined up glumly in front of the table while a sad-faced partner doled out a sum to each of us for train fare that would at least take us out of Vermont.

I stood beside my father and brother in the line. Their reaction to what had happened was typical, in a special way, of each of them. My father remained unruffled and philosophical, his chief regret (or so it seemed) being only that this blissful summer was at an end. He seemed unaware of, or unwilling to face, the fact that our always shaky financial structure had finally and at last hit rock bottom; but I did not press the point upon him. I was grateful enough for his sunny good humor. His lifelong habit of blotting out anything that was "upsetting" or "unpleasant," a trait which I had always found infuriating, I now accepted with relief and gratitude. For the first time I envied and almost admired what I had always considered a cardinal weakness of my father's character.

My brother remained silent as usual, but there was no hint of recrimination in his attitude. I think perhaps we were closer together at that moment than we had ever been before. He knew quite as well as I did how desperate our situation was, and that the sorry fix we were in, to say nothing of this whole miserable summer he had suffered through, had originated with me. But his silence conveyed understanding, not blame. There is a quality of silence quite as verbal as words, and his wordless sympathy formed the first slim bond that had ever existed between us. Though we did not speak, our eyes occasionally met as my father burbled on, and I correctly detected an unspoken agreement between us to share this family crisis together and say nothing. I began to feel better in spite of myself— sharing a common disaster always lightens the burden—and my spirits lifted still further when it turned out that after buying my father a ticket straight through to New York, there would still be enough money left to get my brother and myself as far as Albany.

This was far better than I had dared hope. The sad-faced partners had behaved like gentlemen. With a little luck on the road we might be able to make it in little more than a day and a night.

It was not, as it turned out, either a hard or unpleasant journey. Had we had enough extra money to buy food, it would actually have been a quite enjoyable way of traveling. Hitchhiking was an accepted courtesy of the road in those days, and we thumbed our way from one car to another with no difficulty whatsoever. Hunger, however —real hunger, not the hunger of an appetite waiting with the knowledge that it will soon be appeased—was something that neither my brother nor myself had ever experienced before, and we learned quickly enough what a devilish traveling companion it can be. I discovered on that journey that there is an appetite beyond hunger— an appetite beyond appetite, that comes from the contemplating of hunger itself—and it is an experience I have no wish to repeat, despite the testimony of saints and martyrs of the state of grace that is achieved once the demands of the body are spurned and overcome.

If ever I needed an illustration that I am an earthbound creature, tied to the gross and ignominious demands of my body, I received it on that hitchhike, for when we left the train at Albany, we had little more than the subway fare we would need to get home with. That little we soon spent as the first pangs of hunger attacked us. For the rest of the way, though it was not long in terms of time, we simply did without. It was an unedifying twenty-four hours. Hunger seems to etch each gnawingly empty moment with a remarkable clarity, and I can still recall with acid sharpness the tantalizing picture of a small child seated alone at the roadside, a large box of raisins in its lap, cramming fistfuls into its mouth, while I stood watching it malignantly—and I remember the overwhelming temptation I had to grab the box of raisins and run, though I either lacked the courage or was not yet quite hungry enough to do so.

I remember, too, quite as vividly, watching a man at a gas station toss a half-eaten sandwich onto a rubbish heap, where it lay a little dusty but still quite edible, and considering whether to pick it up surreptitiously after he had moved away. Again I did not possess sufficient courage, or some foolish nicety of pride prevented my boldly snatching at it. But I am certain that, given a few hours more of hunger, no such civilized considerations would have stopped me from making straightaway for that bit of bread and meat and gobbling it up, no matter who was watching. I have always readily understood since then how a hungry man could contemplate cracking a safe or smashing a bakery window, and it has never surprised me that the stark streak of barbarism beneath the surface in all of us is but thinly held in check.

Nevertheless, we arrived back in the Bronx not one bit the worse for our fast, except for an excessive irritability on my part, and on my brother's, an alarming tendency to be sick after each mouthful he ate. There was not much time, however, to waste on either irritability or an upset stomach.

My mother's furnished room, now occupied by my father as well, was luckily paid for until the beginning of the following week, and the landlady had already agreed that my brother and I could sleep on the sofa in her living room for a night or two; she would also trust us for meals. But it was plain that this arrangement, good-willed as it was, could not last for more than a few days at most. The landlady had troubles of her own and could ill afford to add ours to them. We were, if we dared to face the fact honestly, actually homeless, and though a strange roof was temporarily over our heads, we were, except for the remnants of the last ten dollars I had sent her that remained in my mother's purse, penniless as well.

At no one time that I could remember had our fortunes been at this low an ebb. Again my mother surprised me. Her defenses where her family was concerned were paper-thin, and her given way in a crisis was usually to dissolve into helpless tears as a practical method of meeting the crisis head-on. But now, as on the day of our leave-taking for camp, she remained dry-eyed and clear-minded. She had even, awaiting my return, written down on the back of an envelope a list of a number of relatives, and beside each name she had set down a sum she thought it likely we might be able to borrow from them.

I took the envelope and quickly added up the column of figures. It was woefully inadequate for our needs. As closely as I could figure it, we needed not less than $200 to see our furniture out of storage, including the transportation of it to wherever we went, and with the month's rent in advance that was always demanded on a new apartment, plus the amount we would need to live on until I could get my little-theatre work started again in late October—all this could not possibly be managed on less than $200, a sum that would loom large at any time but at this particular moment seemed gigantic.

We knew not a single soul, either relative or friend, who possessed enough ready cash to allow the borrowing of $200. Poor people know poor people, and rich people know rich people. It is one of the few things La Rochefoucauld did not say, but then La Rochefoucauld never lived in the Bronx.

I stared hard at the envelope and hopefully enlarged the sum my mother had set beside each relative's name. It came to no more in aggregate than a paltry $110. I refused point-blank to borrow it. To borrow this money and dissipate it on furnished rooms, I pointed out, critical though our situation was, would only serve to precipitate a worse crisis in very short order. There was, of course, an ever-present alternative, but the thought of it was chilling. The alternative was to face the blunt fact that my scheme of social directing in the summers and little-theatre work in the winters was not going to work. If that was true, there seemed to be no choice but to give up the idea of writing plays and take a regular job in the workaday world tomorrow morning. I did not suggest this. I barely allowed myself to think it. It had taken so long to get this far and, inconsiderable though the distance was, I clung fiercely to the advantage of having my days free to write. It represented the one good chance I had of entering the theatre again, and to give it up, to turn back now, I felt, was to turn away from the theatre forever.

I well remembered Eddie's admonition: Never go back—you're swallowed up if you do! It sounded in my ears again with an irrevocable rightness. Self-pity is not a pleasant emotion and it is a fruitless one as well, for its point of no return is an onset of black despair in very short order. I gave way to both now. I sat silent for so long a time that my mother finally began to clear the dishes from the table. I knew they were all waiting for me to speak, to come to some sort of decision, but I could not. I was dissolved in a kind of wild panic—a new and sudden panic that had nothing to do with our present reality. I could not put a name to it, though I could dimly surmise its content.

I have always had a strong, almost an overpowering, sense of family unity. Its roots are perhaps racial and lost in the atavistic past of a people whose history is a stern one; or it may be that I had inherited a good deal more than I suspected of my mother's own deep feeling of family ties. I felt those ties slipping away now, felt our family, small as it was, disintegrating before my eyes. It was the unreasoning panic one feels as a child, not as an adult. I was gripped by an intense anxiety, by wave after wave of a heart-clutching fear that left me without speech. I cannot recall another emotion so engulfing, so choking in its intensity, and I believe some remnants of that moment remain with me still. It could account in some measure for my curious habit in later years—a habit of such repetitive pattern that it might almost come under the heading of "mania"— of buying apartments and houses, decorating them to the hilt, and then abandoning them with almost the same compulsive ferocity that had given me no rest until they were furnished, with every match box and ashtray in place. It was as if no one apartment, no one house, was ever secure enough against the picture of family dissolution I still carried with me.

The new one . . . the next one . . . and the grander one, was always the house or apartment that would push the panic safely and farther away, and forever shatter the picture of sitting around that table in a stranger's kitchen, with no home of our own. It may be, too, that the buying sprees at Cartier's were tantamount to the endless decorating of houses, the sets of gold cuff links and shirt studs, the countless gold cigarette cases and keys and chains and rings and watches that I bought so heedlessly—all were talismans against a repetition of that moment.

I got up from that table now and walked out of the kitchen and out of the house. The house was about three blocks distant from our old place, and I walked back to where we used to live and stared up at the fourth-floor windows. Our apartment was already rented, the window of the front room, where my brother and I had slept for so many years, inevitably draped with a woman's figure leaning out, a small child on either side of her, all of them staring idly down into the street below, much as my brother and I had done in our early childhood. Even now, with the few coins from my mother's purse jingling in my pocket—all the money we possessed in the world—it was still a comfort, a victory of sorts, to be out of those hated rooms and to know that we would never go back.

I felt decidedly better for having looked at it. Anything, even our present state, was better than living in the symbol of defeat those rooms had become for me. The sight of the familiar windows, the discolored stoop with the broken railings leading down into the janitor's apartment, the fire escapes laden with stunted geraniums and drooping rubber plants, had the tonic effect of clearing my mind of all regret and stiffening the resolve that was already taking shape in my mind. I had only to think of it as our home once again and to envisage walking up those steps into the dirty hallway and of climbing those four flights of stairs, to know that being homeless was not the worst of all possible evils. The real evil was to live on in it, not to fight one's way out, and suddenly I was able to think clearly again. To turn back now was to give up more than just the idea of becoming a playwright—it was to relinquish as well the vision of a way of life. I knew now that I was not prepared to give up my chance at that vision without a struggle. Somewhere in this city must be someone who could lend me $200. There must be someone I had not thought of or had forgotten, someone who must be remembered now.

I thought at once of the richest person I had ever known—Mrs. Henry B. Harris. She had liked me and she was a woman given to impulsive generosity. I turned away and walked quickly toward the candy store on the corner. To the side of it were the same steps I had sat on, in those summers that now seemed of an altogether far-away and ancient time, telling the gang stories of Dreiser and Frank Norris, buying my way with the only coin I possessed. It had seemed easy enough to dream of the theatre then.

There was another group of kids on the steps now, another gang almost indistinguishable from my old one, and I looked at them enviously. Whatever dreams they were having of growing up would be safer dreams than my own had been. The theatre, in more ways than one, is a curse.

I looked up Mrs. Harris' number in the telephone book and gave the number to the operator. The connection was made almost too quickly. Mrs. Harris was out of the city and would not be returning until late November. So much for the richest person I knew.

I thought briefly of Mr. Pitou, but he was not rich in the sense Mrs. Harris was, and I had cost him dearly enough already. He had every reason to refuse me, even if I could think of a good enough reason to ask for the money, and I did not relish the asking. I longed for Eddie to be back from South Africa, not that he was likely to possess $200, but because he was always wildly ingenious in situations that demanded evoking money out of thin air; and I was of a mind, in this present moment, to clutch at straws and miracles, even of Eddie's unsteady kind. I considered briefly going to Washington Heights and asking Eddie's parents for the money. They knew me, of course. But even as I thought of it, I knew that it was unlikely they would have it to give, nor had I any right to ask it of them.

I began to thrash wildly about the back corners of my mind. Priestly Morrison might give it to me, for he had been quite outspoken in his belief that I could write, in spite of his close acquaintance with *The Beloved Bandit,* but I had no idea of where to find him. He did not seem to be listed in the telephone directory; but even as I turned the pages, vainly seeking his name, the name of another who had evinced a belief in my ability flashed into my mind. Joe Hyman. He had come back to camp once more during the summer, and again he had worked the lights and curtains, and again we had talked at length about the theatre. It was stretching our slim summer acquaintance a good deal to call it a friendship, but I had gathered in one of our talks that he was a full partner in the second largest knitwear business in the city, and that was enough for me to know.

For a terrible moment I could not remember the trade name of the concern, and his own name was not listed separately, but then it came to me and I gave the number to the operator in a voice that was considerably more husky than my usual one. The words "last chance" seemed to glow on and off in the glass door of the telephone booth as I gave my name to a voice that said, "Holman Knitting Mills, good afternoon," and waited.

Joe Hyman came to the phone immediately and his voice was warm and welcoming. He would be in the office all afternoon, he said, and he would be glad to see me any time I came. I would be there within half an hour, I informed him, a little breathlessly. I hung up the receiver and bought myself a cherry soda to steady my nerves. I must make sure to present my request for the money correctly. There would be no second chance; no new $200-names flashing providentially into my mind if I failed.

On the subway ride downtown I thought of something else he had said in one of our talks together. I reminded him of it as I sat across the desk from him in his office, although not at all in the way that I had intended. Anyone who has ever sat across a desk from another man and asked him for money knows what an unpleasant and unhappy business it is. Like the effort to end a love affair, there is no nice way of doing it. I struggled through a few minutes of chatter, and then in spite of the fine dignified scene I had played out for both of us in my mind coming downtown in the subway, the words began to emerge quite differently. I was startled to hear myself speaking in a belligerent tone, wholly foreign to the way I felt and which I could do nothing to modify.

"If you meant what you said," I was saying aggressively, "this is the chance for you to get into the theatre. You told me this summer you wanted to sell your share in the business some day and produce plays. Well, I'm going to write plays, and if you'll lend me two hundred dollars you can produce them. This is a good chance for you."

I stopped, as astonished as though someone else had been speaking. Even to my own ears it sounded crude and insufferably patronizing. What a way, I thought numbly, of asking a comparative stranger for money! What in the world had prevented me from telling him simply and truthfully that I was dead-broke and that without his help I might have to give up the idea of play-writing entirely. The

[225]

truth was simple enough, and it had a ring of decency about it in contrast to the hollow nonsense I had just spoken that must have rung as falsely in his ears as it did in my own.

I stared miserably across the desk at him. He had listened to me quite straight-faced, but now he smiled. "All right," he said, "we're partners. Do you want it in cash or by check?"

"Cash," I replied quietly, too surprised to add a "thank you." He reached into his wallet and counted out $200.

"You go ahead and write 'em," he said, handing me the bills, "and maybe I *will* do just that . . . sell this business and produce plays. Not right away, perhaps, but someday. Meanwhile, I'll be around if you need me to manage your fortune."

I said "Thank you" a little lamely and we shook hands.

I rode the subway back uptown, with my hand clutched around the bills in my pants pocket so tightly that I could hardly open it when I arrived safely back in the Bronx. It was more money than I had ever seen at one time; more money than I think my parents had ever seen at one time before, too, when I tossed it on the bed in my mother's room. They stared hard at it and at me, as though to make sure I had not stolen it, but I brushed all their questions impatiently aside. The story of Joe Hyman could wait. What I wanted now was the details of the apartment for rent in Brooklyn that my mother had written to me about a few weeks earlier. I wanted the move made by tomorrow night, if possible. Not one penny of this money was going to be wasted on furnished rooms while we shopped around for an apartment, if I could help it. We had been too close to the edge for me to relish looking over it again.

My mother had not actually seen the apartment. It had been looked at by some Brooklyn relatives and reported on as a pleasant three rooms in a new building, within the price we could afford for rent without taking in boarders.

"Take it," I said without hesitation. "Go downstairs and phone them to take it for us, and tell them we'll be out there tomorrow morning to pay the deposit."

"But we've never seen it," my mother protested. "And it's over an hour's subway ride away—it's only one station from Coney Island."

Brooklyn, then as now, seemed another country to inbred New Yorkers, and to my mother's loyal Bronx ears I might well have been suggesting a trek into the western wilderness.

"It doesn't matter," I insisted. "The only thing that matters is to get settled quickly. I'll phone the storage people while you're talking to Brooklyn. I want to be in that apartment by tomorrow night."

My sense of urgency prevailed. Even Santini Brothers, the storage and moving people, who were generally not prepared to act this quickly in what was their busiest month, succumbed to the bribe of an extra five dollars for hurrying. The infinite speed that only money can buy was not lost upon me. In less than an hour all arrangements had been made, and at eight o'clock the next morning we were on our way to Brooklyn. The furniture, I was assured, would be arriving by ten. It was something to know we would be eating a meal in a kitchen of our own by evening.

Our new home was indeed well over an hour's subway ride from even Times Square, a fact that was to devil me considerably later on, but now I could only enjoy the idea that we were getting almost as far away from the Bronx as it was possible to get. That single fact in itself was of no small moment in my eyes, though the new apartment was something of a shock to all of us. The three tiny rooms on the ground floor dashed the fond hopes we had held after gazing admiringly at the brand-new building they were in, but compared with what we had left they were the Taj Mahal as far as I was concerned.

The building itself had a little forecourt with trees and a tiny fountain, around which was set on three sides, with no protruding fire escapes, the apartment house itself. Our apartment had evidently been designed as a superintendent's or janitor's quarters. It lay directly at the entranceway and conveyed a view from all its windows of moving feet on the street outside; there was no sense of privacy, unless the shades were kept drawn at all hours.

With the six rooms of furniture that my mother had insisted on keeping, those tiny rooms would be overpoweringly cluttered, but no matter. At last there would be no other people moving about in them but ourselves. I paid the deposit to the superintendent, and as the moving van arrived in front of the building, I announced I was going for a walk to explore the neighborhood while the van was being unloaded and our belongings moved in. This was true only in part. The actual truth was that I was ashamed of seeing our shabby furniture brought in under the curious eyes of our new neighbors, and snobbish enough to want to detach myself from the scene.

I walked hurriedly away from the building as the moving men started to unload the van. I stopped after a block or so at a candy and stationery store to buy some pads of yellow paper. I also wanted to know if there was another beach this close to Coney Island. It might be a place to work until we got settled in. There was indeed another beach, eight or nine blocks away, straight ahead in the direction I had been going. I bought a supply of candy bars and a box of cheese crackers and headed for it.

It was a sweet, mild September morning and I was surprised to find the beach deserted. There was not a soul to be seen upon it. It was a stretch of sand that edged the bay, and if it was always as empty as this, I decided, it would be an excellent place to work until the weather drove me indoors. I felt fatigued, but the impulse to get to work was strong. Time presses terribly at twenty, in contradiction to the testimony of the senescent, who claim the years of age fly by with winged speed; or time pressed upon my own impatient spirit with a passionate sense of life passing by that only twenty can feel.

I looked across the bay to Manhattan, and for a moment my high spirits were dampened as I reflected that I seemed to be moving farther and farther away from Broadway instead of closer to it. Only for a fleeting moment, however. For on this special day nothing could dampen my high spirits for long. It seemed to me I had grasped one of the theatre's deepest secrets. Survival. This hidden secret is seldom spoken of in books or schools that teach the hopeful how to act or how to write plays. The Art of Survival is seldom even mentioned. Yet it is as prime a requisite for a theatrical career as talent itself, for with an ability to survive, everything is possible, and without it . . . nothing.

I knew that I would survive now, that I would get on with the business of writing plays, and keep on with it no matter what other Mr. Axelers the future held in store. To be concerned now about whether any of those plays would ever see a Broadway production seemed like an ungrateful repayment for the almost miraculous good luck that had taken me this far. Whatever guardian angel there was watching benignly over me, he had produced Joe Hyman, some pads of yellow paper, and an empty, sunny beach; and in the light of what had happened these last three days, I could ask for no further guarantees.

I fixed a mound of sand to lean against, waggled my backside into it for a more comfortable seat, and settled down to write a play.

PART
TWO

F OUR YEARS later, almost to the exact day and at almost the identical spot on the beach where I had sat four years earlier, I sat again, my pockets stuffed with a supply of candy bars, a pad of yellow paper again on my knees. It seemed to me remarkable that so much and so little had happened since that other September morning when I had first made my way to this same spot.

I had returned only a day or two before from another season of social directing, but this time as social director of the Flagler Hotel, the Fontainebleau of the Catskills. In those four years I had gone, like Kansas City, about as far as I could go. I was now the most highly paid, the most eagerly sought-after social director of the Borscht Circuit. The summer of my novitiate at Camp Utopia and my summer of serfdom at the Half Moon Country Club were bitter but distant memories, something to be told to the staff as laughable but almost unbelievable tales out of the past, considering my present high eminence.

This past summer at the Flagler, I had arrived for the beginning of the season with a personal staff of twenty-six people, not including waiters or musicians. The staff included not only a future night-club headliner and two future soloists of the Philharmonic Orchestra, but it also included as my chief assistant a solemn-faced young man of quiet but unswerving ambition, named Dore Schary. My position as King of the Borscht Circuit was largely undisputed. My chief competitor in the field was one Don Hartman, the social director of Grossinger's Hotel—a curious quirk of circumstance, considering the fact that Dore Schary was to become head of Metro-Goldwyn-Mayer and Hartman the head of Paramount Pictures. Not one of us would have believed this to be in the realm of even remote possibility in that summer of 1929—though we were, all three of us, not inclined to be modest in our estimates of what the future held in store.

A good deal more than just my own status as a social director had changed during those years. Camps and hotels with social staffs had taken an enormous leap forward. Money was plentiful and the competition keen. Both camps and hotels kept enlarging their social staffs and bettering their ability to provide greater social activities, particularly in the realm of shows, with each new summer.

The Flagler Hotel, whose proprietors had begun to feel the cutting edge of displacement by their deadliest rival, Grossinger's, had, the summer before I arrived, decided to build the finest social hall on the Borscht Circuit and engage the best social director, barring Don Hartman, that they could get to run it. They had built what was, when I arrived to take it over, a completely equipped little theatre seating fifteen hundred people, whose electrical switchboard, fly loft and scenery dock compared more than favorably with some New York theatres. It was the pride of the Catskills. Its audience dressed to the hilt for the Friday and Saturday night shows. At the height of the season, such was my weighty reputation as a social director by then, overflow crowds came from other hotels from miles around to see the shows, even though they were charged an admission fee, and on Saturday nights a couple of hundred were always turned away.

As the director in charge of all this grandeur, I had long since disdained to stoop to such primitive means of thievery as sneaking into theatres during intermissions and standing at the back with a pocket flashlight to scribble notes on a program. My seats to theatres were now paid for by whatever camp I chose to give the benefit of my services the following season, and I was accompanied by a stenographer, also paid for, who at the touch of my fingers at her elbow,

[234]

would take down exactly and expertly whatever portions I wanted stolen of the particular show we were witnessing.

Even during the camp season itself, the demands of my time were no longer incessant. I did not participate to any great extent in campfire nights and games nights, and though I still sang "boy and girl" numbers in the musical shows and performed the redoubtable "Mrs. Cohen at the Beach" several times each season, it was the ability, week after week, to present full-length plays like *The Show-Off* and *The Trial of Mary Dugan,* and short ones like *The Valiant*—which Dore Schary played to perfection—that kept the social hall jammed and kept Don Hartman, a few miles away at Grossinger's, well up on his toes.

Had I been prepared to derive any sense of pleasure from these triumphs, I would have been forced to agree that I had come a long way from the days when Eddie and I, and afterward I alone, had dragged the wood for the campfires and the blankets for the guests to sit on out to the woods unassisted; a long way indeed from the indignity of wearing, in lieu of my own clothes, the remnants of the camp wardrobe trunk, and a longer way still from being at the mercy of Mr. Axeler and his ilk, or sitting glassy-eyed with exhaustion through bunk parties I dared not refuse to attend.

But not a long enough way, I thought sardonically, to be any farther than this beach I was still sitting on come each new September. I had now survived six summers of social directing, and six winters of little-theatre work, and with each winter I had faithfully kept to my intent and completed a play. All of them reposed safely and out of sight on the top of an unused shelf in the kitchen. The seventh awaited only the pencil I held in my hand to start taking shape on the yellow pad of blank paper on my knee. I gazed across the bay to Manhattan, as I had done at the start of each of these Septembers, but not quite as hopefully, not with the same certainty that this would be the last September I would be here.

All six plays had been submitted and read by the play readers of the best managements on Broadway, and all six had been speedily refused and returned. Somewhere or other along the line, I was in error; an error either of thinking or of execution. Each successive play had been better than the one before, of this I was convinced, if only in terms of professionalism. I had taken great pains to better each play's craftsmanship. I no longer allowed myself to be seduced by the dangerously sweet music of my own words. I played them back, as it were, and listened with a cold and critical ear. The last two had been written, I thought, with a greater degree of economy and a surer sense of the theatre than I had ever achieved before. Yet these, also, had been promptly and unregretfully returned. Unquestionably, some necessary element or ingredient was missing in those plays, some one aspect of writing for the theatre had escaped me—barring, of course, the unpleasant possibility that I lacked any talent for play-writing whatever. I was altogether unprepared to accept this last assumption as a fact, true or not. At least, not yet, but it seemed to me a reckoning of some sort was not only necessary but long overdue. For one thing, I was aware that social directing could not go on forever. Fads and fashions changed in social directing as much as in anything else, so that this year's top social director might well be the summer after next's assistant, or even a mere member of the staff. Even so, I roughly estimated that I still had three big-league summers left and I was determined to make the most of them. Making the most of them, however, did not include simply doing more of the same, if that meant finishing a play each winter and returning to this beach each fall to write still another.

Continuous and heedless writing, a dogged plowing ahead in spite of failure, represents industry and little else if it does not also include a willingness to explore the anatomy of that failure. I was prepared not to set down another word on paper until I had satisfied myself that I was at least using the tools correctly; and I had reached a point where I was no longer certain, in spite of a growing technical dexterity, that this was so. There was an indication of a kind that I was not. In my pocket reposed a letter that was to have a considerable effect upon me. It was from Richard J. Madden, of the American Play Company, to whom I had sent two or three plays, and his letter was one of two rejections I had received at camp a few weeks earlier. Mr. Madden had written at some length explaining his own refusal, and it was not so much what he said as the fact that his words mirrored, to a great extent, the content of the other letter.

Both readers were kindly disposed to consider future plays of mine, but in Mr. Madden's words, "Since by far the best part of the plays you have sent us have been the comedic moments, why not try writing a comedy? I am inclined to believe very strongly that you could turn out a good one." I read the letter through again, then put it back in my pocket, still as frankly and thoroughly puzzled as I had been at its first reading. It had never occurred to me that any of the six dramas I had written contained any comedic moments at all, other than those demanded by the characters themselves and in very sparse terms at that.

There was a logical reason for this. I was a full-blown snob so far as comedy was concerned. My gods of the theatre still remained Shaw, whom I considered a writer of political and social ideas rather than comedy, and O'Neill, who represented the drama of the emotions. Like all snobs, I dismissed everything in between. I had no taste for the popular comedies of the day and little admiration for those who could turn them out successfully. I had no idea whatever of how to go about writing a comedy, for my own idea of comedy did not seem to be at all the popular conception. Only in the comedies of George S. Kaufman and Marc Connelly did there seem to be a kinship with my own sense of the ridiculous and the outrageous. They were the exception to my snobbishness. I did not look down my nose so far as *Dulcy, To the Ladies, Beggar on Horse-Back* or *Merton of the Movies* were concerned, but it seemed to me utter foolishness to try to ape these two masters of the form. They ruled unquestioned and absolute in the field of satirical writing for the theatre. Nobody else could touch them.

With a bravado I did not feel, I considered Madden's letter again, for if I could bring myself to attempt a comedy it would only be in the tradition of Kaufman and Connelly, or not at all, and I was neither so brave nor so innocent as to consider that an easy undertaking. Nevertheless, if I was going to examine the reasons for my failure realistically, it was pure blockheadedness not to gravely

[237]

estimate the truth of Madden's words. If he was right, then I was wasting my time by turning out pseudo Shaw and O'Neill year after year. If whatever capacity or talent I possessed might lean in quite another direction, I could do no better than try to prove it or disprove it to my own satisfaction. I most certainly had little to lose in trying. Again my predilection toward omens and portents played a decisive part. This would be my seventh play, and seven was a lucky number. I decided to try a comedy.

A little grumpily I removed the mantle of Shaw and O'Neill from my shoulders and regarded the yellow pad of paper on my lap. Without thinking too much about it, I scribbled a title across the blank sheet. I usually came by a title last, sometimes quite a while after the play itself was finished, for titles seemed to me, then as now, the least important part of a play, but I had a slight comedic idea in the back of my mind that this title would fit. It seemed also to suggest neatly what I was certain would be my one and only attempt at writing a comedy. The title I had scribbled across the paper was *Once in a Lifetime,* and staring down at it, I began to block out in my mind the opening scenes of the play.

It will be remembered that talking pictures had arrived with the impact of a thunderbolt in 1928, and by 1929 Hollywood, at first skittish and unbelieving, was shaken to its roots and in the midst of a tremendous economic and artistic upheaval. I had, of course, never been anywhere near Hollywood, but this did not stop me from imagining what might conceivably be happening in Hollywood now with the sudden advent of talking pictures.

A comedy, particularly a satirical comedy, is always conditioned by its author's attitude to the manners and mores of the climate in which he lives, and it would seem that a thoroughgoing first-hand knowledge of what he is writing about would be his first necessity. This is not always true, particularly so far as satire is concerned. It is sometimes far better for a writer to allow a lively imagination to roam over the field he has chosen than to research that field within an inch of its life—the danger being that what emerges is likely to be all research and no play. By and large, an audience usually knows as much as an author does before he starts his research, and that is all they want to know or should know. The author's creative imagination and satirical viewpoint must do the rest. An audience is not interested in how hard the author has worked at his research or how much material he has unearthed, and they do not take kindly to his parading in front of the footlights his hard-earned knowledge. They are quite right. They have not come to a schoolroom; they have come to a theatre.

I did not consider that my complete ignorance of Hollywood or of the making of motion pictures was any bar whatever to my writing about both with the utmost authority, and I proceeded to do so with the invaluable help of that renowned trade paper, *Variety*. A weekly copy of *Variety* was the full extent of the research I did on *Once in a Lifetime,* and I could not have done better. *Variety* viewed the Hollywood scene with a shrewd and shifty eye. Not taken in by Hollywood's boasts or wails of protest, its reporting of the current crisis was first-rate. Between the lines of the special language used by its writers to put a declarative sentence into simple English, a cunning eye could catch an enveloping glimpse of the wonderful absurdity of the Hollywood scene. I read every word *Variety* wrote about it, and no oceanographer or marine botanist ever came up out of the Sargasso Sea with more prime specimens than I did out of those weekly issues. In a very real sense, the play might well have been dedicated "With love" and "Without whom" to that astute and all-knowing journal.

To my surprise, the play itself was finished in something under three weeks' time, a fact which I viewed with something akin to alarm. I genuinely mistrusted the ease with which I had written it, for I had never written a play, barring that first abortive effort for Augustus Pitou, in anything short of four to six months' time. I took it for granted, I do not know quite why, that the more agony a play generated in the writing, the better it was likely to emerge as a play. I am inclined to believe now that the very opposite is likely to be true. Agonizing effort has a way somehow of permeating the stage and drifting out across the footlights.

The airiest comedies, the most delightful ones to watch, are usually the ones in which the author has shared some of the audience's

[239]

delight beforehand, and there was no question that I had had a very good time indeed in writing *Once in a Lifetime*—a good enough time to make me thoroughly suspicious of it. I had no idea whether it was very good or no good at all. I read it over several times, trying to measure its worth against the standards of the Kaufman and Connelly comedies, but I could come to no conclusion. It seemed to me the play had a fresh and impertinent quality, but I had no idea whether it was funny or not. I had arbitrarily set myself the task of writing in a style altogether new to me and in a kind of idiomatic language that was foreign to my ear. I had no yardstick by which I could judge it. There was only one way to find out if the play was any good and that was to see whether an audience laughed at it. I decided to create my own audience. I made the decision in the Hudson Tubes, where I was reading over the play for still another time while on my way to an evening rehearsal of a Newark little-theatre group which I was directing for a second season.

My status as a director of little theatres had changed as sharply for the better as my standing as a social director. I could pick and choose at will which little theatres I would direct now. I had chosen to direct two groups in Brooklyn and one in Newark, and although this necessitated my spending an inordinate amount of time in the Hudson Tubes and the subway, I did not mind. The group in Newark was an interesting one. The people in it were a good deal more mature than any I had ever directed before, and they were in all ways superior to the usual run of little-theatre groups. Dore Schary, the leading spirit of the group, himself engaged in writing plays and short stories on the side, and almost all the others were aspiring scenic artists, directors-to-be or dedicated amateur actors who hoped to graduate into the professional theatre in very short order. They made it their business to see everything worth seeing on Broadway and their critical judgment was generally sound. They would not be an easy or a flattering audience. Quite likely the opposite, which was exactly the test I wished the play to have.

I had never done such a thing before, but I decided suddenly to call off the evening's rehearsal and read *Once in a Lifetime* to them instead. Their reaction, good or bad, would most certainly settle the chief reservation I had in my own mind about the play. I would soon know whether it was funny or not. Laughter cannot be faked, no matter how much good will an audience has toward an author. For an audience, whether it consists of one person or one thousand, shortly becomes a valid one in spite of itself the moment the mechanism of listening starts to operate. Every author, unless he chooses to be willfully self-deluded, carries a Geiger counter in his inner ear that tells him quickly enough whether he has struck the false politeness of hollow laughter or the real thing. There is no mistaking it.

As I opened the door to the rehearsal hall, I hesitated and briefly reconsidered. Like a man with a toothache, whose pain disappears as he sits waiting in the dentist's outer office, I was no longer so certain that I wanted to know if the play was good or not. But my curiosity, to say nothing of my vanity, was far too great to allow me to draw back now. I barely acknowledged their good evenings, and quickly trapped myself by making the announcement that there would be no rehearsal tonight and that I would read them the new play I had just finished.

The announcement was received with considerable excitement. They were well aware that I was a would-be playwright, but it was a part of myself I kept entirely separate from my work with them and seldom discussed. Ever since my first unpleasant experience with little-theatre groups, I had been at some pains to maintain an attitude that was impersonal and scrupulously businesslike, from first rehearsal to last, and I intended, if I could, to keep to that attitude now. I wanted their laughter, not their praise, but I was not unaware of the hushed expectancy in the room as I opened the manuscript and began to read rather nervously. The first laugh was a long time in coming. I was making the mistake, of course, of listening only for laughter, and no play can create laughter at the outset without a necessary exposition of its characters and its premise. Nevertheless, they were a quick and knowing audience. I had not been wrong, at any rate, in one respect. Hollywood and talking pictures were a prime subject for satire, and the time was evidently ripe for it.

Satire, more than any other form of writing for the stage, depends on timing; the audience must be ready to acknowledge that the culture it accepts and lives by is a proper subject for the playwright's sharp stings, and ready for the astringent look the satirical playwright is asking them to take at themselves. I read on, not only greatly encouraged by that first laugh but by their immediate perception of what the play intended to say and the way in which it was going to say it. Laughter was coming more often now, and I began to read less nervously and with greater conviction.

I have always been a good reader of my own work, and that is a danger I have had to make myself aware of and guard against as best I could. If one is going to read a play to a group of people, it is witless to try to read it badly even if one could, and since I read extremely well, I have had to accustom my ear to the nuance of just how much a play's favorable reception was due to my reading of it and how much to the play itself. The process of reading the first draft of the play aloud can be an excellent barometer of its strength as well as its weaknesses. If one listens correctly and refuses to be fooled by the good nature of the listeners, there is a great deal that can be learned from it. There could be no mistaking now, for example, the fact that I had written a very funny first act, a somewhat unfulfilled and commonplace second act and a quite flat third act. Long before I came to the final curtain, I was completely aware that I had sacrificed a good deal to the speed with which I had written the play, although there was no question that in spite of its obvious lacks, the play had a wonderful surging vitality, which was, perhaps, its most valuable asset. Most remarkable of all, however, was the fact that I could make an audience laugh and that I had an unsuspected and surprising flair for the satirical —and that at last, if this audience was any judge at all, I had written what might very well be my first salable play.

I was quite as excited, when I finished, as they were, and in the shouting discussion that followed, my mind was more taken up with how quickly I could manage to rewrite the play and get it into Richard Madden's hands than with what was being said about the play itself. I pricked up my ears, nevertheless, at what Dore Schary was saying now, and I stopped thinking about Richard Madden and, as it turned out, about anything and everything else for the next three weeks, except the name and person of the man he was speaking of. He was speaking of Jed Harris, and in the theatre of the middle and late twenties it was a name to conjure with.

Harris had sprung out of nowhere with the velocity of a meteor streaking across the sky. He had flashed suddenly across the stodgy theatrical firmament of the early twenties with the hard white light of a winter star, and he continued to light up the theatrical heavens with an unerring touch that had something of the uncanny about it. He could seemingly do no wrong. Production after production, whatever play he turned his hand to, was catapulted into immediate success, and his vagaries, his flaring tempers, his incisive way with a script were already a legend and fast becoming Broadway folklore. I do not think it too great a stretch of either logic or imagination to say that every aspiring playwright's prayer in those days probably went exactly along the same lines, to wit: "Please, God, let Jed Harris do my play!"

Above the hubbub in the room, Dore Schary was clamoring for my attention. "Jed Harris would go for this play like a ton of bricks," he was saying, shouting a little to make himself heard above the others. "Don't wait to rewrite it—just send it to him the way it is—tomorrow morning, if possible. I'll make a bet with anybody that he buys it."

"It isn't that easy, Dore," I protested. "Even if I were willing to send it out in this shape—it isn't that simple. Every play written is automatically sent to Jed Harris first. What chance would I have of even getting my play read? And if the play's got anything at all," I went on, "it's got a kind of on-the-nose timeliness. If it kicks around too long it will just evaporate into a collection of old Hollywood jokes. I want to get it read as soon as possible."

"Wait a minute," he cried triumphantly, "suppose I could fix it so that you didn't send it to Jed Harris' office at all, but right to the hotel where he lives? What about that?"

I shook my head ruefully at such innocence in the ways of Broadway, and laughed. "Remember what Judge Brack said when

Hedda shot herself? 'People don't do such things!' he said. Well, unknown playwrights from Brooklyn don't send plays to Jed Harris direct—and don't think his office is going to tell you where he lives, either. They guard that secret with their lives."

"Not his office," he persisted. "His sister. His sister Sylvia lives right here in Newark and I know her. This is where Jed came from originally. I'm going to call her right now." He turned on his heel and walked out.

I shrugged my shoulders and began to gather my things together. He would discover quickly enough, I knew, that theatrical producers were as protected and impregnable as a feudal monarch in a turreted castle. He was back, however, almost before I had finished stuffing the manuscript into my briefcase.

"She says to go ahead and do it," he cried, decidedly pleased with his success and the look of surprise on my face. "He lives at the Madison Hotel," he went on, "and she says to send him a telegram saying you want to bring the play to him personally. Then you can do your own talking and get him to read it right away. Well"—he grinned—"how about that? Got any other excuses for not sending it to him now?"

"No," I replied, catching something of his excitement. "What do I say in the telegram? You've managed everything else so far, you might as well tell me what to say."

The whole thing had somehow taken on the aspect of sending off a prize jingle to a national magazine contest. The racket around the table was tremendous. The entire group crowded around us, offering suggestions at the top of their voices. High-sounding phrases and one or two flagrant untruths were briskly shouted down before we could get enough quiet to compose a telegram that would not obviously find its way into the wastebasket. In the end, what was turned out was a long and rather stiff telegram, its too studied wording, I thought uneasily, having the effect of threatening Jed Harris with the loss of a possible masterpiece. But I was in the mood to go along with anything now. The entire evening's proceedings, beginning with my sudden decision to read the play, had been so unorthodox that by this time it seemed quite in the nature of things to send off a lengthy telegram to Jed Harris, blithely signed by myself.

Nor was this the end of it! Everyone trooped down to the Western Union office to see me dispatch the telegram and then went on to an all-night diner for coffee and doughnuts to celebrate, quite as though Jed Harris, now that the telegram was sent, had already bought the play and set a rehearsal date.

I waited for my train in the Tubes station in Newark, in a foolish and happy daze. I had missed the last express to New York by a good hour and the locals ran on an intermittent and whimsical schedule of their own. The journey home would take a good three hours, but I did not mind. I thought of the telegram winging its way above me as I rode underground and I could not refrain from the warming fantasy of believing that Dore's words had the ring of truth in them. Jed Harris would read the play at once and buy it.

I dozed and came awake again, always with the voice of Jed Harris in my ears and the satisfying phrase, "We'll go into rehearsal in three weeks," ringing loud and clear. By the time the subway local reached my station in Brooklyn, I had cut the time and the words down to, "We'll go into rehearsal Monday."

I T SEEMED THAT I had only been asleep a bare moment or two when I opened my eyes to see my mother standing over me with an unmistakable yellow envelope in her hand. "It came over an hour ago," she was saying, "but I didn't want to wake you. You got in so late last night."

"You should have got me up," I shouted. "Maybe the appointment was for this morning. What time is it?"

"What appointment?" she asked bewilderedly. "It's almost twelve o'clock."

But I had already snatched the telegram out of her hand and was tearing it open. Half asleep as I was, I knew Jed Harris was going to see me. Theatrical producers did not send telegrams merely to say "No." I stared down at the curt message on the telegraph blank: "Be at the Madison Hotel at two o'clock this afternoon. Jed Harris."

The matter-of-fact words sent me leaping out of bed into the kitchen to gulp down some coffee and to read again and again the telegram which I still clutched in my hand. It is an exhilarating experience to witness for the first time one's own name coupled with that of a celebrated one. It heightens the illusion of immediate attainment, even though the juxtaposition of names occurs in so slight a way as on a telegram.

While I shaved and dressed I tried to tell myself that it was absurd to reach this pitch of excitement over what was, after all, merely a summons and nothing more. Obviously, Jed Harris did not produce every play he read. Yet try as I would to keep fact and fantasy from running together, I could do nothing to prevent the laughter of the audience of the evening before from re-echoing in my ears. If the play evoked the same kind of laughter from Jed Harris, then this might well be the last subway ride I would ever take. I had long since known the first use I would make of money. It would be to take taxis whenever and wherever I wished, for so little as a half-block if I chose to, and never ride underground again.

Above the roar of the subway, now, I tried to fashion in my mind the way the interview might go. To be too much in awe would highlight the eagerness of the unproduced playwright. On the other hand, too great an insistence that he read the play immediately might be equally foolhardy.

I tried to recall the pictures I had seen of Jed Harris in magazines and newspapers. It was a face that leaped back into one's memory with razor-sharp definition: the gaunt features, the clean-shaven cheeks thinly ringed even in the pictures by a dark shadow of beard, and the unforgettable hooded eyes, veiled and threatening, with a promise of future rancor even as the lips arranged themselves into the semblance of a makeshift smile. There was no clue whatever as to what to expect or how to behave, for if the eye of the beholder is quite properly the place wherein beauty lies, it is not unreasonable to conclude that the beholder's unconscious carries along as well a vision that is even sharper than what his eye takes in. He carries into a first meeting with the celebrated a prefabricated legend of a thousand bits and pieces, and it is generally never a person he sees or talks to but the reflection of that legend.

It puts both parties at a distinct disadvantage. The celebrated figure is almost always a disappointment in terms of the legend, and it is hard to see how it could be otherwise. A first meeting with the famed generally precludes anything but the most strained of conversations and is equally awkward and uncomfortable for both hero and hero-worshipper.

Nothing, however, could have properly prepared me for the tongue-tied shock of my first visit to the celebrated Jed Harris. Like everything else about him, it was unexpected, perverse, and calculated to disconcert even the most cynical and hardy.

I gave my name to the clerk at the desk of the Madison Hotel and waited nervously while he muttered into a telephone that was just out of sight. "Mr. Harris wants you to wait," he reported after a moment. I glanced at the clock over the desk. It was a quarter of two and I was early for the appointment. It had not occurred to me, in my eagerness, to check the time. I walked to a chair in the lobby that faced the clock and sat down.

The Madison was largely a residential hotel and its walnut-paneled lobby had style and elegance. I watched its well-dressed occupants come out of the elevators and stroll to the desk, to leave keys or receive mail, with the discreet authority and poised assurance of the well-to-do. As I watched, my mind raced ahead ignobly to the pleasantries of behavior that money makes possible. It was a form of daydreaming I often indulged in. A too constant preoccupation with money may seem to indicate the lack of a proper sense of moral values, but I did not consider this to be so. It is not as craven as it may appear to those who have always had money and given little or no thought to its possession. Let them be without it for a while, and they will soon discover how quickly it becomes their chief concern. People with children do not think much about the gift of parenthood, but most childless couples think of little else until such time as they have a child of their own or succeed in adopting one. Parenthood and money are not so disparate as they may seem to be, if one considers how largely these twin obsessions engage the thoughts of a goodly portion of mankind. Once achieved, they soon cease to dazzle and very quickly fall into the natural order of things; but it is surprising how the lack of one or the other, particularly money, can occupy the mind to the exclusion of more noble sentiments. I have always accepted my pleasure in money as something eminently sensible and not as something crass or base in my nature that need be hidden or denied.

I had become so deeply engrossed in my own daydreams of plenitude that when I next glanced up at the clock it was twenty minutes past two. I rushed up to the clerk at the desk and gave my name again. "Mr. Harris knows you're here," he replied. "We're not allowed to ring him until he calls down."

At four o'clock a new desk clerk replaced the one I had spoken to. I tried my luck again, but with no better result. Mr. Harris could not be disturbed. From the clerk's tone I gathered that orders from Mr. Harris were not lightly trifled with. I walked back to my chair and sat down heavily on the newspapers which I had already read from cover to cover. I had long since passed the point of taking what comfort I could from the well-publicized fact that theatrical people are notoriously late for appointments; and, as usual, nervousness had increased my always large appetite beyond its ordinary limits, but the newsstand in the corner of the lobby was elegantly above carrying anything so plebeian as candy bars and I had not dared leave the lobby for fear the summons would come while I was gone.

As the hands on the clock veered toward five, I began to be concerned about my rehearsal in Brooklyn, which was an early one this evening; but I was determined not to jeopardize the chance of having the play read, no matter what. After all, Jed Harris had replied to my telegram with undeniable promptness and I was credulous enough to believe that theatrical history might be in the making upstairs. For all I knew, I told myself reassuringly, a pride of famous names might well be closeted with Jed Harris right now, reshaping the destiny of an as yet unborn hit, and who was I to chafe at being kept waiting.

For want of anything better to do, I took the manscript of *Once in a Lifetime* out of the envelope and began to read it. I soon put it back. The dialogue that had seemed sparkling, impudent and twinkling with humor the evening before now seemed astonishingly tepid. The thought of those intense eyes scanning these pages made the idea of sudden flight extremely tempting; but I had witnessed stage fright too many times to give way to it now. Instead, I sat and stared miserably at the clock.

At twenty minutes past five, the clerk motioned me toward the desk. With what I hoped would appear a casual saunter, I strolled toward him. I might have spared myself the trouble. He was busy riffling through those mysterious bits of red and green strips of paper that desk clerks seem to be endlessly engaged with and did not even look up when I stood in front of him. "Mr. Harris says to leave the manuscript and be here at twelve o'clock tomorrow," he remarked flatly, and held out his hand for the envelope. I handed it over to him without a word. It had not occurred to me that this meeting which I had been bracing myself to face for three and a half hours, would not take place at all. I felt immeasurably let down and curiously cheated.

A little dazed I walked out of the lobby and made my way to the nearest drug-store luncheonette. By the third hamburger, I felt a good deal better and of a mind to believe that the postponement was something of a blessing in disguise. After all, he obviously intended to have the play read by tomorrow morning—otherwise, why the instructions to meet him at twelve o'clock? My mood reverted at once to the great expectations of the night before and it was with some difficulty that I could bring any attention to bear on the evening's rehearsal in Brooklyn.

Sleep that night was an uneasy business also, and I was up and shaved and dressed long before I needed to have been, in order to be on time for my appointment with the great man. Promptly at noon I presented myself to the same desk clerk, and the same business of muttering into a telephone just out of my sight was gone through again. To my immense surprise, however, the clerk was blandly repeating to me the exact words of the day before. "Mr. Harris wants you to wait," he said succinctly and disappeared behind the cashier's window. I stood uncertainly for a moment, not quite prepared to believe what I had just heard, then walked toward the same chair I had sat in yesterday.

"But it can't be the same as yesterday," I thought; "there's no point to it. Why did he answer my telegram? Why did he ask me to leave the manuscript? Why would he ask me to come back?" I had plenty of time to think these and many other thoughts as well, it turned out. The clock over the desk slowly meted out time from twelve to one, from one to two, and then from two to three. As the hours passed, I veered from bitterness to amusement and back to bitterness again. But I was determined to wait it out, now, if I sat there all night and all of the next day. Some time or other Jed Harris must emerge from one of the elevators I sat facing, and when he did, he would find me keeping a grim vigil!

I was on my way over to the newsstand to buy some magazines when the clerk signaled to me. "Mr. Harris," he said, seeming in no way surprised at the extraordinary procedure of the last two days, "Mr. Harris wants to see you at ten o'clock tomorrow morning. Ten o'clock *sharp*," he added—which was to me one of the great under-statements of the time. "Tell Mr. Harris," I began—and then stopped. If Mr. Harris wanted to play games, I would play along with him. I nodded my head solemnly to the clerk and walked out of the lobby once more. It was not yet four o'clock and I had no rehearsal scheduled for this evening.

I made my way from the Madison Hotel to a restaurant called Rudley's at 41st Street and Broadway, where at four o'clock every afternoon a small group, of which I was a member, forgathered for coffee. Whenever I could arrange to be in town from Brooklyn I joined them, and there were many times indeed when I made a special trip in to take part in these daily discussions, for, like myself, it was a group of "have-nots," an acid brotherhood of kindred spirits all desperately trying to fight their way into the theatre and unseat the mighty.

A great deal of the satisfaction and pleasure I derived from these meetings was due to the fact that we were all, almost without excep-tion, a supercilious and malicious lot. Having nothing to lose, we had a great deal to say. No aspect of the theatre pleased us. Let Woollcott praise a play, and we immediately damned it and, in the bargain, accused him of logrolling for his Algonquin friends. Let Percy Hammond jeer at a performance and we were quick to defend it. If an actor or actress pleased the public, they did not please us. Our condemnation and contempt were reserved for success, and our enthusiasm for the calamitous failures, usually of the imported kind. Very few American plays or playwrights, particularly the newer and younger playwrights, met with our approval, and when we did give it, it was grudging and reluctant. We were bitter, jealous,

[251]

prejudiced and thoroughly unfair, and I can recall no discussions on the theatre since then that were as deeply satisfactory.

The most exhilarating theatrical discussions are usually those denigrating success, and I am certain that in all the little restaurants and bars that dot the theatrical district of today, just such groups are stirring their coffee and pouring their spleen into the hides and reputations of the successful. It is a game as ageless and fascinating as the theatre itself, and each time one of the mighty falls, the glad cry of "Bingo!" is joyfully voiced with all the resonance of a hallelujah chorus.

There was already a full quorum at work on somebody's reputation when I entered the restaurant and made my way to the group's usual table. The more or less permanent members, the ones who were usually to be found in their same uncharitable places every afternoon, were already there. Eddie Chodorov, long since returned from his African journey; Oscar Serlin, the only would-be producer among us; Edward Eliscu, a former social director (like Chodorov and myself) now turned lyricist; and a young man by the name of Lester Sweyd, the acknowledged chairman and arbiter of the group, were already at work, derogatives and disrespect flashing like knife blades on the play which had opened the evening before. The only faces missing were those of Preston Sturges, a young fellow who joined us occasionally and whose views on the theatre were so lofty that he looked down upon even us, and that of a disconsolate young actor named Archie Leach, whose gloom was forever dissipated when he changed his name to Cary Grant later on in Hollywood.

As usual, Lester Sweyd was banging furiously on the table and trying to stem the drift into disorder. It was never quite clearly known how Lester had assumed his position of leadership, for he was the only one of us with no clear-cut theatrical ambitions of his own. He was, instead, as he himself phrased it, a "believer" in talent, and to disagree with Lester once he "believed" was to open the floodgates of a Niagara-like power of invective that could overflow for days on end. Very few people chose to disagree with him. How he arrived at his choices, or by what standards he chose to "believe" in the talents of certain people and not in those of others, was his own secret and one that no one dared question, once he announced his annual slate.

He held sway among us for the very good reason that his knowledge of the theatre was boundless and he possessed total recall of everything he had ever seen in a career of theatregoing that had apparently begun at the age of two. Moreover, he kept encyclopedic records and diaries of everything he witnessed and was invaluable as a court of last appeal in a time before theatre yearbooks began to make their appearance. His judgments were not always sound, but the fact that his own ax was already ground and his opinions were untinged with the acrimony and bias of our own separate hobbyhorses and pet hates, allowed him to take precedence in the daily mayhem that went on around the table.

I was anxious to regale the group with my saga of the Madison Hotel, but I hesitated because I had somehow neglected to inform Lester that I had written a new play. This was lese majesty of a very high order indeed! Quite some time ago Lester had indicated that he "believed" in Oscar Serlin, Archie Leach and myself, and this knighthood rested somewhat heavily on all of our shoulders. We well knew that the conferring of this honor implied a scrupulous and immediate reporting to him of every theatrical activity, large or small, on the part of all three of us. Not to do so was not only to incur a wrath that was Jovian, but also to risk upsetting one of his well-laid campaigns to bring at least one foot of his protégés inside a theatrical door. He was forever accosting play readers, secretaries, casting directors, and even office boys, or whomever else he could waylay in the streets and alleys around Times Square, and saying, "The best young actor around right now is Archie Leach"; or, "Keep your eye on a writer called Moss Hart—he's a comer"; or, "If you want to put some money into a play, give it to Oscar Serlin—he's going to be the big new producer." His faith in those in whom he "believed" was touching; but like all true zealots his possessiveness was overwhelming.

He could turn in a flash on one of his selections and toss the crystal ball, through which he had so clearly discerned the talented one's future, smack into the transgressor's face. Not the slightest

[253]

margin for error was allowed. The unspoken rules were expected to be obeyed to the letter, and woe betide the protégé rash enough to break one!

Nevertheless, the temptation to regale the group with my adventures of the last two days overcame even my timidity in facing Lester. I waited until the play under discussion had been thoroughly drawn and quartered, from the first-night audience reaction down to the reviews in this morning's newspapers, then leaped headlong into the refreshing pause that always followed a thoroughgoing damnation and told my story.

Lester's response was immediate and typical. "You're wasting your time," he snapped. "Jed Harris will never do that play."

"That's a damn-fool thing to say," I retorted in spite of myself. "How do you know? You haven't even read the play."

"I don't have to read it," he barked back. "I know he won't do it. And *why* haven't I read it? You let me read all your lousy ones," he added waspishly.

"You can read it," I said placatingly. "I have a carbon copy and I'll bring it in to you tomorrow."

"I'm busy tomorrow," he said blackly, and left the table and the restaurant.

I tried to call him back, but the others were too eager to hear about the new play to let me go after him. They insisted, correctly, that he would be unable to resist reading it—which of course he could not, and he at once became *Once in a Lifetime's* most fierce and passionate champion.

That night I went to the theatre alone. I sat in the balcony of the Broadhurst Theatre and watched *June Moon* being performed on the stage below, much the way a young medical student might sit in a hospital amphitheatre and watch a noted pair of surgeons perform a difficult operation. George Kaufman and Ring Lardner were at their satirical best in *June Moon,* and the experience of seeing two skilled men function at the top of their form is a very special pleasure. I watched *June Moon* that evening with a private admiration of my own, for I could not help comparing it with my own first effort at satire. It was not too far removed in attitude from the play I had just written, and in spite of the identification I made between the two plays I did not feel I had come off too badly.

June Moon was sharp-edged and pointed, where my own play wavered uncertainly, swift and deft, where mine shifted emphasis; and the keen eye and sure hand of George Kaufman were stamped on both play and performance with the indelible professionalism that was his personal trademark. But in spite of *Once in a Lifetime*'s obvious lacks, I did not feel the same sense of inadequacy at the thought of Jed Harris' reading the play that I had felt yesterday. I could look him straight in the eye tomorrow when we met, with no false humility—presuming, of course, that we *did* meet. For I had decided that great man or not, this was the last time I would present myself to that desk clerk.

At ten o'clock the next morning I stood in front of the desk, and while the clerk went about his usual ritual of muttering into the telephone, I composed in my mind the short note I intended to leave in Mr. Harris' box when the usual message came through. "Mr. Harris says to come right up," said the clerk, confounding me and the biting opening sentence I had just contrived. "Suite eight-ten and twelve," he said a little impatiently, as I continued to stare at him. I looked at him blankly for a moment more and then turned toward the elevators.

The upper regions of the Madison were thickly carpeted and elegantly empty. I walked down the silent corridor to the door marked eight-ten and twelve, and knocked softly. The door of the suite was more than half open as though its occupant were waiting just inside the doorway, but there was no answer to my knock. I waited and knocked again. There was still no sound from within. I pressed the bell just at the side of the door and heard it buzz loudly inside the apartment.

After a moment or two, a muted voice, seeming to come from some distance away, called, "Come in; come in." I pushed the door open, walked past the little foyer and into the living room. The room seemed peculiarly lifeless. There was not a stubbed-out cigarette in any of the ashtrays, not a book or newspaper lying about, not a half-empty glass standing on any of the tables, or any of the other little telltale signs of life that give even hotel rooms an air of occupancy. For a moment I wondered if in my nervousness I had not misunderstood the number the desk clerk gave me. While I stood uncertainly, the voice, this time much clearer, and seeming to come from the bedroom, again called, "Come in!"

I crossed the living room and walked into the bedroom. One of the twin beds had been slept in, and its covers were kicked off or pushed onto the floor; the two ashtrays on the night table between the beds were filled with half-smoked cigarettes. The table itself was piled high with a mound of play scripts, and on the opposite bed two manuscripts had been carelessly tossed, one of which I noted quickly was the blue-covered manuscript of *Once in a Lifetime*.

The shades were still drawn and the room was in half-darkness. Its famous occupant was nowhere to be seen. I stood just inside the doorway not knowing quite what to do. A bedroom, particularly the bedroom of someone whom one has never met, is an extremely personal room to move about in. The voice called out again, "Come in; come in," this time unmistakably issuing from the bathroom.

The bathroom door was on the right, just out of my line of vision, and as I turned toward the voice I could see that it was standing open. A little mystified at the strange ways of the celebrated, I moved toward it, and as I reached the threshold I stopped dead. Mr. Harris was in front of the washbasin and mirror, stark naked. He was shaving himself and he did not turn around until he had completed shaving the side of his face he held the razor to. Instead, he addressed my image in the mirror, with the easy politeness of two people greeting each other in a drawing room in Grosvenor Square.

"Good morning," he said. "I'm sorry I couldn't see you until now."

I have no recollection of what I said to this, or even if I made any reply at all. I was suffused with embarrassment. I did not know where to look or what to say. My nervousness at meeting Jed Harris for the first time would have been great in any event, but the shock of coming upon him in this way was overwhelming. I have no idea what the expression on my face in the mirror showed of my feelings, but if he had planned to have my mouth drop open in surprise and dismay, he achieved his goal easily.

He finished the side of his face he was busy with, held the razor under the water tap, and turned his full nakedness upon me. "I read your play last night," he said, still as though he were fully clothed, "and I liked a great deal of it."

Again, I have no recollection of replying. There is nothing so exasperating, or that succeeds in making one feel quite so foolish, as pretending not to see something that one is seeing. I looked up at the ceiling and down at the floor. I stared at the shower curtain and at the light fixtures above the mirror—I looked everywhere but at the uncovered figure in front of me. Finally I fastened my eyes on the part in his hair and kept them fixed there, looking, I knew, exactly as I felt, an acutely embarrassed and tongue-tied fool.

So far as Mr. Harris was concerned, he might have been receiving Lord Chesterfield himself for an early-morning call. He was courteous, almost excessively polite and extremely talkative. Unfortunately, I did not hear a great deal of what was being said. I watched him finish shaving, wash and dry his face, and then sit on the edge of the bathtub and delicately pick some dead skin from between his toes. A word or two would penetrate, but that was all.

If Mr. Harris noticed my dumb-struck and rigid silence, he gave no sign of it. Talking all the while, he passed by where I still remained in the doorway, and began to dress himself in the bedroom. As he stood in his underwear, finally and at last, I began to hear what he was saying—and I regretted every word I had missed. There is no question in my mind but that Jed Harris is one of the finest conversationalists on the subject of the theatre that I have ever listened to. If there is such a thing as "creative" talk, he possessed this skill to its fullest degree. Only one other person I have listened to since matched him in brilliance: the late Irving Thalberg could generate in a hearer the same sense of excitement, the same tingling stimulation, the same feeling of participating in a discussion that was highly charged with the all too rare atmosphere of listening to a first-rate mind talking with the effortless ease of an accomplished master.

Even in my present disoriented state, I could tell that this was theatre talk of a kind I had never heard before, and as the haze of my embarrassment began to lift with each succeeding article of clothing that he put on, I began to listen intently. His criticism of *Once in a Lifetime* was sharp, penetrating, full of a quick apprehension of its potentialities as well as its pitfalls, and included an astonishingly profound understanding of satirical writing in general. His nimble tongue raced from *Once in a Lifetime* to Chekhov, to a production of *Uncle Vanya* that he was contemplating, to a scathing denunciation of his fellow producers, to a swift categorizing of certain American playwrights whose plays were not worth the paper they were written on, and back again to *Once in a Lifetime*—in a dazzling cascade of eagle-winged and mercurial words that left me a little breathless.

I was too deeply fascinated, too strongly impressed by this burst of eloquence to break in upon it and put the question I was burning to have answered: Did he like *Once in a Lifetime* well enough to do it? I could not, however, bring myself to speak and break the spell. I listened with all of my mind alert to the rich and unending flow of imagery that poured forth over every aspect of the theatre. And before I was quite aware of what was happening, his coat was over his arm and he was walking out of the bedroom and out of the suite toward the elevator.

"Are you going downtown?" he asked as he pressed the elevator button. I nodded. "Good," he said, "you can drop me."

In the elevator going down, walking through the lobby, and inside the taxicab into which he leaped as we left the hotel, he continued to talk with the same soaring agility and quick brilliance that sent each sentence blazing vividly into the next. He had a wonderful trick of locution which he used with great effect. No matter how grandiloquent the words, the delivery of them was almost whispered. Whatever he gave utterance to was spoken so quietly, with such deliberate softness, that one leaned forward to catch what he was saying with the most intense concentration.

He was talking still when the taxicab came to a stop in front of the Morosco Theatre on 45th Street. He called out a good-bye over his shoulder and leaped out of the cab. I watched him disappear down the stage alleyway, a little stunned and somehow curiously fatigued. This singular, intensely alive man created so compelling an effect by the sheer dynamic force of his presence, that when it was removed, the remarkable exhilaration and excitement he induced were replaced by a sudden and complete weariness.

I sat in the back of the cab for a long moment after he was out of sight, not yet in full possession of my everyday self, until the taxi driver called over his shoulder, "Where to, buddy?" Only then did it occur to me that Mr. Harris had left me to pay for the cab, and I remembered as I paid off the driver that I had watched Jed Harris put everything else in his pocket but money. I walked toward my more native habitat, the subway, musing on the strange ways of the celebrated and trying to sort out in my mind exactly what this astonishing interview had meant in terms of *Once in a Lifetime.*

In the massive flow of words I had listened to, I could fix on none which expressed his outright desire to produce the play, nor could I fasten on any which showed a complete lack of interest in it. I was at a loss as to what to do next, for having at last met the great man, I was convinced that no such simple procedure as a telephone call or letter would suffice to pin down the slippery and formidable gentleman who had received me in the nude and allowed me to pay his cab fare. I decided to let matters remain as they were for a while and do nothing. It seemed to me that a strategy of silence would have a greater effect on Mr. Harris than almost anything else.

The discussions during the next two or three days on whether or not this was the right thing to do were loud, violent and opposite. The stage-struck group in Newark maintained that as long as contact had been made, it was foolish not to push the advantage; and my own astringent group in Rudley's Restaurant, led by Lester Sweyd at his most intractable, insisted that I withdraw the script immediately and submit it at once to other managers. One of the grave dangers inherent in the various stages of any theatrical career

—whether it be budding, quiescent or diminishing—is the advice of friends.

The frivolity with which all theatrical activity is conducted has one consoling feature—there are no rules of behavior that apply regularly to any part of the theatre. There is nothing that one can say about acting, writing, producing or directing that cannot be revoked in the next breath. Nothing is immutable. The logic of one year is a folly of the next.

Probably the saving grace of the theatre as opposed to motion pictures and television is that unlike those lunatic worlds, repetition in the theatre usually breeds failure. There exists in the theatre, perhaps to a greater degree than in any other art form, a kind of rough justice in that its practitioners receive, if they stay in it long enough, just about exactly what they deserve—no more and no less. It is what makes the theatre the most dangerous of all public forums, but also the most satisfactory—and a field of endeavor where advice, however well intentioned, can never take the place of one's own judgment, good or bad. Every time I have departed from my own values and substituted those of others, I have suffered the inevitable consequences.

I listened to everything that was said by both groups, not always without an inward wavering and uncertainty, but in the end I did exactly what I had intended to do in the first place, which was nothing. I was greatly surprised some two weeks later when Lester Sweyd awakened me one morning with the news that Sam Harris had read the play and that I had an appointment to meet with his general manager, Max Siegel, that afternoon at the Music Box Theatre. The voice on the telephone raced on with such headlong speed that at first and in my still sleepy state I could make no sense at all of what he was saying. When I put the pieces together finally, it was too late to be angry; it had been dim-witted of me to have expected that the copy of *Once in a Lifetime,* which I had dutifully given Lester to read, would lie fallow in his hands.

What he had done was to turn over the play without my knowledge to one of the newer play agents that he "believed" in, a Miss Frieda Fishbein. Miss Fishbein, a season or two before, had succeeded in selling Elmer Rice's *Street Scene* to William A. Brady, after other agents had been unable to dispose of it. And since *Street Scene* had turned into a major success, all theatrical doors now were open at Miss Fishbein's approach and a good deal of red carpet was unrolled for her coming and going. Whatever plays she submitted, good or bad, were read with promptness and alacrity, on the basic and unsound theatrical assumption that where one hit came from another hit must surely lie in wait. Lester had simply disagreed with my strategy of waiting for Jed Harris and had gone ahead on his own.

Far from excusing the *fait accompli* he was presenting to me, he was loud in praise of himself and as loudly insistent that I get into town as soon as possible for a meeting with Miss Fishbein before the afternoon meeting with Max Siegel.

It was not, of course, an unhappy quandary for an unproduced playwright to be in. Though nothing but silence had ensued since my meeting with Jed Harris, my heart was still set on his producing the play. Nevertheless, Sam Harris was a distinguished producer in his own right, and if his interest in *Once in a Lifetime* was a genuine one and not just play-agent's talk, it might serve to heighten Jed Harris' interest or even push him into a decision.

Miss Fishbein, a large lady with a mass of red hair and many rings and necklaces, was given little chance by Lester to do much talking while we lunched, appropriately enough, at Rudley's. But I gathered that she agreed with him that Jed Harris was given to expressing a deep interest in plays he had no intention of doing and took an active pleasure in torturing writers with the promise and lure of a Jed Harris production without ever actually committing himself, thereby keeping the play off the market and out of the hands of other managers. I nodded agreeably, but I had no thought of passing up the possibility of a Jed Harris production if Jed Harris decided to lure me, false promises or no.

We stood outside the Music Box Theatre, a little early for our two o'clock appointment, and with broad grins told one another that of course this was where *Once in a Lifetime* would open. We were not being more than ordinarily fanciful. The Music Box is everybody's dream of a theatre. If there is such a thing as a theatre's making a subtle contribution to the play being given on its stage, the Music Box is that theatre. Except for the Haymarket Theatre in London, I know of no other that possesses so strong an atmosphere of its own, as living and as personal, as the Music Box. Even in broad daylight, as we stepped inside its doors and into the darkened auditorium, there was an indefinable sense that here the theatre was always at its best.

We walked up the stairway to the mezzanine and were shown at once into Sam Harris' office, where Max Siegel was waiting. I looked around me with deep satisfaction. Sam Harris' office was exactly what a distinguished theatrical producer's office should be, but more often is not. There is a vast difference in a producer's office when it is situated in a theatre instead of being contained in a series of chromium and steel cubicles of an ordinary office building. The theatre loses something when its business is conducted in the atmosphere of ordinary trade. Its people are not at their best on the forty-first floor of Radio City or in the high reaches of the Paramount Building, for although it tries very hard to seem so, and every now and then rigorously pretends that it is, the theatre, strictly speaking, is not a business at all, but a collection of individualized chaos that operates best when it is allowed to flower in its proper medley of disorder, derangement, irregularity and confusion. Its want of method, its untidiness and its discord are not the totality of anarchy it so often seems to be, but the natural progression of its own strange patterns, which sometimes arrange themselves into a wonderful symmetry that is inexplicable to the bewildered outsider.

Most of the furniture in Mr. Harris' office had quite obviously been reclaimed from various unremembered failures. Nothing could otherwise sensibly explain the stiff Italian Renaissance chair that stood behind the French Empire desk, or the early American benches that served as end tables for lamps and ashtrays. Even the sofa and easy chairs were a strange conglomeration of Georgian and modern, with wildly contrasting coverings; but the over-all effect of this unholy mixture was somehow wonderfully theatrical and cozy. No stage designer could have contrived a set of such marvelous

[262]

theatricality and correctness, or one that so instantly told the exact function of the room.

Max Siegel, Sam Harris' general manager, was himself a smiling and cozy fellow, who put me at my ease right off. He was cheerful and congratulatory about the play, and explained that after reading it he had sent it off to California to Sam Harris, who was visiting in Hollywood with Irving Berlin, and he had a telegram from Mr. Harris which he wanted me to read. He picked up the telegram from the desk and read it: " 'Like play. Ask the young author if he would be willing to make a musical of it with Irving Berlin. Sam Harris.' "

I was silent for a moment after he finished reading and then I looked at Lester and Miss Fishbein. To my surprise they were smiling delightedly. Without hesitation I rose from my seat and spoke directly to Max Siegel. When I think of the conceit, the self-importance and the pomposity of the words I used, I blush a little still, but I said them then, loud and clear.

"I do not write musical comedies, Mr. Siegel," I said, "I'm a playwright. I write plays—*only* plays." I looked sternly and directly at Lester and Miss Fishbein, then turned toward the door. They stared at me aghast, as well they might have, and since they made no move to get up, I started out.

"Wait a minute," said Max Siegel sharply. He laughed—and his laugh somehow saved the day. "You don't have to write musical comedies if you don't want to," he said. "Let me send Mr. Harris another telegram." He picked up a pencil and wrote hurriedly on a piece of paper. "How's this?" he asked, reading aloud what he had written. " 'Young author says he is playwright and does not write musical comedies. Are you interested in play as play and not as a musical.' What about that," he inquired, "does that say it plainly enough?"

"Yes," I replied, and added boldly, "But another producer is interested in the play just as it is without songs and dances, so he'd better make up his mind."

Miss Fishbein and Lester were shooting deadly looks in my direction, but their annoyance was lost on Max Siegel. "Mr. Harris is a quick decider." He chuckled. "You may have an answer tomorrow morning." He held out his hand. "It's interesting to meet someone who turns down Sam Harris and Irving Berlin in the same breath," he said. "It doesn't happen every day in the week, but I happen to think you're right."

It was my turn now to grin at my furious and still silent companions. I shook hands with Max Siegel and marched out of the office, trailing behind me a cloud of artistic integrity that lasted all the way down the stairs and into the street outside, where Lester and Miss Fishbein found their voices in full and resonant volume. I shrugged my shoulders and remained blandly adamant. The truth was, I suppose, that I still held high hopes that at any moment a message would be forthcoming from Jed Harris, and my courage, if it can be called courage and not unmitigated gall, in so airily dismissing one of the masters of American music, was based largely upon the secret illusion I cherished that Jed Harris would finally decide in favor of Hart instead of Chekhov.

When they move at all, things move with the speed of light in the theatre. There was a message to call Max Siegel waiting for me when I awoke the next morning. "I have a telegram from Sam Harris," said the voice on the phone. "It says, 'Tell young author I will produce his play if George Kaufman likes it and agrees to collaborate. Is he willing to collaborate with Kaufman? Am sending play air mail to Kaufman direct.'"

"Do you mind reading that to me again, Mr. Siegel," I said. I knew very well what the telegram said, but I was sparring for a moment of time to make up my mind, and a moment was all that I needed. "Tell him yes," I said, almost before he had finished reading it again. "When will I know whether Mr. Kaufman likes it or not?" I asked.

"He usually reads a play the day he gets it," replied Max Siegel, "and I'll call you right away. He ought to have it by day after tomorrow, so I should think you'd have an answer by about Thursday. Okay?"

"Okay," I answered.

"I'm going to draw up the contracts now," he said. "That's how sure I am that he's going to like it. Don't write any musical comedies in the meantime!" His laugh came merrily over the phone. "Goodbye, playwright," he added, and the connection at the other end clicked off.

I could hardly wait for four o'clock that afternoon to break the news of what I had done to the group at Rudley's and most particularly to Lester. I thought I knew pretty well what their reaction would be, and if I was right it was the better part of valor, I thought, to brave Lester's wrath among the safety of numbers. I was correct on all counts. Lester's wrath was great, and if the argument about my tactics with Jed Harris had been loud and vehement, the debate on my willingness to collaborate with George Kaufman was now outraged and violent.

"It will be *his* play!" "No one will ever know *your* name is on the program!" "You might just as well say 'By George S. Kaufman' and leave it at that!" "He'll get *all* the credit!" "They won't even know you had anything to do with it!" "A first play is what you establish your reputation with!" "You're just handing your play over to Kaufman and saying good-bye to yourself!"

The voices around the table grew so loud that the manager, accustomed though he was to loud talk from that corner of the room, came over and asked us to quiet down or to leave. It did me no good to protest that I knew very well that all or a good part of what they were saying might more than likely be true, but that what I was seizing was the main chance—the golden opportunity of working with the Herr Professor himself. There would be other plays to write, I argued, and if I emerged with little personal recognition from this one, the apprenticeship was well worth it. My arguments had as little effect on them as theirs did on me. I finally took a cowardly refuge by stating flatly that all this bellowing was largely academic. George Kaufman might be thoroughly uninterested in *Once in a Lifetime,* and even if he was interested, I had not yet signed any contracts; when the moment came for that, there would still be time to reconsider.

This bit of subterfuge fooled nobody, of course, Lester least of all, and I carefully remained absent from Rudley's for the next three days. My mind was made up, and though I had every intention of sticking to my decision, I well knew that continued argument carried with it the danger of making the half-truth seem valid. Eddie in particular was a most convincing and persuasive talker, who could brilliantly pervert any discussion to his own ends, sometimes purely for the pleasure of winning the debate. I did not wish to be shaken, for the more I thought of it, the more certain I became that a chance to work in collaboration with George Kaufman would be of greater value to me in the end than even a production as sole author of the play, by Jed Harris or anyone else.

It seemed imperative that I acquaint Jed Harris with this fact as soon as possible, for so far as he was concerned, he must still believe he held the right to produce the play if he chose to do so. Nevertheless, I let two full days go by before I could summon up enough courage to put through a call to the Madison Hotel. Having seen him plain like Shelley—plainer, perhaps, than ever Shelley was seen—I was aware that his reception of the news that I was withdrawing the play might range anywhere from magnanimity to cold fury, with a likelihood of something fairly bloodcurdling in between. I called the hotel at the unlikely hour of nine o'clock in the morning in the hope that he could not be disturbed and I could leave a message, but to my horror the call was put through immediately.

The low but intensely alive voice of Jed Harris came over the wire with the same vibrant urgency and excitement that any kind of contact with him immediately generated. Even on the telephone that quiet voice contained all the power of his presence. Stumblingly, I blurted out my story. There was nothing but silence from the other end of the phone, while I awkwardly backed and filled and explained and excused, and I finally ground to a halt and waited. I gave thanks to Alexander Graham Bell for an invention that could put this much distance between me and the silence at the other end of the phone.

When he spoke at last, the tone was as hushed as ever, the voice even softer and more silken. "I think you're doing exactly the right thing," he said. "I'm going to do *Uncle Vanya* as my first production

[266]

of the season. Chekhov has never been produced well in this country, don't you agree?" The question was asked respectfully, in the manner of one expert on the Russian theatre consulting another expert on a point beyond the comprehension of the mere layman. My relief was so great that I could do nothing more than grunt some sort of acknowledgment in reply.

There was another little silence and then the voice came softly through again. "Do you know George Kaufman? Ever met him?" he asked.

"No," I replied.

"Has he read the play yet, do you know?" he inquired.

"He may be reading it today," I answered. "He should have gotten it by this morning. That's why I wanted to call you before he read it, just in case he liked it. And I want to thank you, Mr. Harris, for being so . . ."

"Listen," the voice cut in, "this is George Kaufman's home telephone number. Put it down. You call him right away and tell him that Jed Harris says that this is just the kind of play he ought to do. Good-bye."

And before I could utter a word, there was a click from the receiver at the other end. I sat staring at the telephone, wondering anew at the unpredictability of Jed Harris, and for a moment I had a strong impulse to call him back immediately and thank him. I would drop him a note and do it properly, I decided, after I talked to George Kaufman; and I picked up the telephone again.

The number had barely buzzed once when a voice said, "Yes?" Not "Hello"—just "Yes." "May I speak to Mr. Kaufman, please," I said. "This is he," said the voice bluntly.

"Oh," I said and paused lamely. I had expected to give my name and state my business to a secretary before being put through. I had always taken it for granted that a secretary was as much a part of a famous playwright's stock in trade as a typewriter and blank paper. It was disconcerting to find myself talking to George Kaufman without that small moment of preparation beforehand.

"Yes?" said the voice again, this time quite testily.

There was nothing to do but speak up. "My name is Moss Hart,"

I said, plunging. "You don't know me, Mr. Kaufman, but Sam Harris is sending you a play of mine to read." I paused, suddenly overcome with timidity.

"I received it this morning," said George Kaufman. "I am reading it tonight."

"Oh," I said again, and stopped, thereby reaffirming the impression, I thought hopelessly, of what a brilliant conversationalist I was. There was nothing but silence from the other end of the telephone, so I gulped and continued. "Well," I said, "Jed Harris has read the play and he asked me to give you a message. He said to tell you that this was just the kind of play you ought to do."

Even as I spoke the words I was dimly conscious of their peculiar ring. But I was so relieved to have it quickly over and done with, that for a brief moment I did not realize no reply had come from the other end of the wire, and for another moment I thought we had been disconnected.

"Hello? . . . Hello?" I said into the receiver two or three times. But we had not been disconnected. The voice of George Kaufman was glacial when it again sounded over the telephone. Each word seemed to be incrusted with icicles. "I would not be interested in anything that Jed Harris was interested in," he said and hung up.

I put down the telephone and stared stupidly at it in complete dismay.

Not until long afterward did I learn that George Kaufman and Jed Harris were at that particular moment at the climax of a corrosive theatrical quarrel, a quarrel of such bitterness that it has remained irreconcilable to this very day.

Obviously, the motive of that seemingly innocent message was to produce exactly the deplorable result that it had had. There could be only one explanation: If Jed Harris intended to punish me for withdrawing the play, he had deftly accomplished his purpose in the most stinging and hurtful way. It is the only conclusion I have ever come to on this ill-natured and wayward bit of wickedness, for when I next met Jed Harris some three or four years later, the trepidation that awesome gentleman still inspired in me precluded any kind of inquiry on my part. I was still not brave enough to cross swords with him, and by that time it no longer mattered.

It mattered very much indeed at the moment however. I remained sitting in the chair by the telephone, too numbed by the sudden collapse of my hopes of working with George Kaufman, to do anything more than stare out the window and perceive the full idiocy of my behavior. I briefly considered calling Lester, Miss Fishbein, and even Max Siegel, but I doubted if there was anything very much that Max Siegel could do now to repair the damage, and I was in no mood for either "I told you so" or the disclosure of what a complete fool I had been.

I finally went about my business and did nothing. The play might be sold elsewhere, of course, and I supposed that I would be consoled and even console myself with the idea that this had been a blessing in disguise, but I knew I would never believe it. The chance of working with George S. Kaufman was gone, and I could not take the loss of that opportunity lightly. I was then, and am still, all things being equal, a great believer in the element of luck in the theatre—in that strange alchemy of timing that seemingly by chance and little else brings together an admixture of talents which, working in combination, infuses the theatre with a magical alloy that blends it into a mosaic-like junction of play, playwright, actor and director. It was my deep-rooted and perhaps childish belief in the mystique of this process that had made me grasp so eagerly and so unhesitatingly at the chance of working with George Kaufman.

I had felt in that moment when Max Siegel read me Sam Harris' telegram that luck was running my way, and I felt just as strongly now that fortune's wheel had seemingly spun past me. It would be nonsense to suggest that a complete reliance on so dubious and uncertain an element as luck does not imply an evasion of the other substantial realities that go into the making of any career, theatrical or otherwise. But I have seen the element of luck operate conversely too often not to remain convinced that it plays an exceptional and sometimes absurd part in the precarious charting of that thin line that divides success from failure. I am not an optimist where fate is concerned. I do not belive that one's destiny is resolved beforehand. It is a doctrine I have always rejected as indicating a certain poverty of mind or as the excuse of the insolvent, for it is a dogma that allows inaction to become a virtue. Nevertheless, I could think of no action on my part that would retrieve the disaster of that morning, and I went through the rest of that day and evening in a state of real wretchedness.

I was asleep when the telephone rang the next morning, but contrary to my usual custom of putting the pillow over my head and turning over, I got out of bed and answered it myself.

"Is this the young author?" the voice of Max Siegel came cheerfully over the telephone.

"Yes," I answered, thoroughly wide awake in a moment and shaking a little with excitement.

"Can you meet George Kaufman here at the Music Box at three o'clock?" he went on.

"You mean he read it?" I asked incredulously.

"Certainly he read it," said Max Siegel. "That's what he wants the meeting for this afternoon. He likes it very much—I told you he would. What's the matter?" He laughed. "You sound like you don't believe it! It's true. You'll be here at three o'clock then?"

"Yes," I managed to reply. "Three o'clock, the Music Box."

I hung up, and startled my mother, who had just come into the room, by throwing my arms around her and kissing her three or four times soundly.

"We're going to be rich," I said gleefully. "This time next year we may not even be living in Brooklyn." She smiled, pleased at my good spirits, but refrained from asking if they were once again based upon my "homework." She had been through six years of varying forms and degrees of enthusiasm every time I finished a play, and I have no doubt she had heard a version of the same speech before.

"I'm going to work with George Kaufman, *that's* the difference *this* time," I said. "George S. Kaufman," I repeated, rolling out the name luxuriously.

She stared at me blankly, the name having registered nothing at all, and then added hastily, "That's very nice." It was the tone of voice and the expression she reserved, I remembered, for such moments as when I would rush to show her a new stamp I had garnered by barter in my stamp-collecting days.

"You go ahead and do your shopping." I laughed. "I'll make my own breakfast." She smiled encouragingly, obviously pleased that she had not deflated my good spirits by her unawareness of who George Kaufman was.

"If you're going to bring him home to work with you," she said politely, "I hope you won't do it until after next week. We're having the painters next week."

"I'll explain that to him," I said carefully as I made my way toward the kitchen.

While the eggs fried, I composed in my mind a graceful little speech of gratitude I intended to deliver to Mr. Kaufman at the right moment after all the business details were out of the way. It sounded a shade too reverential even to my own ears, I decided, as I tried speaking it aloud while I waited for the coffee to boil, but there was no time to polish it up now. That could be done on the subway on the way into town.

I hurried through breakfast as quickly as possible and got to the telephone to acquaint Lester and Miss Fishbein with the happy trend of events, but more particularly to insist that for this first meeting I wanted to meet with George Kaufman alone. As I suspected, this did not sit any too well with either one of them, but I was firm, and at three o'clock I walked alone up the stairs of the Music Box Theatre to the mezzanine and knocked on the door of Sam Harris' office.

Max Siegel, smiling as usual, stood in the doorway, and behind him, slumped down in one of the large armchairs, I caught a glimpse of George Kaufman. That first glimpse of George Kaufman caught fleetingly over Max Siegel's shoulder made all the caricatures I had seen of him in the Sunday drama sections through the years come instantly alive. The bushy hair brushed straight up from the forehead into an orderly but somehow unruly pompadour, the tortoiseshell glasses placed low on the bridge of the rather large nose, the quick, darting eyes searching incisively over the rims, the full sensuous mouth set at a humorously twisted tilt in the descending angularity of the long face—each single feature was a caricaturist's delight. It was easy to understand why he had been caricatured so often. It was not a handsome face in the way the word handsome is generally used to describe men's looks, but it was an immensely attractive one. He had the kind of good looks that men as well as women find attractive.

Though it was rather a mild October day, he sat in the chair in his overcoat, and around his neck was wrapped a long blue woolen scarf that hung outside the coat and came almost to his knees. His legs were twisted or, rather, entwined one under the other in the most intricate fashion, so that one wondered how he would ever get out of the chair if he had to do so quickly, and one arm was stretched clear around the back of his neck to the opposite side of his head where it was busily engaged in the business of scratching the back of his ear.

"This is the young author, George," said Max Siegel, ushering me to the center of the room.

"Hi," said Mr. Kaufman wearily. He lifted in greeting one finger of the hand that was not engaged in scratching his ear, but he did not move otherwise. Even the one finger was lifted slowly and with infinite lassitude.

"Sit down," said Max Siegel, and smiled reassuringly at me. I retreated to the sofa at the other end of the room, but my eyes remained fastened and expectant on the figure slumped in the armchair.

"You want me to do the talking, George?" said Max Siegel after what seemed to me an unconscionably long time. Again the one finger of the disengaged hand rose slowly in assent. "Mr. Kaufman is willing to work with you on the play and he has suggested some terms for a division of the royalties," said Max Siegel, consulting a typewritten slip of paper on the desk. "Would you prefer to go over them with your agent?" he asked, coming over and handing me the paper. "I think you'll find they're very generous terms," he added.

"I'm sure there will be no difficulty," I said. I took the slip of paper from him and put it in my pocket without looking at it. My eyes were still riveted on the unmoving figure in the armchair. There was another long silence, and a long drawn-out and mournful sigh came from the depths of the chair, followed by a slight but unmistakable belch. It was a somewhat surprising sound—a cross between a prodigious yawn, a distant train whistle hooting over a lonely countryside, and the satisfied grunt of a large dog settling down in front of the fireplace. It was followed by still another silence while Mr. Kaufman's eyes restlessly searched for something they seemed to find missing on the ceiling. He had a perfect view of the ceiling, for he was now sunk so low in the chair that only the top of his head was visible from where I sat. The long legs wrapped one around the other in a tight sailor's knot obscured most of his face, but now the legs moved slightly and his voice issued clearly from behind them.

"When can we have a working session?" he said.

"Whenever you want to," I answered quickly. "Right away—any time—now." The words came out in too great a rush, but there was nothing I could do to stem my eagerness. Behind the legs the arms rose slowly and one hand reached into an inside pocket and withdrew an envelope, while the other hand found a pencil in the handkerchief pocket. I could not see his face, but he was holding up the envelope and evidently regarding some notations on the back of it.

"Would eleven o'clock tomorrow morning be all right?" he asked tiredly.

"Fine," I replied.

"My house," he said, "158 East 63rd Street." The envelope and pencil were moving down and going back into his pocket and one arm was going around the back of his neck again to scratch his ear. I waited and looked inquiringly across the room to where Max Siegel sat behind the desk.

Max Siegel winked at me and addressed the armchair. "Is that all you want of the young author now, George?" he said.

"That's all," came the answer, "except a second act."

Max Siegel made a slight gesture back to me, which seemed to say, Well, that's it, I guess. I cleared my throat and took a deep breath. It seemed that the moment for my graceful little speech had arrived. I had polished it up rather well in the subway, I thought smugly, and

[273]

I knew it by heart. I rose from the sofa and stood in front of the armchair.

"Mr. Kaufman," I said, "I would like you to know how very much it means to me to . . ." and that was all I said. To my horror, the legs unwound themselves with an acrobatic rapidity I would not have believed possible, and the figure in the chair leaped up and out of it in one astonishing movement like a large bird frightened out of its solitude in the marshes. He was out of the chair, across the room, had opened the door and was flying down the stairs, the blue scarf whipping out behind him.

I stared dazedly after the retreating figure until it disappeared down the stairway. "What have I done?" I stammered. "What did I do?"

Max Siegel, to my intense relief, was shaking with laughter. "You haven't done anything," he answered. "Maybe I should have warned you. Mr. Kaufman hates any kind of sentimentality—can't stand it!" He started to laugh again, but controlled himself. "Maybe I should have told you about George over the phone, but it never occurred to me that you were going to make a speech at him. Did you actually prepare a speech of thanks?"

I nodded sheepishly.

"Well, no great harm done," he said. "He had a barber's appointment that he had to get to, and you saw to it that he got there on time." He handed me a sheet of paper with a check attached. "I'm certain Miss Fishbein will agree these are very generous terms, so you can just fill in the contracts and sign them. That's a check for five hundred dollars for your advance royalty. Congratulations." He held out his hand and smiled. "If you want to, you can make the speech to me so it won't be a total loss."

I smiled back and shook my head. "Is there anything else I ought to know about Mr. Kaufman?" I asked.

He hesitated and laughed again. "There is, but if I started you'd never make that eleven o'clock appointment tomorrow morning. Anyway, it's like marriage—nothing anybody tells you about it is really any help. You've got to live it out for yourself; and if I know George, you'll be living it out every day from now on. Get a good night's sleep—that's the best advice I can give you." We shook hands warmly and I walked out into the bright October afternoon.

I stood for a moment outside the Music Box and looked up at its columned façade with a new and proprietary interest, the contracts and the check rustling importantly in my pocket. There could be no doubt of it now; at last I was on my way.

The rest of that shining afternoon had a quality of incontinent pleasure that I can still recall as vividly as though it were yesterday. The jubilant meeting with Lester and Miss Fishbein, the fusillade of congratulations and obligatory misgivings when the group forgathered at Rudley's, and that last look at Times Square lighting up for the evening just before I walked down the subway steps to go home; the same subway steps, I reminded myself, that I had darted up to have my first look at Broadway long, long ago.

I looked back at the lighted canyon, its daytime ugliness softened into something approaching beauty by the magic of the October twilight deepening around it. The knowledge that I was going to be part of it at last brought me perilously close to that wonderful mixture of emotions that makes one want to laugh and to cry at the same time. It is a mistake to dismiss such a moment as maudlin. To do so is to rob oneself of one of the few innocent pleasures the theatre offers. I enjoyed that last lingering look unabashed by its sentimentality and unashamed of its bathos. I deserved that moment, it seemed to me, and I allowed myself to enjoy it to the full.

I was wise to have done so, for my family's reception of the news, when I stood in the doorway and announced in ringing tones that I had sold the play, in no way matched my own triumphant glow. They received the news with an air of amazed disbelief and infuriating calm. Even the check, which I unfolded carefully and placed in the center of the dining-room table to be admired by them and by myself all over again, was viewed with an irritating detachment and a quite evident distrust.

"I suppose you know what you're doing, taking all that money," said my mother warily, "but I wouldn't touch it until after you've worked with this Mr. Kaufman for a while—in case he asks you to give it back. I certainly wouldn't go around spending it with Eddie Chodorov."

I lost my temper, picked up the check and what remained of my triumphant glow, and spent the rest of the evening on the telephone rekindling the embers of my triumph with Lester, the unsuspecting Eddie, Joe Hyman, and Dore Schary. And as a consequence and in spite of Max Siegel's advice I spent an almost sleepless night, chewing over and sorting out the insistent but contradictory advice I had received from each one on how to meet the first test with George S. Kaufman on the morrow.

THE NEXT MORNING at five minutes of eleven, I rang the bell of 158 East 63rd Street. The rather modest brownstone house was a little disappointing to my fancy of how a famous playwright should live, but the street was fashionable and the maid who opened the door was a reassuring sight. She was in uniform, a starched white cap perched correctly on her head. More like it, I thought, as she held the door open for me to pass her. I walked in and glanced quickly down the hall at a dining room leading out into a little garden. There was a bowl of flowers on the polished table flanked by silver candlesticks. Just right, I told myself satisfactorily and looked inquiringly at the stairway.

"Mr. Kaufman is waiting for you," said the maid. "The top floor, just go right up."

I walked up the stairs and stopped briefly at the second landing to look at a drawing room and library divided by the stairwell. Both rooms might have come straight out of the movies as far as my innocent eyes were concerned. I knew at once that my first goal the moment the money began to roll in, beyond the taking of taxicabs wherever and whenever I wanted to, would be to live like this. It was an illuminating and expensive moment.

The doors on the third floor—evidently bedrooms—were all tightly closed, and as I reached the fourth-floor landing, Mr. Kaufman stood awaiting me in the doorway of what turned out to be his own bedroom and study combined. After the elegance and style of the drawing room and library, this room was a great blow. It was a small, rather dark room, furnished sparsely with a studio couch, a quite ugly typewriter desk and one easy chair. It was hard for me to believe that a stream of brilliant plays had come out of this monk-like interior. I am not certain what I expected the atelier of Kaufman and Connelly would be like, but it most certainly was the opposite of this. There was no hint of any kind that this room was in any way concerned with the theatre. Not a framed photograph or program hung on its walls, and except for an excellent etching of Mark Twain, it might well have been, I thought regretfully, the bedroom and workroom of a certified public accountant. My initial disappointment was to deepen into an active loathing of that room, but at the moment, my eyes after the first quick look were focused on its occupant.

Mr. Kaufman was in the process of greeting me with what turned out to be his daily supply of enthusiasm so far as the social amenities were concerned; that is to say, one finger was being wearily lifted and his voice was managing a tired "Hi." He had moved to the window after this display of cordiality and now stood with his back to the room and to me, staring out at the gardens of the houses on 62nd Street. I had not been asked to sit down, but I was too uncomfortable to remain standing and after a moment of waiting I sat down in the armchair and stared at his back. His arm now reached around his neck to scratch his ear, a gesture I was to come to recognize as a prelude to a rearrangement of a scene or the emergence of a new line; now he remained for a few moments engrossed in the movements of a large cat slowly moving along the garden fence as it contemplated a sparrow on one of the leafless trees. This backyard spectacle seemed to hold him in deep fascination until the cat leaped up into the tree and the bird flew off, whereupon he turned from the window with a large sigh.

I looked at him, eager and alert, but there were still other things of moment that caught and held his attention before he addressed me directly. As he turned from the window, he spied two or three pieces of lint on the floor, and these he carefully removed from the carpet with all the deftness of an expert botanist gathering specimens for the Museum of Natural History. This task completed, he turned his eye toward a mound of sharpened pencils on the desk, found two whose points were not razor-sharp or to his liking, and ground them down in a pencil sharpener attached to the wall. In the process of doing so, he discovered some more lint at the side of the desk and this, too, was carefully picked up, after which he held up and inspected a few sheets of carbon paper, found them still usable, and placed them neatly beside a pile of typewriter paper, which he neatly patted until all its edges were perfectly aligned. His eyes darted dolefully around the room again, seeming to be looking for something else—anything at all, it seemed to me!— to engage his attention, but the carpet being quite free of lint, his gaze finally came to rest on the armchair in which I sat, and he addressed me at last.

"Er . . ." he said, and began to pace rapidly up and down the room. This, too—the word "Er" used as a form of address and followed by a rapid pacing—I was to come to recognize as the actual start of a working session: a signal that lint-picking, cat-watching and pencil-sharpening time was over and that he wanted my attention. During all the time we were engaged together on *Once in a Lifetime,* he never once addressed me by any other name but "Er," even in moments of stress or actual crisis. Perhaps he felt, being the innately shy and private person he was, that "Moss" was too intimate a name to call me; and to address me as "Mr. Hart" seemed a little silly, considering the difference in our ages and positions. But somehow or other I recognized at this first meeting that "Er" meant me and not a clearing of the throat, and I waited attentively until Mr. Kaufman stopped his pacing and stood in front of the armchair looking down at me.

"The trouble begins in the third scene of the first act," he said. "It's messy and unclear and goes off in the wrong direction. Suppose we start with that."

I nodded, trying to look agreeable and knowing at the same time; but this, like my disappointment with the workshop of the master, was my second blow of the morning. After the brilliant peroration on satire in the modern theatre that I had heard from Jed Harris,

[279]

I had been looking forward with great eagerness to that first talk on play-writing by the celebrated Mr. Kaufman. I had expected to make mental notes on everything he said each day and put it all down every evening in a loose-leaf folder I had bought expressly for that purpose. But this flat, unvarnished statement that something was wrong with the third scene of the first act seemed to be all I was going to get, for Mr. Kaufman was already moving past me now on his way to the bathroom. I turned in my chair and looked at him as he stood by the washbasin and slowly and meticulously washed his hands, and I was struck then and forever afterward by the fact that his hands were what one imagines the hands of a great surgeon to be like.

This impression was further implemented by the odd circumstance that he invariably began the day's work by first washing his hands —a ritual that was, of course, unconscious on his part, but which he would sometimes perform two or three times more during each working session, usually at the beginning of attacking a new scene, as though the anatomy of a play were a living thing whose internal organs were to be explored surgically. I watched him dry his hands and forearms carefully—he took the trouble, I noticed, to undo the cuffs of his shirt and roll them up—and as he came back into the room, walked briskly toward the desk and selected a pencil with just the right pointed sharpness, I was again startled by the inescapable impression that the pencil held poised over the manuscript in those long tensile fingers was a scalpel.

The pencil suddenly darted down onto the paper and moved swiftly along the page, crossing out a line here and there, making a large X through a solid speech, fusing two long sentences into one short one, indicating by an arrow or a question mark the condensation or transference of a section of dialogue so that its point was highlighted and its emphasis sharpened; the operation was repeated with lightning-like precision on the next page and the next, until the end of the scene. Then he picked up the manuscript from the desk and brought it over to me.

"Just cutting away the underbrush," he said. "See what you think." I took the manuscript and read with astonishment. The content of the scene remained the same, but its point was unmuddied by repetition, and the economy and clarity with which everything necessary was now said gave the scene a new urgency. The effect of what he had done seemed to me so magical that I could hardly believe I had been so downright repetitive and verbose. I looked up from the manuscript and stared admiringly at the waiting figure by the desk.

Mr. Kaufman evidently mistook my chagrined and admiring silence for pique. "I may have cut too deeply, of course," he said apologetically. "Is there something you want to have go back?"

"Oh, no," I replied hastily, "not a word. It's just wonderful now. Just great! I don't understand how I could have been so stupid. The scene really works now, doesn't it?"

It was Mr. Kaufman's turn to stare at me in silence for a moment, and he looked at me quizzically over the rims of his glasses before he spoke again. "No, it doesn't work at all," he said gently. "I thought the cuts would show you why it *wouldn't* work." He sighed and scratched his ear. "Perhaps the trouble starts earlier than I thought."

He took the play from my lap and placed it on the desk again. "All right. Page one—Scene One. I guess we might as well face it." He picked up a pencil and held it poised over the manuscript, and I watched fascinated and awestruck as the pencil swooped down on page after page.

If it is possible for a book of this sort to have a hero, then that hero is George S. Kaufman. In the months that followed that first day's work, however, my waking nightmare was of a glittering steel pencil suspended over my head that sometimes turned into a scalpel, or a baleful stare over the rims of a huge pair of disembodied tortoise-shell glasses. I do not think it far-fetched to say that such success as I have had in the theatre is due in large part to George Kaufman. I cannot pretend that I was without talent, but such gifts as I possessed were raw and undisciplined. It is one thing to have a flair for play-writing or even a ready wit with dialogue. It is quite another to apply these gifts in the strict and demanding terms of a fully articulated play so that they emerge with explicitness, precision and form. All of this and a great deal more

I learned from George Kaufman. And if it is true that no more eager disciple ever sat at the feet of a teacher, it is equally true that no disciple was ever treated with more infinite patience and understanding.

The debt I owe is a large one, for it could not have been easy for him to deal with some of my initial blunderings and gaucheries, particularly in those first early days of our collaboration. He was not at heart a patient man or a man who bothered to tolerate or maintain the fiction of graceful social behavior in the face of other people's infelicities. In particular, easy admiration distressed him, and any display of emotion filled him with dismay; the aroma of a cigar physically sickened him. I was guilty of all three of these things in daily and constant succession, and since he was too shy or possibly too fearful of hurting my feelings to mention his distress to me, I continued to compound the felony day after day: filling the room with clouds of cigar smoke, being inordinately admiring of everything he did, and in spite of myself, unable to forbear each evening before I left the making of a little speech of gratitude or thanks. His suffering at these moments was acute, but I construed his odd behavior at these times as being merely one more manifestation of the eccentricities that all celebrated people seem to have in such abundance. And the next morning, as I sat down, I would cheerfully light a cigar without pausing to wonder even briefly why Mr. Kaufman was walking as quickly and as far away from me as it was possible for him to get within the confines of that small room.

It did not occur to me, I cannot think why, to be either astonished or confounded by the fact that each time I rose from the armchair and came toward him to speak, he retreated with something akin to terror to the window and stood breathing deeply of such air as was not already swirling with blue cigar smoke. Nor could I understand why, after I fulsomely admired a new line or an acid turn of phrase that he had just suggested that seemed to me downright inspired, he would scratch his ear until I thought it would drop off and stare at me malignantly over the top of his glasses, his face contorted with an emotion that seemed too painful to find expression.

[282]

Even his passion to remove each dead cigar butt from the room almost before my hand had reached the ashtray with it, and his obsession with keeping the windows wide open on even the most frigid days, did nothing to alert me to his suffering, and I was, seemingly, deaf as well as dense when his diatribes against people who made speeches at each other took on added strength and fervor with each passing day.

I suppose his worst moment of the day came at my leave-taking, when he could sense another little speech coming on. I know now that he evolved various stratagems of his own to escape these eulogies, such as rushing into the bathroom and with the water taps turned full on calling out a good-bye through the closed door, or going to the telephone and with his back to me hurriedly calling a number; but with something approximating genius I nearly always managed to find the moment to have my say. He seldom escaped!

Mr. Kaufman spent a good deal of his time, particularly in the late afternoons, stretched out full length on the floor, and it was usually at one of these unwary moments when he was at his lowest ebb and stretched helplessly below me, that I would stand over him and deliver my captivating compendium of the day's work. Something like a small moan, which I misinterpreted as agreement, would escape from his lips and he would turn his head away from the sight of my face, much the way a man whose arm is about to be jabbed with a needle averts his gaze to spare himself the extra pain of seeing the needle descend.

All unknowing and delighted with my eloquence, I would light a new cigar, puff a last fresh aromatic cloud of smoke down into his face, and cheerfully reminding him of the splendid ideas he had had for the scene we were going to work on tomorrow, I would take my leave. I have never allowed myself to think of some of the imprecations that must have followed my retreating figure down the stairway, but if I was torturing Mr. Kaufman all unknowingly, the score was not exactly one-sided. Quite unaware that he was doing so, he was on his part providing me with a daily Gethsemane of my own that grew more agonizing with each passing day, and though his suffering was of the spirit and mine was of the flesh,

I think our pain in the end was about equal, for I was as incapable of mentioning my distress to him as he was of mentioning his to me.

The cause of my agony was simple enough. Mr. Kaufman cared very little about food. His appetite was not the demanding and capricious one mine was—indeed, his lack of concern with food was quite unlike anyone else's I have ever known. The joys and pleasures of the table seemed simply to have passed him by in the way that a dazzling sunset must escape the color-blind. He apparently needed very little food to sustain him and cared even less when and how it was served. He had his breakfast at ten o'clock in the morning, and work was enough to nourish him thereafter until evening. His energy, unlike my own, seemed to be attached not to his stomach but to his brain; and his capacity for work, which was enormous, seemed to flourish and grow in ratio to the rattle of a typewriter.

True, every afternoon at about four o'clock, apparently as a concession to some base need he knew existed in other human beings but did not quite understand himself, tea would be brought in by the maid. Six cookies, no more and no less, and on gala occasions two slices of homemade chocolate cake would lie on a plate naked and shimmering to my hunger-glazed eyes; and, as I could sniff the tea coming up the stairs or hear the teacups rattling on the tray outside the door, my stomach would rumble so loudly and my ravenousness would be so mouth-watering, that I would get up and walk about the room, pretending to stretch my arms and legs, in order to control myself, for it was all I could do not to grab and stuff the minute the maid set the tray down.

My predicament was further complicated by the fact that Mr. Kaufman was always scrupulously polite and devilishly insistent that I help myself first, and since I was only too aware that he took only a sip or two of tea and never more than one cookie, which he absent-mindedly nibbled at, I could never bring myself to do more than slavishly follow his example for fear of being thought ill-mannered or unused to high life—until one day, maddened by hunger, I gobbled up every single cookie and the two slices of chocolate cake while he was in the bathroom washing his hands. Whether it was the mutely empty plate or my guilt-ridden and embarrassed face staring up at him as he approached the tea tray, I do not know; but from that day onward, little sandwiches began to appear, and tea time to my vast relief was moved up an hour earlier.

Meanwhile, in spite of the separate and unwitting mortifications which we daily afflicted on each other, work proceeded with a grueling regularity and an unswerving disregard of endurance, health, well-being or personal life that left me at first flabbergasted and then chastened and awestruck at his unrivaled dedication to the task in hand. It was a kind of unflagging industry and imperturbable concentration that anyone, not just myself, might well marvel at, for this eminently successful man labored each day quite as though our positions had been reversed and this were *his* first play, not mine; his great chance to make his mark as a Broadway playwright, not my own. There was an element of the demoniacal in his tireless search for just the right word to round a sentence into its proper unity, for the exact juxtaposition of words and movement that would slyly lead the audience along the periphery of a scene to its turning point and then propel them effortlessly to its climax.

His ear for a comedic line was faultless and his zeal for the precise effect he wanted boundless. No moment, however small, seemed unimportant enough to escape his almost fierce attention, and his grasp of the play's latent values was immediate and complete. My eyes and ears were opened anew each day to the thousand-and-one endless details that go to make up the subtle and infinitely fragile clockwork of a play's interior mechanism, and to the slow cultivation of its subsoil that gradually makes it blossom into something vital and alive. I watched and listened with the consecration of a yogi, and yet in awe of him though I was, it never occurred to me not to disagree when I thought he was wrong, whether on the reshaping of a scene or even on a newly coined line which he liked and I did not. This was not a special bravery on my part or some noble effort at keeping my own identity intact—it had simply never entered my mind to be timorous with him or to be in any way discomforted by his manner.

I was all the more amazed to discover later on that this gentle man with whom I had been at once thoroughly at ease and completely comfortable, this same kindly and understanding man at whose side I worked each day, could instantly succeed in disquieting the most formidable men in the theatre or out of it and, by his mere presence in a room, frighten the daylights out of half the people there. There could be no doubt about the effect his presence created. Head waiters cowered and the wits of the town watched their tongues as he loomed up in a doorway, the eyes over those tortoise-shell rims seeming to examine the room for a sign of the inept, the fake or the pompous.

Famous raconteurs seemed to wither and dwindle under that penetrating glance, for he could puncture pretense or bombast with an acid verbal thrust that would be repeated with malicious glee in every corner of the so-called charmed circle before the sun set. Even such rugged specimens as New York taxi drivers or talkative barbers quailed at his stare and were silent until he was safely deposited out of the cab or the chair, and so fearsome a practitioner of the art of discomfiture as Alexander Woollcott admitted that George Kaufman was the one person who could always make him uncomfortable and ill at ease.

This side of him at first bewildered and astonished me. I never ceased being surprised at the startling and sometimes numbing effect he created among even the most seemingly secure and self-assured people, for unquestionably he did indeed intimidate even his close friends. But the result, though trying on the more timid of them, was not without its compensations. People took pains to be at their best with him, and just as a mediocre tennis player will sometimes play above his game when he is matched with a superior opponent, people were generally stimulated into their level best when he was about. It is my own guess that his somewhat terrifying manner, far from being any sort of pose, stemmed from the fact that he more than most men simply refused to resort to the banalities of what usually passes for polite conversation; faced with some of the cant and nonsense that a good deal of theatre talk consists of, he allowed himself the luxury of saying exactly what came into his mind as the only proper answer to the extravagant claptrap and twaddle he was often forced to listen to. It is not difficult to acquire a reputation for asperity and irascibility, particularly if one has the courage to indulge this luxury as a matter of principle and it is accompanied by a tart and ready wit.

These he had and the audacity to use them, for unlike most of us, he was not driven by a savage necessity to be liked. He cared little for the good opinion or the admiration of the special world he moved in and was a celebrated part of. He adhered strictly to his own standards and judgments, and they were stern ones. The most striking characteristic of the personality he presented to the world at large was an almost studied aloofness and indifference, and it struck me as remarkable how the world at large continually tried to break through this wall and win his approval on any terms he chose to make. Indifference can be a wonderful weapon— whether it is used as ammunition in a warfare between lovers or as a mask for timidity and shyness, for behind that mask of disdain and unconcern lay the diffident and modest man whom it never entered my mind to be afraid of.

Perhaps better than most I came to know that this seeming in-difference was the protective coloring of a temperament whose secret and inmost recesses held a deep reservoir of emotion; that it was the superficial exterior of a man who chose to reveal himself only to a very few, but whose emotions could be fervent and profound. I knew how quickly he could be seized and touched emotionally and how susceptible he was to the dark doubts that licked at other men's souls. Somehow or other, I do not know why, or quite under-stand how, I seemed to have managed from the very beginning to by-pass both the façade and the legend and immediately to fall into a warm-hearted and gay relationship in which he bore no re-semblance to the tales I heard or to the scenes I witnessed of his cantankerous behavior with other people.

He was not, of course, without his own mischievous and annoying qualities, even for me. He could be willfully stubborn on small

[287]

things with a dogged and inflexible obstinacy, and perversely fair and just on large issues to the point of exasperating saintliness; and he had an abundant share of inconsistent and crotchety prejudices that extended over a wide area and included, most particularly and actively, waiters who never seemed to be able to take down his order correctly, people who tried to tell him jokes, and any fellow passenger he happened to find himself next to when he was in an elevator or on a train and who had the misfortune to recognize him and attempt to engage him in conversation. If I was with him at one of these awful moments, his churlishness would make me cringe and I would move away and pretend we were not together, but to my unfailing amazement it was always him they apologized to and me they glared at. Like "the man who came to dinner," whom he resembled in a muted way more than he ever suspected, he suffered daily from the gross inadequacies of the human race; but these failings, however infuriating, were seldom sufficient—after a small but satisfactory explosion of irritation—to keep him from walking toward the typewriter with alacrity. Nothing in the world, as far as I could tell, ever stopped him from doing that—and as he walked toward the desk I would marshal my wits and try to think of a bright line to begin the day's work.

By the end of the first month of our working together, however, I was in a state of constant weariness. I attributed a great deal of my brain fag to simple malnutrition, but actually what I was suffering from was insufficient sleep. Our working hours were from eleven o'clock in the morning until five thirty or six in the evening, at which time I would eat a walloping dinner and rush off to Newark or Brooklyn for my little-theatre rehearsals, which began at seven thirty and usually continued until midnight and sometimes past. By the time I reached home again, after the obligatory socializing with the cast over coffee and cake, it was usually three or four in the morning. Since I had to be up shortly after eight o'clock in order to allow enough time for the long subway ride, which would get me to 158 East 63rd Street at five minutes of eleven, by the end of the month I was desperately trying, in those archaic days before Benzedrine and Dexamyl, not to let Mr. Kaufman notice that my brilliance seemed to diminish with startling abruptness at about two o'clock in the afternoon.

I did not dare, however, give up my little-theatre work. Apart from the necessary weekly income that it provided, the basket I carried most of my eggs in was too precariously balanced to shake, even with a Broadway production in the offing. I knew well enough that failure is the norm of the theatre, not success.

It was fortunate for me that Mr. Kaufman was the most incurious of men. The state of my health or the vagaries of my personal life held little interest for him, nor did he seem to connect my afternoon lassitude with either one or the other. It did not seem to surprise him that I grasped the smallest opportunities to take quick cat naps, sometimes even while he was washing his hands in the bathroom or taking a telephone call, and though he was vaguely aware that I was engaged in some sort of amateur theatricals in the evenings, it never seemed to occur to him to ask exactly what it was that I did. How he imagined I earned a living I do not know; but it was just as well that he was without curiosity on that score, for I had dropped Shaw and O'Neill from my repertoire and was now enthusiastically rehearsing the pirated works of Kaufman and Connelly.

I had switched to Kaufman and Connelly shortly after seeing *June Moon* and before I had the faintest idea that I myself would be working with one-half of the famous team. Now that I miraculously was, there was no way of changing back even if I wanted to. I breathed a sigh of relief, nevertheless, as each day passed and Mr. Kaufman's lack of interest in my personal life remained untouched, for it was the practice in those days for directors of little-theatre groups to escape, by any means they could devise, the payment of royalties to authors, for the good enough reason that no royalties to an author meant more money to the director, and I had long since hit upon the simple expedient of taking whatever play I wanted to do and giving it a new title of my own. Thus, *Beggar on Horseback, Dulcy* and *To the Ladies,* all three of which I was busily rehearsing each evening after I finished the day's work with Mr. Kaufman, were being presented as: *Dreams for Sale,*

Mrs. Fixit and *The Superior Sex,* by James L. Baker and Michael Crane.

I had never dared face what I would say if he ever questioned me about my evening activities; only once, when I asked if we might stop work early that particular afternoon because I had a dress rehearsal in Newark, was Mr. Kaufman's interest sufficiently aroused to inquire, "What play are you doing?" I was able to gulp an answer, *"Dreams for Sale,"* and as I saw his eyebrows arch questioningly at the title of a play he had never heard of, and as my heart began to race with the lie I was about to tell him—at that same moment his eye, luckily, spied a new piece of lint on the carpet and his interest in my personal life vanished.

As best I could and as much as I dared, I tried to end my nightly rehearsals earlier, but my weariness persisted. I had about reached the decision that I would have to borrow money enough to live on from Joe Hyman until *Once in a Lifetime* was produced, when the weariness disappeared as if by magic, never to return in quite the same degree. The magic was accomplished by two events that took place one after the other on the same day, and they instantly banished not only weariness, but also any idea I may have been cherishing of how hard my lot was. In quick succession, I met Beatrice Kaufman and I took a headlong plunge into the off-stage private world of the theatre that I had read about and mooned over for so long and of which I longed to be a part. Even the brief glimpse that I had of it was sufficient to keep me awake for quite a while afterward, for it came at just the right moment.

One morning, as I reached the fourth-floor landing at eleven o'clock as usual, I was surprised to see Mr. Kaufman in conversation with a handsome woman whose luxuriant hair, brushed straight back from her forehead in a high pompadour, was tinted a bluish-gray. I was aware, of course, that other people occupied and moved about in the rooms below us, but I had no idea who they might be. Mr. Kaufman had never spoken of a wife or child, and he did not, to me at least, appear to be a married man—but then it was hard for me to conceive of Mr. Kaufman as a man who had ever had a mother or a father, much less a wife! He seemed like a being who sprang full-grown out of the typewriter each morning and went back into it at the end of each day. I had as little knowledge of his personal life as he had of mine. Once the door closed behind us at eleven o'clock, no person other than the maid who brought up tea ever appeared and I had never glimpsed anyone other than the same maid as I walked down the stairs in the evening and let myself out the door.

I must have stared at them both in open-mouthed surprise, for their conversation ceased as I appeared on the landing and they both turned toward me. Mr. Kaufman lifted the usual one finger in greeting, and then seeming to summon up all the social graces he possessed for the effort, he said, "Moss Hart—Beatrice Kaufman." We smiled at each other and I stood uneasily on the landing, uncertain as to whether I should go into the room. I am a little loath to record that I at once took it for granted that Beatrice Kaufman was Mr. Kaufman's sister, but that, indeed, is what I did assume. For one thing, I had never heard anyone introduced in that fashion before. In the Bronx or Brooklyn, introductions always took the form of, "This is my wife, Mrs. So-and-So," or even more simply, just, "My wife." For another thing, in Brooklyn or the Bronx, a man and wife always occupied the same bedroom, and I knew Mr. Kaufman did not share his room with anyone else. Incredibly simple-minded though it seems, I did not discover that Beatrice Kaufman was Mrs. George Kaufman until a good deal later on, so that the mildly confused look that came into Mr. Kaufman's eyes when I politely inquired now and then how his sister was, is easily accounted for.

They picked up the threads of their interrupted conversation after that somewhat less than revealing introduction, and I stood watching Beatrice Kaufman admiringly. She was not in the conventional sense a beautiful woman, but she had uncommon distinction, an individual style, and a unique and singular quality of her own that lent to everything she said and did a special radiance. She had the gift of imbuing even the smallest of daily undertakings with an enkindling gaiety and an intoxicating flavor. It was a gift which was peculiarly hers and hers alone. I had never listened to or looked at, at such close quarters, anyone quite like her. I eavesdropped shamelessly. To ears used to listening to the female chatter of the Bronx and Brooklyn, her talk seemed to come straight out of Somerset Maugham, and though I could make little of what she was saying in terms of the people she was talking about, I knew she was recounting some tale of the world I had read about for so long in F.P.A.'s column. I marveled at the grace and ease with which she sent Mr. Kaufman into willing and ready laughter—no small feat in itself—and I was fascinated and charmed by the vibrancy and force of the woman herself.

This is the kind of woman I will get to know, I thought, when I become a part of that world myself. It was worth any sort of weariness a thousand times over.

I stared at them enviously and thought, How wonderful to have a sister like that—and as I watched and listened, hoping she would not finish the conversation too soon, to my surprise she suddenly turned to me and said, "I've left strict orders with George, and I'm depending upon you to see that they're carried out. He's to stop work early today and come down to tea. You're to come with him to make sure he gets there." She gave me a quick conspiratorial smile and then she was gone. I looked after her and then at Mr. Kaufman, who was already making his way toward the typewriter.

"Beatrice is having people for tea," he said grumpily as he removed the cover. "And of course the world is supposed to come to a full stop." Not, "My wife is giving a tea this afternoon," mind you—just, "Beatrice is having people for tea." I took it for granted anew that his sister was having a cousin or an elderly aunt, whom he was reluctant to see, in for a family tea—but that she was arranging it, nevertheless, in a devoted, sisterly fashion.

The sparkling flood of light her presence seemed to create remained in the room like an afterglow long after she had gone. It took me a while to settle down to work after the door closed behind her, and then I was brighter for having caught even that fleeting glimpse of her than I had been in days. The creative impulse is a mysterious one. It ignites and flourishes under the strangest of stimuli. I do not know precisely why the sight of Beatrice Kaufman should have unlocked my creative mechanism and set it wildly in motion, except that she seemed to be so striking a symbol of the world which lay just behind success in the theatre that she made the goal itself seem tantalizingly nearer and the drudgery and the weariness worth while. Both drudgery and weariness seemed to have vanished now. I could have worked right through the night.

It came as something of a shock when Mr. Kaufman glanced at his watch and said, "It's quarter of five." The day had sped by without my usual battle to keep awake or of my even being aware that no battle had taken place. He walked to the door and opened it. A babble of voices came up the stairway from the rooms below. "They're here," he sighed. "We'd better go down." He ran a comb through his hair, adjusted his tie, and motioned me to follow him. I was mystified by the number of voices that came more clearly now as we walked down the stairs. It did not sound at all like a family tea party. With some little alarm I realized I was not dressed for anything more than that—indeed, I was hardly dressed suitably for even that. I was wearing my ordinary working and rehearsal clothes, an old sport coat with brass buttons, and a pair of faded, unpressed brown flannel trousers. It was too late to think about the way I looked, however, for we were on the second-floor landing now and I was following Mr. Kaufman toward the drawing room. I drew back at the threshold and stopped dead. The room was alive with people and I recognized every single one of them. It seemed to my dumfounded eyes as if one of those double-page murals of the great figures of the theatre and literary world that *Vanity Fair* was always running had suddenly come to life.

Everyone I had ever read about or hero-worshipped from afar seemed to be contained within my awestruck gaze, from Ethel Barrymore and Harpo Marx to Heywood Broun and Edna Ferber, from Helen Hayes and George Gershwin to F.P.A. and Alexander Woollcott—as though some guardian angel of the stage-struck had waved a wand and assembled a galaxy luminous enough to make the most insatiable hero-worshipper's hair stand on end. I had the feeling that mine was doing exactly that, for I was seized with a kind of stage fright that made my tongue cleave to the roof of my mouth,

[293]

and I was horribly conscious of my clothes. Only a stare from over those tortoise-shell rims made me move forward into the room.

"Alfred Lunt—Moss Hart," said Mr. Kaufman. Alfred Lunt held out his hand and I managed to shake it. "Leslie Howard—Moss Hart," and again I smiled and shook hands, not yet daring to trust my tongue to come unstuck. "Get yourself a drink and bring Miss Parker one, will you?" said Mr. Kaufman. "Dorothy Parker—Moss Hart." I presented Miss Parker with the same glazed smile and stood grinning crazily at her, unable to get my upper lip down over my teeth. Neysa McNein—it was unmistakably she—called to Mr. Kaufman, and he turned away, mercifully releasing me from any more introductions.

"Don't bother about the drink," said Miss Parker. "Mr. Benchley and Mr. Sherwood are arriving with reinforcements." Her own slight smile seemed to indicate a willingness to talk, but Mr. Benchley, arriving with the drinks at that moment, came between us, and someone I could not see was putting a pair of arms around her in an embrace. With an inward sigh of relief, I moved toward the center of the room and stood by myself, watching and listening. To my further relief, no one paid the slightest attention to me, and the room was so jammed I felt my clothes would not be much noticed if I made myself as unobtrusive as possible.

A butler nudged my arm and said, "Tea or a drink, sir?" "A drink, thank you," I replied and took one from the tray. I took a long swallow and looked around me delightedly. Six months ago, I thought contentedly, even six weeks ago, this would have been pure fantasy. Maybe this time next year I'll be talking to everybody here. A group of people in front of the tea table moved away, and Beatrice Kaufman seated behind it suddenly caught sight of me, smiled brightly and waved her hand. I smiled and waved back.

At the far end of the room someone began to play the piano, and though I could not see who was at the keyboard, I knew that it was probably George Gershwin. I smiled to myself. I remembered how I had stolen some of the songs from *Lady Be Good* to use in camp, and I listened to him play with a special pleasure of my own. I began to enjoy myself hugely. It was far better, this secret enjoyment, I thought, than any kind of chatter could possibly be, even if I could manage to bring myself to talk to someone. The butler moved by me again and I relinquished my empty glass and took a fresh drink. Herbert Bayard Swope, on his way to join a group near the fireplace, found me directly in his path and said with great heartiness, "Hello, there, how *are* you?" He had obviously mistaken me for someone he thought he knew; but I smiled back and said, "Fine, how are *you*?" Speech had not only returned, but I was able to match his own heartiness in reply. I took a long swallow of the drink and looked around the room carefully. Why not talk to someone after all? What a fine, juicy bit it would make to report to the group at Rudley's. I could already hear myself artfully working a celebrated name into the conversation and then casually remarking, "Oh, yes, I was talking to him just the other afternoon." It would be a gratifying moment. Whom could I talk to, I wondered, that would impress them the most? There was almost too great a selection of the celebrated to choose from; for nearly all of the figures, which were damned and envied at the table at Rudley's every afternoon, were scattered around the room.

There was no question, however, as to who would impress them most. I had noticed him at once, even while I stood gaping at the threshold. And my eyes had searched him out several times since then, but always he was the center of a group that seemed to ring him in and roar with laughter at whatever he was saying. I looked around the room once more, and this time to my surprise Alexander Woollcott was alone. He had moved as far away from the piano as he could get and was sitting in a chair in the opposite corner of the room, calmly reading a book amidst all the hubbub. It seemed to me an astonishing thing to be doing at such a time, but then the celebrated seemed to be full of endless and varied eccentricities. By the same token, I reasoned, taking another large swallow of whiskey, he probably would not think it strange if I interrupted his reading and engaged him in conversation.

I made my way slowly over to where he sat and stood for a moment gathering my courage and my wits for the proper opening gambit. I glanced sideways at the title of the book he was reading and saw that it was a new mystery novel that I had just finished reading a few days ago myself. What better opening than that could I possibly have? Alexander Woollcott was a famous connoisseur of murder and mayhem and I was also an aficionado of this particular form of literature. We had that in common to start with, anyway, and then we could branch off into the theatre and all his various enthusiasms, every one of which I knew by heart. I moved closer until I was right beside him, then coughed discreetly to attract his attention.

"You'll like that very much, Mr. Woollcott," I said, pointing to the book, and smiled engagingly down at him.

Mr. Woollcott withdrew his gaze slowly from the page, and his eyes, owlish behind the thick spectacles, fixed themselves on mine. "How would *you* know?" he said.

The tone was so acid that the words seemed to ferment as he delivered them. The owlish eyes gleamed fiercely behind the glasses for a moment more and then removed themselves from mine and returned to the book, quite as though I had splattered against the walls and was no longer visible. I devoutly wished I could have done so. I would indeed have given anything to be able to vanish into thin air in front of him, but I could only stand for still another harrowing moment, rigid with embarrassment, until my legs were able to move me away. I retreated to the center of the room in a cold sweat of self-consciousness. There are moments so mortifying that one's inner sense of confusion and shame seem completely exposed to the eyes of every passing stranger. I knew well enough that no one had overheard this passage with Woollcott, but I began to tremble with apprehension lest anyone else speak to me. Suddenly, I began to be painfully aware of how raw and unqualified I was to move among these people, and how ludicrous it was to fancy myself ever becoming a part of this exclusive, tight little world. As quickly as I could, I threaded my way through the jammed room and fled down the stairs.

The next morning, my determination to be part of Woollcott's world more firmly strengthened than ever by the preposterous beginning I had made, I was galvanized into a kind of working fury. Out of just such ignoble moments and motives, do plays and novels sometimes emerge. For I do not think that these vain and foolish spurs to creativity obtained only in my own case. On the contrary, I am inclined to believe that just such petty considerations often seductively quicken the wheels of creation. If we could ever glimpse the inner workings of the creative impulse, coldly and without pretense, I am afraid that to a larger degree than we choose to admit of so exalted a process, we would discover that more often the siren enticements of worldly pleasures and rewards spark it into life than the heroic and consecrated goals we are told inspire it.

I have noticed that the lofty and lonely pinnacles inhabited by the purely creative are sometimes surprisingly and most comfortably furnished by Westinghouse, and a new convertible generally waits outside. There is nothing necessarily unacceptable or unworthy about this, but the pious nonsense that regularly issues from those domiciles—about the lacerations to the spirit that the throes of selfless creation impose and the unworldliness of the rewards these artists seek—is irritating to listen to. I knew what I wanted and why, at any rate. And crass as it may sound, it not only left my creative spirit unblemished but it heightened my capacity to enjoy unashamed the inglorious but satisfying mess of pottage that success offers to the less honorably inspired of us.

I SET SUCH a furious pace in the weeks following Beatrice Kaufman's tea party that to my own amazement and to Mr. Kaufman's as well, I think, the second act was completed and the structure of the third act was planned and roughly committed to paper in scenario form. To my further surprise, Mr. Kaufman called a halt. I had begun to think of ourselves as a great force of nature, like Victoria Falls, pouring forth and stopping for nothing. "I think a little breather is indicated before we plunge into the third act," said Mr. Kaufman. "We'll take tomorrow off." And then, accurately gauging the expression on my face to be the onset of a forthcoming burst of eloquence to commemorate the completion of the second act, he added wickedly, "There must be *somebody* else you want to say a few words to," and he rushed into the bathroom and turned the water taps full on!

While he was washing his hands, I eased my way over to the desk and stealthily turned over an envelope lying on top of the pile of manuscript to steal a look at the notations typed on the back of it. Mr. Kaufman's appointments and reminders to himself, which he typed out daily and later stuck in his breast pocket, always fascinated me, and whenever I could, I would shamelessly rubberneck, for they invariably listed meetings with a number of people whose juxtaposition on the same day never ceased to tickle my fancy. The list for tomorrow, freshly and neatly typed, with three dots between appointments, said in part: "Francis Fox . . . Scalp Treatment";

"Aunt Sidonia . . . Gloria Swanson." The jump from Aunt Sidonia to Gloria Swanson was just the kind of unlikely contiguity that delighted me, and there was an even more satisfying conjunction farther down on the envelope, for later in the day, which read: "Inlay . . . Croquet mallet . . . Norma Shearer." Satisfied that Mr. Kaufman's day would be as piquant and provocative as I had hoped it would, I turned the envelope over again and moved away to consider what my own one-day's respite would be. It took no great amount of searching to know what would give me the most pleasure. My day would not be as colorful as Mr. Kaufman's, but it would from my own point of view be equally diverting. I planned simply to stay in bed all day and eat! I would eat until I fell asleep, and when I awoke I would eat again until I dozed off. The very thought of the amount of food I would down filled me with content; but Mr. Kaufman, emerging from the bathroom, put an end to it.

"By the way," he said, "Sam Harris is back from California and he wants to meet you. I told him we wouldn't be working tomorrow, and he'd like you to come to the Music Box at eleven o'clock. Is that all right? I'm going to call Max Siegel now."

I nodded agreeably but seethed inwardly, and instantly made another solemn resolve. From the very first moment I could arrange to do so, I would never put a foot out of bed until noon. The solemn vows of our youth are fervently pledged but usually kept with inconstant faithfulness. This one, however, along with my resolve never to ride in the subway again once I had money enough to take taxis, I have had no trouble in remaining faithful to—and with no little pleasure and profit to myself.

There is ample evidence, I am certain, that the early-morning hours are the golden ones for work, and the testimony of such loiterers as myself on the enduring joys of late-rising carries little weight with folk who are up and about at dawn, busily improving those shining early hours. They continue to have my blessing from the depths of a warm and skeptical bed. I accept their data on the beauties of the early morning along with their thinly veiled scorn of my own pitiable indolence; but the truth is, I have never been able to understand the full extent of my loss. The Bay of Naples

[299]

and the harbor at Rio de Janeiro were still there at one o'clock in the afternoon when I first laid eyes on them, and were even more beautiful, it seemed to me, for my being wide awake and thoroughly refreshed when I did look upon them. So far as I know, anything worth hearing is not usually uttered at seven o'clock in the morning; and if it is, it will generally be repeated at a more reasonable hour for a larger and more wakeful audience. Much more likely, if it is worth hearing at all, it will be set down in print where it can be decently enjoyed by dawdling souls, like myself, who lumpishly resist the golden glow of dawn.

I was not, therefore, in the best of moods for a first meeting with Sam Harris as I climbed the steps to his office the next morning at a little before eleven o'clock, and it is not a small compliment I pay him when I say that after a few minutes in his presence, I no longer regretted that my dream of stuffing and sleeping had come to nothing. Sam Harris was an irresistible human being. From the moment Max Siegel offered his usual introduction, "This is the young author, Mr. Harris," and Sam Harris came from behind the desk with his hand extended and said, "Hello, kid," I was in love with him and his willing slave.

This was not, I was to discover, an unusual occurrence. Few people in the theatre or out of it remained aloof to the wise and tender sense of life that seemed to envelop Sam Harris and to touch everything about him. The extraordinary effect he produced on people was somehow made all the more striking by the fact that at first glance he gave the impression of being a most ordinary little man. He was short and chunky, with a pushed-in face that was saved from downright ugliness by a pair of the brightest and kindliest eyes I had ever seen, and a smile of such warm-heartedness and amiability that words like "goodness" and "humanity" leaped foolishly into the mind.

Most amazing of all, perhaps, was how immediately one was persuaded that this ordinary-appearing little man, of obviously little education or learning, was a man of impeccable taste, with a mind of vigor, clarity and freshness. He was elegantly turned out, from the pearl stickpin in his chastely hued tie to the fine linen cuffs appearing with studied correctness from under the sleeves of his beautifully tailored suit. He spoke softly, but with a pithy and trenchant conciseness, and his replies to a question were sometimes startlingly laconic. It made the first few moments with him difficult, for neither Mr. Kaufman nor Max Siegel had forewarned me before this first meeting that Sam Harris was more than a little deaf. He pretended, however, to hear everything, and some of the elliptical conversation that I was puzzled by on that first day was due to the fact that he was as vain about his growing deafness as he was about his appearance. It was the only vice, if vanity is indeed a vice, that I ever discovered he possessed.

He was exceptional also in the sense that a man without vices is usually humdrum and dull, and Sam Harris was anything but dull. He had color and gaiety and humor, and a most marvelous bonhomie with theatre people that extended all the way from stagehands to stars. Everyone in the theatre adored him. In a jungle profession, where the petty snipings of envy and mean-spiritedness are the passports to everyday conversation, the reverence in which he was held was a little awesome. So, too, was his renown for the way he could handle the most difficult of stars. On these vulnerable and trigger-tempered creatures the effect he produced was especially astonishing. An actor locked in a tantrum of rage and frustration at the end of a disastrous dress rehearsal would fall into sweet reasonableness at the sound of the first soft-spoken words uttered by Sam Harris. In a twinkling the hoarse words of rage would be muffled and the gentle voice of Sam Harris would take over. His secret, I think, was a simple one. Violence is strongly attracted by serenity, and Sam Harris was by all odds the most tranquil human being I have ever known. The world he lived and worked in was a world whose daily climate was governed by the uproar of hysteria and turmoil, and against this howling calliope of egomania he moved with a calm and a quietude that instantly subdued the most savage and ungovernable outbursts of temper and temperament. No matter how loud the blast or how extravagant the explosion, his untroubled serenity was the balm that allowed the bluster to die down and the bellowing to slacken into something that approached a common ground peaceable enough for rehearsals to continue.

I would be doing him a disservice to suggest that his nature was entirely saintlike or that he did not possess a good-sized temper of his own. He was too merry a fellow to accommodate much of saintliness, and when his temper flared, as it did occasionally, it was marvelous to see him wrestle with it, for it was a rip-snorting affair while it lasted. Actors themselves seldom provoked it, for he was excessively sentimental about theatre people and notoriously soft-hearted about actors in particular. Their lawyers or agents, however, were the worm in the heart of the rose, and about these he would fulminate with unsentimental gusto. Other than that, little else about the theatre daunted him. He was a gambler of unwavering courage, once he placed his bet on an author or star he believed in; and his single-minded passion to give a good play a fine production remained undiminished to the end of his life. He was a great gentleman of the theatre and, so far as I am concerned, its last aristocrat.

We got along famously, once the first moment or two of stiffness had passed and my enjoyment of him outran my shyness. "How are you two fellows getting along?" he asked. And when I replied, "I'm starving most of the time, but I think we've got a good second act," he roared with laughter. After that, I rattled on unrestrained, telling him all sorts of things about myself I could not recall ever having told anyone else; for it was quite evident that he liked me immediately, and there is nothing that so quickly opens the floodgates of friendship and intimacy as that light in the other person's eye that unmistakably signals a delight and pleasure in one's company.

I must have talked on interminably, for Max Siegel finally reappeared and, surprised to see me still chattering away, said, "You got an appointment at the booking office, haven't you, Mr. Harris?" Sam Harris nodded and came from behind the desk. He led me toward the door and rested a hand affectionately on my shoulder. "We'll be seeing more of each other, kid," he said. "I hope a lot more. I think you're going to write some interesting

[302]

plays." He smiled that special smile of his and waved as I started down the steps. I waved and smiled back and walked out of the Music Box lobby curiously jubilant and elated, though I could not understand why until a few minutes later. Suddenly I knew. Sam Harris had made up my mind for me.

For some two or three weeks past I had been shirking the making of a decision that had to be made, and now, still without knowing quite why I was doing so, I knew that I had made it. This hour with Sam Harris had pushed me over the brink. The decision was not an easy one to make. It was already March, and the owners of the Flagler Hotel had been pressing me since early February to sign a new contract as social director for the coming summer at the largest salary I had ever received and one which they claimed, truthfully I believe, to be the largest sum ever to be offered a social director in the history of the Borscht Circuit. I had backed and filled and excused and put them off in every way I could think of, but eager as I was to put that part of my life behind me, I had to face the possibility of what I would do if the spring tryout of *Once in a Lifetime,* which was planned for the last two weeks in May, was a failure. No camp or hotel, of course, could wait until the end of May to engage a social director, no matter how sought-after he was—March, indeed, was the very latest they dared wait and they had so informed me. But suppose *Once in a Lifetime* was only half-good and needed to be rewritten over the summer—what then? Some plays—in fact, a major proportion of them as I well knew—were summarily abandoned in Asbury Park or Atlantic City and never came to New York at all. If *Once in a Lifetime* were to meet this same fate on its tryout, how would I get through the summer and what would we live on until the little-theatre groups started up again in November? For though I was earning a good deal more money now, both summers and winters, than I ever had, it seemed to disappear with annoying swiftness—a phenomenon, I might add, that has plagued me down the years with dogged persistence. That morning, however, I had finally come to a decision of sorts—a safe compromise, so it seemed to me: the bright idea of

[303]

having Dore Schary substitute for me as social director until mid-June, when I would certainly know which way the wind was blowing; and then I could take over myself.

This was actually what I was on my way to try to do as I walked out of the Music Box. I was fairly certain the proprietors of the Flagler, anxious to have me as they were, would agree to these terms, and I had made the appointment to meet them and sign the contract at two o'clock this afternoon. Instead, I turned into the Piccadilly Hotel, next door to the Music Box, and marched resolutely toward a telephone booth. I dropped a nickel nervously into the slot, and as I closed the door of the booth, I knew I was going to burn the last bridge behind me. Fresh from the presence of Sam Harris, it seemed a simple and easy thing to do—and somewhat shakily I did it. I emerged from the booth and walked out into 45th Street again, a social director no longer, but a playwright come hell or high water—though no one on the street seemed to notice the startling change in me.

The next morning, arriving for work, I was conscious of a subtle difference in the atmosphere. Even before I had settled myself into the armchair and surreptitiously unwrapped the first Hershey bar in my pocket, Mr. Kaufman said, "Er . . ." and was pacing rapidly up and down the room. Cat-watching, lint-picking, ear-scratching and the straightening out of typewriter and carbon paper seemed to have been dispensed with. Even the pencils had all been sharpened before my arrival, and though Mr. Kaufman proceeded to wash his hands as usual before opening the pile of manuscript on the desk, he washed them hurriedly and kept up a running fire of comment about the third act from within the bathroom. We had long since agreed upon the opening scene and he quickly typed a description of the set, read it aloud, and then turned toward me with a tentative opening line of dialogue. I nodded and suggested a following line, and the opening pages of the third act began to spin from the typewriter.

I have always been more than a little puzzled by the fascination that the mechanics of collaboration seem to hold for most people, fellow playwrights and laymen alike. I have been endlessly questioned about how one proceeds to write a play in collaboration, a good deal of it on the basis, I am sure, of trying to ferret out just who wrote which particular amusing line in what particular play. But since I considered that no one's business but our own, I have always deepened the mystery by smiling inscrutably and pointedly turning the conversation into other channels. Actually, the process of collaboration is exactly what the dictionary says it is: a union of two people working in agreement on a common project.

It requires no special gift except the necessary patience to accommodate one's own working method harmoniously to that of one's collaborator. In *Once in a Lifetime,* it is true, there was a complete play to start from; but other plays were started from scratch and every line and idea, including the idea of the play itself, was so tightly woven into the mosaic of collaboration that it would be impossible to tell who suggested which or what, or how one line sprang full-blown from another. When the basic idea of a play was a good one, our collaboration worked well, and when it was not, it did not work at all. The mechanics of collaboration in the plays we did together remained as simple as putting a fresh sheet of paper into the typewriter and laboriously plugging away until that page satisfied both of us. It pleased me to make a mystery of our playwriting partnership, for the sole reason that the mechanics of two people writing together are no less dull and flat than the mechanics of one person writing alone, and I preferred to let the inquisitive lady on my right drink her demitasse with the idea still intact in her mind that I was a young man of rare and mysterious gifts.

There can be no mystery, however, about the fact that collaboration is an infinitely more pleasurable way of working than working alone. Most human beings fear loneliness, and writing is the loneliest of the professions. Writers agonize a great deal about the loneliness of their craft, and though the wailing is apt to be a little deafening at times, they are telling the truth. The hardest part of writing by far is the seeming exclusion from all humankind while work is under way, for the writer at work cannot be gregarious. If he is not alone, if he is with so much as one other person, he is not at work, and it is this feeling of being cut off from his fellows that drives most writers to invent the most elaborate and ingenious excuses to put work aside and escape back into the world again. Collaboration cuts this loneliness in half. When one is at a low point of discouragement, the very presence in the room of another human being, even though he too may be sunk in the same state of gloom, very often gives that dash of valor to the spirit that allows confidence to return and work to resume. Except on the rarest of occasions, writing is a cheerless business. I have not the least doubt that some young writers of promise have retreated to Hollywood or television simply because they hated being alone. I do not blame them, just as I am never unmoved by the suffering of a fellow writer when he cries out that he is "blocked." It is a protest, I think, against his unalterable fate of being alone, and it is a desperation I can understand and give full sympathy to. When later on I went back to writing plays by myself, I looked back to the warmth and companionship of collaboration with the nostalgia of the exile for his homeland, and I confess that I have moments of missing it still.

Some of the formal quality of our collaboration began to thaw slightly as we approached the end of the third act. For one thing, Mr. Kaufman suddenly grew talkative as he picked lint off the carpet or watched the cats in the backyard gardens across the way. This was formerly a silent business and I generally used the time to stuff Life Savers and bits of Hershey bars into my mouth, for I knew that nothing was expected of me until Mr. Kaufman was ready to say, "Er . . ." and begin his pacing. Now, however, he grew downright loquacious for a man of his taciturn bent, and to my vast surprise, I discovered that he loved gossip, the more indiscreet the better. It was a most unlikely side for a man of his nature to have, but there could be no question that he relished and delighted in the peccadilloes and indiscretions that float about the world of theatre folk like motes in the air on a hot summer's afternoon. He was aware that I was personally unacquainted with most of the people he gossiped about; but I knew the names, of course, and that seemed to be enough for him.

To my further surprise, he turned abruptly toward me one morning and said, "Let's have lunch out today. There seems to be a slight household crisis going on at the moment."

Lunch! I stared at him—we had never had lunch, as I understood lunch, in the four months I had been sitting starved in that chair. He must have caught my look, and completely misunderstood it, for he added, "You'll be able to eat something by about one thirty or so, won't you?" I nodded slowly at him and wondered what in the world he thought the constant chomp-chomp of Hershey bars in my jaws could have meant all through those long afternoons. Obviously, he was still totally unaware that some form of food was a necessity to most ordinary human or animal organisms. A dog, I reflected bitterly, would have slim pickings in Mr. Kaufman's house if he could not provide himself with a few Hershey bars on the side, or whatever the equivalent of Hershey bars is in dogdom.

The lunch he provided that afternoon, however, was a full one. During the course of it, I was somewhat startled to sense that he wanted to ask me a question but that he was embarrassed to do so and was hesitating. He seemed to dismiss it from his mind for a moment, but I could see he was going to ask it after all.

"What would you think," he finally said, "if I were to play the part of Lawrence Vail? We ought to begin to think about casting pretty soon, now."

In spite of myself, I laughed. Scratch a playwright and you find a frustrated actor!

He joined in my laughter, then added hastily, "Of course, it's a bit of a trick because I've never acted professionally, but I think I can do it and it would give that part the kind of authenticity it should have."

"It's a *wonderful* idea," I said, "it couldn't be cast better." I meant what I said. The part of Lawrence Vail was that of a famous Broadway playwright who is brought to Hollywood with frantic pleas and pressures for his immediate arrival, and then is kept waiting for six months without being able to see anyone at all or to find anybody who seems to know what he is even there for. The part, though it appeared in the second act only, provided a Greek chorus of sanity

[307]

to the lunacy prevailing all around it, and it was important to the play that it be played well. Some of my favorite lines in the play were contained in that part, and I knew they would never be acted better than the way Mr. Kaufman had read them in the privacy of his bedroom when he tried some of the scenes aloud for himself and for me. Not all but certainly some playwrights can give a better performance of their plays in a bedroom or study than those plays ever receive on the stage; just as some composers can sing their own songs far better sitting alone at the piano than any great star of the musical stage can sing them with a full orchestra at her feet.

Mr. Kaufman seemed inordinately pleased at my enthusiasm. So much so, that he seemed to want to hurry me through my cheese and apple pie in order to get back to the typewriter, but I was not to be pushed! I rightly guessed that the next full-sized lunch would be a long time in coming, and I took my own sweet time with each mouthful—in spite of the fact that he called the usual terrorized waiter for the check, paid it, and sat impatiently piling up little blocks of sugar all around the sugar bowl.

"If you take larger bites," he finally remarked, "we could finish the third act in a week."

He was right to the exact day. A week later he typed "The curtain falls on Act Three" and quickly dashed into the bathroom to escape what he correctly surmised would be a few grandiloquent words from me to set the occasion more firmly in his mind. This time, evidently suspecting a whopper, he turned not only the washbasin taps on full, but the bathtub faucets as well, and began to take off his shirt and tie. He smiled and lifted one finger in farewell, knowing it was impossible even for me to make a speech to a man who was stripping down to get into a tub.

"The usual time tomorrow," he called out over the noise of the running water. "We'll have to let Sam Harris know what we'll want in the way of actors. We'll go over the list together up here and then go down to the Music Box," and a little too pleased with himself, he nudged the door with his foot and carefully closed it.

[308]

M R. KAUFMAN and Sam Harris, in the days that followed, seemed to me to be casting the play a little too quickly for comfort, but as the inexperienced member of the trio I kept my reservations to myself. They were scrupulous about consulting me on every final selection, but I could sense when they both agreed completely on an actor or actress, and for the most part I remained silent or agreed with them. The fact was, I was enjoying these days of preparation for rehearsals far too much to worry over anything. These days were the dividends I had awaited with growing impatience to collect.

A play for me never really takes on an aspect of reality until it has left the dry air of the study and begins to sniff the musty breezes of a bare stage, with actors reading aloud at auditions. Only then does it begin to come alive. I have never quite understood playwrights who find auditions and rehearsals a grueling bore, or whose real pleasure in their work ends as it leaves their typewriters. For me, the excitement of auditions, the camaraderie of actors in rehearsal, the tight and secret conspiracy against the world, which begins to grow between actors and authors and directors and is the essence of putting on a play—this, to me at any rate, is the really satisfying part of the whole process, and the only thing, I think, that ever persuades me to walk toward a typewriter once again.

After the grind and imprisonment of those months in 63rd Street, the lazy freedom of sitting through auditions at the Music Box was glorious, to say nothing of the bliss of being able to dash into the little drug store next to the theatre between readings and gorge myself on chocolate malteds and hamburgers. I more than made up for the Spartan diet of tea and cookies I had been on for so long. Each day was a holiday so far as I was concerned, and almost before I was aware of it, or would have dreamed it possible, the play was cast and I was walking toward the Music Box for the first rehearsal. My excitement was intense. The bits and pieces of scenes I had heard read aloud at auditions had whetted my appetite to the bursting point to hear the play read in its entirety and in sequence.

My impatience was such that I was, unhappily, the first person to arrive. The stage was empty except for the two stage managers who were setting out chairs in a wide semicircle and placing a table in front of the chairs where Mr. Kaufman, Sam Harris and I would sit. They stared at me, surprised at my undignified promptness, and I thought I saw a good-humored wink pass between them, for I had evidently violated by my early arrival one of the major tenets of the code of first rehearsals. There seems to be a rigid code of behavior for the day of a first rehearsal that is as stately and as set in its pattern as a minuet. The minor actors are always the first ones to arrive. Then the principals stroll casually in, depending upon the order of their billing, timing their arrival by some inner clockwork of their own. Just before the appearance of the author, director and producer, the star appears—or if the star is of sufficient magnitude, she will appear last. The wink between the stage managers was a testimony to my newness as an author, but I did not mind. This was where I wanted to be, and it was a mark of what patience I had left that I had not arrived even before the stage managers themselves!

Gradually, the bit players and minor principals began to arrive; then, since there were no stars in *Once in a Lifetime,* the leading players—Aline MacMahon, Hugh O'Connell, Blanche Ring and Grant Mills—came onto the stage and took their places in the semicircle of chairs, all of them shining with that false brightness that actors seem to bring to a first rehearsal along with their cigarettes. I could hear Sam Harris and Mr. Kaufman talking in the back of the theatre, and now they came down the aisle together and up onto the stage, Sam Harris greeting all of the company even to the bit players, with a word or two or a pat on the shoulder. Mr. Kaufman muttered something to the first stage manager, and then sat down at the table and motioned me to sit beside him. Sam Harris sat down on the other side of Mr. Kaufman, with Max Siegel in the chair next to him. The stage manager called out, "All right, ladies and gentlemen—will you please be sure to use the fire buckets next to your chairs for your cigarettes. Thank you." He sat down again and turned toward Mr. Kaufman. I found it difficult to breathe; I cleared my throat with what sounded to my own ears like an artillery barrage.

Mr. Kaufman opened the manuscript on the table before him and quietly pronounced what have always seemed to me to be the four most dramatic words in the English language: "Act One—Scene One." There was a fractional pause and then the first line of the play came from the semicircle of chairs. It came rather listlessly and quite flatly, and so did the second and third lines. My own nervousness is affecting my hearing, I thought—and I brushed aside the impression I was receiving of the way the play was being read and tried to listen less nervously. It was not, however, just my own taut nerves that were making the opening lines sound so trite. The lines that followed were coming out dull and flat as well, and the play itself sounded entirely lifeless even in this opening scene. It seemed increasingly lifeless as the second scene droned on. I glanced sideways at Mr. Kaufman to see if his face was mirroring my own disturbance, but he seemed to be unaware of how badly the play was emerging. He was busily making notations on each page of the manuscript and seemed not to be listening at all. I looked past him at Sam Harris and Max Siegel, but they too seemed undisturbed. I could not understand it. Surely they were hearing what I was hearing—the sogginess and downright dullness of the play must certainly have been as apparent to them as it was to me. How, then, could they sit there so placidly unconcerned while my own ears were rejecting every line as it was read!

What I did not know, of course, was that all plays sound frightful at the first reading. It appears that still another aspect of the code of behavior of a first rehearsal is that actors, for reasons known only to themselves, consider it a breach of professional etiquette to read the play well the first time through. The stars or the principals mumble through their parts in a hopeless monotone, and if one of the minor players, new like myself to the proper procedure, reads his one or two speeches with a semblance of performance peeping through, he is stared at and contemptuously dismissed as a "good reader" or "radio actor," and the mumbling goes agonizingly on. The result of this witless but unshakable convention is that a new playwright will listen to his play being read for the first time by the company that is going to perform it and quake in his boots, wondering as he suffers through it what in the world he has wasted two years of his life on. Actors, of course, maintain that no such code exists at all and that their own nervousness and nothing else makes them read so execrably, but I have never quite believed it. They may well be telling the truth, but twice I have listened to a first reading in which the stars gave as brilliant a performance at the first reading as they subsequently gave on the stage, and I have never ceased to be grateful to them for it.

Gertrude Lawrence, at the first reading of *Lady in the Dark*, and Rex Harrison, at the first reading of *My Fair Lady*, plunged into their parts with an electric excitement, from the first line onward, that was contagious enough to make their own excitement spread through the rest of the cast like a forest fire; it made this usually dispiriting experience a thing to be set apart and remembered with gratitude.

As the end of the first act of *Once in a Lifetime* ground down to what seemed to me to be a slow death rattle, not only my undergarments were drenched with perspiration but my suit as well. I could feel my jacket sticking wetly to the back of the chair. The stage manager finally called, "Ten minutes, ladies and gentlemen," and I rose from the chair and looked miserably at Max Siegel, not daring to look at either Mr. Kaufman or Sam Harris. Max Siegel came over to me.

"What's the matter," he asked. "Not feeling well?"

"It sounded so terrible," I said, "so plain *awful.*"

He laughed and his laugh never sounded more reassuring. "But it always sounds terrible at a first reading," he replied. "Didn't you know that? The second act will sound a little better, and by the third act they'll begin to forget themselves and even act it a little bit. You watch."

He was correct. The second act did indeed sound like something that mildly approximated a play, and the third act even began to have a hint of amusement in it. I began to breathe again instead of wheezing, and when the stage manager dismissed the company for lunch at the end of the third act, I was amazed to find I even had an unmistakable sign of an appetite. It had seemed to me in the middle of the first act that I would never touch a morsel of food again, and I knew that to be a sign of how badly I had thought things were going.

By the time the company reassembled for the afternoon rehearsal at two o'clock, I was in high spirits once more and considered myself a hardy veteran of rehearsal behavior. Nothing would throw me now, I thought. But I still had two other disappointments to face that afternoon, one after the other in quick succession, and these I did not recover from as quickly. Mr. Kaufman was famed as a topnotch director and I had been eagerly looking forward to the moment when I would see him in action. I considered I had been cheated out of those little talks on play-writing I had expected to have from him and on which he had remained silent through all the months of working together. I could not see how he could very well do me out of the obligatory discussions he would now have with the cast, however. A day or two of these informal but enlightening talks from the director to the actors, on characterization, motivation and the level of performance that would best express the tone and attitude of the play itself, were what I had been given to understand every noted director did as a matter of course, and I had again come armed with a little notebook in which I intended to jot down the salient points he made while I sat in the back of the darkened theatre. I was an old hand at taking down my own homemade brand of shorthand at the back of dark theatres, and I expected to store up a good deal of valuable information for further use from these first rehearsal seminars.

To my surprise, the floor of the stage was already marked out with chalk, and the chairs and an old sofa were set out to represent the first scene of the play when the cast returned from the luncheon break. There was, apparently, to be no discussion at all! I could hardly believe what was taking place, but without so much as a word to the actors Mr. Kaufman already had the script in his hand and with no further ado was staging the opening scene of the play. Nor was this all. He spoke in so muted a tone that I could gather nothing of what he was saying—not that he was saying much of anything. He seemed mainly to be seeing that the actors did not bump into each other. The first scene, though not a long one, was nevertheless a scene which I took for granted would take at least two full days to stage, but it was staged in a little less than an hour. I watched astonished and disgruntled. The movement of the first scene marked out, Mr. Kaufman came from the stage down into the auditorium and asked for the scene to be run again so that he could see it from the front. The actors ran through the scene and he walked back up onto the stage once more. Aha, I thought, *this* is his method, to stage it roughly and *then* have his talk with the actors. It was merely a question of approach. Now, with the mechanics out of the way, would come the discussion of the playing of it. The motivations of the movement, the psychological background of each character in relationship to the actor himself, and all the rest of it.

Nothing of the sort occurred. Mr. Kaufman sidled up to Aline MacMahon in what seemed to be some slight embarrassment and began a whispered colloquy with her. She nodded in agreement to whatever he was whispering; then he moved to Hugh O'Connell and began to whisper in *his* ear. I began to squirm around in my seat with irritation. I had carefully sat myself down about three rows from the back, well over to one side of the theatre, so as not to have Mr. Kaufman feel that I was breathing down the back of his neck while he worked, but now I got up and moved down to the third row on the aisle. He had walked over to Grant Mills and was

[314]

now whispering into his ear in the same infuriating fashion. Even in the third row I could not hear one word of what was being said. It would not have done me any good, either, to move up onto the stage itself, for he spoke so quietly that not a word of what he was saying could be overheard even at arm's length away.

He proceeded in just this fashion not only for the rest of that afternoon, but for the rest of the three weeks' period of rehearsal. By the third day I glumly put my notebook away before I left the house to go and sit morosely through still another day of watching what might well have been a silent movie of a man directing a play —directing the first play, moreover, about the "talkies," I thought resentfully.

Gradually, however, and in spite of my annoyance, I could begin to see the pattern of his direction emerge. He gave no lessons in acting nor did he use the power some directors wield to hold a cast helpless before him while he discusses his own interpretation of the playwright's meaning, or with becoming modesty performs each part for each actor in turn to show how easily it might be played to perfection with just a modicum of his own talent. Instead, he seemed to allow the actors to use him as a sounding board. He watched and listened and without seeming to impose his own preconceived ideas of how a scene should be played, he let each actor find a way of his own that was best for him; and slowly, with no more than a whispered word here and there, the scenes began to take on a directorial quality and flavor that was unmistakably his. The sovereign motif of his direction seemed to be an artful mixture of allowing actors the freedom to follow their own instinctive intelligence and taste, and then trusting his own ear for comedic values—an ear that had the unerring exactness of a tuning fork. With no directorial vanity or ego of his own, he was able to indulge the actors in theirs, and an actor's ego in the early days of rehearsal is like a blade of new spring grass that will grow and reseed itself if it is not mowed down too quickly by a power-driven lawn mower—the lawn mower in most cases being the overenthusiastic imposition of a famed directorial hand. Unlike a newer school of directors, he made no pretense of being either

[315]

a built-in psychoanalyst, a father figure or a professor in residence of dramatic literature—a combination of roles which is sometimes assumed by directors and which always plays havoc with the stern business of getting a play ready to open.

The results of what seemed to be his detached and reticent direction were remarkably effective. The actors, a little at sea at first, gradually found their own balance; and since it was theirs and not a false one imposed by the director, they flourished and blossomed, and the play quickly began to establish an architecture of its own. All too often, or so it seems to me, a play has been so minutely directed to within an inch of its life early on in rehearsal, that some of its more simple and basic values are sacrificed to a showy but costly series of brilliant directorial moments, and these values are never thereafter recaptured. To my jaundiced eye, the best-directed play is the one in which the hand of the director remains unnoticed —where the play seems not to have been directed at all, but merely mirrors the over-all perception and sensitivity of a hidden hand that has been the custodian of the proceedings on the stage, not the star of them. Though it was dull to watch and I continued to feel that I had somehow been cheated out of my just due, I could not deny that each day he accomplished more than I would have thought possible, and on the evening of the eighth day of rehearsals, the first complete run-through of the play was given for Sam Harris.

Max Siegel, as usual, accompanied him, but no other person was allowed in the theatre. Mr. Kaufman did not hold with the theory or the practice of having run-throughs for his friends or friends of the cast, or even for people whose judgment he respected and trusted. He held firmly to the idea that no one person or collection of persons, no matter how wise in the ways of the theatre, could ever be as sound in their reactions as a regulation audience that had planked down their money at the box-office window, and in the main I think he was correct. There is perhaps something to be learned from a run-through for friends or associates; but more often than not, it can be as fooling in one way as it is in another. I have witnessed too many run-throughs on a bare stage with nothing but kitchen chairs and a stark pilot light and seen them go beautifully, and then watched these same plays disappear into the backdrop the moment the scenery and footlights hit them, to place too much reliance on either the enthusiasm or the misgivings of a well-attended run-through. The reverse can be equally true. However well or ill a play may go at a run-through, there are bound to be both some pleasant and some unpleasant surprises in store for the author when it hits its first real audience.

We received neither enthusiasm nor misgivings from Sam Harris at the end of the first run-through of *Once in a Lifetime* that evening. I was disturbed by his silence, but his curious non-communicativeness did not seem to disturb Mr. Kaufman at all. "You'll seldom hear praise from Sam Harris," he explained, "you'll only hear what he *doesn't* like. I don't think he was too displeased tonight or we'd have heard a little more from him. I imagine he's waiting until the play shakes down into a better performance before he says anything much." And with that I had to be content. Mr. Kaufman was too busily engaged with all the many details of production that engulf a director from that moment onward to give much time to the business of reassuring an increasingly nervous collaborator. The end of the afternoon rehearsal usually saw him in conference with the scenic designer, the costume designer, the prop man or the electrician, and the same conference with one or more of these same gentlemen took place again at the end of the evening rehearsal.

Once in a Lifetime was a large production. It called for six elaborate sets, a flood of costumes and a quantity of rather bizarre props, including a half-dozen live pigeons and two Russian wolfhounds. The pigeons and the wolfhounds were already being used in rehearsal to allow the actors to grow used to them, or to allow them to grow used to the actors. But since neither the pigeons nor the two wolfhounds seemed to respond as readily to Mr. Kaufman's whispered murmurings as the actors did, and as his patience with humans did not spill over into the animal world, I thought it politic under the circumstances not to add to his burdens by voicing my own moments of uncertainty. Part of the daily panic I was feeling, I suppose, was due to the fact that after the first easygoing week, the production of a play suddenly increases in tempo until it becomes a headlong rush

to meet the deadline of opening night, and with a complicated production there is never enough time to do the necessary little things—
mainly because of some impossible rulings by the unions that hedge
the theatre in on every side and effectively strangle the concentrated
and creative work a play should be allowed to have in rehearsal.

It was all going too fast; there were a hundred things still undone
that I knew could not be done now before we opened. What I had
not yet learned, and would have to learn the hard way, was that once
in rehearsal a play—and everyone and everything connected with it—
is sent spinning down a toboggan slide on which there is no stopping
or turning back. Whirling down the slope one can only take the
twists and turns as they come and hope to have sufficient luck to
land safely. It is a marvel to me that so many do, for there are no
exceptions made—the same rule applies to everyone—and the toboggan slide is especially iced for each new play.

Before I could believe it was happening, I was dazedly packing
my suitcase to go to Atlantic City for the dress rehearsals and the
opening. My own numbing anxiety was in no way helped by the
attitude of my family, all of whom had made a complete turnabout.
After their early conviction that the $500 I had received as advance
royalty on *Once in a Lifetime* was highly suspicious and that eventu-
ally I would be asked to give it back, they were now as firmly
convinced that the rosiest of futures awaited only the rising of the
curtain. My mother in particular was in a state of blissful certainty
that somehow I had at last stumbled into a profession which, while she
did not profess to understand it, at least gave the appearance of being
respectable; and in the eyes of her friends, a profession that was perhaps only a rung or two below that of lawyer or dentist. For quite
some years now she had labored under the burden of being unable
to explain to her friends exactly what it was her elder son did for
a living. My summers were not too difficult to explain, though
nothing, God knows, to be proud of, measured against sons who
were studying medicine or dentistry or the law; but the work I did
in the wintertime completely defied explanation or understanding.
She had maintained for a while that I gave "speech" lessons in the

evenings; but a son who lay around the house all day and did something so outlandish at night was obviously nothing to boast about. She had, I knew, always refrained from any mention of my "homework" as seeming to put an official stamp on my difference from other people's sons, but now suddenly she could point to that difference with pride.

Once in a Lifetime was booked to play a week in Atlantic City and a week in Brighton Beach, and the theatre in Brighton Beach was not too far from where we lived. The neighborhood was already well plastered with billboard posters announcing its coming, and my name, along with George Kaufman's, was prominently displayed. My name had also appeared in newspaper announcements of the play, and even the more theatrically obtuse of her friends could no longer be unaware that her son might be of some consequence at last! I truly believe that it was not the possibility of anything so unbelievable as riches coming out of all this, but simply the fact that my activities, always so mysterious and faintly spurious in the eyes of her friends, had taken on the aura of respectability. I knew very well that, having now seen my name on those billboards, she would be unable to accept the fact that my brand-new "respectable" profession might easily vanish within the space of two weeks, and I did not mention it. Her pleasure and her satisfaction were so apparent that I could not bear to disillusion her, and for much the same reason I said nothing to discourage my father's and my brother's equally unrealistic optimism and high expectations.

I kissed them all good-bye and took the subway to Pennsylvania Station, where I joined the company on the Atlantic City train. The "opening night" glaze already filming my eyes was apparent enough to make Max Siegel take one look at me, laugh, take a flask from his hip pocket and usher me quickly into the club car for a stiff drink.

ATLANTIC CITY in the spring of 1930 was bursting at the seams. Every hotel seemed to be filled to capacity and overflowing into the boarding houses that dotted all the side streets. The boardwalk, always crowded during the fashionable strolling hours, was even jam-packed during the late afternoons, so that the people on its outer edges seemed in some danger of being pushed onto the sands below.

I stared down from my hotel window at the sparkling ocean and at the pleasant pattern the strollers made along the sun-splashed boardwalk, and alert as always for omens, good or bad, I told myself that these holiday-minded folk were bound to be a good audience for a new comedy. Though I could not see their faces clearly, I preferred to imagine them as already wreathed in smiles of good will. After all, I thought reassuringly, Atlantic City was the top tryout town of the Eastern Seaboard, and the audience that would file into the Apollo Theatre on Tuesday night would not only be a knowledgeable one but an understanding and forgiving one as well, for they were used to tryouts here and did not expect a new play to be airtight. They would accept its lacks as part of the whole holiday spirit that pervaded the resort itself. And unlike that bitter winter's day in Rochester that ushered in the opening of *The Beloved Bandit,* today was mild and balmy and sweet with a lovely tang of freshness as the breeze rolled in from the ocean.

I stood by the open window breathing in the day and looking

down at the bright panorama spread out below me, and for a few moments my spirits soared and my faith in omens worked its usual magic. Yet as I turned away from the window and walked toward the bed to unpack my suitcase, I could begin to feel gloom settle over me once more, and try as I would, I could not shake it off. It was a misery as unreasoning and persistent as it was unshakable. I had wrestled with it all through the last week of rehearsal, through the wakeful hours of each night, on the train coming down, and now I could feel the same unmistakable flicks of anxiety and panic uncoiling and welling up within me.

"No one," I said aloud to the empty room as I slammed my things furiously into the bureau, "no one is worried but *you,* and they all know a hundred times more than *you* do, so stop it!" Saying it out loud helped for a moment, but for no more than a moment. The gloom deepened into the frozen panic that Max Siegel had seen clearly mirrored in my eyes as I stepped onto the train a few hours earlier. I threw myself on the bed and lay staring up at the ceiling. I knew little of psychoanalysis—its methods and its meaning were unknown to me—but instinctively I felt that I must make a final effort to try to understand the state of terror I was locked in, or it would take over and immobilize me completely. I lay on the bed for almost an hour, and the conclusion I came to, while not a very satisfactory one, at least had the virtue of presenting me with a calmer exterior and the ability to get out of the room and go to the theatre to face whatever I might have to face with some degree of composure.

What I was finding it impossible to face, I concluded, was the possibility of failure. Too much was riding on the success of *Once in a Lifetime* for me to be able to bear the idea of its failure with ordinary fortitude or even common sense. I was discounting the dread possibility in a way that Dr. Freud would have understood at once. I was obviously arranging an unconscious barter with the gods —offering up, as it were, my pain as a token of worthiness, making my suffering a silent plea for their clemency. It is not, I believe, uncommon behavior for people under strain and tension awaiting the outcome of an event upon which all their hopes are based; but as I dimly perceived that this was what I might be doing, some of

[321]

the pain eased, and consumed with the idea that I had divined a startling new truth, I walked out of the hotel and toward the theatre. Like all major discoveries made in a hotel room on the eve of an opening, however, this one lasted exactly the same amount of time—that is, it survived until I reached the theatre and walked through the stage door, where it evaporated and merged into the anxiety-ridden atmosphere backstage.

The first dress rehearsal, already well under way by the time I reached the theatre, although no one seemed to have noticed my absence, was going badly. The actors, without make-up and in their street clothes, sat numbly in their dressing rooms or hung about in disconsolate silent little groups in the wings, waiting to be called on stage when and if the stagehands had changed a set or after the electricians had adjusted and focused the lights. Little mounds of cardboard coffee containers, of half-eaten sandwiches and stale doughnuts had already begun to pile up in odd corners of the stage, in the dressing rooms and on the empty seats of the dark theatre. A false gaiety, as depressing and as soggy as the doughnuts themselves, punctuated intervals of equally false camaraderie between the actors and the stagehands, and finally disintegrated into a hollow shell of silence in which no one spoke at all.

The first dress rehearsal, in short, was proceeding in quite the usual way, being neither better nor worse than it usually is, for a large production in the throes of a first dress rehearsal is a dis-spirited and agonizing process. With it begins the age-old battle to allow the play to emerge in spite of the production, for at this stage of the game each bit of technical virtuosity or stagecraft—that extravagant effort by the lighting expert to suggest a pearly dawn, which takes a good three hours to achieve, and is thoroughly disturbing to the scene being played in front of it; that charming but useless conceit of the scenic artist to have a terrace where none should be, thereby limiting the acting area to a cramped boxlike space in front of the footlights; the extraordinary concoction by the costume designer that does not allow the leading lady to sit down in her evening gown, or a hat that completely covers her face from all but the first three rows of the orchestra—all of these in the first hours of putting a large production together seem to matter more than the play itself, and unless the battle is met head-on with a tough mind and an iron will and the sheer physical endurance to keep constantly alert, fiercely watchful and thoroughly ruthless, a play may be smothered or defeated by the intricacy, the trickiness or even the downright beauty of a production.

Perhaps sheer physical endurance is the prime requisite. It is almost impossible to convey to an outsider the atmosphere of a theatre during those endless hours of unrelieved tedium. The dismal waiting about, the awesome hopelessness of shouting at stagehands who can hear nothing and are obviously blind as well, the whispered but venomous arguments in the back of the theatre with the scenic artist, the lighting expert and the costume designer—all of this, strung out over a period of three days and nights, is my own private conception of what hell or eternal damnation must be like. There exists among the laity a mistaken idea that dress rehearsals are exciting and glamorous. It needs correction. They are pure hell! This particular hell, fortunately, was Mr. Kaufman's, not mine, although as an anguished onlooker I seemed to be doing a good deal more turning on the spit than he was.

I prowled uneasily around the theatre, moved about in the wings among the little groups of weary actors, wandered back and forth between the auditorium and the dressing rooms, finding little comfort on either side of the footlights and growing increasingly more certain that the play would never open by Tuesday, if at all. Mr. Kaufman walked silently up and down the aisle, a dim blue-suited figure, talking softly now and then over the apparatus that connected him with the stage manager backstage; or sat quietly in a seat in the very last row of the theatre, seemingly undisturbed by the chaos that was taking place in front of his eyes; and when I hoarsely whispered to him that the change from the first scene into the second had taken twelve minutes instead of two, he looked at me over the rims of his glasses and replied with a kind of lunatic logic, "I know. I've been right here all the time," and let his unconcerned gaze wander back to the stage again.

The comforting figure of Sam Harris was nowhere to be seen. I learned from Max Siegel, smiling as usual, that Mr. Harris had cast an experienced eye on what was obviously going to be a rocky series of dress rehearsals and had retreated to a chair on the boardwalk or to his hotel room and would not be visible now until curtain time on opening night. "He likes to keep himself fresh," said Max Siegel. "Why don't you do the same thing?" he added. "You can't do any good here standing around and looking green. You're just scaring yourself and the actors. Why don't you go out and get some air?"

I turned away without answering and wandered backstage again. In a little while I wandered listlessly back into the auditorium and slumped down into a seat for what I thought was to be five minutes of closing my eyes against the mayhem that was taking place on the stage, but which turned out to be two hours of the best sleep I had had in two weeks.

I seem to have no clear recollection of the next forty-eight hours. The scenic and light rehearsals went on, the dress parade took place, the actors began to appear in their proper costumes in the right scenes and at the right time. My memory of those hours is actually of a feeling or a sensation—of a curious illusion which is still vivid and remains remarkably clear in my mind to this very day. During those last two days before the opening I seemed to be under a constant hallucination that I was floating down an underground stream whose dark waters seethed and eddied with the faces of actors, stagehands and Mr. Kaufman—where the shore was lined with endless mounds of discolored coffee containers, half-eaten sandwiches and doughnuts—and that I was being borne swiftly and implacably toward an improbable island over which the precise, invariable voice of Mr. Kaufman echoed and re-echoed with a sepulchral clarity, although I could not always understand what he was saying.

I returned to reality, if indeed it may be called that, with the arrival of Joe Hyman in my hotel room at six thirty on the night of the opening. He found me standing in my underpants in front of the washbasin in the bathroom, with my hands outstretched beneath the electric light bulb over the washbasin mirror; I had pulled the cord of the light bulb, then fallen into some bemusement of my own, and instead of turning on the water taps I had remained standing with my palms upturned under the bulb waiting for water to gush forth. "Of all nights for the water to be turned off without warning," I said bitterly to him by way of greeting. "How am I going to shave? I can't go to the opening looking like this!"

Joe Hyman turned on the water tap and said, "Hurry up and shave and I'll buy you a good dinner. If things are as terrible as you look, you'll need one."

There was always a gentle hint of mockery in everything Joe Hyman said, even when he was being most grave. It was the most immediate and personal thing about him and it either attracted or repelled people who knew him only slightly. It was just what I needed right then. It cleared the air of actors, stagehands, even of Mr. Kaufman himself, and brought the real world back into focus. To my surprise, I ate and thoroughly enjoyed the large lobster dinner he bought me, and aided by his brisk matter-of-fact presence I even talked sensibly for the first time in weeks about the play. I had been right to allow him and no one else to come down to the opening. By urgent pleadings and a few not so veiled threats, I had persuaded all of my little coterie—Eddie Chodorov, Dore Schary, Lester Sweyd, et al.—not to come down to Atlantic City for the opening, but to wait until the following week at Brighton Beach. I wanted Joe Hyman and no one else with me tonight.

The initial performance, the raising of a curtain on a play before its very first audience, is for me at least the worst two hours of that play's existence, whatever its subsequent fate may be. No one really knows anything much about a play until it meets its first audience; not its director, its actors, its producers, and least of all its author. The scenes he has counted on most strongly, his favorite bits of fine writing—the delicately balanced emotional or comedic thrusts, the witty, ironic summing up, the wry third-act curtain with its caustic stinging last line that adroitly illuminates the theme—these are the things that are most likely to go down the drain first, sometimes with an audible thud. The big scene in the second act, or the touching speech that reflects all of the author's personal philosophy—that cherished mosaic of words on which he has secretly based his hopes for the Pulitzer Prize or at the very least the Drama Critics Award— such things the audience invariably will sit silently but politely through, patiently waiting for the reappearance of that delightful minor character, who was tossed in only to highlight the speech, or for an echo of that delicious little scene which was written only as a transition to the big one.

It is a humbling process, and the truculent author whose pride or vanity seduces him into believing that his play is above the heads of its out-of-town audience, is due for a rude surprise when his play reaches New York. There are, of course, plays that have withered out of town and then blossomed in New York, but they are the exceptions rather than the rule. By and large, an audience is an audience is an audience, as Gertrude Stein might have said, and the acid test of a play is usually its very first one. It is that first audience that I most fear, for regardless of what miracles of rewriting may be undertaken and even brilliantly carried out, the actual fate of a play is almost always sealed by its first audience.

A New York opening night is not something to be borne with equanimity, but after four weeks out of town, unless one is willfully blind and deaf to the unmistakable signs that an audience gives to even the most sanguine of authors, the ballots are already in and counted—the ball game has already been played and lost. Audiences do not vary that widely, nor for that matter, do critics. The New York notices will generally be more perceptive of the author's intent, more astute in distinguishing the first-rate from the cleverly contrived, but they will fasten on the weakness of a play or a performance with the same kind of exasperating genius that out-of-town audiences have shown from the first performance onward. It is permissible, of course, to believe in miracles as one makes one's way to the theatre on the night of a New York opening; but it is safer and less painful in the end, I have found, to continue to believe that miracles, like taxi accidents, are something that happen to other people, not oneself.

We strolled slowly along the boardwalk to the theatre, my dinner-table calm suddenly giving way to a mounting excitement and dread, distributed in equal parts at the pit of my stomach Even Joe Hyman, walking beside me, lapsed into a strange loquaciousness to cover, I realized, his own excitement. Neither of us said one word about the play. I discoursed learnedly and at length on one of my favorite topics, the evils of poverty; and Joe Hyman, paying no attention whatever to what I was saying, held forth on the superior taste and chewing consistency of salt-water taffy in the days of his childhood over the present poor makeshift specimens that we passed in store after store as we walked along. The lobby of the Apollo Theatre, when we reached it, was a reassuring sight. It contained within its jammed confines that happy buzz that I had come to associate with an audience about to enter a theatre for an evening of already assured pleasure. Pushing my way through, I heard "George S. Kaufman" and "He always writes hits" with punctuated regularity, and just before I reached the ticket taker a man behind me announced loudly, "I'll lay you two-to-one right now this show is a hit—I'll put my money on Kaufman any day of the week."

Joe Hyman presented his stub to the ticket taker, who nodded his head to me in recognition as I passed through. Joe and I shook hands silently, and I watched him proceed to his seat in the fourth row on the aisle, with the lingering, beseeching look a child gives to its parents when he is about to have his tonsils removed, but Joe did not look back. I turned and looked over the heads of the crowd at the back of the theatre for a glimpse of Mr. Kaufman. Mr. Kaufman, Max Siegel had informed me, never sat for the performance of a play—the first performance or any other one. He stood at the back of the theatre, not looking at the stage, but pacing furiously up and down and listening. Under the mistaken idea that he might expect me to do the same thing, I had not arranged for a seat, but stood dutifully waiting, anxiously casting about for him to make his appearance.

The house lights dimmed to the halfway mark, warning latecomers to get to their seats. There was still no sign of Mr. Kaufman. I wondered if I had misunderstood Max Siegel—I had not been understanding more than half of what was said to me these last few days—and I had a moment of wild panic, feeling certain Mr.

Kaufman had met with an accident on his way to the theatre and that the curtain would rise without him, leaving only me in charge. Then, from somewhere over my shoulder quite close by, came an unmistakable snarling voice: "Stop talking and sit down, you son-of-a-bitches." A group of latecomers, rather a large group, gave one startled glance at the grim figure staring at them over the rims of his glasses and scurried silently down the aisle. If Mr. Kaufman saw me, he gave no indication of it.

His wild pacing had already started. Back and forth across the back of the theatre he paced at a tremendous clip, staring down at the carpet and heedless of what or who might be in front of him. The ushers threw him a sidelong look and gave him a wide berth. He paced up and down like a man possessed, as indeed he was possessed at those moments, by a demon that only the laughter of an audience in the proper places could exorcise. For an uncertain moment I considered falling into step beside him, but another look at that formidable figure made me think better of it. Instead, I started my own pacing from the opposite side, so that we passed and repassed each other as we both reached center.

Thus began accidentally, for me, at any rate, a ritual that has persisted ever since. I have never since that night sat in a seat for a performance of one of my own plays. How many hundreds of miles I have paced in how many countless out-of-town theatres I hesitate to think. The mileage, to say nothing of the wear and tear, has been considerable. Moreover, my ear and my brain, at-tuned since that first memorable pacing, have never had the en-joyment of hearing the audience laugh—they are trained to hear only the silences when laughter is supposed to come but does not. It may account for my look of very real surprise when people have said to me, "It must be wonderful to hear a theatre full of people roar with laughter at something you have written, isn't it?" I have always answered, "Yes, it is," but actually I have never really heard it. I have always been listening ahead for the next line or the next scene, when laughter may not come.

The theatre went dark and the audience fell silent as the foot-lights glowed on. The curtain rose to a spatter of polite, obligatory applause, but I resolutely kept my face from the stage, fiercely determined to emulate my hero, whose eyes were glued to the carpet and whose legs were taking even longer strides as he came toward me. Aline MacMahon made her entrance and a second or so later, with her third line, the entire audience broke into a roar of laughter. It marked the first time I had ever heard an audience laugh at something I had written.

I stopped dead in my tracks as though someone had struck me hard across the mouth, and the Lobster Newburg resting fitfully in my stomach took a fearful heave and turn. I was near the stairway fortunately, and I raced down to the men's room, making it only just in time, and there I remained for the next fifteen or twenty minutes. I could hear applause and knew that the first scene had ended, and could tell by the other kind of applause that Blanche Ring had made her entrance in the second scene, but I dared not go upstairs. Each time I tried to leave I got only as far as the bottom of the stairway, and then returned to be sick again.

Finally, in the middle of the second scene, I could bear it no longer. The audience was laughing almost continuously now and it was intolerable not to be able to drink it all in. I raced up the stairs and for a few seconds stood gaping at the stage, grinning foolishly and then breaking into delighted laughter myself as the audience laughed.

I might have stayed that way for the rest of the act, or indeed the whole show, but for the figure that loomed up suddenly beside me and interrupted his pacing just long enough to remark thinly, "There were plenty of places where they didn't laugh while you were doing whatever the hell you were doing." He made a grenadier-turn and was off like a whippet to the opposite side of the theatre. Thoroughly ashamed of myself, I resumed my own pacing; and we passed and repassed each other without a word until the curtain fell on the end of the first act.

I could barely wait for Joe Hyman to get up the aisle, but I could tell from the applause and from that wonderful buzz that came from the audience itself on all sides as the house lights went on, that the first act had gone wonderfully. Joe Hyman did not stint.

For once he "gave satisfaction," as my mother would have said. "If the rest of it keeps up like this, my boy, you can give up the lecture on the evils of poverty," he said, his face wreathed in one big satisfied grin. I looked around for Mr. Kaufman, but of course he had gone backstage. He was to be discovered already seated as the curtain rose on the second act, and he would be putting on his make-up now. I moved about trying to find Max Siegel or Sam Harris; but Max Siegel was nowhere to be found and Sam Harris was surrounded by a large group of people. He caught sight of me over the edge of the group and winked broadly. There could be no doubt that he was immensely pleased.

The ushers began to shout, "Curtain going up, second act . . . Curtain going up . . ." and the audience started to stream back down the aisles with avidity. The pace with which an audience returns to its seats after an intermission is always a dead giveaway on how the play is going. If they linger to chatter in the lobby or sip their orangeades at the back of the theatre, it is always a fairly good sign that things are not going any too well. I am always infuriated by stragglers, but one cannot blame an audience for being reluctant to return for more of the same if what they have already sat through has been dreary and dull. It seemed to me that this audience could hardly wait to get back to their seats.

Mr. Kaufman's reception, when the curtain rose on the second act, was the biggest of the evening. That gaunt, saturnine figure, his eyes peering malignantly over the rims of his glasses, seemed to amuse them before he even spoke—and the very first line he uttered got the biggest laugh in the play so far. Indeed, they laughed twice at it, so to speak—once a great roar, and as the roar died down they gave another burst of delighted laughter. Then they broke into applause, completely drowning out his next line, but he craftily waited them out, then signaled with his eyes to Leona Maricle, to give him the cue again. He was quite wonderful in the part and in complete control of the audience. His timing was perfect, he looked exactly what he was supposed to be—a New York playwright venomously dedicated against all things Hollywood—and he played with the resourcefulness and skill of an actor who had been all his life on the stage. In my opinion he never received enough credit for his performance. Not being a "real" actor, he was received by the critics with the good-humored tolerance reserved for a theatrical trick or a parochial joke; but it was far above anything of the sort. Every line he uttered, even some of his pantomime, drew huge laughs, and when he made his exit in the middle of the second act a resounding round of applause followed him off.

And then a terrible thing happened. An extraordinary quiet settled over that eager, willing audience!

There were laughs, of course, during the rest of the act but they were scattered and thinnish and sounded as though the audience were forcing themselves to laugh at things they didn't quite find really funny. It was as though they wanted the play to keep on being as good as it had been and were eager to help as much as they could by playing the part of a still delighted audience. The second-act curtain, nevertheless, descended to a polite but disappointed hand.

I did not wait for Joe Hyman to come up the aisle this time. With grim foreboding I made my cowardly way to the stage alley around the corner, where I stood miserably biting my nails and saying silently over and over, "Oh, God, is it going to be like Chicago again?"

I went back to the theatre after the curtain had risen on the third act, to find Mr. Kaufman already pacing furiously up and down. I resumed my own pacing and we passed and repassed each other, though he did not speak to me nor I to him. The third act played more or less like the latter half of the second—scattered thinnish laughs—and finally in the last scene, a scene made all the more lethal because the scene itself was more elaborate in decor and lavish in costume than any other in the play, no laughs at all. It was the scene we had labored hardest on, and true to form, the scene which we both liked the best and were secretly the proudest of. With a silent and disgruntled audience watching it, the elaborate set looked ridiculous and the expensive costumes foolish and a little vulgar.

A deadly cough or two began to echo hollowly through the auditorium—that telltale tocsin that pierces the playwright's eardrums, those sounds that penetrate his heart like carefully aimed poison darts—and after the first few tentative coughs a sudden epidemic of

[331]

respiratory ailments seemed to spread through every chest in the audience as though a long-awaited signal had been given. Great clearings of the throat, prodigious nose-blowings, Gargantuan sneezes came from all parts of the theatre both upstairs and down, all of them gradually blending until the odious sound emerged as one great and constant cough that drowned out every line that was being uttered on the stage.

I stopped pacing and stared balefully at the serried rows of heads and the backs of necks that stretched straight down to the footlights, as if my fury could spray itself over those heads and throats like an insecticide and make them stop. And my eye was immediately struck by the changed postures of that audience. In the first act they had sat erect in their seats and leaned forward a little, attentive and eager for every word coming over the footlights. Now they sprawled every which way. Some of them had even slumped down in their seats as far as they could get, and their heads rested on the back of the seats. I have watched the same silent spectacle since then, and even without coughs, it is as good and grim an illustration of a disappointed audience as I know of, and another excellent reason why a playwright should never sit through one of his own works. Looking at the heads of an audience from the back of the orchestra will tell him a good deal more than sitting in a welter of well-wishing friends in the third row. I walked away and leaned against the wall, waiting for the coughing to stop, but of course it did not stop. It continued growing in volume for the rest of that lumpish and hulking scene. The curtain finally and at last came down on what at best could only be described as reluctant and somewhat fugitive applause.

Mr. Kaufman had disappeared at least five minutes before the curtain fell, and I remained where I was at the back of the theatre waiting for Joe Hyman to come up the aisle. I could see his face long before he reached me. It looked sad, sullen, and somehow five years older than when he had come up the aisle at the end of the first act. He reached my side and, never a man to mind putting the obvious into words, said, "You got an act and a half of a hit. What you need pretty badly is the other half." I stared dumbly back at him without replying. "Shall I wait for you back at the hotel and go home tomorrow morning, or would you rather I went home tonight?" he asked.

I found my voice, though it sounded squeaky and high-pitched and the words came out almost like a bleat. "Better go home," I said. "There's a conference in Mr. Kaufman's room right away and I think he'll want to go right to work after we finish. Looks like there's quite a lot to do, doesn't it?" I asked needlessly.

Joe Hyman nodded, and the gentle note of mockery was in his voice again. "While you're working tonight, just keep thinking 'Well, at least I'm not up at camp doing "Mrs. Cohen at the Beach." ' That'll help." He held out his hand and I took it. "It's an awful good act and a half, though," he said. "I'll call you from New York tomorrow or the next day. I better run now if I'm going to catch that train back." And he was gone.

I waited until the last stragglers had left the lobby and then walked slowly up the boardwalk toward the hotel. I was in no hurry to get there, even at the risk of keeping Mr. Kaufman waiting. Had it really gone as badly as I feared it had, and if so, what would Mr. Harris and Mr. Kaufman do? Sam Harris was no Augustus Pitou, but I remembered I had heard him say to someone or other during rehearsals, "You can't pinch pennies in show business, but the great secret is to know when to cut your losses. Make up your mind quickly, take your loss and run. Just not doing that little thing has caused a good many managers to die broke." I shivered a little in the warm night air and found that I was already in front of the hotel.

Inevitably some of the other passengers were talking about the show as the elevator ascended. "What did you think of that thing tonight?" said a fat suntanned man addressing another fat suntanned man standing next to me. "I saw you in the lobby, didn't I?"

"Yeah," said the man at my side, "after the first act everyone could have stayed in the lobby. They got a big juicy flop on their hands if you ask me."

[333]

Who's asking you, you fat, overfed, overdressed son-of-a-bitch, I thought sullenly as he pressed himself against me.

"You're Beacon Sportswear Sweaters, aren't you?" said the first man to the man at my side. "I'm Ladies Cashmere Woolens."

"Yeah, Beacon Sportswear. You know the line?" the man next to me asked.

I longed to answer him myself, but I lacked the courage. "I know the line," I ached to say; "and your sweaters are lousy—lousier than our third act. I'm wearing one of them right now. They stretch and they unravel. And if you know so much about plays, why don't you make better sweaters, you pompous bastard?" I added silently and illogically as I pushed past him to get off at my floor.

I made my way miserably down the corridor, but in front of Mr. Kaufman's room I turned away and walked a few doors further down to my own room. Whether because of the tension of the evening or because of what Mr. Sportswear had just said in the elevator, my face and forehead and eyes were burning as if with a high fever. I let myself into my room, and without turning on the lights—I had no wish to be mocked by the little pile of telegrams, stacked neatly on the bureau, which I had opened with such amusement and pleasure earlier in the evening—I walked through the dark room to the bathroom. I filled the washbowl with water as cold as I could get it to run and dipped my face and finally my whole head into it. In the dark bedroom I changed my shirt, which was limp and dank with perspiration, and as I stood buttoning it the telephone rang. With a pang I remembered I had told the family to call me in my room at eleven thirty sharp, before I went to the conference, so that I could tell them how the opening had gone. It rang again, and I let it ring without moving to answer it. There was no point in giving them bad news until I knew just how bad the news might be. Still less point in trying to put a good face on it or attempting to whitewash the evening's calamity—my mother would catch me out at once. Better to let them think they had missed me.

I walked out of the room, with the telephone still ringing, and down the hall to Mr. Kaufman's room again and knocked on the door. Mr. Kaufman's voice called, "Come in, come in," and I walked into the room to find no one there, surprisingly enough, but Mr. Kaufman himself. I had expected to see Sam Harris, Max Siegel, the stage manager, the company manager, and even some of the group I had seen talking to Sam Harris during the intermission. Mr. Kaufman's conferences were evidently not going to follow the prescribed ritual. The wrecking crew and even Sam Harris were apparently barred.

Mr. Kaufman, in pajamas and bathrobe, was seated on the sofa, the script already on his knees, a pencil poised above it, and a sheet of yellow paper and carbon stood ready at the typewriter. He did not look up but gestured toward a table on which stood a Thermos of coffee and two thin sandwiches. "Those are for you," he said. "We'll be working all night, and room service closes at one o'clock." I stared hungrily at the sandwiches, but another gesture had motioned me over to the sofa. I sat down beside him.

"You know what didn't go as well as I do," he said. "Curing it is another matter. We'll get to that later. Let's cut right down to the bone first, to give us a clean look at what we've got. It won't fix what's wrong, but at least it will improve the good stuff that's there." Nothing in his tone or manner indicated that there was any thought of abandoning the play. I could easily have thrown my arms around him and hugged him, and my sigh of relief must have been so audible that he turned to me and said, "Did you say something?" I shook my head. The pencil in his hand began to make quick, darting marks on the manuscript, bracketing the cuts on page after page. It was astonishing to find how much of what we had written was unnecessary, how we had underestimated an audience's ability to grasp what was needful for them to know without restating it not once but sometimes two or even three times. It was reassuring to find that so meticulous a craftsman as George Kaufman himself still had to learn the hard way the ever-constant lesson of economy.

There was a knock at the door and I opened it to find Max Siegel standing in the doorway with a number of typewritten sheets in his hand. "Mr. Harris' notes," he said, handing them over. "How's the young author? Not discouraged, I hope." He waved to Mr.

Kaufman over my shoulder and walked away. I presented the notes to Mr. Kaufman. He placed them on the table beside him without so much as a glance. "Later," he remarked, without looking up from the manuscript, and the pencil darted surgically over the pages.

I could only guess at the passage of time by the increasingly loud rumblings of my stomach. That large lobster dinner I had eaten with Joe Hyman seemed some years away. Moreover, I had returned it to the sea early in the evening and I was beginning to grow a little dizzy with hunger. I waited until Mr. Kaufman found it necessary to go to the bathroom and then dived for the sandwiches and coffee, stealing a look at my watch at the same time. It was almost four thirty in the morning and we were only just past the middle of the second act.

Mr. Kaufman, returning from the bathroom, walked toward the bureau instead of going back to the sofa, and rummaging under a pile of shirts he brought out a large brown paper bag. "Fudge," he said casually, "for energy. Have some." He held the bag out in front of me and I tentatively picked out the daintiest piece I could find, conscious as always in his presence of my undisciplined appetite. "Have a good-sized piece," he said sharply, "you won't even taste it that way. I make it myself," he added, with a satisfied chuckle.

I looked up at him in surprise. What was even more surprising was the fact that his eyes were shining with the first hint of pride I had ever seen glisten in them. I had tried once or twice to discuss some of his work that I particularly admired, but careful as I had been to keep any hint of admiration out of my voice, his replies had been so lackluster and his indifference so obvious that I had quickly dropped any mention of the plays and never returned to it. To my astonishment, he was now standing over me, waiting as eagerly for me to taste the piece of fudge in my fingers as he might wait for a notice in the *Times* the morning after an opening night. I bit into it and carefully let it melt in my mouth before I gave my report, for his eyes were intent on mine and the expression on his face was so childishly expectant that I knew my judgment must be a considered one before I pronounced it.

The very first bite told the whole story! It was awful fudge—

[336]

gummy and sickly sweet. I did not have the heart to tell him so. "It's just wonderful," I lied. He smiled delightedly and popped a large piece into his own mouth, still looking at me with the look of fevered expectancy that a favored relative fixes on the family lawyer about to read the will. Evidently "just wonderful" wasn't going to be enough. "I didn't know you could make fudge," I said thickly, trying to make the words sound enthusiastic, for the horrible stuff was sticking to the roof of my mouth and had worked its way around my back molars and gums.

"Can't buy it *this* way anywhere," he said, deeply pleased with himself. "Never the right consistency or not sweet enough. Matter of fact"—he went on chewing contentedly—"This isn't quite sweet enough either. I'll make a new batch to take to Brighton Beach next week."

Oh, God, I thought . . . not sweet enough! If he makes me take another piece I'll be sick right in front of him. "Have some more," said Mr. Kaufman, helping himself to another piece and holding the bag out in front of me. "Best thing I know of to keep you awake."

It'll keep me awake all right, I thought, as I plunged my hand in the bag and tried to pick out the smallest possible piece. Just keeping it down will keep me awake. "Thanks," I said brightly, "it certainly does seems to give you energy, doesn't it?" And I walked into the bathroom. I flushed the lump of wretched stuff down the toilet and emerged from the bathroom falsely chewing away like the traitor I was.

Through the years the brown paper bag full of that terrible fudge emerged from a good many other bureau drawers. Mr. Kaufman rarely traveled without it. It was as much a part of his traveling equipment as the sharpened pencils, the carbon paper, the typewriter and the special hand soap. And the memory of that brown paper bag coming toward me at four or five in the morning is still enough to engender a slight feeling of queasiness. His staunch belief in the energy-giving properties of his own fudge, however, worked like magic—at least, for him—for he worked through the rest of the night without so much as a pause or a single yawn.

It was just after seven thirty in the morning when he closed the manuscript and walked to the windows to draw the curtains and pull up the shades. The bright sunlight made me blink my eyes and made me realize that I ached all over with weariness. "I've called rehearsal for eleven o'clock. We never got to Sam Harris' notes," he added with a regretful sigh. "Oh, well, we'll get a chance to go through them between the morning and afternoon rehearsal. Good night—or good morning—whichever you prefer." He opened the windows, then pulled the curtain and shades to once again and was taking off his bathrobe and making for the bed as I murmured a good night and closed the door after me.

The rest of that work-filled week in Atlantic City was a testimony to the remarkable continuity with which George Kaufman functioned—to the unity of purpose and dogged persistence with which he cut away every superfluous word of the play until its bare bones lay exposed. It was a striking illustration of his dictum "First things first," for he refused to be swerved or stampeded by anyone, Sam Harris and Beatrice Kaufman included, until he had achieved what he chose to call "A naked look at the play itself—I don't care if the curtain comes down at ten o'clock." Indeed, at the Friday evening performance, the final curtain actually did come down at ten fifteen—he had cut a little too deeply, he grudgingly conceded—and some of the cuts were quickly restored for the Saturday matinée; but for that one alarming evening the play must have given the impression to the bewildered and stunned audience of being hardly a play at all, but merely a series of loosely connected scenes strung causelessly together.

There is always one performance in the life of a play that is in trouble out of town, where the entire enterprise, from the idea of the play itself right down to its settings and its actors, succeeds in looking utterly ridiculous and gives to everyone connected with it a sense of deep and complete humiliation. We had apparently reached that terminal point in record time. It was on that black evening also that both Sam Harris and Beatrice Kaufman returned to New York, leaving behind them, or so it seemed to my apprehensive ears, an impression of extremely cautious and guarded optimism as to the play's ultimate chances, in spite of the careful way they phrased everything they said. Nevertheless, that savage and ruthless cutting job accomplished exactly what he had meant it to do: it revealed as nothing else could have the deep trouble we were in, for stripped of its excess verbiage *Once in a Lifetime* emerged as a play of sound satiric viewpoint but very little substance. It was possible, it seemed, for an audience to laugh long and loud at a play, and yet leave the theatre dissatisfied and disappointed—a phenomenon that I have noted in a good many other plays through the years, sometimes in plays of sound enough ideas, but which remained unhappy casualties because of this fundamental lack of what an audience compellingly demands.

I was learning in that memorable week still another aspect of how baffling a quarry an audience can be. Some basic human element or ingredient was missing in *Once in a Lifetime,* and in spite of its high sense of fun and rollicking good spirits, the sum total of the evening did not add up to that magical sense of enjoyment that sends an audience out of the theatre completely satisfied and breeds long lines at the box office afterward. Each night after the labor of cutting was over, we sat in Mr. Kaufman's room and discussed the nature of the disease, but curing it, as he had tartly remarked after the opening performance, was another matter. The gravity of the trouble we were in was obvious enough; the remedy was not so easily come by. We discussed and quickly discarded any number of devices which we sensed were palliatives rather than the pure oxygen the play needed, and as I watched Mr. Kaufman stride toward the windows at the end of each night to pull aside the curtain and let the dawn streak in, I marveled anew at his resiliency—at his uncommon ability to stand up under the punishing load of work he was carrying and still retain his full zest and vigor.

I had ceased to be astonished by the freshness with which he would attack each new day's rehearsal after a night of little or no sleep, but as I made my own weary way down the corridor to my room, my befuddled brain continued to marvel at him. I still do, and I continue to wonder why I have allowed myself to follow the same foolish path. The playwright who directs his own work is playing a

[339]

fool's game. The schedule he must keep and the load he must carry is an inhuman one and it does not always work to the advantage of his play. If the play is in trouble—and trouble is the out-of-town norm—he will more often than not be forced to rewrite whole scenes during the night, have the rewrite typed and ready for an eleven o'clock rehearsal, rehearse throughout the day, watch the performance that evening, making his notes to give to the actors after the curtain comes down, as well as judging how well or ill the new scenes played, and then go back to his room to repeat the same procedure over again every night until such time as he is lucky enough or clever enough to have rescued his play. Apart from the labor and tension of the original rehearsals, after two or three weeks of this grueling schedule on the road, the playwright who is his own director would be wise not to go to a doctor for a checkup at the end of it. He is very likely to be unpleasantly surprised at the results of his cardiogram. Yet there is no recovery, it is only fair to say, as quick as the recovery from a hit. The roses appear in the playwright's cheeks again with amazing swiftness, and the sparkle of health in his eye gives the lie to the lunatic battering he has just put his physical and nervous system through.

Perhaps it is precisely this unholy knowledge that has caused me to persist in continuing to direct my own plays against all the dictates of common sense, considering that I have teetered along the edge of that porcupine path so many times before. Vanity, I can only presume, inevitably triumphs over plain common sense, for I am certain that some of my plays have suffered at my own hands as director. I have long since reached the conclusion that I am a better director of another's work than of my own—yet I very much doubt if my egoistic sense of pleasure in directing my own plays would allow me to let another man stage them. It is strange that this should be so, for the rewards to a playwright as the director of his own plays are minor compared to the awareness he has of the price he must pay for this indulgence, but vanity is part of a writer's strength as well as his weakness. Without vanity a writer's work is tepid, and he must accept his vanity as part of his stock in trade and live with it as one of the hazards of his profession.

Something of the sort must have held true for George Kaufman, for as I saw him toil under the grind of rewriting and rehearsals I wondered why he usually chose to bear the double burden of playwriting and directing at the same time. It seemed to me a sleeveless errand that vanity alone could explain. More than once as I watched him labor, the thought crossed my mind, "What a social director he would have made," for he was seemingly immune to weariness and his capacity for working around the clock would have made him the loved and envied of the entire Borscht Circuit. By the end of the first week's tryout of *Once in a Lifetime* at Atlantic City, the rigors of social directing seemed to me in retrospect like so much child's play.

On the journey back to New York, I wondered sleepily not if or how we were going to be able to fix the play—my brain seemed to go dry and my wits to scatter if I attempted to focus on it—I wondered instead if the new social director at the Flagler was as dog-tired as I was! There was one salutary thing about social directing, I morosely concluded. "Mrs. Cohen at the Beach" did not need a second act, and if I had to pick up social directing again next season, I would remember it. It was cold comfort, and the sight of Max Siegel, unsmiling for the first time, did not make it a particularly warming journey.

For the first time in my life I found myself walking down to the subway at Times Square with a sense of actual relief. I needed to be alone, to escape from *Once in a Lifetime*—to look at no one connected with it, to have no one ask me about it, or ask me to think about it. I needed to shut it out of my mind and psyche, if only for the measure of a subway ride back to Brooklyn. Brooklyn, however, was holding a surprise in store that I had not quite reckoned with and one that was hardly likely to promote forgetfulness.

I KNOW OF no group of people as idiotically confident of success as a playwright's family while his play is still in its tryout stage. In spite of everything I had said over the telephone to my mother from Atlantic City, in spite of my insistence that they must all think of the play as still "trying out" and not as an assured success, I was welcomed home on a note of unqualified triumph. Everything short of flags and a brass band greeted a returning hero, whose own doubts about the play jangled like sleighbells in his ears as he listened to the neighbors' fulsome congratulations and their repeated assurances that they could hardly wait to get to the theatre. My mother could barely wait to get me inside the apartment to proudly parade for my inspection the two new dresses she had bought to celebrate. These twin purchases were explained by the fact that since she expected to attend every performance throughout the week, as well as the opening one, it was hardly to be expected that she could appear all week in the same dress. My father and brother had settled for new ties and shirts and would wear their best blue suits every night, but since different neighbors would be attending the play on different nights it was no more than seemly that she be dressed as the occasion merited. I could only gather that she meant to alternate the dresses, as alternate neighbors attended the performance, for at the end of an hour of listening to light-headed plans and dreams of the rich, full life we were going to live, I nodded "yes" to everything. It was plainly hopeless to try to persuade her or my father or brother, for that matter, that *Once in a Lifetime* might turn out to be a little less than the shower of gold they had already concluded it was.

To do them justice, this conviction, which seemed so firmly rooted and fixed in all of their minds, was not entirely without a basis in reality. For one thing, the notice in *Variety* had been a surprisingly good one. If one took the trouble to read the notice carefully, however, the reviewer's certainty that a hit was in store for Broadway the following season was based almost entirely on George Kaufman's accepted wizardry of being able to pull a large number of rabbits out of his play-doctor's hat. For another, Dore Schary, Eddie Chodorov, Lester Sweyd, in fact everyone who should have known better and curbed his tongue, had called and offered congratulations in my absence. To my vast surprise, they continued to misread the *Variety* notice when I talked to them myself on the telephone, and they put down my reservations and rumblings to what they laughingly termed, "success modesty." Obviously, the reports that had seeped back to Broadway from Atlantic City had all been good: "Kaufman is working on it night and day," the grapevine had reported—and that was enough for Broadway to know.

By Monday afternoon, the day after my return and the day of the opening at Brighton Beach, I too had succumbed to the general elation. The same self-delusion that had enveloped everyone connected with *The Beloved Bandit,* as it transferred from Rochester to Chicago, fell into place again and operated with equal magic. I reread the *Variety* notice and managed to translate what it plainly stated into something it did not say at all. By the time I left the house that evening and took a trolley car to Brighton Beach, I was in high spirits. I got off the car four or five blocks before I reached the theatre, for I was early and I wanted to enjoy this sudden and unexpected tranquillity. I wanted also, in my usual way, to seek some omen that would make secure my high hopes for tonight. Reason or logic has little to do with these moments of self-deception, which come into play at moments of crisis. We all wear these atavistic wishing caps in one form or another. I still search for opening-night omens, good ones or bad ones, and I invariably find one. I found one now.

Hurrying along the boardwalk I came suddenly upon the bathhouse that had once been the night club my grandfather had taken us all to on that far-off midsummer night. The façade had been altered almost beyond recognition, but there could be no doubt that it was the same building. That night and this place had been too sharply etched in my memory for me to mistake it. I stopped and stood in front of it for a few moments. Everything else but the memory of that night and of my grandfather vanished from my mind. It had been a long time since I had consciously thought of him or of my Aunt Kate, but they came back sharply now. Much of what I was and what I had done, this very journey that was taking me along this boardwalk and past this bathhouse, to a theatre where a play of mine was to raise its curtain in less than an hour—a great deal of both of them was embedded in every step of that journey. And if I needed an omen for tonight, there could scarcely be a better one. This shabby relic of middle-class gaiety had been for my grandfather a cry from the heart against his lot. He would be pleased at the journey I was making, no matter what happened tonight. I hurried past it, my spirits soaring higher than ever.

The crowd that filled the lobby of the Brighton Beach Theatre looked surprisingly like a cross section of a Broadway opening night. I was startled by the turnout. It was stupid of me to have forgotten that the Broadway regulars would of course have waited to test themselves against the play at Brighton Beach, rather than make the journey to Atlantic City. The sight of them lowered my spirits by a good fifty per cent. Agents whose clients had been turned down for parts in the play buzzed softly to scenic and costume designers, who likewise had lost out on their own bids. Even some of the very actors who had auditioned for us, unsuccessfully, were present, to prove to themselves, I suppose, how prejudiced and unseeing authors and managers can be. They would be bringing no great good will down the aisles with them when they went to their seats. Rival managers whose agenda for the new season also included a topical comedy had come to have an appraising look at the possible competition. They would judge and compare silently, without benefit, if possible, of laughter. The jungle drum beaters were also represented in almost their full strength—those faceless folk on the periphery of the theatre to whom it is all-important to be in the know and to know in advance just how good or how bad the incoming merchandise is likely to be.

I stared resentfully at the ones I knew and realized with something of a start that I myself had been an enthusiastic member of the same club, though it did not seem possible that my own eyes could ever have glistened with the same cannibalistic glee that seemed to shine from every countenance at the possibility of imminent failure. This same anticipatory buzz would have sounded equally in key, it seemed to my ears, rising from the throats of a group of savages grouped around a tribal pot, over whose rim rose the steaming heads of George Kaufman and myself. Ticket brokers, columnists, a delegation of some of Mr. Kaufman's Algonquin set, as well as the faces of some of my own friends, appeared and disappeared in the throng. One heart-sinking look was enough to send me quivering backstage, my pulses pounding. I crouched against a piece of furniture that I knew would not be used until the third act and I remained there until I heard the curtain rise and the first laugh waft backstage.

Mr. Kaufman was already pacing furiously when I stole back into the theatre and he did not recognize my presence by even that one lifted finger in traditional greeting. His race across the carpet was if anything more frenzied than it had been at Atlantic City. His long strides had a hint of the pursued in them and his head seemed sunk into his shoulders. He knew, of course, far better than I did, the composition of tonight's audience, and that the closer one drew to Broadway, the larger the lacks in a play loomed. Tonight was as close as one could get without actually opening on Broadway, and this audience would pounce on every lack. I listened for a moment or two and then stopped my own pacing and stared at him. The actors were giving a nervous and strained performance—cutting into their own and each other's laughs, their timing sky-high, and their voices pitched at that taut level that always heralds a shaky

[345]

performance. Yet the audience, even this audience, was responding to the play with unrestrained laughter. "They like it," I whispered to him as he passed me. He did not reply, but continued his pacing.

As he passed me again a moment or two later, he stopped long enough to state flatly, "They'll like it better when they stop laughing. They haven't long to wait." I looked after him wonderingly. Was he never satisfied? What more could he want or ask? He was right, however. The ethics of the wrecking crew, curiously enough, are as strong as their malice. They adhere to a strict code of theatre behavior that contains its own kind of rough justice. The two things are not mutually exclusive, though they may seem so. In operation it is unfailing. If in the first fifteen minutes a play begins to play like a hit, no matter what ill will or personal animus they may have brought to it as single members of the audience, they give it as an entity their unalloyed blessing and reward it with laughter. This does not deny the fact that individually they might be better pleased if the opposite were true, but once the indications are clear that a hit is about to be revealed before them, the excitement of being present and part of the event itself is enough to outlaw their personal feelings and make them a good audience—sometimes better, in fact, than an audience of friends and well-wishers. For one thing, they are sharper and more acutely aware of the skills of the playwright and the actor, and their very malice creates an electricity of its own. It heightens and sparks both play and performance, so that a positive crackle of wills and wits pervades both sides of the footlights, and when the battle is joined, the evening is a memorable one for all concerned.

The first act of *Once in a Lifetime* played like a hit of vintage rare, and when the curtain descended at the end of it, it was greeted with spontaneous and ungrudging applause. As Mr. Kaufman had prophesied, the faces coming up the aisle were not particularly happy faces. It was as though a hundred pairs of shoulders had shrugged in unison with the unspoken message: "A hit is a hit. You can't stop it. Might as well get on the bandwagon early." But their faces relayed in the same silent fashion that they didn't have to be happy about it either, by God. "Just be patient—it won't be too long," I thought, paraphrasing Mr. Kaufman's cynical assessment of their laughter and their applause, and scurried backstage to avoid the folly of the premature congratulations I saw plainly mirrored on the faces of some of my friends as they struggled up the aisle toward me. They caught a glimpse of me and raised their arms above their heads in congratulation, but I turned on my heel and ran. Let them put it down to nerves, mock modesty, or what they would—I preferred not to face them just yet.

The second act played exactly as it had in Atlantic City, with the exception that from Mr. Kaufman's exit onward the silence was deadlier. There were no willing, scattered laughs now. There was instead a kind of rapt attention, as though they must make thoroughly certain that no sound disturbed the passengers while the crew sank the ship. This, in a sense, was what they had come for, and their silence had the breathless hushed quality of a death watch. The curtain fell to a thin round of obligatory applause, but the faces coming up the aisle were relieved and smiling this time. It did not comfort me or make me feel any the less bitter to know that I had been guilty of exactly the same behavior at other people's plays. The theatre breeds its own kind of cruelty, and its sadism takes on a keener edge since it can be enjoyed under the innocent guise of critical judgment. Charity in the theatre usually begins and ends with people who have a play opening the week following one's own. Their unlikely benevolence is not so much a purity of heart as the knowledge that they face a firing line with rifles aimed in exactly the same direction.

I waited now for Eddie and Dore and the others to come up the aisle. They, at least, wished me well and I wanted desperately to hear something good about the play, no matter what, in spite of what my eyes and ears so plainly told me. They were slower this time in coming up the aisle and their faces were the unsmiling ones. For a brief moment I felt sorry for them. Greeting an author on the opening night of a play that is going badly is in some ways comparable to taking a marriage vow. You are damned if you do and you are damned if you don't. Not to greet him if he catches your eye is impossible as well as painfully obvious, and to murmur evasively when one stands face to face with him is nothing short of out-right cruelty. Yet the truth is too painful for him to hear, even if one has the courage to state it, and the truth is exactly what he least wishes to know. It is an impossible moment. Politeness does not suffice and good manners are somehow an affront. I have evolved a credo of my own which serves the occasion but does not attempt to solve the insoluble. Simply stated, I tell the truth to an author on an opening night out of town, and on an opening night in New York I do not. The truth is not always a virtue. There are times when the truth is unnecessary as well as needlessly cruel, and a New York opening night is one of those times. By then the die is cast, and at that moment the author is at his most vulnerable. It is unfriendly not to tell him the truth out of town when it may yet do some good, but by the same token it is nonsense to do so at a time when it can be of no service whatever. The truth at that moment can only succeed in giving the teller the smug satisfaction of virtuous honesty and do the author no good at all. The truth will be his soon enough and he will nourish it for a long time to come.

My friends cushioned the truth and made it as palatable as they could—there was no way of making it pleasant and I did not press them. What, after all, was there to say after that painfully weak second act? It was Joe Hyman, as it turned out, who bore the brunt of my explosive behavior that evening, when he gravely remarked, with that edge of mockery in his voice, "What happened to all that work you were supposed to be doing? This is the same play I saw in Atlantic City." My rage found a target. The defeat of my hopes uncoiled like a cobra within me and I lashed out at him with almost a sense of relief at no longer having to repress the black sense of fury and defeat I had kept concealed from everyone, myself included, until that moment. He did not answer, nor did anyone else inter-rupt me. When I finished I turned and walked out of the theatre. I felt strangely better. The worst had become true and there was only one more act to live through. I had the courage not to return to the theatre for the third act. Not until I had seen the last of the audience, including my family, leave the theatre and the lights on the marquee go out, did I venture to go backstage to find out what Mr. Kaufman's working plans might be for the following day.

Mr. Kaufman was not there nor had he left a message for me. Neither Sam Harris nor Max Siegel was to be seen either, all three of them, it seemed, having driven back to New York together immediately after the third-act curtain had fallen.

As usual, there was that minor player, about to deposit his dressing-room key with the stage doorman, who informed me brightly that he thought the play had gone wonderfully and that all of *his* friends were certain we were in for a long run on Broadway. I am ashamed to record that my ego was so limp and my spirit so impoverished that I walked him to the subway to hear in greater detail just how wonderful his friends had thought it was. I willingly paid the blackmail of having to listen to how his own part could be strengthened to the greater good of the play. At that particular moment it was worth it.

There is this much to be said for the value of out-of-town notices. If they are good, they can be acknowledged as good for business and for the morale of the actors. If they are bad, they can be brushed aside as out-of-town notices and what do out-of-town critics know anyway? My mother achieved this solid professional viewpoint in exactly one night, or by the time I had awakened the next morning. Standing over me she announced that she had read the local papers and compared their notices to the review in *Variety*. Her pronouncement was professional and exact. "What do Brooklyn papers know about a play, anyway? If they were real critics they wouldn't be here in Brooklyn!" She handed them over, and my own professionalism being neither as steadfast nor as flourishing as her own, I read them avidly and not without a painful twinge or two. The worst, naturally, was the paper I happened to pick up first. "It is probably unfair," the notice ran, "to infer that the good parts of a play are written by one man and the inferior parts by another, but judging by the records of both names listed on the program last night, the first act and a half of *Once in a Lifetime,* which is very good indeed, was written by George S. Kaufman, and the rest by

Moss Hart. Mr. Kaufman's witty hand is everywhere in evidence during the hilarious first part, but he seems to have left the type-writer in the custody of Mr. Hart for the rest of the play. He had better get back to it as fast as he can, if the lavish Sam H. Harris production unveiled at the Brighton Beach Theatre last evening, etc., etc." The other Brooklyn papers were less damning, but meager indeed in their praise, which consisted mainly of listing the actors and saying they were all good. "Well, bully for the actors' morale," I thought briefly. "I hope it's in better shape than my own."

I glanced sourly up at my mother, who stood rereading the *Variety* notice and smiling and nodding her head in agreement, and got out of bed and out of the house as fast as I could. I had no wish to hear how much the neighbors had liked it or how violently they disagreed with what the local papers said, which I could see she was firmly determined to tell me, neighbor by neighbor. I went to the drug store on the corner and telephoned Mr. Kaufman from there. If the news was going to be bad, I wanted to be alone to hear it. "Were you planning to work today, Mr. Kaufman?" I asked with as much casualness as I could summon into my voice when his hello came through the receiver.

"I think we both need a respite for a couple of days before we tackle it again," he replied. "By the way," he went on, "don't let your-self be upset by what that silly bastard said. How the hell would he or anyone else know who wrote which parts of a play? It's damned infuriating."

"I'm not upset," I said almost jubilantly. As long as we *were* going to tackle it again, what difference did it make what anyone said?

"Good," he said. "See you there tonight." And the connection clicked off.

I made another telephone call to apologize to Joe Hyman and then returned home to eat a huge breakfast, my mind tumbling with ideas about the play and as refreshed as though I had returned from a month in the country. It is possible that fear in one form or another is as much responsible for that occupational illness, writer's block, as any of the traumatic experiences a writer may have gathered in his childhood.

The second night's performance of a comedy is generally a letdown for both actors and audience. It is a letdown, that is, unless the second-night audience has been told by the reviewers in their morning newspapers that the play is funny. Having thus been relieved of having to exercise their own judgment, they then enter the theatre laughing at the ushers as they receive their programs, and the actors have only to stroll through their parts to be hilariously accepted and applauded. It is a sheeplike exhibition and a dispiriting one to watch. The second-night audience of *Once in a Lifetime,* having been told what to expect, entered the theatre feeling already cheated. One could almost feel them stiffen against the play as they settled into their seats. They opened their programs with an air of preparing themselves not to be amused. Actors can do little with a disgruntled audience. They can win over a cold audience, but not a disapproving one. Even the first act, which contained genuine laughter if an audience met it halfway, played soggily. Moreover, the actors, keyed to the quick perception of the audience of the night before, suddenly found themselves adrift in a sea of unknowing silence, where before waves of laughter had always safely borne them along. Perhaps even more disconcerting than this unexpected stillness was the sound of a single laugh that kept staunchly and hollowly resounding through the silences. It was my mother's laugh, and I could easily have throttled her! The actors gave up when the biggest laugh in the first act was again met with a thudding silence, and played from that point onward with an air of undisguised martyrdom that made the play seem endless.

Mr. Kaufman, other than giving me his traditional single finger lifted in silent greeting, spoke not a word during the first act nor throughout the rest of the evening. If he was dismayed by the dismal reception the play was receiving, he gave no sign of it. His pacing continued, but it was neither more nor less fervent than it had been on any of the other evenings I had watched him. I chose to interpret his silence as a tacit agreement that this was one of those evenings and one of those audiences that must somehow be lived through and on which comment was superfluous. One could only blot it out and hope that by tomorrow evening the memory of those notices would be partially dimmed. Not everyone in Brooklyn, I thought grimly, reads the newspapers or they would vote more sensibly and spend less time at the ball park.

To a large degree this was true. As the week wore on, the audiences grew noticeably better, though increasingly smaller in number. There were, it seemed, just so many friends and neighbors of my mother and they apparently all sat in the balcony. Her faith in the play remained unshaken and her ringing laughter cut through each silence, but her influence on the Brooklyn theatregoing public was obviously negligible. By Thursday evening the gaps in the back rows of the orchestra were alarming. I had another and deeper cause for alarm by Thursday evening, however. Sam Harris and Max Siegel had appeared only once since the opening night at Brighton Beach. They sat through the second performance, but I had purposely evaded meeting them on that depressing evening. Their absence was unsettling, but I refused to let it or the fact that Mr. Kaufman had given no sign of being ready to go to work yet disquiet me unduly. Perhaps it was pointless for them to keep coming back to look at the play until we knew how we were going to fix it, and Mr. Kaufman had said he had wanted a respite before we tackled the play again. He was not a man to equivocate or to give his word lightly where work was concerned. I could not completely down, however, a feeling of haunting uneasiness as each night's performance came to an end and there was no suggestion of a meeting for the following day, and I took what comfort I could in the fact that he still gave notes to the actors after each performance and continued to make little cuts in scenes. There was, moreover, the solid certainty of his presence in the theatre each night as the curtain rose and the reassuring sight of his pacing back and forth until the last curtain fell.

When he did not appear as the house lights dimmed for the final performance on Saturday night, my stomach took a nasty turn. The absence of that familiar figure pacing to and fro in the dark suddenly exploded all the gnawing doubts I had been able to keep within bounds until now. I paced back and forth alone for a while and then gave it up. I realized that I was hearing not one word that came across the footlights. I left the theatre and scanned the street outside.

The street had that special emptiness of streets outside of theatres after the curtain has risen. For some inexplicable reason no one seems to pass by after curtain time. The street goes as silent and dead as it might in the middle of the night. The only sign of life now on either side of the street was the Negro attendant sweeping up the ticket envelopes and cigarette stubs in the lobby behind me. I walked to the corner and stood there aimlessly, chilled by the emptiness around me but unable to go back into the theatre until I could stem the sense of unease Mr. Kaufman's absence had stirred up. He would have to be there, I knew, in time for his appearance in the second act, but his failure to turn up in time for the first act took on a growing but deadly significance in my mind. It was unlike him not to appear tonight of all nights. He was a bitter-ender, for one thing, and for another he was scrupulous about watching each performance from the beginning, no matter how well or how badly the play might be going. Short of a traffic accident, I could not account for his absence, and the longer I waited the more forbidding his lateness seemed to become.

I did not see a car pull up and stop in front of the theatre until I became aware that the figure helping someone alight from the car was Mr. Kaufman himself and the woman he was helping out was Beatrice Kaufman. He looked quite startled, as well he might have, when my own figure dashed out of the shadows and ran toward him yelling, "The curtain's up," in a tone of wild jubilation. I stood in front of them both, grinning foolishly, so relieved at seeing him that I was unconscious of how idiotic my behavior must seem.

Beatrice Kaufman gave me a puzzled hello, and after a moment Mr. Kaufman recovered himself sufficiently to ask, "How is it going?"

"Great," I found myself unexpectedly replying, though I had barely seen any of it.

"Well, that'll be a nice change," he remarked and started toward the lobby.

Fortunately, they entered the theatre on a burst of laughter, so that I was not made out a complete fool—but laughter, even with this easily pleased Saturday night audience, stopped exactly where

[353]

it had always stopped before. At Mr. Kaufman's exit, dead center in the middle of the second act—almost as though some hand had pulled a hidden switch that controlled the audience's mirth—all laughter ceased abruptly. For the first time, however, I listened for the expected silence, and when it came I did not, as I had done throughout every other performance, quail inwardly. That long-awaited signal from Mr. Kaufman had been given and it remained in my ears now, filling in the silence. At the end of the first act he had approached me and said, "Come back to the dressing room at the end of the show so that we can talk for a few minutes, will you?" And from that point onward I had hardly bothered to listen to the play at all.

In the middle of the third act, a portion of the evening's listening that was always the hardest for me to bear, I walked out into the lobby for a smoke. Now that I knew we were actually going to work I could spare myself the needless pain of watching scenes that were going to be tossed out or completely rewritten.

A playwright is almost invariably to be found in the lobby throughout one of the bad scenes of his play—during the very scenes, in fact, that warrant his most serious attention; but these are the scenes, of course, that he finds the most painful to watch. No matter how inveterate a smoker he may be, he will somehow manage to contain his longing for a cigarette through the good scenes. Indeed, it would be hard to drag him out of the theatre then under any pretext. Ten lines before a bad scene approaches, however, his need to smoke becomes savage beyond endurance and he gives way to it. He remains puffing away in the lobby until the scene is over, timing his re-entrance with a splendid ingenuity. He can somehow manage to escape the scenes most in need of work until the last possible moment. His excuse to himself and to others is a valid one— he needs the solace of a smoke. It is hard after all to deny a man the steadying influence of a cigarette. The practiced "out-of-town" eye, however, can tell to a nicety just how badly a play is still in need of fixing by the length of time an author spends smoking in the lobby.

I felt no sense of guilt about stealing out to the lobby, for we obviously were going to arrive at an entirely new last act, and I began to sort out some possibilities in my mind. I have had the good fortune of being able to work almost anywhere at all. I have written in subways, on shipboard with people chattering away in deck chairs on either side of me, in theatre lounges with actors rehearsing on the stage above, in kitchens, in automobiles, and on beaches or beside swimming pools with children cavorting about in the water. No particular exercise of discipline is inherent in this ability to work in whatever setting happens to fall my way—it is a lucky or accidental gift of concentration and I have always been grateful for it.

I walked up and down the empty lobby, hardly conscious of where I was, and when one of the doors of the theatre opened, I was so immersed in a tangle of thoughts for a new last act that I stared unseeingly at Beatrice Kaufman for a good thirty seconds before I recognized her and smiled back. She stopped to light a cigarette before she moved toward me, and I was conscious once again that she somehow managed to infuse even so small an action as the lighting of a cigarette with a distinctive quality of her own—just as the way she puffed on the cigarette in its green paper holder was peculiarly hers, fastidious and feminine, yet with a delicate sensuality. The gray smoke curled lazily around her face until it blended with the color of her hair, and she seldom removed the holder from her lips while she talked, so that her entire head was usually haloed in a haze of smoke that made her own bluish-white hair seem to rise out of the smoke and become a part of it. It lent a frisky and rakish air to everything she said and made it sound faintly reckless.

We talked for a few moments about the play, easily and lightly. Her very presence was enlivening after the dreariness of this past week—there had been little chance to talk to her in Atlantic City— and as always, her effect on people and certainly on myself was to induce a sense of exhilaration and gaiety.

I heard myself saying now with the intimacy of old acquaintance, "We'll probably be seeing a good deal of each other during the rewrite this summer."

She did not pause in her reply, but her expression changed slightly. "I won't be here this summer," she said. "We've taken a villa in France for three months—in Antibes—Woollcott and Harpo and

Alice Miller and I. I'm leaving next week." I sensed she was about to go on, but my face must have shown such open mouth-watering envy that she burst into laughter instead, and said, "I hope it's as good as all that! Will you tell George I've gone on to the Dietzes' and that I'll send the car back for him?" She held out her hand. "Good-bye," she said and started for the street door.

She had half opened the door when she turned and came back. She hesitated and seemed to be searching for the right words, but they eluded her, for she sighed and somewhat nervously, I thought, lit another cigarette. She smiled uncertainly for a moment before she spoke. "You'll be spending summers in Europe yourself some day," she said. "You're going to be a very successful playwright. You'll be writing other plays."

Again it seemed to me she seemed to be regretting the impulse that had made her return and speak at all. She moved quickly to the door, smiled another good-bye over her shoulder, and was gone.

I looked after her for a moment, a little warning flick of panic beginning to flutter once more. I suppose the difference between the chronic worrier, the man who seizes on words or even nuances of voice to feed the mainstream of his fears, and the man who worries not at all until catastrophe is full upon him, is only an apparent difference, since both attitudes are aspects of the same neurosis. Given a choice, I should unhesitatingly choose the latter kind, for if catastrophe is inevitable it is at least less painful to meet it in one piece rather than in sections, but one is given little choice in such matters. I seem to have been born a chronic and fretful worrier with an antenna capable of picking up stray words and looks that to a nature other than my own would be imperceptible or nonexistent. I picked up the phrase, "You'll be writing other plays," and bit into it, turning it over and over, screening it from every angle of the disquiet that I felt mounting within me. I seized on the word "other" and could not let it go. The word had an ugly connotation. What did it mean? There were no "other" plays but this one, so far as I was concerned. Why had Beatrice Kaufman turned back, and having decided to speak, why had she been reluctant to say what she evidently had meant to say, except in those veiled and shadowy terms?

[356]

There had been an undercurrent of downright compassion in her tone that I did not like. I liked it less and less, the more I thought about it.

I waited impatiently for the third act to end. I watched Mr. Kaufman take his bow and then hurried backstage. Actually, I think I knew what he was going to say before he spoke. He was experiencing the same difficulty finding the right words that Beatrice Kaufman had encountered, and his first words confirmed the truth that I was already half prepared for.

"This has not been an easy decision for me to make," he said slowly and then paused. "It's taken me all week to come to it," he went on, "but I'm certain now that I haven't anything more to offer to this play. Someone else, or maybe you alone, would be better than I would be from here on. I've gone dry on it or maybe I've lost my taste for it. That happens sometimes."

He picked up a towel and began to wipe the cold cream from his face, waiting for some kind of response from me. I stared at his image in the mirror, unable to utter a sound.

"I'm sure you'll get it done again," he said finally. "There's a lot of good stuff there and you may suddenly get an idea that will crack the second and third acts. I wanted you to know that I want no part of any rights or royalties for whatever work I've done. It's yours free and clear. I've spoken to Sam Harris and he'll make a very generous arrangement on the scenery and costumes with any producer who wants to do it. Sam Harris would like you to come in and see him on Monday, by the way. I imagine he wants to tell you himself that . . ."

He left the sentence eloquently unfinished. I had my breath and my wits back again and I could see he was embarrassed and unhappy. He was waiting for me to speak but I could still find nothing to say. At least he had spared us both such grubby phrases as, "I'm sorry it had to turn out this way," or, "I hope you'll call me some time," and I was silently grateful to him for it.

"You're sure you've gone dry on it, Mr. Kaufman?" I finally asked.

He nodded slowly. "I'd be no use to you any more," he said and looked longingly at the door.

"I see," I said and moved toward the doorway. He looked grateful in his turn that there were to be no speeches on my part, and he solved the question of how to have the agony over and done with as quickly as possible by raising that one finger in a gesture of good-bye. I murmured, "Good-bye," and closed the door behind me.

There is a certain excitement about bad news that is curiously sustaining and in a strange way almost stimulating. Until the shock of it has worn off and reality comes back into focus again, there is a heightened sense of being alive, almost a buoyancy of the spirit, until its import reaches through the walls of self-defense and what has seemed impossible to accept becomes an actuality. I walked along the boardwalk surprised and then astonished to find that I was not feeling bad at all. Other than that first crushing moment in the dressing room, I had felt nothing except the pressing necessity of getting out of the room and the theatre as fast as possible. Now I was conscious only of a weariness that held something akin to boredom in it. If *Once in a Lifetime* had reached a point of no return, so had I. It was almost a relief to know at last that it was over, for there was no doubt in my mind that this was the end of it.

Mr. Kaufman had colored the truth more than a little when he said that there would doubtless be another production under a different management. It was understandable that he should do so under the stress of the moment, but it was not true and he must have known it was not true with the same certainty that I did. If George Kaufman and Sam Harris relinquished a play as unfixable, there was little or no likelihood of another management's picking up the challenge. George Kaufman was usually the man they called in to fix the unfixable. His reason for dropping *Once in a Lifetime* was obvious, and since there are no secrets in the world of the theatre, this one would be common gossip up and down Broadway by Monday morning, no matter what carefully worded announcement from the Harris office appeared in the theatre columns of the *Times*. I leaned over the railing and looked out at the ocean and began to whistle an old camp song. I would be back in camp next summer no doubt, but by the following winter I might have another play. *Once in a Lifetime* had ended, but the world hadn't and neither had I. It was the mark of a professional, I decided, to be able to take it this easily.

It was not until I sat down on a bench and, for want of anything better to do, began idly to watch the passers-by, that my mood changed, with a swiftness that at first startled and then overwhelmed me, from one of relief to one of black despair. The charge that detonates the explosions of rage or bitterness which occur within us is often disguised quite innocently. The boardwalk that evening was full of couples my own age and younger, for though it was only the end of May, it was like a midsummer night. They strolled slowly and happily along, hand in hand or arms around each other's waists, heads pressed closely together. Without knowing that I was doing so, I must have made a bitter identification with them and with my own youth. I stared at these strangers passing in front of me, and all the hopelessness I had been unable to feel before welled up now, transformed into a rage that was like pain. I had had no youth as these young people were having it—no idle sweet time to savor the illusion that life was beginning and that love was the key to its mystery and its flavor. I had let the theatre rob me of mine. With a stab of grinding jealousy I realized I had never gone "steady" with a girl—the small fugitive attempts I had made had always ended quickly, with the knowledge that I had neither the time nor the money necessary for it. Time that was free I had hoarded as something to be used only for work, and money that could be spared was already earmarked for plays that must be seen. I had walked through the years, single-minded, shutting out everything but the goal I had seen shining so steadily in front of me—averting my eyes from everything but the glow of footlights—and now those years were over and done with, as irretrievably finished as *Once in a Lifetime*. These light-hearted couples seemed to crystallize the waste I had made of them—a waste that seemed to have led me nowhere but to this boardwalk tonight.

In the bleakness of that realization it seemed to me that this lifelong intoxication with the theatre had been a barren and unprofitable waste. I could hardly bear to look at those unconcerned carefree figures. Regret and even self-recrimination are bearable emotions. The unbearable one, for me at least, is the hatred of one's self that follows waste, the waste of one's talent or one's affections. The self-hatred that destroys is the waste of unfulfilled promise—the sterility of a thankless affection. I leaned over the back of the bench and turned toward the sea again to shut out the sight of those couples passing before me.

I have no idea how long I remained there, staring out at the ocean, but if I were asked to pinpoint the exact moment or moments that have marked a turning point for me, I should unhesitatingly choose this as one of the decisive ones. In every career, in every profession, there must occur a like moment: when the will to survive falters and almost ceases to exist—when the last reserves of ability to pick up and go on seem to have been used up. This was that moment for me, and its saving grace was a strongly developed sense of irony that began to break through and give me a glimpse of the truth. It rescued me then, and it has come to my rescue many times since. A sharp sense of the ironic can be the equivalent of the faith that moves mountains. Far more quickly than reason or logic, irony can penetrate rage and puncture self-pity. It can be, as it was for me then, the beginning of the first small steps toward clarity; for the truth, of course, as I began to glimpse it slowly, was that it was more than a little ironic for me to envy now what I had never envied before and nonsense to consider as wasted the years in which I had chosen to do exactly what I wanted to do.

It was not accidental that I was sitting on this bench, nor would I have had it otherwise. I had never wanted any idle sweet time to savor anything other than the mystery of how to get through a stage door. I had what I wanted even now, just as I had always had what I wanted, and just as these boys and girls had exactly what they wanted. I would be no whit happier in their shoes, and never would have been, than they would have been in mine. The true waste of these years would be to let them slip through my fingers tonight—to accept as final the decision that George Kaufman had lost his faith in the play or had gone dry on it. If he had gone dry, he must be led to the well again—if he had gone stale, he must be refreshed. Just how this was to be accomplished I had no idea, but it must be done speedily. Delay would produce a finality of its own. I got up from the bench, walked back along the boardwalk to where the streetcar stopped and waited for one to take me home. The streetcar was full of the same young couples, but I looked at them now with neither envy nor jealousy. I could hardly keep my eyes open. I wanted a good night's sleep more than anything in the world right now, and fortunately I got one. I slept as though someone had hit me over the head.

My relationship with George Kaufman did not include intimacy. His nature did not allow him those easy interchanges between people that ripen into swift friendship. The paradox was that he had a quick sympathy and understanding that made one feel at times that one was on the brink of intimacy, but he invariably retreated behind a barrier of cool detachment that he either chose to maintain or could do nothing about. I had sensed this quickly and had respected it, and I had never tried to pass beyond the limits he himself set. Ours was purely a working relationship that was comfortable and friendly during working hours, but remained aloof and distant away from the typewriter. It precluded any personal appeal to him on my part on the basis of sentiment. Mr. Kaufman would be reached, if indeed he could be reached, on the specific level of work or not at all. Anything else was a waste of time or plain wishful thinking.

Early the following morning I walked back to the little beach where I had written *Once in a Lifetime* and arranged to go to work —a supply of yellow pads in one hand and a bag of sandwiches and soda pop in the other. The one good chance of winning Mr. Kaufman back to the play was to devise new second and third acts that might strike him as worth the extra gamble of picking up the pieces again, considering the time and effort he had already put into it. The difficulty lay in the fact that they must be invented today and presented to him if possible not later than tomorrow, or it might well be too late. He was the most sought-after director in the theatre, and for all I knew might already have embarked on some other venture. He usually went from one play right on to another, sometimes being represented by two or even three plays in the same season. It was unlikely that he would remain inactive with the new season stretching this far in front of him. His telephone was probably jingling with offers right now. It was an unpleasant thought and I did not allow myself to linger on it. I put it firmly out of my mind and stared down at the yellow pad resting on my knees. I had enough to think about otherwise. To ask him to rewrite two full acts, even if I were lucky enough to come up with them, was rather a large order, but there was time enough to do it if I could get him to agree. It had been done before—that was what spring tryouts were for, or some of the solid hits of every other season would never have reached Broadway, and a number of new playwrights would have expired with them.

The formula of the spring tryout was a boon to a new playwright. The two or three months' layoff for rewriting, after which the play was reopened, was economically possible to the theatre of those days; and it gave the playwright a decent chance to redo his play and, more important, to learn his craft without the shadow of theatre party dates that must be met, booking jams on the road and the scarcity of New York theatres looming constantly over his shoulder. There are plays that can be rewritten in two or three weeks on the road and there are plays that cannot. It takes time to unravel the mechanism of a play without destroying its over-all structure, time to think through and select the good and bad of audience reaction and friendly advice, and more time still to reach a fresh viewpoint or attitude on the work to be done if one is not to make the same mistakes all over again. It is difficult for the new or even the practiced playwright to work well under conditions which include the in-evitable deadline of a New York opening only two weeks away, let alone to learn anything worth knowing in the only laboratory where the art of play-writing can be successfully taught, which is back of the proscenium. I was fortunate to have been a new playwright in a time when the theatre contained a reasonable continuity and did not resemble a wild game of roulette played on the lucky chance that a play either opened in not too great trouble or closed a month later in New York. In the theatre of today, it would have been impossible to do what needed to be done within the limits of the lunatic immediate-hit or immediate-flop procedure that now prevails; nor would I have had the irreplaceable opportunity of learning my profession with the proper tools, the most important of which is not a pencil or a typewriter, but the necessary time to think before using them.

It was almost dark when I started for home, my pockets stuffed with pages of yellow paper scribbled over with a rough scenario of new second and third acts. That there were still great unresolved holes in it, I knew, but what it lacked in finesse it made up for, I thought, in new invention. Of necessity I had had to leave certain troublesome areas untouched and plunge ahead, but I had had a bit of luck now and then along the way—enough at any rate to make me feel that there was an outside chance that Mr. Kaufman might accept it. The trick now was to smooth it out and be able to present it to him as skillfully as possible. There is nothing deadlier than having someone read aloud the outline of a play, and it is equally deadly to read a typed résumé full of careful omissions that only serve to highlight the weaknesses and bury the good points. It was far better, I knew, to memorize the scenario completely and rely on my ability to present it sharply and adroitly, covering its lacks and taking advantage of ever one of its virtues. I was convinced it had several, and I did not intend to ad lib them tomorrow or trust to the inspiration of the moment.

I chased my mother out of the kitchen, with the supper dishes still unwashed in the sink, put a chair against the door to bar any interruptions and sat down to memorize the outline incident by incident, strengthening its weak spots and heightening its strong points as I went along. It held up well, even under my anxious testing. The thinking was fresh, the invention seemed amusing and the construction was sound. If only I could tell it to Mr. Kaufman tomorrow as well as I was telling it to the kitchen sink now, all would be well.

I presented myself to the maid who opened the door of 158 East 63rd Street at ten o'clock the next morning, and smilingly walked past her into the house. She had no reason to suppose that I was not simply reporting again for work with Mr. Kaufman as I had done all winter, and this, of course, was what I had counted on. I had decided it was much too risky to telephone for an appointment first, and I had come early enough to insure his being in. She returned my good morning and indicated that Mr. Kaufman was upstairs as usual, and I walked up the stairs and into his room without knocking.

He was having his breakfast and in the middle of a phone call, and he was very surprised indeed to see me. The startled look he gave me over his glasses was quite as though he had seen a ghost or some forgotten figure out of the dim past. While he finished his telephone conversation I walked over and stole a sideways glance at the pile of manuscripts on his night table. The top one was titled *Grand Hotel,* and the pile was thick enough to make me feel I had been wise not to let another day pass in getting here. He hung up and said, "Good morning," pleasantly enough, though his voice still held a tone of puzzled surprise in it.

I knew better now than to make any kind of prefacing speech. Instead, I took out an envelope from my inside pocket, much like the one he himself used each day, and glanced briefly at the notes I had typed on one side of it as a guide to help me begin. "I worked out a new second and third act, Mr. Kaufman," I said, "and I'd like you to hear it."

"Right now?" he asked, looking quickly at his watch.

"It won't take long," I lied, knowing full well it would take at least an hour or as long as I needed to finish.

"Mind if I keep eating?" he said.

"Not at all," I answered. "I'll just keep talking."

I started right off. The crackle of cornflakes followed by the crunch of toast is not the most helpful of accompaniments to the telling of a story, particularly of so crucial a story as this one represented to me. The sound was terribly disconcerting, but there was no help for it. I was lucky to catch him and have him listen, and the very fact that he was willing to listen I took as a sign that he was still un-committed to any one of those manuscripts on the night table. I consciously slowed down until he had finished the second cup of coffee, though he was giving me all of his attention, and mentally noted that memorizing the scenario had been a stroke of absolute genius! I could watch him intently now, the outline thoroughly in my head, hastening the telling when his interest seemed to flag or matching the glint of interest that came into his eyes occasionally with an excitement of my own. He smiled once or twice and laughed outright at an old line of dialogue we had discarded and which I had purposely stuck back in a new place when it fitted perfectly. It had been a favorite line of his which had never worked, and I used it craftily. I knew it would please him. Had there been other little wiles I could have thought of or used I would have used them all shamelessly. Sometimes play-writing only begins when "End of Act Three" is typed on the manuscript.

I finished at last, flushed and a little breathless. I looked at my watch. It had taken just over an hour, even rushing it a bit now and then. Toward the end Mr. Kaufman had retreated to his favorite position, stretched out flat on the floor, and now he slowly and silently arose. He walked to the window and stood staring out at that damned cat which seemed to hold such fascination for him. He turned back toward the room and picked a few bits of lint off the carpet before he looked directly at me.

"What's the matter?" he asked suddenly, giving me a strange look.

I must have been holding my breath without being aware of it and I imagine it gave my eyes a somewhat bug-eyed expression. "Nothing is the matter," I answered. "I'm just waiting."

"How soon could you move in here?" he said.

"In here—with you?" I asked stupidly.

"Not in this room, no," he said not unkindly. "In the house. Beatrice goes to Europe today and Ann is leaving for camp. I meant Ann's room. That's a full summer's work you've laid out, you know, with evenings included. We could get into rehearsal by August, I think, if you moved in here and we worked straight through."

"I'll go home and pack a suitcase and be right back," I said and started for the door.

"Tomorrow morning will do," he called sharply after me. "I'll be looking at you all summer."

"You had a whole day off yesterday," I called back and closed the door behind me.

It was done—and I had also achieved the first moment of intimacy I had ever been able to allow myself with him. I celebrated both victories by having a full-course steak dinner as a second breakfast. The occasion seemed to call for nothing short of that.

PLAY-WRITING, like begging in India, is an honorable but humbling profession. I had privately decided that with an outline before us and armed with the knowledge those two weeks of playing before audiences had given us, we could finish the revision in a month or very little more. I soon saw, however, that Mr. Kaufman was not far wrong in his estimate. He did indeed look at me almost all summer long, including most of the evenings. What I failed to take into account was that an outline or scenario is an imprecise instrument at best. It cannot be followed slavishly, for as the outline is translated into dialogue, it shifts mercurially under one's fingers, and the emphasis of a scene or sometimes a whole act will twist out of control, taking with it large parts of the carefully plotted scenario that follows after.

We spent the first few days painstakingly setting down and enlarging the outline I had memorized, but by the third day of actual work many of the things that had seemed so promising on yellow paper disappeared under the harsh glare of the sheet of white paper in the typewriter. Nevertheless, some of the better invention remained and even what was unusable served a purpose; but it was apparent not only that there was a full summer's work ahead but that we would actually be lucky to complete it by August. Mr. Kaufman accepted the fact without complaint, and for my own part I was too pleased and grateful to be back at work to mind, however long it took. What I minded, as we settled down into a daily grind, was not work, but the heat and hunger, one or the other of which seemed to be ever present, and which in combination became my chief concern. New York, that summer, was teaching those unlucky enough to have to remain in the city that the Upper Reaches of the Amazon, though not in the same latitude, were perhaps no hotter than the Jewel of the East could be if it chose to rub its inhabitants' noses into a bit of subtropical weather. Heat wave after heat wave broiled the buildings and the pavements with almost no respite, so that even in the evenings the baked brick and stone seemed to give off a heat much like that of a baker's oven that had not yet cooled. The tar in the asphalt paving melted each day and oozed blackly from the cracks, and the parched people still trapped in the city walked heavily along the streets looking wilted and beaten. The weather made the headlines in every edition, and the heat headache I awoke with every morning seemed to throb a little more dully as I read, "Heat Wave Unbroken" or "No Relief in Sight."

The heat became a living and evil thing, for air conditioning, that most glorious of mankind's inventions since the discovery of the wheel, was not in general use—and if it had been, I doubt whether Mr. Kaufman would have considered it anything more than an unnecessary or unworkable toy. He seemed impervious to the heat, and other than washing his hands more often than usual, his only concession to it—made, I think, more for my sake than for his own —was a small electric fan that tiredly plop-plopped around in an uneven contest with the waves of hot air that came in through the windows from the furnace outside. This useless object was placed on the floor in a far corner of the room so as not to ruffle the papers on the desk. Once, *in extremis*, I moved it to a chair where I fancied some of the slight air it circulated might blow directly on me. Instead, it blew the papers from the desk all over the room and four or five pages blew right out the window and skittered into the adjoining yard. I had to hurry downstairs and retrieve them under Mr. Kaufman's baleful eye, and to make matters worse, I got stuck trying to climb back over the fence of the house next door and had to call for the maid to help me down, while Mr. Kaufman watched from the upstairs window. It was an ignominious performance, and after that I let the fan remain where it was and sat as still as I could in the leather chair trying not to think of either the heat or food.

Heat, of course, is supposed to diminish or even rob one entirely of appetite, but my unfortunate appetite was apparently sturdy or robust enough to defy, like the United States mails, heat or sleet or snow and let nothing deter it! There were even times when I grew hungry enough to forget about the heat and to see mirages of food heaped in front of me, for Mr. Kaufman's delicate appetite, slim enough in the winter, seemed to all but disappear with the first robin. With warm weather, long before the first heat wave enveloped the city, a salad and a not too lavish plate of thinly sliced cold meat became the unvarying menu of each day's main meal, and when on a coolish day lamb chops occasionally appeared, my old struggle not to grab and stuff was like a man wrestling with his faith. I had made the terrible mistake, when he asked me the first evening of my arrival what I took each morning for breakfast, to reply genteelly, "Oh, just orange juice, toast and coffee." And I had watched him write it down on a slip of paper and hand it to the maid to give to the cook, knowing even as the words left my lips that I had made a fatal error. It was impossible after that to fill up with a decent breakfast to fortify myself against the rest of a day where lunch remained as always tea and cookies and little cucumber or watercress sandwiches served in the middle of the afternoon, and though cookies and a full pitcher of iced tea were left on the desk, when evening came and that tidy little salad and platter of cold meats stared up at me from the table I was always ravenous.

By the third week of my sojourn, when I was not lying awake all night cursing the heat and my ungovernable appetite, I sat staring during the day at Mr. Kaufman from the depths of the leather chair, not thinking of the next line or scene, but torturing myself with fantasies of thick roast-beef sandwiches or chicken soup with the chicken still floating around in it. He must at times have thought I had taken leave of my senses, for I caught him once or twice staring at me malignantly over his glasses. My own eyes were glazed, not with inattention or boredom, but with hunger.

[369]

By Thursday evening of each week, which was the evening Mr. Kaufman played poker and I returned to Brooklyn to visit my family, even my mother's cooking, ordinary at best, seemed positively Lucullan, and the relish and appetite with which I ate everything set before me must have given her the impression that she had turned into Escoffier, or at the very least the best cook in Brooklyn. I was always sprightlier and more nimble-witted on Friday morning than on any other day during the week, a fact which seemed to puzzle Mr. Kaufman considerably.

By the middle of July, Mr. Kaufman became aware that something was wrong with the weather. Even an extra washing of the hands did not quite do the trick, and toward the end of an unbroken two-week stretch of scorching days and nights he suddenly announced that he was taking the weekend off to play in a croquet tournament in Long Island. I could hardly believe my ears. I had been sitting glassy-eyed all that day, watching the perspiration from his forehead drip slowly onto the typewriter and marveling at the fact that he would pass his limp handkerchief over his face and never once make the slightest reference to the weather. It was positively inhuman, I had been thinking to myself just before he spoke, not only to be nobly above man's baser appetites, but to be hermetically sealed in against the weather as well! I was human enough to be meanly delighted that the heat had finally got him. He was pale and drawn, and looking at him, I decided I probably looked even worse. I had not realized that after six years of camp—of being out of the city all summer long—I was now starving for the feel of grass under my feet instead of pavement and longing for the sight of trees and water and an expanse of sky. I could barely wait for the day's work to end.

Five minutes after he placed the cover over the typewriter I telephoned the Flagler and asked if they would have me as guest performer for the weekend. They would be delighted, it seemed, and I managed to catch the evening train for the Catskills.

That weekend was the last time I did a boy-and-girl number in a revue, "To be or not to be" at the campfire, "Mrs. Cohen at the Beach" in the Saturday night musical, and used my full bag of social-director tricks in the dining room, at the indoor games and around the swimming pool. I was welcomed back like a reigning opera star and I did my stint gladly to pay for my free weekend; but even while I performed, and afterward when I mingled with the guests and staff, I wondered how I had ever lasted through six summers of it. I shuddered to think that I might have to come back and do it again, if *Once in a Lifetime* failed. The things that are bearable at a certain period of one's life, out of necessity or made possible by youth itself, are unbearable to contemplate doing again when that time is over. By Sunday night I was champing to return to the city. Those three days, though I did not realize it at the time, did more than just rescue me from the city's heat—they were a blessing in disguise. That weekend, and all that it implied, was just what I needed to see me down the home stretch, for without wanting to or meaning to, I had been faltering and dragging my heels.

As a rule, the writing of a second act seems to drag on forever. It is the danger spot of every play—the soft underbelly of play-writing, as Mr. Churchill might put it—and it is well to be aware of it. A first act carries an impetus of its own that is almost sufficient to carry the writer along with it—the excitement of a new play seems to supply the energy and freshness needed for each day's work at the typewriter, and there are some first acts that literally seem to write themselves. That is why, perhaps, Bernard Shaw is said to have remarked, "Anyone who cannot write a good first act might just as well give up play-writing entirely." It is second acts that separate the men from the boys. We were still mired in the second act when Mr. Kaufman gave way to the heat, and I suspect his giving way to it may have been partly due to his sensing that a point had been reached where a halt might be not only helpful but downright necessary.

Whatever the reason, he returned from his own weekend refreshed and fired as I was with brand-new first-act energy. Cooler weather also coincided with our return—an omen I was quick to seize on as a good one and which was borne out by the fact that lamb chops as well as dessert appeared on the table twice that week. By the middle of the following week, the second act was finished and we both seemed to breathe more freely.

With the beginning of the third act the pace accelerated. We were due to go into rehearsal the beginning of the second week in August, and Mr. Kaufman passed up several of his poker evenings and worked straight through. We were losing part of each day's working time now for recasting and sessions with the scenic artist and costume designer. Two new scenes had been added, one of them quite elaborate and calling for the interior of a Hollywood night club called the Pigeon's Egg, where the patrons sat at tables encased in huge cracked eggs and the waitresses were attired as pigeons, feathers and all. This was one of the new inventions I had concocted during my solitary day on the beach.

There was some doubt now in both our minds that we would finish in time, and Mr. Kaufman grew noticeably edgy. But four days before rehearsals were scheduled to begin he turned toward me and said, "I think you ought to stand up or lie down or shut up or go away or something—I'm about to type 'The End.'" He typed the two words and grinned. "No farewell speech to the troops?" he asked. He was delighted, I could tell, to have finished with a few days to spare.

I shook my head and grinned back, but I did not share his pleasure. I had secretly hoped that we might have to work right through until the evening before rehearsal. The truth was, I hated the idea of this four-day wait, for eager as I had been before to have rehearsals start, as each day brought them closer, I pushed the thought firmly out of my mind and tried to maintain the illusion that they were still far off. While one is in the throes of work it is easy to hold to the fantasy that success is almost certain to crown so sterling an effort, but as the day of rehearsal relentlessly approaches, the fantasy begins to chip away around the edges and the certainty seems to grow slimmer and slimmer until it is swallowed up by a new dogmatism—the certainty of failure. It is commonly called "rehearsal jitters" and I evidently had a severe case of it. I packed my suitcase reluctantly and went back to Brooklyn to wait.

It is not the best time in the world to be around one's family, and

I mooned about the house for those four days, succeeding in making both my family and myself utterly miserable. Only those who have lived at close quarters with a bad case of pre-rehearsal nerves understand in some measure the unbalanced behavior of the schizophrenic. Brooklyn is a large borough, but it seemed to me that I walked over most of it in those four days, for there was not enough money to do much else but walk, and when I could no longer stay in my skin and remain in the apartment I got out and walked. In the evenings I twisted the dial of the radio from station to station until it drove them all crazy, or flew out of the house in a temper when I was asked to stop. In a decently arranged world playwrights would be allowed, or even made, to go, a week before rehearsals begin, to some isolated spot not even within flying distance of their families, where their wants would be attended to in silence and their lunacy understood.

I think even my mother was glad to see me leave for rehearsal on Monday morning. She reminded me that a mother's heart went with me, but its balm did not last out the subway ride to Times Square, and I walked through the stage door of the Music Box with that age-old mixture of foreboding and cowardice that marks the true professional. It seemed to me I was some light-years removed from the wide-eyed hopeful who had walked shyly through this same stage door last spring, overawed by the stage managers, embarrassed at being too early, and ridiculously eager for a sniff of the excitement and glamor of a first rehearsal. I was arriving now not ahead of the actors but with the management this time, and I would not panic at that mumbled first reading of the play, but behind my professional manner lay the cowardice gained by a knowledge I had not had before. I knew now that beyond this first rehearsal lay those minutes alone in the hotel room before going down to the theatre to face the first performance. I knew the torment of pacing up and down in the dark, waiting for the sting of an audience's silence when laughter did not come, and the pain of watching those faces come up the aisle. I could almost feel the fatigue of night-long revisions and the weariness of waiting for dawn to come through the blinds so that we could stop rewriting and get some sleep before the next day's rehearsal— and I shrank from facing it all again. I longed to settle back into my ignorance of last spring. It was all to be gone through once more, but this time there was the added knowledge of knowing that the stakes were higher. I had had my second chance.

Sam Harris, coming through the stage door just behind me, phrased it neatly with that facility he had for putting everything there was to say into a short sentence. "Hi, kid," he greeted me, "we're playing for keeps this time, eh?" I nodded glumly and walked to the table where Mr. Kaufman already sat waiting, and a few moments later the stage manager rapped on the table and called the company to attention.

All the little absurdities and affectations of a first rehearsal were again present, but I did not suffer from them too greatly. The actors heaved and mumbled, and Max Siegel smiled sunnily at everything. Mr. Kaufman made his coded chicken marks on the manuscript, seeming not to listen to a word that was being said, and Sam Harris sat rigidly in his chair, his face inscrutable. There were the usual long pauses that had maddened me before, where the parts had been typed incorrectly, and the resultant frenzied search for a pencil by the actor whose part was wrong and who had apparently never thought of bringing a pencil to rehearsal, though he had been in the theatre for forty years. An actor's pained surprise at the need of a pencil at a first rehearsal runs parallel to his bewilderment at having to open a door or a window for the first time at a dress rehearsal in the actual set. He seems never to have opened a door or a window in his life, or even to have seen one before, and he will fiddle with one or the other and delay the proceedings until one has the impulse to leap over the footlights and hit him—or better still, push him straight through it. The rococo politeness and hoary theatrical jokes that always accompany the search for a pencil, while the sense and meaning of the scene being read is lost entirely, is hard to bear, for of course the actor who now has a pencil cannot then find his place.

I sat patiently through it all. My chief interest was in listening, or trying to listen, to Jean Dixon, who had replaced Aline MacMahon in the leading role, and Spring Byington, who had taken over the role of the Hollywood gossip columnist played in the tryout by Blanche Ring. Miss Dixon was a prime mumbler and nervous as a cocker spaniel to boot, but every so often in spite of her mumbling an incisive manner and a corrosive delivery of a line with just the right emphasis shone brilliantly through, and Spring Byington's motherly, wide-eyed mendacity hit the exact fraudulent key the part called for.

I tried now and then to gauge how the new second and third acts might be going by darting overt glances at Sam Harris' face, but I might have spared myself the trouble. It remained throughout like something carved out of stone on Mount Rushmore, nor could I much blame him. It was hard to tell from the way it was being read whether those two acts had been improved or were even worse than they had been, though the actors laughed helpfully as actors always do. They had laughed just as appreciatively last spring and were just as surprised as we were when the audience did not laugh after the curtain was up. Reliance on actors' laughter is the furthest reach in self-deceit, and I shut my ears to it. The second act actually did seem better, but I could tell nothing whatever about the new third act because the typist's errors were so numerous and the scrambling for pencils and the hemming and hawing of correcting parts so distracting that it made any kind of judgment impossible. I gave up listening entirely and made chicken marks of my own on the stage manager's pad until the reading was finished. I would have to contain myself as best I could until the play was roughly staged. The typist had either been typing some other play or we had worked badly. What little I heard sounded terrible.

The rehearsal period of *Once in a Lifetime*'s reopening was perhaps the worst three weeks I have ever spent in rehearsal in the theatre. I knew well enough by now that Mr. Kaufman's directorial method of whispered consultation with each separate actor was unendurable to watch for more than one or two days at the most, and where before I had been content to watch the play grow slowly, sitting through the false starts and the fumblings until play and performance developed, now I wandered restlessly in and out of the theatre and even tried staying away from rehearsals for two full days, in order, so I told myself, to get a fresher look. It was a useless dodge. I was unhappy in the theatre and miserable away from it.

The truth of the matter was that I was no longer willing or able to trust my own theatrical instinct or judgment—it had been wrong before, so my reasoning went, therefore how could I judge what was good or bad now? I had not thought the old second and third acts were bad originally—ergo, how could I tell now if they were any better? I walked to rehearsals under an umbrella of disquietude and held it open over my head in the theatre through every rehearsal that I watched. When this happens, the playwright is incapable of judging a baby contest at Asbury Park, much less a play. Everything takes on the coloration of his own anxiety, and what he sees invariably looks not better but worse. I longed for Mr. Kaufman to break his rule and allow a few friends in for the first run-through, but I did not have the courage to suggest such a thing—indeed, I barely had enough courage to come to it myself!

At the end of the first week, the same slim audience of Sam Harris, Max Siegel, Mr. Kaufman and myself sat solemnly through the first run-through and solemnly said good night afterward. It was a little more than I could bear, and I found enough courage when Mr. Kaufman was out of earshot to grab Max Siegel firmly by the lapels and whisper, "What did Mr. Harris think of it?"

"He didn't say," was Max Siegel's unsatisfactory reply. "But I think he liked it or he would have said something. I liked it, if that's any consolation."

It was not—and I realized dully that it would not have mattered if Sam Harris had gone out of his way to praise it, for his praise in my present state of mind would have lasted only long enough for me to tell myself that neither he nor anybody else would really know anything until the curtain rose in front of that first audience in Philadelphia.

I seemed to have spent the final two weeks of rehearsal almost continuously in the company of Max Siegel. I would dutifully appear at the beginning of each day's rehearsal, remain long enough to make Mr. Kaufman aware of my presence, and then streak upstairs to the Sam Harris office and by hook or crook inveigle Max Siegel to come with me to the drug store next door. I used his sunny nature and God-given optimism the way a dentist uses novocaine on a throbbing

[376]

molar. Max Siegel had apparently emerged from the womb liking the world and everything in it, and he liked everything we had done to the play. He liked everything he saw at every run-through, and every actor in the cast; and seated on a stool next to him at the drug-store counter I ate hamburger after hamburger and let him dull my pain. Each day I increased the amount of anesthesia he provided, so that finally not only was he having lunch and dinner with me, but he was walking me around the streets at night after rehearsals were over and until he had to go home to his wife. I think if he had not been married I would have insisted that he come home with me, and the night of the last run-through in New York I almost asked him to take me home with him!

THERE IS a phrase that has gone out of fashion now, but it aptly describes the mood of my leave-taking for Philadelphia: the "white feather" was not painted on my suitcase, but it might just as well have been, or stuck in the band of my hat. I said good-bye to my family, a far soberer good-bye on their part this time than the roseate good wishes that had sped me off to Atlantic City. Even my mother now dimly realized that my new profession was largely a gamble in uncertainties so far as eating and paying the rent were concerned, for we were once again coming to a dangerously low ebb financially. Indeed, without my brother, who had his first job that summer, I doubt that we could have managed at all. It seemed to me that the white feather fluttered in the breeze for all to see as I walked down the subway steps to take the train to Pennsylvania Station.

This time I did not need Max Siegel's invitation to join him in a drink. I borrowed his flask and had two stiff drinks before the train was well out of the tunnel. They helped considerably; and the atmosphere of a company on the way to an out-of-town opening is always so sanguine and high-spirited that it is hard to remain downcast, surrounded by so much good cheer and hopeful expectation. Apart from the buoyant spirits actors carry with them on any journey, they usually carry along as well for these three or four weeks out of town their cats, their dogs, their parakeets and canaries, and sometimes even their tropical fish, all of which lend a carnival air to even a journey to Philadelphia. By the time the train pulled into the Broad Street Station I was feeling surprisingly cheerful. I had been too greatly dispirited during rehearsals to try to restore my lack of confidence by searching for a good omen, but I felt so much better now that I began the search as the train slowly moved into the station. I did not have to search far or for long. The heat, as we stepped down from the train onto the station platform, was grisly. The dogs and cats began to pant at once, and their owners drooped visibly, along with my new-found cheerfulness. The true believer does not pick and choose his omens. The range is limited and the selection strict. The first one is the one that counts, and according to the rules of the game this was it.

I picked up my suitcase and followed Mr. Kaufman heavily toward the taxi stand, my shirt already beginning to stick to my back. Cool and unwilted, Mr. Kaufman ordered our bags dropped with the doorman at the hotel, then drove straight on to the theatre to have a look at the new set which he had ordered to be put up first. I could not believe, as the taxicab stopped in front of what looked to me like an armory, that this was the theatre we were going to play, in spite of the posters outside. It seemed to cover a square block. The Lyric Theatre in Philadelphia, now mercifully torn down, was a great barn of a place, about as appropriate for the playing of a comedy as the interior of a steel mill in Pittsburgh and just about as hot. It was, in fact, where large touring musicals generally played, but it was the only theatre on the road at this time that was free and Sam Harris had taken it.

It seems incredible now that theatres in New York and all the other major cities of the East remained open all summer long without benefit of air conditioning, but they did, and people astonishingly enough went to them uncomplainingly. Two giant-sized electric fans on either side of every theatre proscenium were kept running until the house lights dimmed, and were turned on again for each intermission, but the heat generated by an audience on a hot night was still formidable. The make-up ran down the actors' faces, and the audience itself was a sea of waving programs and palm-leaf fans, the rustle of which sometimes drowned out the actors altogether.

[379]

Nevertheless, summer-long runs in Philadelphia, Boston, Washington and Chicago, with every theatre in full swing, were an accepted fact, and the new season in New York actually began on August 15, or at the latest Labor Day, heat waves or no heat waves.

I followed Mr. Kaufman through the stage door and wandered aimlessly about while he conferred with the carpenter and electrician. The Lyric Theatre backstage smelled stalely of that last touring musical, and the auditorium, of its last perspiring audience. I looked up and counted what seemed to me to be at least seven balconies running clear up to the roof, and I wondered briefly why anyone would climb up there in the heat and how they would manage to hear anything if they got there. The back rows of the huge orchestra seemed difficult enough to reach with the loudest human voice, and my heart sank as I visualized subtle comedy lines being shouted into that vastness. I slid down into a seat and stared at the asbestos curtain. It would have been far better, it seemed to me, to open cold in New York and take our chances than to try the play out in this monstrous cave. It would not have astonished me to see a covey of bats fly down from the balcony or out of one of the boxes. As if to illustrate my thoughts, two moths rose slowly from the red plush a few seats away from me and flew languidly off. I watched them settle on the back of the seat in the row in front and was suddenly in good humor again. I think the idea of the animal or insect world ultimately taking over this rookery delighted me. It was certainly the last place for humans to witness a sparkling new satirical comedy, but my cheerfulness had returned.

A good many of the company had wandered into the auditorium from backstage to have a first look at the Pigeon's Egg from out front, and in a few minutes Mr. Kaufman came through the fire door and the asbestos curtain was taken up. The company burst into laughter and then into applause. It was a remarkable set—an immense baroque affair that in terms of decor and good taste might have been termed Early Frankenstein—and a wonderful conception of Hollywood extravagance at its wildest. Even without the actors in it, it was preposterous enough to be amusing all by itself. I was delighted with it. It seemed to me that every funny line in the scene would be

[380]

enhanced by this setting, and fortunately it was the last scene in the play. Everything seemed suddenly and miraculously better. Though it was tempting fate to switch omens, I decided that those two moths were the omen I had been looking for and moreover that it would be foolish to dampen my sudden good spirits by sitting through hours of scenic and light rehearsals where nothing much happened except the slow rotting of my mind. I got up from my seat and walked out of the theatre, leaving Mr. Kaufman in full charge of the drudgery that lay ahead. I had read somewhere that some playwrights filled in these useless hours by visiting a museum or even going to a movie, and while I was incapable of such blithe behavior, I had a pleasing enough prospect of my own in view. An author's living expenses out of town are always paid for by the management, including the food he eats, as long as he eats it at the hotel, and the hotel was just where I was going. I could do nothing about the heat, but this time at least I would not go hungry.

Some of the world's pleasantest reading is contained in a good hotel menu, and I sent for one before I even unpacked my suitcase; I also found out just how late room service remained open at night. I had eaten scarcely anything through the four days and nights of dress rehearsals in Atlantic City, though I had known that Sam Harris was footing the bill, and I was not going to be the same kind of fool again. Fresh from Mr. Kaufman's Spartan teas of watercress and cucumber sandwiches, I ordered an afternoon tea of my own. It was extraordinary how much smaller the Lyric Theatre seemed in my mind's eye after Lobster Newburg and Baked Alaska, and I took care to see to it that my mind's eye remained on that same crystal-clear level.

I ate my way through four days and nights of dress rehearsals in Philadelphia and slept beautifully in spite of the heat. Everyone noticed my changed demeanor, and Max Siegel commented on it, but I could hardly explain that a midnight snack each night, and a waiter staggering through the door with a loaded breakfast tray every morning, was the source of my wholesale enthusiasm for everything about the play and the performance. The company manager might have a nasty moment when he looked at my bill, but it was certainly to Sam Harris' advantage to have me as fresh as possible for whatever work needed to be done after we opened. My soaring good spirits had even dissipated my fears about facing the opening—never, in fact, had the play's chances seemed so bright. This almost fatuous optimism was not entirely due to food, I suppose, but to the fact that anxiety had taken a manic swing, as anxiety has a way of doing, but I have an idea that a full stomach was not unhelpful in keeping the swing upward.

I was not even particularly unhappy when Joe Hyman telephoned on the morning of the opening to say that he had a bad summer cold and would have to come down to Philadelphia later in the week. He was surprised at how cheerful and well I sounded, and indeed it was hard for me to recall the abject terror in which I had spent the hours waiting for his arrival in Atlantic City. I felt entirely capable of going through this opening alone and actually impatient of the hours that remained until it was time to go to the theatre and see the curtain rise.

I sat pleasantly through a final light rehearsal and spent the rest of the afternoon trying to find a dozen different ways of working the title of the play into those traditionally funny telegrams to the cast. I was surprised to find that it was suddenly six o'clock and time to get ready. I looked out the window and saw, of all things, a rainbow. To a man who was willing to believe that moths constituted a good omen, that rainbow seemed to be the ultimate sign that everything now seemed to be conspiring in our favor, including the weather. A fierce thunderstorm late in the afternoon had bathed the city in coolness and I leaned out the window and felt the first breeze that hinted of fall. That fresh cool air would certainly put any audience in the best of possible moods, and while I was not yet ready to accept such a heresy as a painless opening, I could not deny the fact that contrary to the way I'd expected to feel, I was not only feeling no pain at all but a distinctly pleasant excitement. The rainbow seemed to call for something more than just staring at it, and obeying a sudden impulse, I went to the telephone and asked the bell captain if he could get me a bottle of Scotch. Rich people in the movies were always sipping Scotch highballs while they dressed for dinner, and though Sam Harris was paying for this one, I sipped it slowly in the bathtub and mused on how pleasant might be the shape of things to come—large sums of money in particular. I was sorry now that Joe Hyman was not here to lift a glass to the future with me and then walk serenely off to the opening.

Even Mr. Kaufman seemed to have an unwonted air of gaiety when I ran into him backstage on my rounds of wishing the cast good luck, and Sam Harris in the lobby gaily reported that the absence of a full quorum of the wrecking crew tonight was due to the fact that so many plays were opening out of town all at once that they had to make a choice of the one that would give them the most pleasure to see fail. "Looks like they've written us off already." He laughed. "But I have an idea we may fool them." It seemed to me that he exuded a note of confidence tonight that had not been there before, and the Lyric Theatre, with its orchestra almost entirely filled, did not seem nearly so barnlike or impossible to play in. I looked impatiently at the last stragglers going down the aisle. I wanted not so much for the play to begin as to have the first act over and done with. I knew they would laugh at the first act. What happened after Mr. Kaufman's exit in the second act would be the test of how well we had worked. I kept watching the giant fans on each side of the proscenium, and at last they slowed down to a whirr and the house lights dimmed and the footlights came on.

I don't know whether it was because this was the largest audience we had ever played to or because it was an uncommonly generous one, but the volume of laughter was greater than it had ever been before, even for the first act. The revisions we had made in it to make it of a piece with the new second and third acts had tightened some of the arid spots and made the laughter almost continuous. It had always played well, but now it played thunderously. The applause lasted a good half-minute after the curtain came down. It was a little too early to gloat; but if the second act was right, it was going to have its best chance with this audience, and I could hardly wait for them to get back to their seats. Sam Harris made no comment other than a laconic, "That act's been improved, kid." Like myself, he was marking time.

It seemed an unconscionably long intermission until the house lights dimmed again. Mr. Kaufman received his usual reception as the curtain rose on the second act and his usual round of applause as he made his exit. I held my breath—the next few minutes would tell the story.

I did not have to hold it for long. They were laughing loudly now in all the places where there had been only silence before, and as the laughter kept on without any sign of diminishing I began to bang delightedly on the back of the orchestra railing with my fists. A blue-suited figure was immediately at my side. "Don't interrupt them, you fool," hissed Mr. Kaufman, but I could tell he was as delighted as I was. The wonderful sound of laughter kept coming in wave after wave, and in spite of that pacing figure nearby, I began to laugh with them myself. It seemed impossible not to. I was, I suppose, a little light-headed with relief. The second act came down to even greater applause than the first and an unmistakable buzz filled the theatre even before the house lights came up.

There is something almost touching about the way an audience comes up the aisles when it has been thoroughly satisfied with a play. They beam at each other with pleasure, as though they had been given an unexpected present. It is a rewarding sight. Sam Harris, caught in the crush coming up the aisle, saw me and winked broadly, and right behind him Max Siegel's smile seemed to be running straight off his face and into his ears. I waved and indicated I would meet them in the lobby.

I was eager to eavesdrop and hear what the audience was saying about the play, though lobby-listening is a dangerous occupation. A playwright is likely to hear last night's bridge game being discussed instead of his play, or how well little Robert is doing since he changed schools. Lobby-listening even at an acknowledged hit in New York is likely to yield no more than, "I don't know what they're raving about, do you?" or, "It's just an evening's entertainment, that's all," to a playwright's outraged ears. But tonight they

[384]

were actually talking about the play. I threaded my way from group to group and heard them saying, "Funniest play I've seen in years," and, "Wait until this hits Broadway," and reminded myself that this was the time I usually spent in the stage alley, afraid of what I might hear if I remained in the lobby.

I listened so avidly that I failed to meet Sam Harris and Max Siegel—the ushers were already calling out "Curtain going up" by the time I had had my fill. I followed the audience back into the theatre, gathering up the last morsel of comment and relishing every word. I suddenly realized I had also neglected to say a word to Mr. Kaufman, until I saw him beginning to pace back and forth as the house lights began to dim. I went over to him and tried to modulate my excitement to a pitch that would match his own usual conservatism. "They seem to like it, Mr. Kaufman," I said.

To my surprise, he put a hand on my shoulder and said, "You deserve it," and then quickly walked away. Only the rising of the curtain saved him from one of my commemorative speeches.

The audience's response to their first sight of the Pigeon's Egg was almost excessive. They gave a great whoop of laughter and then broke into applause that lasted through the first few lines of dialogue. I took my place at the back of the orchestra rail, prepared to behave with a little more decorum this time and not laugh along with them, even though this was the act we were both certain contained the funniest moments of the play.

Their laughter came promptly as the applause died and the scene went on, but it was not, I quickly noticed, of the same kind. The ear could tell the difference almost immediately. It was a little forced, as though they were unwilling to believe that so good an evening might be going downhill and were perfectly prepared to laugh at costumes and props until the play came to life again. But the play was not coming to life again, even with the best of intentions on the part of this eager-to-laugh-at-anything audience. In spite of themselves, their laughter was growing weaker and more fitful, and finally at about the middle of the act it ceased altogether. I looked around for Mr. Kaufman. For once he had stopped his pacing and was standing staring at the stage as aghast as I was. We had gone

[385]

terribly wrong somewhere and there was no point in going over and asking him how or why.

He came over to me just before the third act ended and whispered, "We're too close to a hit now not to get this right. Meet me in the room in half an hour."

I watched a bewildered and disappointed audience file out of the theatre, and on my way back to the hotel I walked behind a man and a woman discussing something in so aggrieved a tone that I knew they must be talking about the play.

"It sure as hell didn't hold up, did it?" I heard him say.

And the woman, equally offended, replied, "I don't understand how the same two people could have written that last act, for the life of me."

I was tempted to join them and say, "May I introduce one of the idiots, madam?" In a way I felt quite as victimized as they did.

We had both largely recovered, however, from our own shock and disappointment with the third act by the time we sat facing each other in Mr. Kaufman's room half an hour later. One thing was inescapable. Two acts were right now, where only one had been right before. It seemed impossible not to be able to lick a last act that was all that seemed to stand in the way of a smashing success. That had been Sam Harris' sanguine conclusion, Mr. Kaufman reported, and he was staying right on in Philadelphia, a sure sign that he believed it could be done. Mr. Kaufman's own belief that we could do it was tonic.

He brought out a new box of fudge, placed the manuscript on his knees, poised a pencil above it for the first cuts, and went right to work without further discussion. It was the same old method— cuts down to the bare bones of the last act to get a clean look at it, until we could glimpse what was wrong and had an idea of how to solve it. It was dawn as usual before we finished, for although there was only one act to cut, we spent the last two hours writing a new scene that might get the act off to a better start, and we were encouraged the next evening to find that it did.

We worked through the following night on another scene, and

that, too, was an improvement; but nothing we wrote seemed to provide a clue for that straight line we were seeking. New scenes, even if they are wrong, will sometimes point out the direction in which a play should move, but nothing seemed to offer us the slightest hint that we were on the right track. There was something stubbornly wrong with the basic idea of the last act that evaded all our efforts to fix it.

Mr. Kaufman, never a man to spare himself or his collaborator where work was concerned, worked like a man possessed. Something more than just a play seemed to be at stake. His professional pride was involved now and made insupportable the fact that he was this tantalizingly close to a hit and not quite able to achieve it. He drove himself, and me along with him, at a merciless pace and to a point where each night we worked until it appeared that not another word could be dredged up, yet the night's work was far from being ended. After flinging himself on the sofa for a few minutes and closing his eyes in exhaustion, he would get up and walk to the typewriter again. I lost count of the number of new scenes that were written every night, staged the next day, and played, rough or not, that same evening, only to be tossed out after one performance.

The actors accomplished prodigious feats of memory, learning and unlearning new scenes for performance after performance, but as a consequence the first two acts were becoming a little shaky and were not playing nearly as well as they had played. When actors walk into a first act with a new last act in their heads almost every night, it is not unnatural that it should play havoc with their over-all performance. Actors cannot be expected to remember new lines each night and still give the old ones their proper value.

By the end of the first week the first two acts had begun to lose that wonderful sheen and precision of the opening performance. On Monday night of the second week there was scarcely a third of the orchestra filled, and the theatre again began to take on that cavelike quality which had appalled me so when I had had my first look at it. A week of disappointed audiences and uncertain performances was beginning to take its toll at the box office. Out-of-town audiences are extremely sensitive and well aware of the role they play. They do not resent being used as guinea pigs to test out a new play, but they pride themselves on their ability to pick winners. Word is passed around rapidly among out-of-town theatregoers, and they can stay away from a play on which the report is bad with an obstinacy that borders on the sinister. The word had evidently gone out on *Once in a Lifetime,* although we told each other that the heat was actually the villain that had caused our business to drop with such frightening swiftness. A new heat wave had engulfed Philadelphia with such scorching intensity that it dwarfed the New York heat waves I had grumbled about and made them seem almost elfin by comparison. The city emptied under our eyes. By the third day of it, offices and shops were sending their employees home at one o'clock in the afternoon, and the baking streets seemed to be bare of everything except traffic policemen, children dousing themselves under fire hydrants, and water sprinklers endlessly sloshing water over the dusty pavements.

No one could work through such heat and remain unaffected by it, but I began to doubt that the heat was the sole cause of Mr. Kaufman's moody and restive manner with the company as he rehearsed during the day or his increasingly pessimistic air as he watched the play each night. Imperceptibly at first, and then unmistakably, I began to detect little telltale signs of discouragement which seemed to grow larger as I watched for them. He worked through the nights and days without letup, but he was strangely silent now when the result of all our labors was being played night after night to audiences of sometimes less than a hundred people. It was disheartening to watch a new scene that had seemed promising in rehearsal spin itself out before rows of empty seats, and programs waving listlessly to and fro in the heat. Laughter is contagious and does not spread easily among people huddled together as if in self-protection against the emptiness around them. We were literally working in the dark —it was impossible to tell from these audiences what was good and should be saved or what was bad and should be tossed out. What little laughter there was came strangely and in curiously isolated spots, and sometimes laughter came where none at all was called for. Though I would not have admitted it to anyone, I began to mistrust everything we were doing. We had either lost control of the play or the last act was incurable. Mr. Kaufman's silence might very well mean that he had come to the same conclusion and was as loath to put it into words as I was, but while it remained unspoken, miracles were still possible. Self-deception is sometimes as necessary a tool as a crowbar.

As our third and last week in Philadelphia began, however, I could sense that whatever his thoughts might be they were not too far from my own. Very few plays are without faults of one kind or another, but few plays succeed with a bad last act. The best kind of fault for a play to have is first-act trouble, and the worst kind last-act trouble. An audience will forgive a slow or even a weak first act, if the second act grows progressively better; and a third act that sends the audience up the aisles and out of the theatre with the impression of a fully rounded evening, can sometimes make that hair's-breadth difference between failure and success. A bad third act or even a poor last fifteen minutes of a play can be ruinous. It can somehow wipe the slate clean of all that has gone on before and completely negate the two acts preceding it, and if a playwright is not in control of his last act in the final week of the tryout, it is unlikely that he ever will be.

Mr. Kaufman brought it out into the open finally on the Tuesday night of that last week. He was taking the midnight train to New York to meet the boat that was bringing Beatrice Kaufman back from Europe the following morning, and he would return in time for the matinée tomorrow. He tossed the new scene we had played that evening into a wastebasket in the corner of the dressing room and removed the last of the make-up from his face before he turned to me directly.

"I think we ought to face the fact that we may have to settle for what we've got," he said. "We must give the company a chance to play the same show four nights in a row before we open in New York," he went on, "and I've got to have a good crack at getting back the performance of the first two acts to where it was when we opened here or we'll stand no chance at all. I'm going to freeze the show as it stands on Thursday night—no more changes—that's it. Hot or cold. That all right with you?"

"What do you think our chances are in New York with this last act, Mr. Kaufman?" I asked.

"Not wonderful," he replied, "if you have to have my honest opinion." He was silent for a moment and then continued. "Comedies usually have to be ninety-five per cent airtight—at least that's been my experience. You can squeak by with ninety per cent once in a while, but not with eighty-five, and according to my figures, not to keep any secrets from you, this one just inches over the seventy mark. I don't know what son-of-a-bitch set up those figures, but there you are. Well, no one can say we didn't try. We're freezing the show Thursday night, Sam," he called over my shoulder to Sam Harris, who had appeared in the doorway. "And good-bye—I'm just going to make that train."

Sam Harris looked after the figure hurrying down the stairs and laughed. "You know, I think he's glad to duck out of town, kid. He runs down those stairs like he just heard tonight's receipts." He laughed again. "A hundred and four dollars and eighty-five cents," he said. "We jumped eighty-five cents over last night. That just about pays for what the actors eat in that night-club scene." He glanced briefly at the wastebasket and the typed pages scattered over the floor around it. "Come on out with me and have a beer, kid. This is your first night off, isn't it?" I nodded. "Do you good to forget the show," he said and started down the stairs. "Never saw two guys work harder. That last act's a little bastard. I've sat through quite a few tough ones in my time but this one is something special. A couple of beers will do us both good."

Serendipity is a word that has fallen into disuse, but there are few words in the language that so graphically characterize the combinations of fortuitous and random circumstances that make up the behind-the-scenes history of almost every play. It describes precisely what happened that night and afterward as a result of my evening with Sam Harris. In the little speakeasy just around the corner from the Ritz Hotel, we sat drinking beer after beer, our tongues loosened and our minds, a little drunkenly after a while, going over the play, scene by scene and almost line by line.

I was surprised in the beginning at Sam Harris' loquaciousness, for I had never before heard him talk at such length. His comments on the play were usually tersely worded typewritten notes, delivered to Mr. Kaufman's room by Max Siegel every evening after the performance. Mr. Kaufman did not suffer gladly a nightly conference with a producer, even if that producer was Sam Harris. It occurred to me for the first time to wonder if even Sam Harris might not be a little intimidated by George Kaufman. Tonight, with Mr. Kaufman on a train bound for New York, Sam Harris' criticism of the play was far more explicit than his notes had ever been, and I listened as intently as my fuzzy-mindedness would allow after the third bottle of beer. He was a sound and shrewd judge of a play and an old and crafty campaigner in evaluating its chances, but his talk—pithy though it was, and full of the insight of his years in the theatre—did not always make clear his meaning. His turn of phrase was somewhat cryptic and his conversation followed an enigmatic and circuitous course. Though I kept nodding my head in agreement, I was not always certain that I had grasped the significance of what he was saying.

Just before the place closed, when the waiters were piling the chairs up on top of the tables all around us in a last despairing gesture of getting us to leave, my ear caught a phrase he had used once or twice before, but whose meaning had escaped me. "I wish, kid," he sighed, "that this weren't such a noisy play."

"Noisy, Mr. Harris?" I said, determined to understand what he meant by that word. "What do you mean by a noisy play?"

"It's a noisy play, kid," he reiterated without explanation. "One of the noisiest plays I've ever been around."

"But why, Mr. Harris?" I persisted. "It's no noisier than any other play."

"Oh, yes, it is," he replied. "Just think about it. Except for those two minutes at the beginning of the first act, there isn't another spot in this whole play where two people sit down and talk quietly to each other. Is that right, or isn't it?"

I looked at him, a little stunned, and said, "Is that what you mean by noisy?"

"Maybe *noisy* is the wrong word," he said. "But I've watched this play through maybe a hundred times, and I think one of the main things wrong with it is that it tires an audience out. It's a tiring play to sit through, kid . . . I can almost feel them begin to get tired all around me. That stage is so damn full of actors and scenery and costumes and props all the time they never get a chance to catch their breath and listen to the play. Sure they laugh, but I think they're longing to see that stage just once with maybe two or three people on it quietly talking the whole thing over. Give them a chance to sit back themselves and kind of add the whole thing up." He signaled the waiter for the check, then laughed. "Once this show gets under way nobody ever talks to each other. They just keep pounding away like hell and running in and out of that scenery. It's a noisy play, kid, you take my word for it."

I stared at him silently, my mind racing back and forth over what he had said, an odd excitement beginning to take possession of me. He got out of the elevator at his own floor a little tipsily, but I was wide awake now. I took the elevator down again and began to walk. Far from clutching at straws, it seemed to me that Sam Harris in his own paradoxical fashion had put his finger straight on that unfathomable fault in the third act that had defied all our efforts. The more I thought of it, the more certain I became that he was correct, though I could not define why. A curious kind of interpenetration occurs when one watches a play night after night. Impressions are registered unconsciously that emerge as full-blown concepts—sometimes when a chance word or phrase is spoken by someone else. What Sam Harris felt, so closely matched some of my own unconscious thinking, though I had not been able to put it into words, that it had almost a quality of revelation about it.

I was much too stimulated now to think of going to sleep. It was a fine moonlit night and I kept walking. I tried to find my way toward the park, for the air in the streets was still stifling, but I stumbled instead upon a children's playground. It looked a little weird in the moonlight, but it was an open space among the buildings and something approximating a breeze seemed to be blowing through it. I walked to a swing and sat down in it. I swung back and forth, and the higher and more wildly I made the swing go, the greater impression of coolness it created. I was a little apprehensive that a policeman might happen by and wonder what a grown man was doing in a child's swing at four o'clock in the morning. I became absorbed in threading my way through the labyrinth of that third act, and with a shock of recognition I thought I saw clearly where we had gone wrong, and then, in a sudden flash of improvisation, exactly the right way to resolve it. I let the swing come to a full stop and sat there transfixed by the rightness of the idea, but a little staggered at the audacity of it, or at what it would entail.

It called for tossing the Pigeon's Egg out of the show entirely—the specially constructed tables, feathered costumes and all—and bringing the part of the New York playwright, which Mr. Kaufman played and which disappeared from the play after the second act, back into the third act, for a quiet scene with Jean Dixon. The train scene of the first act, which had brought them all out to Hollywood, could be repeated and was the logical setting for it.

I began to examine it slowly and meticulously, fearful that like most four-o'clock-in-the-morning inspirations, it would explode in my face, but it did not. Its very simplicity was its virtue, for while at first glance it seemed like a deceptively simple idea—if tossing $20,000 worth of scenery into the alley may be termed simple—it was, like all simple ideas, startling in how much it would accomplish by its very simplicity. Everything clicked into place with an almost mathematical accuracy. New lines began tumbling into my mind faster than I could remember them, and the new scene on the train began to blossom and grow in a way that not only convinced me of its rightness, but made me itch to call Mr. Kaufman in New York and get him out of bed to tell it to him, but my audacity had limits and common sense told me to wait and present it to him face to face. It would be difficult enough even then, I suspected, to persuade him to make so drastic a change at this stage of the game; but it seemed so singularly right that I could barely wait for his return.

[393]

I WAS WAITING for Mr. Kaufman in his dressing room when he came back the next afternoon. He was late and the first act was almost over, but there was no time to waste and I talked quickly while he put on his make-up. It would have been better perhaps to wait until after the matinée and to be able to tell it to him less hastily, but if he agreed to do it, every moment was going to count. Simple idea or not, it still had to be written, and I had had time enough to realize that more work was involved than at first met the eye. He listened attentively, but I could tell he was rejecting it long before I had finished. Sensing his rejection, I presented the idea in the worst possible manner—it began to sound lame and foolish, even to my own ears.

"I see what you mean," he said when I had come to the end, "and I see what Sam Harris meant, but it's too risky. It's too big a change to make with only three days left. Suppose we did it and it didn't work? We could never go back to a third act we had so little faith in that we discarded it the last three days in Philadelphia, and ask the company to open with it in New York. We've unsettled this cast enough as it is. Whatever chance we've got is going to depend on how good a show the company gives on the opening night. I don't think we dare take this kind of a gamble now. It's too late."

I had no ready answer, and even if I had been prepared to argue, the stage manager was already knocking at the door and calling out, "Second act, Mr. Kaufman." I followed him down the stairs and went straight back to the hotel. It seemed to me doubtful that even if my very life depended upon it I could watch that third act again. At four o'clock in the morning I had seen a new third act playing brilliantly, and it was still lodged hopelessly in my mind.

I threw myself on the bed and stared up at the ceiling, turning over bit by bit everything Mr. Kaufman had said. I was no longer so certain of my own brilliance or that I had found an inspired way of snatching victory from defeat. In the excitement and enthusiasm of last night I had never stopped to consider the possibility of the idea's not working and the consequences if it did not. There was no guarantee that it would, however right it seemed to me, and everything he had said was true, of course, but I was stubbornly sure that the consequence of not taking the gamble would be equally disastrous. I looked at my watch and decided to take a final gamble of my own. The matinée had been over for half an hour and Mr. Kaufman would be in his room. He was not an easy man to tackle once he had said no to anything, but there was little to be lost now in trying to make him change his mind. I was certain that unless we at least made the attempt, the fate of the play was already sealed.

I walked down the hall and knocked on his door. For a moment there was no answer, but then his voice called out, "Who is it?" and I called back, "It's me." "Come in—I'm in the tub," his voice called again, and I walked through the suite to the bathroom. For once he looked beaten and exhausted, as though my old enemy, the heat, had finally claimed even him. He lay in the tub, his head resting on the back of it; his eyes were closed, and he barely opened them when I came in. They remained closed all the while I talked, a small boon for which I was grateful, for I could not judge how well or how badly I was succeeding, and I took my time. I went over the same ground I had covered in the dressing room, but I presented it well this time—so well, in fact, that I convinced myself all over again— and was making an impassioned plea for taking the gamble, in spite of everything, at the end.

When I had finished he did not move, but reached for his glasses on the edge of the tub and put them on; he seemed reluctant to stir even an arm from the coolness of the water. Now he regarded me silently over the rims of the glasses. "You have as much right to say yes to anything about this play as I have to say no," he said slowly. "It may be that my timidity at making this big a change, in the time we've got left, is too great," he went on. "You know what's at stake as well as I do, but if you feel this strongly, why don't you skip the show tonight and stay here and make a rough draft that we can work on when I get back. Maybe I'll be able to see what you see—or at least see it more clearly than I'm able to see it now." He sighed. "I'd like to play my part of the show tonight right from this tub. Might help business, too." He closed his eyes wearily again.

I forgot about dinner and went right to work. When an idea is sound it writes easily, and I struck pay-dirt early. All the old stumbling blocks that we had uselessly battered our heads against seemed to resolve themselves smoothly and naturally once the Pigeon's Egg had been pried loose from the play. The price we had paid for an audience's momentary laughter and applause at a set had been enormous. Freed from the inflexibility of that scene, exposition that had lacked subtlety became manageable and scenes that had remained lumbering and clumsy seemed suddenly skillful. A play can be blackmailed by its scenery more often than anyone connected with it is likely to realize.

The rearrangement of the third act was too involved to do anything more than attempt the sketchiest of rough drafts, but by the time Mr. Kaufman returned from the theatre I had something ready to show him. A good deal of it had to be indicated in a kind of code, with arrows pointing from my own yellow sheets of paper to the manuscript, but he was reading it with more than just polite interest, and when he had finished he carried the yellow sheets and the manuscript with him toward the typewriter. "Well, here goes twenty thousand dollars' worth of scenery," he said and inserted a new piece of paper in the roller.

I sat staring at him, mesmerized. Instead of the elation I had expected to feel, I was seized by a sudden panic at the enormity of what I had started and of what we were about to do. "If this doesn't work and we can't go back to the old third act, Mr. Kaufman, what happens then?" I asked.

He looked at me quizzically over the glasses. "I sue you," he replied. "Hand me that box of fudge and let's get to work."

I watched the rehearsal the next day with feelings not unlike, I suspected, those held by the company itself. The company received the news of the change in glum silence and went about the business of rehearsing it as though each new line brought them closer to a bog of quicksand. It was a messy job of restaging, and I admired more than ever Mr. Kaufman's forbearance and patience, with time running against him and a reluctant and dissatisfied company to rehearse. The combination of old and new was confusing and there was no question but that the cast was seriously disturbed and its morale at a low ebb.

The morale of a company is one of a play's hidden assets and sometimes its most valuable one. If it remains high in spite of a rocky time out of town, an electric opening-night performance in New York can cover a multitude of sins. A company with high morale, whose faith remains unshaken in its author and director, can accomplish incredible feats of memorizing new lines and business overnight, but it asks in return, and rightfully so, sufficient time afterward to perfect the performance. Nothing contributes more strongly to a company's insecurity than desperate last-minute changes that rob them of the chance of being at their best on an opening night. Their faith in Mr. Kaufman did not waver, but their alarm at being asked to make so drastic a change, with a New York opening less than a week away, was quite evident. It made itself apparent in a dozen different ways, and I could not tell whether the new scheme had any real merit or was just a hodgepodge of the old and new that might play less well than what we were discarding.

The company's unease seemed to fill the theatre and communicate itself even to the stage managers, who took forever placing the chairs for each new scene. It was a long rehearsal and rough on everyone, Mr. Kaufman included. He had to learn new lines himself, as well as redirect some of the old stuff, and stage the new train scene—and all of it had to be done for the evening's performance. Everything had to be tried this night or not at all. The next day was Saturday matinée and the last performance but one in front of an audience before we opened in New York the following Wednesday night. I did not blame the actors for feeling that the old third act with all its faults was less hazardous for them than running the gantlet of a New York opening night with untried material. At least they had played the other and knew all of its pitfalls.

As the afternoon wore on I slumped farther and farther down in my seat, and finally I could sit still no longer. I made for my usual refuge, the stage alley, but after one grim look at the Pigeon's Egg set stacked up against the wall waiting to be carted to the storehouse, I beat a hasty retreat back into the theatre. I had looked at the set triumphantly on my way into rehearsal this morning, happy to be seeing the last of it; but this morning's courage seemed to be oozing out of my fingertips, and there was no Max Siegel this time to anesthetize me for these next few hours of waiting.

Along with Sam Harris he had been in New York for the last two days wrestling with the opening-night ticket list, for the laws by which the theatre is governed remain immutable. Hallowed by time they are not susceptible to change—and the two most inviolate are opening-night tickets and pictures in the lobby. However dire the straits a play may be in, they take precedence above all else, and although they seem almost purposely absurd, any appeal from their divinity is useless. A company is kept up until five or six in the morning during one day of the out-of-town tour—thereby making a rehearsal call, however urgent, impossible the following day—so that pictures may be had in time to fill the lobby frames on the opening night; and management and author alike must rid their minds—at this most vital time and no matter how critical the state of the play—of everything but the crucial dilemma of who shall be seated next to whom and where on the opening night. Since not one person out of a hundred ever bothers to look at the pictures in the lobby on opening night and almost no one at all is ever satisfied with his opening-night's seats, it is difficult to understand why these rites remain undisputed, but they are as reverently preserved and as imperishable an idea as the Kingdom of Heaven.

I would have given much for a Max Siegel smile right then, no matter how illusory or mistaken, and Sam Harris' presence would have halved the burden of guilt I was beginning to feel, since in a way he was as much to blame for that set sitting in the alley as I was, but they would not be back until curtain time, and then only with luck. I did not believe my taut nerves would stretch the distance until then, and I did the first two things that occurred to me. I telephoned Joe Hyman and asked him to get on the six o'clock train for Philadelphia, and I sneaked back to the hotel and ordered the largest dinner even I had ever had the gall to order. Terror, as always, had increased my appetite, and the amount of time it would take to consume that mass of food would fill in the waiting until it was necessary to go to the theatre and face what had to be faced.

I was almost comatose with food by eight o'clock. I walked to the theatre swaying slightly and hiccuping as though I were drunk. I stopped at a drug store and slowly sipped two glasses of plain soda water, but the spasms seemed to grow worse instead of better. I have since learned that a serious attack of hiccups can be caused by anxiety or fear, and this must have been true in my case, for by the time I reached the theatre I could barely talk. I wheezed a few words to Joe Hyman and Sam Harris, but the hiccups were coming with such intensity and with so few spaces to breathe in between that I fled gasping back to the drug store. I gulped some paregoric under instructions from the pharmacist and then held my breath while he pressed his fingers behind my ears, and even blew into a paper bag while I counted slowly up to one hundred—but to no avail. I had drawn an interested little group of bystanders during these experiments; an old lady at the drug counter offered the suggestion that the best way to cure hiccups was to scare the living daylights out of the victim, a method which had invariably worked, she insisted, when she was a little girl. Since I was not a little girl, and frightened enough already, it seemed to me, I left the drug store and returned to the theatre.

The first act was nearing its end by the time I arrived and not going too badly so far as I was able to make out, but each body-shaking hiccup I gave, no matter how hard I tried to strangle it before it emerged, echoed with such resonance in the emptiness of the theatre that it seemed to roll down the unfilled rows, across the footlights, and punctuate every other line the actors were speaking. To my horror, a few people in the audience began to laugh at the unearthly sound I was making, for by this time my wheezing and whistling must have sounded like a dog baying at the moon. I ran out of the theatre and walked around the corner to the stage alley. One look at the Pigeon's Egg set, which had not yet been carted away, set me off again and I fled the alley to the street. I walked up and down, cursing the heat, the hiccups, Philadelphia, the food I had eaten, the Lyric Theatre, and anything else that came into my mind. I was growing frantic that I might have to miss the new third act if the spasms did not subside, but they gave little sign of doing so and I dared not go back into the theatre. It seemed to me I was roaring like a calliope. Every few minutes I kept glancing at my watch, knowing by the time exactly what portion of the second act was being played, and finally I could bear it no longer. I walked in the balcony entrance and ran up the stairs.

The exit doors on each landing were dimly lit but I saw no sign of an usher anywhere, and I kept on going. I came out into what must have been the topmost gallery; there was not a soul in it, and it was so far from the stage that I could well believe that even my hurricane gusts would not echo down. I took a seat in the last row and watched the puppet-like creatures on the stage playing out the last scene of the second act. I knew by heart every line they were mouthing, of course, so it mattered little that I could not hear much of what they were saying—and if I could not hear them they probably could not hear me. Looking down from my aerie there seemed to be not more than twenty or thirty people in the orchestra. Actually there must have been a hundred or so, and we might well have jumped another eighty-five cents, but I was well past caring about the nightly receipts.

During the intermission I opened an exit door and walked back and forth along the platform of the iron stairway outside the gallery, taking deep breaths of air. I came back inside and sat down, hiccuping as noiselessly as I could, and waited for the house lights to dim. I was terrified when the fans stopped whirring and in the sudden silence I gave the loudest and longest series of hiccups I had given vent to all evening. But nothing, I was now determined, was going to get me out of the theatre. The audience must have been talking among themselves as they settled back into their seats after the intermission, for there was no sign that anyone had heard me, and I was thankful that in the new arrangement of the third act Mr. Kaufman was already safely backstage. The third act opened now, not with the Pigeon's Egg, but in the Hollywood film studio, and the second scene of the third act was the new train scene with Mr. Kaufman and Jean Dixon. The first scene seemed to be playing better without the Pigeon's Egg, but the train scene, of course, would tell the whole story.

The first scene ended, and as I waited for the lights to come up on the train scene I began to wonder if the old lady at the drug counter might not have been correct; for at that moment I felt as though the daylights had indeed been scared out of me—the palms of my hands were icy and wet with perspiration and my stomach had twisted into a hard knot—but my hiccups had miraculously subsided.

The curtain rose on the train set, and immediately that most accurate of all barometers gave an unmistakable sign that we were on the right track at long last. The audience broke into understanding and appreciative laughter—not the whoop of laughter that the Pigeon's Egg always dazzled them into giving, but the more valuable laughter of an audience that was taking the play into its own hands and carrying it along with them. Jean Dixon was seated alone in the Pullman car, but her aloneness in a train that was obviously headed back to New York told them all they needed to know without a line's being spoken. They made the leap for us themselves without a word of exposition, and the stage, quiet and silent for once, seemed to create by its wordlessness the exact sense of drama and climax that we had previously tried so hard to achieve, without success. The vital scenes of a play are played as much by the audience, I suppose, as they are by the actors on the stage. As surely as one can sense that an audience is lost, I could tell that this one had been captured. The Pullman porter entered and a moment later Mr. Kaufman followed him on. The biggest laugh that tiny audience was capable of giving greeted his appearance, and I knew that our search for the right last act had ended.

I could barely hear the words being spoken on the stage, but I did not need to. I sat back and listened to the audience. The quiet scene Sam Harris had asked for was playing line after line to the biggest laughs in the play. Even some of the perfectly straight lines seemed to evoke laughter, and the laughter mounted until it became one continuous roar. I closed my eyes and just listened until the scene was over, then I walked downstairs and watched the final scene of the play from the back of the orchestra. With the momentum of the train scene behind it, it played flawlessly. That small audience actually broke into applause once or twice. Those crucial last few minutes had been redeemed. *Once in a Lifetime,* in Philadelphia at least, was playing like a hit right up to the curtain.

I left the orchestra rail and leaned against the back wall. The exhaustion I felt was due in large part no doubt to that violent attack of hiccups, but neither hiccups nor the strain of sweating out the last act could entirely account for the almost overpowering weariness that had taken possession of my mind as well as my body. It was a strange inner tiredness of a kind I had never experienced before. I watched Sam Harris and Max Siegel applauding along with the rest of the audience as though they were seeing the play for the first time, and I saw Joe Hyman leave his seat and dash up the aisle in search of me. But I was suddenly too tired to want to hear what they had to say, or to care. I had finally touched bottom so far as *Once in a Lifetime* was concerned. I wanted the New York opening and *Once in a Lifetime* itself over and done with, whatever the outcome. For the first time, success or failure seemed not to matter. Without any sense of elation or triumph, I stared at the curtain going up and down and listened to the audience applauding. I seemed to have used up the last reserve of response or emotion. I wanted of all things to go home, and I wanted to go home with the passionate unreasonableness of a six-year-old.

I T IS ALWAYS a little dismaying to discover that the truth, as one explores it, consists largely of a collection of platitudes. More often than we suspect, the old wives' tales are not merely a caricature of the truth, but its faithful echo; and among the most banal in a profession where old wives' tales are commonplace are the proverbial tales of the anguish and frenzy of the last few days before a New York opening. These hours have been portrayed in movies, in novels, and even upon the stage itself, in such hackneyed and platitudinous terms that their banality grates upon the ear with the brassy clink of a worn-out cliché. The distraught playwright, the nerve-torn actress, the harried stage manager, the tight-lipped director, the stubbornly optimistic producer, all are such familiar and stock figures that their anguish has been robbed of reality and their frenzy skirts the edge of farce. Yet the truth in this instance is substantially the same as the parody of itself it has become.

As the train from Boston or Philadelphia pulls into Grand Central or Pennsylvania Station, returning a company from its tryout tour for the New York opening, each member in this changeless drama relinquishes his sanity, takes his place as a stereotype, and begins to live out his own cliché with almost clocklike precision. The uneasy discovery that the truth bears a strong resemblance to travesty, or to every bad movie or play about the stage one has ever seen, does not alter the nature of the role each performs or the misery which he feels while he performs it. However trite the sufferings of the last few days before a New York opening may seem to the outsider, they usually contain enough real anguish to make them the Book of Common Prayer of the Theatre—and I began to learn it chapter and verse even before the train from Philadelphia reached New York.

I had watched the last two performances of the play in Philadelphia with a detachment and self-possession that I had never been capable of before. I had been able to look at the matinée and then the night performance, not with indifference, but with so great a loosening of the emotional tie between the play and myself that it made the turmoil of my usual watching seem foolish and remote. It was an experience so new and so enjoyable that I boarded the midnight train for New York convinced that I had come of age. No one, however, comes of age in the theatre. If he does, he takes his place among the disenchanted—or joins the ranks of those Philistines who mistake the theatre's incoherence and fanaticism for muddle and moonshine. My self-delusion lasted as long as it took me to walk the length of the Pullman car to my seat. Almost every member of the company had bought an early Sunday edition of the *New York Times* at the station newsstand, and they had the drama section spread out on their laps, revealing, as I walked by, the pictures of the opening on the front page, or the large opening advertisement on the inside page. My detachment and self-possession vanished after the first quick glance, never to return. By the time I turned the key in the lock of our apartment in Brooklyn, I had taken my rightful place in the old wives' tale, and I played my part exactly as it had always been played—with every platitude intact!

One thing, however, was never to be the same again. My brother and I became friends at last, and that simple fact did much to see me through the time-honored anguish and frenzy of the next few days. It is hard to estimate the way or the moment in which two human beings are able to reach one another. The process, of course, is a gradual one, and perhaps my own unreadiness had always been as great as his; but the moment of my homecoming from Philadelphia marked the beginning of closeness between us. Perhaps events themselves create their own readiness, for I was immediately conscious the moment I opened the door, that this homecoming was different from any other. I had lived for so long as a stranger with my family that it had never occurred to me to seek counsel or comfort among them, but tonight I was secretly pleased to find them all waiting up for me. I am by no means certain that blood is thicker than water, but an opening the following week can thicken it as nothing else can. I warmed my hands and my heart in their affection and wondered why I had never found solace with them before. There is nothing like tasting the grit of fear for rediscovering that the umbilical cord is made of piano wire.

I felt closer to my mother and father than I had in years, and my brother in particular was a surprising source of comfort. I began to look at him and to listen to him with a sense of wonder and discovery. The last year had changed him greatly, and it was the year, of course, that I had seen the least of him. His diffidence had vanished and with it his withdrawal from me and his silence. We sat at the kitchen table talking together for almost an hour after my mother and father had gone to bed, drinking the last of the coffee and finishing off the sandwiches. It was the first time such a thing had happened between us, and as we talked, I became slowly aware that behind his unusual talkativeness, behind his innumerable questions about the play, lay a secret pride in me. He had cut out all the picture spreads and ads from the Sunday papers, and presumably as a joke, had tacked them all over the kitchen walls for my homecoming. He had also collected every word that had appeared anywhere about *Once in a Lifetime,* and as I turned the pages of the neatly pasted scrapbook he presented to me, it was my turn to be silent. I, who was never at a loss for words, suddenly could not find my tongue. The stranger at whose side I had slept for so many years was offering his friendship and I did not know how to bridge the gulf between us. I managed to thank him, after a moment, and we talked on easily enough, but behind the casual words we spoke, each of us in his own way was reaching out across the years to the other. I lay awake for a while in the dark after he had gone to sleep, relishing the new idea of having a brother. It was enjoyable enough to send me off to sleep for the first time in many a long night without thinking about George Kaufman.

The golden rule for the last three days before an opening is that a company must be kept together as constantly as possible, even if some of the rehearsals that are called are purely trumped-up ones and fool nobody, including the company itself. If it is impossible to rehearse on the stage because the scenery is not yet set up, or the scenic designer is still lighting it as he always interminably is, then the rehearsal is held in the lounge of the theatre or in a rehearsal hall. Almost nothing is accomplished, for the actors walk through these rehearsals in a state approximating somnambulism, but the rule and the theory behind it is a sound one. Left to their own devices, a company might conceivably gain the impression that the world had not stopped in its tracks for these three days and that all life did not hang in the balance of those two and a half hours three nights hence. Moreover, misery does indeed love company, and there is nothing so soothing, not to say downright invigorating, as the shared misery of people in the same boat. Tempers may flare and patience reach the vanishing point, but temper or even the drudgery of walking through the play in an empty rehearsal hall can be a safety valve for taut nerves, can prevent the panic that can rise in a company left to wander too loosely in these last days.

If I had been inclined to doubt the rightness of this procedure, all of my reservations would have vanished by the afternoon of the day following my return from Philadelphia. I had passed the morning easily enough in telephoning, but by mid-afternoon I could scarcely stay in my skin. Though I knew no rehearsal was scheduled until the next morning at eleven, I could not remain away from the theatre. I had no idea why I felt it imperative to be there, but I took the subway into town, and at the first glimpse of the scenery piled up on the street outside the Music Box as I turned the corner of 45th Street I felt immediately better. I moved toward it with a lift of the heart and hurried through the stage door as though I were leaving enemy territory for the safety of the U. S. Marines. There are few things duller to watch than scenery being set up on a stage, but that afternoon I found this dull business comforting beyond measure. I watched every bit of it with pleasure and even fascination. I sat or walked up and down in the aisles of the empty theatre hour after hour, or wandered bskstage and swilled coffee with the stagehands, and knew that this peace I felt would last only as long as I remained here.

It must have been eight or nine o'clock in the evening when to my surprise I saw Mr. Kaufman wander slowly across the stage, and I immediately rushed back to talk to him. He seemed equally surprised and a shade embarrassed to see me and quickly mumbled something about wanting to ask the stage manager if we could use some hand props at tomorrow morning's rehearsal, but I knew at once that he, like myself, had been impelled to seek such comfort as he could find, and the only place to find it was here. We had been talking for only a moment or two, when Sam Harris appeared suddenly from behind a piece of scenery, and our presence was evidently as disconcerting to him as mine had been to Mr. Kaufman. He muttered something about stopping by on his way to dinner and beat a hasty retreat. Mr. Kaufman disappeared shortly afterward, but I was delighted to know that as the time drew near for each one to take his place on the firing line, veteran and neophyte alike was affected in much the same way; I had merely arrived earlier in the afternoon.

The company, when they assembled for rehearsal the next morning, greeted each other with the hungry affection of exiles returning to their native land. They had evidently spent a completely miserable day with their husbands, their wives, their cats or their tropical fish, and were happy to be back among their own kind, amidst people who were using the only language they cared to hear spoken at this particular moment.

Unfortunately, it was also the moment that saw the end of Mr. Kaufman's forbearance and patience. The frenzy, in other words, was starting exactly on schedule. Its cause was simple enough. Though the stagehands had worked through the night, it now turned out we could not get the stage, although more than enough time had been allowed and a free stage had been promised for eleven o'clock this morning. The lighting as usual had held everything up, and Mr. Kaufman, who hated to rehearse in a hall or in the lounge, was furious. This was just the sort of small crisis that threw him into a temper—and Mr. Kaufman in temper was a formidable figure. A genuine crisis he met head-on and with enviable calm, but small irritations he had no capacity whatever to meet. In addition, his chief weakness, even beyond inept waiters and people who insisted on telling him jokes, was what may be best described as "inanimate object trouble," and a rehearsal hall or a theatre lounge inevitably brought out the worst in him. His difficulty with inanimate objects seemed to be that all kinds of furniture contrived to take on a malevolent and almost human design the moment he entered the room. Chairs, lamps, ashtrays and tables seemed to move imperceptibly out of line and craftily place themselves in his path. His progress through a room would begin peaceably enough, but by the time he had stumbled against a chair, knocked against a lamp and banged his elbow against the ashtray as he sank down onto the sofa, his threshold of irritation had been breached. He would sit muttering oaths under his breath and stare malignantly at the furniture, and the same pattern more or less would be repeated when he left the room. It put him in foul humor for a good while afterward, and I had learned to steer clear of him until he had rubbed the bruised knee or elbow sufficiently and was out in an open space where no furniture could move toward him.

I held my breath now as we all filed into the rehearsal hall, for a rehearsal hall is just that—a large empty hall with nothing but chairs in it, and usually old and rickety chairs at that. Every one of them seemed to perk up and form an invisible phalanx of enmity as Mr. Kaufman entered the room, and then move quickly into position. I cannot swear that I saw them move, but they seemed to tremble with anticipatory glee. Mr. Kaufman usually surveyed the furniture in a strange room with equal enmity and distrust, trying to gauge, I always thought, from which side the attack would come or which chair he would bang himself against first. But he was deeply engaged in conversation at the moment with the two stage managers and he passed through the doorway without looking up. He did not go very far. Though the stage manager on either side of him did not so much as even brush against a chair, Mr. Kaufman ran smack into one before he was ten steps into the room. He gave a howl of surprise and rage and kicked the offending chair clear across the room, stubbing his toe, of course, in the process. He snarled viciously at one of the stage managers who tried to help him and limped toward the table, where he promptly banged his elbow as he sat down; and, as he sat, there was a sound of ripping cloth and one and all knew that a protruding nail in the seat of the chair had torn a hole in his trousers. Not a soul laughed. Indeed, everyone looked stricken. His whole aspect in these moments was so terrifying that I firmly believe that if he had ever slipped on a banana peel in Times Square the entire area would have been clear of people before he rose to his feet again, for he somehow managed to convey a sense of individual blame to anyone who happened to witness this unending warfare with inanimate objects.

There was complete silence in the hall now, for there was every indication of heavy weather ahead, and to make matters worse, Mr. Kaufman began to sneeze and could not stop. He was susceptible to drafts and convinced that the merest puff of air could lay him low, and a great scurrying took place to close the offending windows. Some of them would not close, others were too high to reach, a window pole could not be found, and the two stage managers were wet with perspiration by the time the windows were wrestled with and all the chairs shifted to the far end of the hall away from the draft.

It was not the best of circumstances in which to start the final days of rehearsal, and Mr. Kaufman's mood was not improved by the news which arrived in midafternoon that the stage would not be available until tomorrow. It was the company's turn now to lose their tempers, and they proceeded to do so each in turn and according to the size of their billing in the program. It was hard to blame them. Actors like to adjust their voices and pitch their performance to the size of the theatre they are going to play in, and the sooner they are able to do so, the more secure they feel. They are correct, of course, for a performance suited to the Lyric in Philadelphia might well be out of scale in the Music Box. The news that they would have only one day on the stage of the Music Box, instead of the two days they had every right to expect, cut through, for good and all, the heavy cream of false politeness that had so far acted as a cover for panic and nerves.

Miss Dixon promptly broke out in hives, Miss Byington grew waspish, Hugh O'Connell sulked, and Grant Mills could not remember a line. Mr. Kaufman, with a real crisis at hand, was instantly all patience again and at his most winning and understanding; but even he could not save the evening rehearsal from the depressing and unmistakable walk-through that it was. I rode home with the uncomfortable knowledge that tomorrow's rehearsal, though it would take place on the stage of the Music Box, might not be very much better. Everything was obviously proceeding according to schedule. Frenzy had arrived on time. The next step, according to the timetable, was anguish. There was evidently going to be plenty of it around, or enough, it seemed to me, to justify those foolish plays and movies about the theatre that I would never laugh at so easily again.

On the day before a New York opening, a company moves within a solar system of its own. It is a planet in outer space, detached from the moon and stars, and its orbit is the stairway from the dressing rooms to the stage. Each actor sits at his make-up table, staring into the brilliantly lit mirror at his own image, making the proscribed movements that will detach him still further from the world of reality and allow him to achieve the anonymity of complete disguise. The more he becomes at one with the part he is to play, the less of himself that peeps through it, the further he sinks into the atmosphere of make-believe and unreality, the safer he feels. He is seeking a judgment from the real world, not of himself but of the hidden image he carries within him that is both his goal and his refuge. The general conception that all actors are born exhibitionists is far from the truth. They are quite the opposite. They are shy, frightened people in hiding from themselves—people who have found a way of concealing their secret by footlights, make-up and the parts they play. Their own self-rejection is what has made most of them actors. What better way to solve the problem or to evade it than to be someone other than the self one has rejected, and to be accepted and applauded for it every night. They have solved the problem, but not its torment. It is what makes every opening night so painful an experience. Little wonder that on the day before an opening the atmosphere backstage reflects each actor's anxiety at meeting the test anew, for the judgment does not lessen but is compounded by the years, and it is always agonizing no matter how many times an actor has walked out onto the stage to meet it.

It was just as well that I had reconciled myself to a bad rehearsal, for the proceedings on the stage of the Music Box were more like a series of nervous explosions than anything else. Hats and dresses that had fit perfectly well in Philadelphia seemed to have come back from the cleaners a size too small. Entrances were missed or exits bungled, and doors that had opened with ease and props that handled without difficulty before, now presented mysterious problems each time one was opened or picked up. Mr. Kaufman rode out the storm like a pilot searching out the eye of a hurricane—unruffled, detached and ready to report back to the weather bureau that the storm was not a dangerous one. But by the end of the afternoon rehearsal I was in no such state of calm. If the final run-through tonight emerged looking anything like this one, I doubted my capacity to sit through it, or perhaps even to live through it. Mr. Kaufman's composure would have to do for both of us. I intended to hijack Max Siegel and make him walk the streets with me at the first flash of thunder.

There is no need to try to understand the eternal perverseness of the theatre, or to attempt to explain why an afternoon rehearsal can be a shambles and an evening rehearsal on the same day be orderly, smooth and perfect in every detail. Like a good deal of the theatre's disorderliness, it defies explanation. It is simpler to say that the evening run-through of *Once in a Lifetime* was flawless. Every mistake of the afternoon had corrected itself; every error in light cues, every blunder in props, every imperfection in costume had vanished. The rehearsal was faultless except in one particular: the acting was completely hollow. Its emptiness may have been due to the difficulty of playing comedy in an empty theatre, for a preview audience the night before an opening was the exception, not the rule, in those days. But granting this difficulty and making all allowances for it, it was hard not to be aware of the falsity of the playing. Not one performance carried conviction. Each actor seemed to lack fluidity, bounce or humor, and in consequence the play very soon took on the

[411]

patina of its acting. By the time the final curtain fell, the play seemed to me to be as brittle and humorless as the performance. I walked up the aisle and stood a little away from where Mr. Kaufman and Sam Harris were talking, not eager to have my judgment corroborated. I was more than willing to attribute my feelings about the play to my own unsteady nerves. It would be small comfort to know that they were steadier than I gave them credit for being and that the play was as frail as it looked.

Mr. Kaufman started backstage with his notes for the cast, and Sam Harris was about to follow him when his eye fell upon me. He walked over to where I stood and peered at me closely before he spoke. "I think you need a drink, kid," he said. "Come on up to the office." I followed him meekly, though I did not want or need a drink, and had it been anyone other than Sam Harris I would have refused. What I wanted was to crawl into the subway and get home as fast as possible. I hated the play and every actor in it, and my mood was far too truculent to chance talking to anybody, Mr. Kaufman included. I did not, as it turned out, utter a word for the next four hours. Mr. Harris' intentions were kindly and I have no doubt that the color of my face must have seemed ashen even in the semidarkness of the theatre, but it was very soon apparent that Mr. Harris' invitation was not altogether altruistic. Mr. Harris badly needed a drink himself for his own reasons. He wanted someone to have it with him, and what was more to the point, he had evidently been having a few drinks on his own all through the evening.

It occurred to me that he walked up the stairs a little strangely, and now he seemed to be having considerable trouble finding the ice and the glasses. As I watched the amount of liquor he was pouring into each glass I realized he was determined to find a happy oblivion for these next few hours and that it was to consist largely of his self-conceived mission of cheering me up. Though his movements were uncertain, his sense of dedication was not. He plunged immediately into the task at hand. "You worried about this play, kid?" he asked.

I nodded, deciding that the quicker I let him cheer me up the sooner I would be on the subway. Unfortunately, there is almost no protection against being cheered up and I have always been sadly unfitted for dealing with people who have had a drop too much. My nodded agreement to his question was unwise. He mistook my silence for emotion too deep to be expressed and changed his tactics accordingly. I could tell by the way he looked at me that he felt that stronger medicine was going to be needed, and with the first spoonful I knew I was going to get the full dose.

"Did I ever tell you about George M. Cohan and the first play he ever wrote?" he began. "Felt just the way you do now, kid. He was just about your age, I think, and I was still managing Terry McGovern, the prize fighter. The theatre was easier in those days, but the people got just as scared. Let me tell you first how George Cohan and I happened to meet . . . "

He settled back comfortably in the large chair behind the desk, clinked the ice merrily against the glass for a moment, and told the tale with loving attention to detail. The theatre may have been easier in those days, but everything apparently took a great deal longer, for by the time Mr. Harris reached George M. Cohan's first play and Mr. Cohan's triumph over his fears, a good hour had gone by, two or three more drinks had been consumed by Mr. Harris in the telling, and we were only just approaching the beginnings of the famous partnership of Cohan and Harris, which I could sense I was going to receive a full account of. I dared not look at my watch or appear to be restive, for Mr. Harris' mind was completely unclouded and his eye, like the eye of most deaf people, was an inordinately keen one. Obviously, the only attitude to assume was to indicate that some of Mr. Harris' cheerfulness had communicated itself to me and that I was no longer so much in need of his ministrations.

It was a second fatal error! Like my silence, my sudden cheerfulness again decided him on a new tactic. He stopped the Cohan and Harris saga abruptly, mixed himself another drink, and sat down next to me on the sofa. He fixed his eyes rather sternly on mine and said, "All of this stuff I've been telling you was just to take your mind off things so you could listen to what I really wanted to say." He cleared his throat importantly and paused before he continued.

"Now, I'm going to tell you why you shouldn't worry too much about this play, kid."

I returned his gaze hopefully and for a few moments it seemed that we would be leaving the office very shortly, for after a preamble on why most dress rehearsals are bound to be disappointing to the author, he stopped as if to marshal his thoughts. I was so certain that this would be his final few words of wisdom and cheer, I was already calculating whether or not I had missed the last express to Brooklyn and would have to take the long ride by local.

To my amazement he rose from the sofa, planted himself in front of me, and announced firmly, "The reason you shouldn't worry about this play, kid, is because it's got a good story. Let me tell it to you . . ."

I stared helplessly up at him, convinced that I must now say something even at the risk of hurting his feelings, but he had already moved away to the center of the room and was launched into telling me the full story of *Once in a Lifetime*. He was not a man to skimp, and liquor seemed to sharpen his memory rather than curtail it. He started with the rise of the first curtain, described the set and the lighting meticulously, and then proceeded to act out each part with every bit of stage business intact. Where he did not remember the exact line, he ad libbed his own interpretation of it, and since he was his own audience and enjoying his own performance immensely, he laughed loudly at all the appropriate places. I sank back into the sofa, horror-struck, as it dawned on me that nothing could prevent him from going through the entire play, scene by scene and line by line, and that I would sit here trapped until the final curtain. At the end of the first act he took an intermission by mixing himself another drink and describing why the audience would like what they had seen up until then, and after a refreshing swallow he placed the glass on the desk and said, "Second act. Now, listen to what happens now!"

There was little else to do but listen with awe-struck attention. In spite of the fact that my eyes occasionally closed, it was somehow fascinating to watch Sam Harris pretending to be Jean Dixon and George Kaufman, mimicking their readings and even falling into a good facsimile of Miss Dixon's slouching walk and Mr. Kaufman's grim leer over the tops of his eyeglasses. His performance was giving him such unalloyed pleasure that at another time I might actually have enjoyed watching him, for all of the sweetness of his nature shone through his innocent enjoyment of himself.

By the time he approached the end of the second act, however, I could keep awake only with enormous effort. I dared not lean back on the sofa, for I would have gone promptly to sleep, and though I shifted my position constantly, my head kept dropping down onto my chest. Only the fact that one of my feet kept going to sleep, sending shooting pains up and down my leg, saved me from drifting off. I roused myself for the intermission, and while Mr. Harris explained why the audience was still liking it, I stood up and stretched discreetly. It helped a little, but not enough. As I watched him fill his glass and get ready for the third act, his enthusiasm and vitality not one bit abated, I was overcome anew with sleepiness. I gave a terrible shudder and so loud a sigh when he announced, "Third act; here's what happens now," that he looked at me sharply and asked, "Not getting a chill, are you, kid?"

I shook my head and went back to my seat. I sat on the very edge of the sofa this time, planted my elbows firmly on my knees and placed one hand at each temple for the double purpose of keeping my head upright and holding my eyelids open with my fingertips. I could do nothing about the enormous yawns that were issuing from my mouth, one after the other; but Sam Harris was so deeply immersed in his attempt to do full justice to the third act that he seemed not to notice or even to be aware of my presence.

He was in full swing again, roaring through the train scene with tremendous verve and gusto, and that last drink seemed to have unleashed a hitherto unrealized athletic capacity for playing comedy. He bounced from one chair to the other as he switched parts, and finally, to illustrate Hugh O'Connell's moment of triumph just before the final curtain, he leaped onto a stool in front of the fireplace with the agility of a mountain goat. I had noticed that the light was changing through the curtained windows behind the desk, and now I saw the first faint streaks of daylight beginning to filter through

[415]

them. There was silence suddenly and the silence startled me into wakefulness. Sam Harris was standing in front of me, placing his straw hat on his head.

"Go on home and get a good night's sleep, kid," he said. "I think you'll sleep better now."

I got up stiffly from the sofa and followed him out of the office and down the stairs. As we came into the street, he stopped dead and blinked with surprise at the daylight. "What the hell time is it?" he asked.

I glanced at my watch. It was just a few minutes short of five o'clock. "It doesn't matter, Mr. Harris," I said. "I wouldn't have slept much tonight anyway."

He shook his head ruefully and laughed. "That play still needs cutting. That's all I can say, kid," he said and we started toward Broadway.

Even in my close to sleepwalking state I could see we were going to have a fine day for the opening. The morning sky was cloudless and there was a hint in the air that the day would be warm but not too hot. It was pleasant to know that much about tonight anyway. We stood silently at the corner of 45th Street, waiting for a taxi to appear. It was strange to look up and down a Broadway whose every square foot I thought I knew and find it looking completely different. The long ugly thoroughfare looked clean and friendly. I thought I had seen Broadway in all of its various guises, but I had never seen it like this. It looked, of all things, sleepy and innocent. The tawdriness and the glitter were gone. It seemed to stand hushed and waiting—as if eager to welcome all the new actors and playwrights struggling to reach it.

"Well, you can't go home now, kid," said Mr. Harris, breaking the silence. "By the time you get to Brooklyn you'll just have time to turn around and get back to rehearsal. What time did George call rehearsal for?"

"Eleven o'clock," I replied.

"There you are," he said, "no use going home. Better go to a hotel."

"No," I said, "I'd better go home."

"What for, kid?" he persisted. "What's wrong with going to a hotel? You'll get a few hours' sleep, anyway."

"I'd rather go home, Mr. Harris," I replied carefully and with emphasis, and stepped away from him to signal a taxi I saw in the distance. I could feel him looking at me, and as the taxi drew up he came toward me and held out his hand.

"So long, kid," he said, "see you at rehearsal," and stepped quickly into the cab.

I looked down at my hand and stared at what he had slipped into it. It was a one-hundred-dollar bill! He had, it appeared, gathered the reason for my insistence on going home. I stared down at the lovely banknote in my hand for a long moment before I made my decision. After tomorrow night, I might well be able to afford to stay at the best hotel in town; but then again, I might not. After to-morrow night—or rather tonight, I suddenly realized as the dawn grew brighter—it might be a very long time before I even saw a hundred-dollar bill again. Now was the time to live richly and fully, if only for a few hours, and not waste this lovely windfall of fate on a small side-street hotel. It might actually be an excellent omen for the opening if I had the good sense to make full use of it.

I crossed the street and walked up the steps into the Astor Hotel. There was no question that I had chosen the right omen the moment I entered the lobby. I felt better in every stiff joint. The night clerk looked at me suspiciously, but I was ready for him.

"I want a suite on the Forty-fifth Street side—just until tomorrow morning. My play is opening tomorrow night at the Music Box and I've got a rehearsal at eleven—we had a longer dress rehearsal than I expected. By the way," I added, with the proper touch of casualness, "could you change this for me? I seem to have nothing small to give the bellboy." I handed the hundred-dollar bill to him across the desk.

His attitude made a quick turnabout from the suspicious to the reverential. He pushed the register card toward me respectfully and held the pen out deferentially.

"Would you like to leave a call and your breakfast order with me, sir?" he asked as he brought me the change.

"Yes," I replied. "And is there a masseur in the hotel, by the way?"

He nodded. "Have him come in at nine o'clock and wake me up for a massage, and I want a barber and a manicurist at a quarter of ten. I'll have breakfast at ten thirty—orange juice, toast, coffee, bacon and eggs. I think that will be all."

"Thank you, sir," he said, and pressed a buzzer under the desk. "Take Mr. Hart to ten-fourteen," he said as he handed a key to the bellboy, "and wait and find out if the suite is satisfactory. I think you'll like it, sir—it's one of our best. If not, the bellboy will show you another. Good night, sir. I'll take care of all of this for you." We bowed slightly to each other and I followed the bellboy toward the elevator.

There can be no false economies in the rich full life. Excess is the keynote or it cannot be enjoyed at all. I gave the bellboy two brand-new one-dollar bills and was rewarded by a rich full bellboy smile. We both knew that I was overtipping outrageously and we both enjoyed it, each for his own reasons. The bellboy bowed himself out and closed the door, and I walked to the window, opened it and then leaned over the sill staring at the marquee of the Music Box across the street. There was an impersonality about my name looked at from this height. This is the way my name would look to strangers. I stared down at it with the utmost pleasure. Only three short city blocks separated the New Amsterdam Theatre from the Music Box, but the journey between them had been a long one. Whatever the outcome of tonight, my name next to George Kaufman's on that marquee represented triumph. I remained at the window for quite a while. I lowered the shade reluctantly, afraid that I would have trouble getting to sleep now, but my head had barely touched the pillow before I was off into the kind of sleep that only babies and old dogs in front of fires are supposed to enjoy.

THERE ARE more expert masseurs, I have since found out, than the gentleman who woke me up at nine o'clock the next morning and proceeded to go to work on me, but it was the first massage I had ever had and I have never enjoyed any since then as much. Every twist and stroke of his fingers represented part of that hundred-dollar bill, and my muscles seemed to know it and respond with pleasure. The barber and the manicurist timed their arrival perfectly to his departure, and I sat contentedly for my first manicure and my first shave in a private suite. The barber and the manicurist were somewhat startled to find their client with a bedsheet wrapped around himself toga-fashion, but I explained that I had needed to have my suit pressed immediately, and the reason for my overnight stay. They were at once all solicitude and understanding. Barbers and manicurists who cater to theatre folk are a special breed—they know how to be silent after failure and talkative following success, and the Astor made a specialty of caring for theatre people. Those two knew all about every new play coming in. They had taken care of Sam Harris, Arthur Hopkins, Charles Dillingham and practically everybody else for years. The barber insisted on calling down to the men's shop in the lobby and ordering me a new shirt for the opening, once he caught a glimpse of my wrinkled and soiled one hanging over the chair, and after they had finished, all three of us stood by the window and looked down at the marquee of the Music Box as they wished me good luck.

No day of an opening, it seemed to me, could possibly be starting better than this one.

I could easily have eaten two full breakfasts, but there was barely time to get downstairs, pay my bill, and be across the street for rehearsal at eleven. I took a last look out the window and a quick glimpse at myself in the mirror before I closed the door. There was no question but that the rich full life agreed with me. I looked as smoothed out and as fresh as I felt. Whatever I had spent, I had had more than full value in return. It did not occur to me until I was going down in the elevator that what with overtipping the barber, the manicurist, the valet and the masseur, I might very well have overspent, but I had not. I had fifteen dollars left, and I walked through the stage door of the Music Box the most relaxed and satisfied of mortals. Appropriately enough, Sam Harris was the first person I saw.

"Get any sleep, kid?" he greeted me, and grinned.

"Best sleep I've had in years, Mr. Harris," I replied truthfully enough.

George Kaufman, standing beside him, remarked, "That's the time to sleep—before the notices."

But nothing could shake my eighty-five dollars' worth of well-being. I turned a Max Siegel smile on everyone in sight.

The rehearsal was a short one—a last unnecessary running over of lines in the lounge of the theatre. Actually, there was no reason for a rehearsal at all, except to provide a common meeting ground for opening-night nerves, and the cast was dismissed at one o'clock. It left a long afternoon stretching ominously in front of me and my high spirits, which I was determined not to lose. Once again I turned to Joe Hyman. I called him and asked him to please drop everything and meet me in front of the Plaza Hotel at two o'clock.

There are certain days when everything one touches, when every idea that comes to mind, is completely right, just as there are certain years in the theatre when one can seemingly do no wrong. They are balanced by those other years when it seems impossible to do anything except to do it badly; but I did not know this then. Today anything I chose to do seemed inspired. I had often longed to take a hansom cab for a ride through the park, and it had always seemed a ridiculous indulgence, but I had fifteen dollars left out of that hundred-dollar bill, it was a beautiful September afternoon, and this of all days seemed the proper time for extravagance. I could not have hit upon a better way of weathering these hours of waiting.

We rode around the park together, Joe Hyman and I, by turns talkative and silent, but the awareness in each of our minds of the opening just a few hours away seemed to heighten the color of the leaves on the trees and etch the buildings more sharply against the sky. There is a kind of inner excitement, of pain that is somehow pleasurable, that adds an extra dimension to our awareness of the visible world—the eye seems to look at old scenes and see them with a new depth and clarity. I looked at the Central Park I had always taken for granted and watched it unfold before me with unexpected and surprising beauty. We rode four times around the park and might easily have gone round a fifth time, for Joe Hyman refused to let me pay for anything today and the time seemed to flash by with unnecessary speed. It was suddenly time to send telegrams to the company and to meet the family for dinner, and just as suddenly, in the way time seemed to be rushing headlong toward eight thirty, it was time to leave them in Joe's charge and go on ahead to the theatre to wish the company good luck. Time seems to quicken on opening nights and take on a velocity of its own, just as, I imagine, time must seem to hasten for the very old, accelerating with a swiftness imperceptible to the rest of us.

I walked toward *Once in a Lifetime* for the last time—that final walk every playwright takes toward his play, knowing that it is no longer his, that it belongs to the actors and the audience now, that a part of himself is to be judged by strangers and that he can only watch it as a stranger himself. The main consideration of his day, the keystone that has dictated his every waking moment, the cause that has enlisted his being for all these months, is at an end. He moves toward his destination with mixed emotions—it is the completion he has sought, but there is the ache of finality in it. He is at last a spectator—a spectator with the largest stake in the gamble of the evening, but a spectator nonetheless.

There was already quite a sizable crowd of first-night gawkers and autograph hounds in front of the Music Box as I hurried toward it, and the two mounted policemen trying to herd them to the opposite side of the street were having rather a hard time of it. The crowd ducked out of the way of the policemen and their horses with practiced skill, and the few who were pushed to the opposite curb were smartly back at their old positions in front of the theatre in no time at all. It had the brisk and innocent liveliness of a children's game, with no malice on either side, and as I pushed my own way through the crowd to the stage door I was tempted to turn and shout, "It's not so wonderful being on the inside as you think—you're better off out here!" The panic I had managed to postpone all through the day had suddenly caught up with me. The timetable of the theatre is never very far off. It may vary a little, but opening-night nerves always arrive more or less as promised. Mine had merely been delayed.

I took the bundle of telegrams the stage doorman handed me as though he had put a red-hot poker in my hands and then promptly dropped them on the floor. He picked them up and stuffed them into my pocket without a word, as though he had performed the same service several times before this evening and expected to do it a few more times as well, and I started up the stairway for the dressing rooms on legs that seemed to have no relationship whatever to my body. Two sticks carried me along, and the hand with which I tried to open the first dressing-room door shook so that I could not turn the knob. Hugh O'Connell opened the door from the inside and then stood there looking at me like a rabbit trapped in the glare of automobile headlights. He kept wetting his lips to speak, but no words emerged, or it may be that I did not hear them, for my ears had gone the way of my legs.

It was just as well that my high spirits had vanished in one fell swoop. Even false cheerfulness would have withered quickly in those dressing rooms. The atmosphere in each varied from calm to controlled hysteria, depending upon the opening-night temperature of its occupant. Jean Dixon, vacant-eyed and pale in spite of her make-up, stared at me for a long moment as if trying to focus on who I was, nodded abstractedly, and then resumed a panther-like stalk up and down her dressing room.

Next door, Grant Mills sat looking at himself in the mirror and grinning idiotically. He kept bobbing his head up and down and rubbing his hands together in some silent colloquy with himself. Spring Byington looked so near to being embalmed as she sat solemn and still amidst the mounds of flowers in her dressing room, that I decided to go downstairs and sit on the stage for a while before continuing the rounds.

I seemed to be having a little difficulty breathing myself. I sat on a chair in the stage manager's corner and took the bundle of telegrams out of my pocket, and by purest accident the first two telegrams I opened were from the barber and the manicurist of the Astor Hotel. It was just the sort of happy coincidence to steady the nerves and to restore the faith of a believer in omens. Immediately some of the bright promise of the morning, some of the buoyancy of that ride around the park, began to return.

My spirits lifted with each telegram that I opened. Opening-night telegrams may seem a foolish and perfunctory convention, but they are not. However naïve or fatuous their phrasing may be, those words are the only ones likely to penetrate the minds and warm the hearts of the people who receive them at this particular moment. They may seem dull-witted and senseless the next morning, but opened backstage in that chill interval of waiting for the house lights to darken and the curtain to rise, they perform the admirable function of saying that hope still runs high. Far-fetched little jokes seem uncommonly humorous in opening-night telegrams, and ten words with an unexpected name signed to them can be strangely touching.

There were a good many unexpected names in the telegrams I opened now, as touching to me as those two from the barber and the manicurist. That bundle of telegrams seemed to contain a cross section of the years: the names scrambled the years in wild disorder —George Steinberg and Irving Morrison; the box-office man at the Mayfair Theatre, where I had played *The Emperor Jones;* guests from camp I had all but forgotten; Augustus Pitou; a group of the boys to whom I had told those stories on the stoop outside the candy store, who carefully explained who they were; Priestly Morrison and Mrs. Henry B. Harris; some old neighbors in the Bronx; all the little-theatre groups; Mr. Neuburger of my fur-vault days; Mr. Perleman of the Labor Temple; the tongue-tied athletic instructor who had taught me how to swim, Herb of the Half Moon Country Club . . . The years leaped out of each envelope with quicksilver flashes of memory, the old jumbled with the new. Time seemed to stop as I looked at each name and the years each name recalled, and something like calm began to settle over me.

In the darkness of the stage manager's corner the years that I held in my hand seemed somehow to have been arranged in a design of marvelous felicity, all of them taking me to this hidden corner tonight. I looked around me with an air of wonder and of disbelief. The green shade of the electric-light bulb on the stage manager's stand was focused not only on the prompt script of a play, but on what had once been an impossible dream and was now a reality. The muted sound of the audience out front, the muffled gabble of the stagehands as they called a reminder to each other of a changed light cue or prop, the colored gelatins in the banks of the lights above me, the stage manager's checking the set for the last time, the minor players already beginning to hover in the wings, the voiceless hum of excitement all around me—these were the sights and sounds that no longer belonged to an old dream, but to this corner where I sat and was part of them. I sat on in the chair, riffling through the telegrams again, forgetting that I had not wished the rest of the cast good luck, that I had not yet seen Sam Harris or Mr. Kaufman—I sat on, unwilling to relinquish the serenity this spot seemed to give me.

Not until I heard Max Siegel's voice saying to the stage manager, "They're all in; take the house lights down," could I bring myself to move. I walked through the pass door into the theatre, and in the half-light I peeked through the curtain below the stage box to steal a quick look at the audience—that foolish and hopeful look a playwright sometimes takes in those last few minutes before the curtain rises. What he sees is almost always the same sea of faces—the same well-wishers and ill-wishers, the same critics, the same agents, the same columnists, the very same first-night faces in exactly the same seats they have always sat in, the old faces a little older, the young faces a little stonier—and why he expects some miracle to have changed them into tender and benevolent faces I do not know, but he does. Perhaps the miracle lies in the fact that he should persist in thinking that tonight, for this opening, the miracle will have occurred; but as he anxiously scans row after flinty row, he sees that no miracle has taken place, except the dubious one that the same people have managed to be sitting in the same seats again, and he closes the curtains hastily. No group of people can look as hard and unyielding as first-nighters seem to look, viewed from that vantage point. Even the faces of one's friends seem to be set in concrete, and each critic as one spots him appears to be hewn from the same block of granite as his heart.

I fled up the aisle and almost collided with Mr. Kaufman, whose pacing had already begun. He muttered something that might have been either "Good luck" or "God damn it" and was on his way again. Applause turned me toward the stage. The curtain was rising, and Hugh O'Connell and the set were receiving their regulation round of applause. Jean Dixon made her entrance, the applause swelled, and as it died down she spoke the opening lines. I held my breath to wait for the first laugh, which always came on her second or third line. No sound, however, appeared to be issuing from her lips. One could see her lips moving, but that was all. No sound came forth. Hugh O'Connell spoke, but no sound came from his lips, either. They seemed to be two people talking to each other behind a glass wall.

The audience began to murmur and turn to each other in their seats. My heart skipped a beat and I looked wildly toward Mr. Kaufman. He stood frozen in his tracks, staring at the stage. Jean Dixon and Hugh O'Connell were talking steadily on, unaware that they could not be heard, but aware that something was gravely wrong, for the murmur from the audience was loud enough for them to hear it now and I could see Jean Dixon's hand shake as she lit a cigarette. Still no sound came from the stage, and in the silence

[425]

a man's voice from the balcony rang out loud and clear: "It's the fans—turn off the fans!"

The audience broke into relieved laughter and applause. I saw Mr. Kaufman make a dash for the pass door that led backstage, but before he was halfway down the aisle, the fans on either side of the proscenium began to slow down. In the opening-night excitement, the electrician had simply forgotten to turn off the fans—one of those simple little opening-night mistakes that lessen the life span of everyone concerned by five or ten years! The nightmare had lasted no more than a minute in all, but it is not one of the minutes I should choose to live over again. Invariably, when horrors of this kind occur, the audience behaves admirably and they did so now. They not only applauded that unknown hero in the balcony, but they rewarded Jean Dixon with a generous round of applause when she went back and started the scene all over again. She could not, of course, go off the stage and re-enter, but aware that not a word of the scene had been heard, she calmly took a puff or two of her cigarette, waited until the fans had stopped, and began the scene anew.

From that moment onward, both play and audience took on something of the quality of fantasy—it was being played and received like a playwright's dream of a perfect opening night. The performance was brilliant and the audience matched it in their response. One of the theatre's most steadfast beliefs is that there is never again a sound of trumpets like the sound of a New York opening-night audience giving a play its unreserved approval. It is a valid belief. Bitter words have been written about the first-night audience, but the fact remains that there is no audience ever again like it—no audience as keen, as alive, as exciting and as overwhelmingly satisfactory as a first-night audience taking a play to its heart. It can unfurl the tricolor of its acclamation and make flags seem to wave from every box; just as in reverse its dissent can seem to dangle the Jolly Roger from the center chandelier and blanket the auditorium in leaden disapproval.

The sound of the audience's approval was unmistakable, even

to my own anxious ears. At the end of each act the applause broke before the curtain had quite touched the floor. The second act played better than the first, and the third act—that vulnerable, exasperating third act, the act which had held the play in jeopardy for so long—seemed to have written itself, so effortlessly and winningly was it playing. It was almost irritating to watch it play with such inevitable rightness and ease, remembering the bitter struggle it had given us. The final lines of the play were being spoken now, and then it came—an explosive crash of applause as the curtain fell. It came like a thunderclap, full and tumultuous. I tried to disengage myself and measure the kind of applause it was, but I could not. It sounded like hit applause to me, and it was keeping up. Except for one or two critics with early deadlines dashing up the aisle, the entire audience was remaining in its seats and keeping the curtain going up and down. The cast stood bowing and smiling—they had taken their individual calls and the entire company was lined up on the stage. No other calls had been set, and the company was bowing and smiling somewhat awkwardly now, in the way actors do when they are no longer in the frame of the play; but still the applause showed no sign of diminishing.

To my amazement, I saw Mr. Kaufman step forward and signal the stage manager to keep the curtain up. I stared at the stage in disbelief. He was about to do something so implausible that I could hardly conceive of his doing it—he was about to make a curtain speech. I could not believe my eyes. More than once he had expressed his scorn for authors who made opening-night speeches, and he had expressed it in such scathing terms that it seemed impossible that he was about to make one himself. The audience seemed almost as surprised as I was. The applause stilled immediately and an eager "shushing" took its place. He came forward another step, peered at them over his glasses, and waited for complete quiet.

"I would like this audience to know," he said carefully and slowly, "that eighty per cent of this play is Moss Hart." That was all. He stepped back and signaled the stage manager to lower the curtain. The audience sat bewildered for a full moment and then broke into perfunctory applause. They had expected a witty speech in the manner of the play—or in the caustic tradition of George S. Kaufman. Their disappointment and their lack of interest in what he said was clear, but they obligingly applauded for another curtain.

I stood staring at the stage and at George Kaufman. Generosity does not flower easily or often in the rocky soil of the theatre. Few are uncorrupted by its ceaseless warfare over credit and billing, its jealousies and envies, its constant temptations toward pettiness and mean-spiritedness. It is not only a hard and exacting profession but the most public one as well. It does not breed magnanimity, and unselfishness is not one of its strong points. Not often is a young playwright welcomed into it with a *beau geste* as gallant and selfless as the one that had just come over those footlights.

A hand was tugging at my sleeve and Max Siegel was whispering some words in my ear, but I moved quickly away without answering. I did not trust my voice, and I was ashamed to have him see that my eyes were blurred.

THE PROCEEDINGS which take place backstage on an opening night, immediately following the fall of the curtain, follow a set pattern and are almost a law unto themselves. At least half of the audience hurries through the stage door to jam the stairways, throng the dressing rooms and overflow onto the stage itself. A kind of formalized bedlam ensues in which the same words echo up and down the halls and float out the open doors of every dressing room. No one is expected to believe the words which are being spoken or the emotional kisses and embraces which usually precede them; they are always the same and are used for both failure or success. Not to come backstage and speak them, however, is considered a remission of friendship or downright cowardice. Both sides know exactly what is expected of them, and the performance backstage sometimes equals or betters the one which has just taken place in front of the footlights. With an obvious failure, or what seems to be an obvious failure, the embraces and kisses are of necessity a little more flamboyant, the words a little more belligerent, and the recurring phrase, "Well, *I* loved it," uttered with great vehemence, is to be heard on all sides. No one is actually lying, for short of a blatant or outright fiasco, everyone is aware of the complete untrustworthiness of critics. Everyone knows that it is just as likely for the certain failure to be greeted the following morning with glowing and triumphant notices as it is for the apparent success to receive its death sentence.

There are some opening nights, however, when a play seems

[429]

destined for success in spite of critical perfidy, and on these nights the backstage throng assumes the proportions of a hysterical and unruly mob. On these occasions a backstage appearance is no longer an unpleasant duty, but a vital necessity—it seems to contain some basic need of human beings to identify themselves or to be identified with success. On such nights the dressing rooms and stairways are a solid mass of humanity crushed one against the other into every available inch of space. *Once in a Lifetime* must have had all the earmarks of such an evening, for I could hardly fight my way through the stage door. I struggled up the stairway to reach Mr. Kaufman's dressing room, but there was a great horde of people clustered in front of it waiting for the crowd within to come out. Beatrice Kaufman caught sight of me, blew me a kiss and waved to me to make my way in, but I shook my head. What I wanted to say to him could not be said in front of strangers. I shouted back, "Tell him I was here," and pushed my way down the stairs again.

Each dressing room and every landing was jammed—swarms of people surged in and out of the densely packed rooms, all talking at once. I caught a glimpse of Jean Dixon and Hugh O'Connell over the tops of heads and started toward them, but the congestion was too great, and as I reached the stage I heard Sam Harris' soft laughter rise from the crowd that surrounded him; but I made no attempt to go toward him.

I felt unaccountably disconnected from the uproar that was taking place all around me; none of it seemed to have any connection with what had made the evening possible—with hotel rooms, a typewriter and curtains drawn against the light; with pacing up and down in the dark; with actors in bathrobes standing on a stage after a performance, the pilot light etching the exhaustion on each face under the make-up—none of this seemed to have anything to do with any of the people who had been part of all that had gone before. Those people were disappearing under my eyes, had vanished already in fact, and suddenly I knew what was vanishing along with them: that tight little cabal against the world—the conspiracy that had begun with the first day's rehearsal and had been pledged in stale sandwiches and cold coffee in cardboard containers, the unspoken compact of long days on dim stages and dirty out-of-town dressing rooms, the common bond of the same shared hopes and fears—that sustaining conspiracy was over and the world had moved in. That old secret world removed and remote from everything but the play and ourselves had ended.

I walked across the stage to where my family and friends stood waiting, a little knot of alien corn in the mass of black ties and jewels and evening gowns that swirled all around them. I felt as alien as they looked. We stood uncomfortably together, not quite knowing what to do. After I had kissed my mother and father and listened to the congratulations of Dore and Lester and Eddie and the others, I stood helplessly rooted to the spot. I felt my face freeze into an apelike grin and tried to unleash my tongue, but I could not; nor could I think of what to do next. I had lived for this moment for so long that it was difficult to accept it as reality— even now it still seemed frozen in fantasy. I have always understood the unbelieving look in the eyes of those whom success touches early—it is a look half fearful, as though the dream were still in the process of being dreamed and to move or to speak would shatter it.

It was Joe Hyman, not I, who finally shepherded all of us toward the stage door and took everyone to a restaurant to wait for the notices. Somewhere or other along the line of that long wait I began to believe that a play of mine had opened on Broadway and that the notices I was waiting to read might transform that lifelong fantasy into a reality that would change my life from this moment onward. Someone gave me a drink and I began to shake so that it was impossible to lift the second drink to my lips—a fortunate moment of panic, I believe, for two drinks under the circumstances might easily have made me quite drunk and would have robbed me of the pleasure of being able to hear the notices read aloud. That fateful moment is not one to be missed. Whatever the state of one's nerves, it is wise at all costs to remain clear-headed on the gambler's chance that the notices will be good, for good notices read aloud are a joy not to be cheated out of. In that first reading, each word is glorious, and no words of praise afterward will ever shine with the same splendor.

The notices of *Once in a Lifetime* as I listened to them were a blaze of glory—each word incrusted with a special luster of its own, and I made the sound decision never to look at them again. They could not possibly be as brilliant, as peerless, as superlative or as downright wonderful as I now thought them to be, and I paid them the honor of letting them remain an imperishable memory. When the last notice had been read, I took that second drink, for I knew now that my life was indeed changed forever—and I drank a silent toast to the new one.

Is success in any other profession as dazzling, as deeply satisfying, as it is in the theatre? I cannot pretend to know, but I doubt it. There are other professions where the rewards are as great or greater than those the theatre offers, there are professions where the fruits of success are as immediate, and still others where the pursuit of a more admirable goal undoubtedly brings a nobler sense of fulfillment. But I wonder if success in any of them tastes as sweet. Again, I am inclined to doubt it. There is an intensity, an extravagance, an abundant and unequivocal gratification to the vanity and the ego that can be satisfied more richly and more fully by success in the theatre than in any other calling. Like everything else about the theatre, its success is emphatic and immoderate. Perhaps what makes it so marvelously satisfying is that it is a success that is anything but lonely—everyone seems to share in it, friends and strangers alike—and a first success in the theatre is the most intoxicating and beguiling time imaginable. No success afterward surpasses it. It roars and thumps and thunders through the blood the way that second drink seemed to be coursing through my veins right now, so that it seemed hardly bearable to have to wait until tomorrow to start savoring it.

I asked someone what time it was and blinked my surprise when I was told it was four thirty in the morning. It seemed but a few short minutes since we had waited impatiently for two thirty to come to be able to read the first notice in the *Times*. The morning editions appeared very much later in those days, and it was the custom to go directly to each newspaper in turn and wait for the first copies to roll off the presses. Everyone in the theatre knew what time each paper would appear and where to go for them. The *Times* appeared first at about two thirty, the *Tribune* about three, and the *Daily News* last at four o'clock in the morning. The *World* was far downtown on Park Row and would have to wait until tomorrow, but with three ecstatic notices under my arm, the *World,* in more ways than just the name of a newspaper, could wait.

We were all standing outside the News Building, where the last notice had been read—or, rather, acted out brilliantly by Dore Schary—and just as it seemed to me but a few moments ago that he had read aloud those exalted words in the *Times,* so it seemed now to be some years ago and not just yesterday that I had watched another dawn lighten the sky, as it was about to do once more. It seemed impossible that it could have been only yesterday that I had sat listening to Sam Harris tell me the story of *Once in a Lifetime—* it seemed to have been someone other than I who walked out of the Music Box with him to see that other dawn beginning. That other I now seemed someone infinitely different from my present self— a fearful, inept, wretchedly uncertain fellow. He was someone I knew and remembered very well, but it was a memory already growing shadowy and dim.

Can success change the human mechanism so completely between one dawn and another? Can it make one feel taller, more alive, handsomer, uncommonly gifted and indomitably secure with the certainty that this is the way life will always be? It can and it does! Only one aspect of that other self remained to spill over into the new. I was once again wolfishly, overpoweringly hungry. It would take at least two more successes to make me lose my appetite, and it is only fair to point out that success can and does accomplish this, too. Everyone but me, however, had eaten during the long wait for the notices, and only that bitter-ender, Joe Hyman, was not too exhausted by this time to declare himself ready to sit through a full meal with me. The others were visibly wilting and I did not press them to stay. My family had long since gone home on the strength

[433]

of that first glowing notice in the *Times*—indeed, their own glow must have sped the train halfway to Brooklyn with no help from the subway system at all.

I protested a little during the good-byes, but I was secretly relieved that the others were going now, too, for a childish reason of my own. It satisfied my sense of drama to complete the full circle of *Once in a Lifetime* alone with Joe Hyman—the circle that had begun with a dinner alone with him before the opening in Atlantic City and would end with this dinner alone with him now after the opening in New York. It is a childish game I have always played and have never been able to resist—a game of arranging life, whenever possible, in a series of scenes that make perfect first-act or third-act curtains. When it works, and it often does, it lends an extra zest and a keener sense of enjoyment to whatever the occasion may be where my thirst for drama has contrived to make life imitate a good third act. It worked beautifully now.

I cannot recall one word that was exchanged between us, but it must have taken a fairly long time to satisfy my sense of the dramatic entities, for when we came out of the restaurant it was six o'clock in the morning and broad daylight. For the second dawn in a row I peered down the streets of a sleeping city, searching for a taxi. This dawn, however, was going to usher in an historic moment. My last subway ride was behind me. Never again would I descend those dingy steps or hear those turnstiles click off another somber day behind me.

Joe Hyman asked, "Got enough money to get to Brooklyn?"

I nodded. That fifteen dollars was still intact—there could not be a better way to spend it than to keep that long-ago promise to myself, and a taxi ride to Brooklyn was keeping it with a vengeance.

A cab pulled up beside us and Joe Hyman and I silently shook hands. The driver eyed me warily when I gave him a Brooklyn address, and I was conscious, looking at Joe Hyman, of how disreputable I too must look. I looked at him again and burst into laughter. His eyes were red-rimmed with excitement and weariness, his face grimy with a full day-and-night's growth of beard, and his suit looked as though he had slept in it. The driver obviously and quite rightly was wondering if there was enough money between us to pay for that long ride, or if we had not already spent every cent in some speakeasy. I took a ten-dollar bill out of my pocket and waved it at him and climbed into the cab. I waved at Joe Hyman through the rear window until the cab turned the corner, and then settled back in the seat, determined that I would not fall asleep. I had no intention of dozing through the first ride to Brooklyn above ground—I intended to enjoy every visible moment of it and I very shortly reaped the reward for staying awake.

No one has ever seen the skyline of the city from Broooklyn Bridge as I saw it that morning with three hit notices under my arm. The face of the city is always invested with grandeur, but grandeur can be chilling. The overpowering symmetry of that skyline can crush the spirit and make the city seem forbidding and impenetrable, but today it seemed to emerge from cold anonymity and grant its acknowledgment and acceptance. There was no sunlight—it was a gray day and the buildings were half shrouded in mist, but it was a city that would know my name today, a city that had not turned me aside, and a city that I loved. Unexpectedly and without warning a great wave of feeling for this proud and beautiful city swept over me. We were off the bridge now and driving through the sprawling, ugly area of tenements that stretch interminably over the approaches to each of its boroughs. They are the first in the city to awake, and the long unending rows of drab, identical houses were already stirring with life. Laundry was being strung out to dry along roof tops and fire escapes, men with lunch boxes were coming out of the houses, and children returning from the corner grocery with bottles of milk and loaves of bread were hurrying up the steps and into the doorways.

I stared through the taxi window at a pinch-faced ten-year-old hurrying down the steps on some morning errand before school, and I thought of myself hurrying down the street on so many gray mornings out of a doorway and a house much the same as this one. My mind jumped backward in time and then whirled forward, like a many-faceted prism—flashing our old neighborhood in front of me, the house, the steps, the candy store—and then shifted to the skyline I had just passed by, the opening last night, and the notices I still hugged tightly under my arm. It was possible in this wonderful city for that nameless little boy—for any of its millions—to have a decent chance to scale the walls and achieve what they wished. Wealth, rank or an imposing name counted for nothing. The only credential the city asked was the boldness to dream. For those who did, it unlocked its gates and its treasures, not caring who they were or where they came from. I watched the boy disappear into a tailor shop and a surge of shamefaced patriotism overwhelmed me. I might have been watching a victory parade on a flag-draped Fifth Avenue instead of the mean streets of a city slum. A feeling of patriotism, however, is not always limited to the feverish emotions called forth by war. It can sometimes be felt as profoundly and perhaps more truly at a moment such as this.

It had suddenly begun to rain very hard and in a few minutes I could no longer see much of anything through the windows. All too quickly I made that swift turnabout from patriotism to enlightened self-interest. I closed my eyes and thought about how I would spend the money that would soon start to pour in. To my surprise, affluence did not seem nearly as easy to settle into as I had always imagined it would be. Try as I would, I could not think of how to begin or in what ways I wanted to spend the large sums that would now be mine to command. I could think of little ways to spend it—new suits, new shirts, new ties, new overcoats—but after that my mind went disappointingly blank. In some ways sudden riches are no easier to live with than poverty. Both demand artistry of a kind, if one or the other is not to leave the mark of a sour and lingering cynicism, and opulence in many ways is harder to manage than penury. It is, however, one of the pleasantest problems with which to drift off to sleep. It is a problem that apparently also induces the deepest and most refreshing kind of sleep. I cheated myself out of the major portion of that first taxi ride by sleeping soundly through the rest of it. The driver had to leave his seat and shake me awake to collect his fare.

I was wide awake again, thoroughly wide awake, and disappointed to find the shades still drawn and the family fast asleep when I unlocked the door and stepped into the apartment. It was, of course, only a little after seven o'clock in the morning, but today was too memorable a day to waste on anything so commonplace as sleep. I was tempted to wake them up at once and show them the other notices, but I went into the kitchen instead and fixed a pot of coffee. I wanted a little more time alone to think about something.

I stood in the doorway of the kitchen while I waited for the water to boil and gazed at the sleeping figure of my brother on the daybed in the dining room, and beyond it at the closed door of the one bedroom where my parents slept. The frayed carpet on the floor was the carpet I had crawled over before I could walk. Each flower in the badly faded and worn design was sharply etched in my mind. Each piece of furniture in the cramped dim room seemed mildewed with a thousand double-edged memories. The ghosts of a thousand leaden meals hovered over the dining-room table. The dust of countless black-hearted days clung to every crevice of the squalid ugly furniture I had known since childhood. To walk out of it forever—not piecemeal, but completely—would give meaning to the wonder of what had happened to me, make success tangible, decisive.

The goal behind the struggle for success is not always one goal, but many—some real, some hidden; some impossible to achieve, even with success piled upon success. The goal differs with each of us in the mysterious and wonderful way each human being is different from any other, in the way each of us is the sum total of the unexpressed longings and desires that strew the seas of childhood and are glimpsed long afterward from a safe distance—a submerged iceberg, only the tip of which is seen.

Whatever dominant force in my nature shaped the blind demands that made it imperative to me to make the theatre my goal, had taken possession of me early and I was still possessed by it. What fulfillment it held I would know only when I walked resolutely out of one world and into another. I poured myself a cup of coffee, and by the time I had finished it, my mind was made up.

[437]

It is always best if one is about to embark on a wild or reckless venture not to discuss it with anybody beforehand. Talk will rob the scheme of its fire and make what seemed mettlesome and daring merely foolhardy. It is easier on everyone concerned to present it as an accomplished fact, turn a deaf ear to argument, and go ahead with it.

I awakened my brother by dumping the papers on the bed for him to read and then called through the bedroom door to my mother and father to get up right away. I gave them barely enough time to read the notices and then plunged. "We're moving into New York today —as soon as you have a cup of coffee—and we're not taking anything with us. We're walking out of here with just the clothes on our backs and nothing else. The coffee's on the stove, so hurry up and get dressed."

My mother stared at me and then spoke quietly, as if a raised voice at this moment might send me further out of my senses. "Where are we going?" she asked logically enough.

"To a hotel," I said, "until we find an apartment and furnish it." There was a stunned silence and before anyone else could speak, I spoke again, not impatiently but as if what I was saying was inarguable. "There's nothing to pack; we just walk out of the door. No," I added in answer to my mother's mute startled look around the room, "not a thing. We leave it all here just as it stands, and close the door. We don't take anything—not even a toothbrush, a bathrobe, pajamas or nightgown. We buy it all new in New York. We're walking out of here and starting fresh."

My mother walked to the window and pulled up the shades as though she might hear or understand what I was saying better with more light, and then turned helplessly toward my father.

He was the first to recover his breath and his wits. "We just paid two months' rent in advance," he said, as though that solid fact would help me recover my own.

"That gives us the right to let this stuff sit here and rot, or you can give it to the janitor," I replied. "We're walking out of here with just what clothes you put on and tomorrow we'll get rid of those, too."

[438]

This second bit of information created an even more astonished silence than the first. "Don't you understand?" I heard myself shouting. "All I'm asking you to do *now* is—"

"I'm not walking out of here without the pictures," my mother said with great firmness.

It was my turn to be astonished. "What pictures?" I asked.

"*All* the pictures," she replied. "The baby pictures of you and Bernie and the pictures of my father and my sister, and Bernie's diploma and your letters, and all the other pictures and things I've got in the closet in that big box."

I threw my arms around her and kissed her. I had won. It was being accepted as a fact—incomprehensible but settled.

"One suitcase," I ordered. "Put it all into one suitcase, but one suitcase—that's all."

I looked at my brother, who had remained silent through all of this. He handed the papers back to me with a flourish and winked. "Don't you have to give *some* of the money to George Kaufman?" he said.

"Half," I replied. "But my share will be over a thousand dollars a week."

"That'll buy a lot of toothbrushes," he said. "I'm going to get ready." And he climbed out of bed.

My mother and father stared at us as if to make sure we were not indulging in some elaborate joke for their benefit.

"It's true," I said soberly. "It's not a salary. I get a percentage of every dollar that comes into the box office. Don't you understand how it works?"

Obviously, they did not, and I realized somewhat belatedly that it had never occurred to either of them to translate good fortune in the theatre into anything more than what my mother's friends defined as "making a good living." No wonder my proposal had sounded lunatic, but now as the belief came to them that what I had just said might be the literal truth, they were suddenly seized with some of my own excitement. My mother's reaction was a curious one. She burst into a peal of laughter. She had a merry and ringing laugh

[439]

and it was contagious. My father and I joined in her laughter, though we would have been hard put to tell exactly what we were laughing at. I was reminded of that moment and of her laughter long, long afterward, when I heard someone say, "Nothing makes people laugh like money—the rich get wrinkles from laughing." It was said sardonically, of course, but it is not without an element of truth. Money does generate its own kind of excitement, and its sudden acquisition creates an *ambiance* of gaiety and merriment that it would be nonsense to deny or not to enjoy. It induces, moreover, a momentum of its own. Everything moves with an unaccustomed and almost miraculous speed.

We were all ready to leave in less than an hour, despite the fact that there were more things of heaven and earth in that box in the closet than could be contained in one suitcase. I carried the box, my father and brother each carried a suitcase, and my mother, her victory complete, hugged a brown paper parcel of last-minute treasures that had turned up in an old tin box. We walked out of the door and waited in the lobby while my brother hurried out in the rain to try to get a taxi. The rain was pouring down in a great solid sheet now and gusts of wind were slashing it against the building. I watched it burst savagely against the glass doors of the lobby and was seized by a sudden and irresistible impulse.

"I forgot something," I said shortly. "I'll be right back."

I unlocked the door of the empty apartment and closed and locked it again carefully behind me. I took one quick look around to keep the memory of that room forever verdant and then walked to each window and threw it wide open. The rain whipped in through the windows like a broadside of artillery fire. I watched a large puddle form on the floor and spread darkly over the carpet. The rain streamed across the top and down the legs of the dining-room table and splashed over the sideboard and the china closet. It soaked the armchair and cascaded down the sofa. It peppered the wallpaper with large wet blotches and the wind sent two lamps crashing to the floor. I kicked them out of my way and walked over to the daybed, which was still dry, and pulled it out into the middle of the room, where a fresh onset of wind and rain immediately drenched it. I looked around me with satisfaction, feeling neither guilty nor foolish. More reasonable gestures have seldom succeeded in giving me half the pleasure this meaningless one did. It was the hallmark, the final signature, of defiance and liberation. Short of arson, I could do no more.

I slammed the door behind me without looking back.

To everyone's surprise, including my own, a strange silence fell upon us in the taxi, in spite of the fact that my brother read aloud the glowing notice in the *World,* which he had picked up on his way to get the cab. Instead of heightening our excitement or reinforcing our high spirits, it seemed, curiously enough, to put a damper on them. My brother stared out the window and my mother and father stared straight ahead, silent and solemn. I talked on for a moment or two and then grew silent myself. Perhaps there was in all of us, including myself, a feeling of unreality in what we were doing or a separate awareness in each of us that this great change—this almost too great change in our life—would change us, too, as a family; that the struggle which had welded us so tightly together was over now, and success in some mysterious way might separate us, each from the other.

My mother, still silent, took out her handkerchief and wiped her eyes. They were not, I suspected, tears of joy for my success. They were not tears for the beginning of something, but for the end of something none of us could name. Not until we came within sight of Brooklyn Bridge did anyone speak. Then, as suddenly as it had fallen, the silence lifted. Crossing the bridge, as it had for me earlier that morning, seemed to put an old way of life behind us and make inevitable the new one we were rushing headlong into. We started to talk, all of us at once, almost at the same moment, as if crossing the bridge had cut the ties irrevocably and was a symbol of entry into a world as dazzling as the skyline in front of us.

Suddenly no one seemed to have an unexpressed thought. Everyone talked incessantly, oblivious of what anyone else might be saying. We were at 34th Street before I thought to glance out the window. I had told the driver to take us to the Edison Hotel on 47th Street, for no other reason except that it was practically around the corner from the Music Box and seemed more of a family hotel than any other I could think of; but as the cab moved into Times Square, I asked the driver to stop first at the Music Box.

Even through the rain-splashed windows of the cab, I could see a long double line of people extending the full length of the lobby from the box office. The line spilled out under the marquee where another line was patiently forming under umbrellas. I got out of the cab and walked into the lobby and stood gaping at all the people. It was not yet half-past nine in the morning. How long I stood there, forgetful of everything else but the wonder of that line, I do not know, but the box-office man, looking up for a moment to glance across the lobby, caught sight of me and smiled. There is no smile as bright as the smile of a box-office man the morning after a hit. It flashes with the iridescence of stage jewelry under spotlights and is as wide as the proscenium itself. His smile did not waver—it grew more brilliant as the telephones jangled behind him and visions of ticket speculators, like sugar plums, danced across his mind. He waved me over to the head of the line and stuck his hand out through the opening in the grille to shake my own.

"A year at least," he said, "It's the hottest ticket in town. What can I do for you?"

"I wanted to draw $500.00," I said quickly. "I'm moving into town."

"Sure, sure—anything you want," he said. He reached for an I.O.U. slip and rapidly filled it in. "How do you want it?" he asked.

"A few fifties," I replied, "the rest in twenties and tens."

I signed the slip as he counted out the money, conscious that the people immediately in back of me were whispering to each other. "It is *not* George Kaufman," I heard a woman's voice say. "It must be the other one."

As nearly as I could, I tried to achieve a look of modesty with the back of my head while I waited for him to finish. He pushed the rather formidable stack of bills toward me and his smile floodlit the box office. "Come around any time," he said, "we'll be here for a long, long time."

I doubled the bills in my fist and walked out and into the taxi. Without a word I went through the pretense of counting the money, thoroughly aware of the awed silence around me.

"When," my brother said quietly, "do they change the name of the theatre to the Money Box?"

It was the first of a perpetual and unremitting series of bad puns that he was to launch and send racketing down the years, and the effect of this historic first one was not only uproarious but explosive. We started to laugh and could not stop. We laughed as though we were out of our wits, uncontrolled and breathless with laughter, and startled because we could not stop laughing, try as we would. My brother's words seemed to have touched off the edge of hysteria our overwrought state had brought us to. The exhaustion and excitement of the last few days and of this morning needed a release, and that atrocious pun had been both a means and a blessing. We laughed as though we might never stop.

The driver, too, started to shake with laughter and turned around apologetically. "I don't know what you're laughing at, folks," he said, "but it must be pretty good to make people laugh that way." No one could answer him; we were all still helpless. He burst into laughter again himself and turned the cab toward Broadway.

My fatal weakness for standing aside from whatever was happening around me and translating it into vignettes of drama overcame me once more. I could hear myself telling the whole story to Sam Harris. Unresisting, I let it assemble and take shape in my mind. The wait for the notices, the first taxi ride home, the decision to walk out and leave everything behind us, the trip back to open the windows and let the rain pour in—I could hear myself telling it all to him, right down to counting the money in the cab, our paroxysm of laughter, and the cab driver turning around to add the final touch. I could see myself some time later this afternoon standing in his office in the Music Box and telling it to him with the proper embellishment, making it all come out a rounded, dramatic entity.

[443]

I could see his eyes squint with amusement as I told it and hear his soft laughter afterward. I could even, I thought, hear his comment. "Not bad, kid," he would say. "Not a bad curtain for a first act."

INTERMISSION

About the Author

MOSS HART and the American theatre of the last twenty-five years seem to be synonymous. Alone, and with George S. Kaufman, he has written some its most successful plays; and, with scores provided by Irving Berlin, Cole Porter, Kurt Weill and Ira Gershwin, some of its more memorable musicals. His *Lady in the Dark,* starring the late Gertrude Lawrence, remains one of the musical theatre's most cherished memories; *You Can't Take It with You* and *The Man Who Came to Dinner,* written with George Kaufman, are still two of the highlights of American stage comedies. Mr. Hart is the director of his own plays and musicals, as well as the works of others, his latest directorial effort being the now legendary *My Fair Lady.*

He is married to Kitty Carlisle, actress and television star, and is the father of two children, aged eleven and eight; they live in New York City, where he was born.

Mr. Hart was, for seven years, president of the Dramatists Guild and is now president of the Authors League of America.